HOW PEOPLE EVALUATE OTHERS IN ORGANIZATIONS

SERIES IN APPLIED PSYCHOLOGY

Edwin A. Fleishman, George Mason University,
Jeanette N. Cleveland, Pennsylvania State University
Series Editors

HOW PEOPLE EVALUATE OTHERS IN ORGANIZATIONS

Edited by

Manuel London
State University of New York at Stony Brook

LAWRENCE ERLBAUM ASSOCIATES, PUBLISHERS
2001   Mahwah, New Jersey   London

Lawrence Erlbaum Associates, Inc., Publishers
10 Industrial Avenue
Mahwah, NJ 07430

Cover design by Kathryn Houghtaling Lacey

Library of Congress Cataloging-in-Publication Data

How people evaluate others in organizations / edited by Manuel London.
     p.   cm. — (Applied psychology)
    Includes bibliographical references and index.
    ISBN 0-8058-3611-X (cloth : acid-free paper) — ISBN 0-8058-3612-8 (pbk. : acid-free paper)
    1. Psychology, Industrial.   2. Social perception.   I. London, Manuel.   II. Series in applied
psychology.

HF5548.8 .H65   2001
158.7—dc21

                                         00-065402

Printed in the United States of America
10   9   8   7   6   5   4   3   2

Contents

Series Foreword

Edwin A. Fleishman
Series Editor

There is a compelling need for innovative approaches to the solution of many pressing problems involving human relationships in today's society. Such approaches are more likely to be successful when they are based on sound research and applications. This Series in Applied Psychology offers publications that emphasize state-of-the-art research and its application to important issues of human behavior in a variety of social settings. The objective is to bridge both academic and applied interests.

Much of industrial and organizational psychology and human resource management, and indeed much of business in general, requires people to evaluate and make decisions about others. Psychologists develop methods to eliminate human error in interpersonal judgment to the extent possible. However, many judgment processes are not systematic and are conducted by managers and employees who are not trained for the task. This book helps readers understand and improve person perception processes in personnel selection, appraisal, development, and a host of important interpersonal interactions.

The book begins with two foundation chapters on basic theory and research of person perception, including such concepts as cognitive schemas, social stereotypes, attribution processes, automatic/mindless information processing, individual motivations and feelings that affect judgment, and situational conditions. The book then builds on these concepts in 13 application chapters and a concluding overview. Topics cover how person perception influences standard methods in industrial and organizational psychology, such as the employment interview, assessment centers, performance appraisal, and upward and peer ratings. Other topics address less systematic applications that are critical in today's dynamic organizations, such as executive selection and promotion decisions, perceptions employees have of their leaders, coaching, managing problem employees, intercultural relationships, negotiations, in-person group dynamics, and interactions in geographically dispersed teams limited to technology-based communication.

The book is for students, researchers, and practitioners in industrial and organizational psychology, applied social psychology, and human resource management. All chapters are original and written by leading researchers and practitioners. Manuel London is particularly well qualified to bring these basic and applied topics together. He is currently professor at the State University of New York at Stony Brook and has carried out research and written extensively on these topics, teaches graduate courses on these issues, worked on human resources programs for AT&T for 12 years, and continues to serve as a management consultant in these areas.

Preface

An important part of human resource management and industrial and organizational psychology is the way people evaluate and make decisions about others. Selection, appraisal, development, and interpersonal interaction are key processes in organizations, and human resource experts design systematic methods to ensure the reliability and validity of these processes. Dynamics of basic social psychology are the foundation for these processes and the tools and procedures that make them rigorous. In particular, these methods depend on how people perceive and evaluate others—the social psychological processes of person perception and social cognition. This book links the social psychology of person perception to interpersonal interactions, evaluations, and decisions in organizations. It applies current theory and research in social cognition to formal and informal assessments used in personnel selection, appraisal, development, and key interpersonal interactions, such as teamwork, negotiations, and cross-cultural relationships.

The book addresses ways to improve the practice of personnel selection and performance appraisal and ways to educate employees so that they make more accurate interpersonal judgments in informal situations. This includes ways to enhance raters' accuracy by helping them understand cognitive processes, in general, and their own judgment processes, in particular. The focus is on how raters and decision makers develop a frame of reference based on performance dimensions that are important for the job and how they can avoid rater biases and other errors. The book is meant for use by graduate students, practitioners, and researchers in the fields of social psychology, industrial and organizational psychology, and human resource management.

This book stems from my general interest in applied person perception. From my research as a graduate student in the early 1970s, I investigated information processing in employment interviews and the role of the rater in performance appraisal. This developed into research at AT&T in the late 1970s and early 1980s on how promotion decisions are made by department managers and the importance of managers' insights into themselves and organizational opportunities as components of career motivation and development. I then began a program of research on multisource (360-degree) feedback surveys and explored factors that influence rater agreement and ratee use of the results. The current book extends this work to a comprehensive examination of how person perception and social cognition influence a wide variety of organizational human resource processes. I invited leading experts to examine basic concepts in social psychology and the application of these concepts to human resource methods. These applied processes are formal mechanisms for making decisions, such as employment interviews (which may be conducted by personnel experts or by managers without formal human resource training), judgment and decision-making aids (such as performance appraisal surveys), and general interpersonal processes.

The book is divided into five parts. The first introduces basic theory and research on person perception, social cognition, interpersonal judgment, and stereotypes. It reviews such topics as dispositional and attributional inferences and judgment biases, indicating how these processes can be functional as well as dysfunctional. The next four parts of the book cover applications of person perception. Part II deals with employment interviews, promotion decisions, and assessment centers. Part III examines performance appraisal and multisource feedback surveys. Part IV focuses on developmental processes, including leadership, career dynamics, coaching, and managing problem performers. The final part examines the role of person perception in interpersonal situations, such as multicultural relationships, negotiations, face-to-face work teams, and "virtual" teams (geographically dispersed teams that use electronic means of communication). The concluding chapter summarizes and integrates the major themes in the book and outlines directions for applying social cognition to understanding organization and individual decision processes.

I am indebted to the contributors to this volume for agreeing to participate in the project and submitting papers that were on target in content, length, and time frame. Their contributions should enhance the fields of industrial and organizational psychology and human resource management by calling attention to the social psychological components of our methods and using this knowledge to enhance the value of our techniques to organizational and individual success.

Manuel London

About the Authors

Herman Aguinis is Associate Professor of Management and Director of the M.S. in Management Program at the Graduate School of Business Administration of the University of Colorado at Denver. He has a graduate degree in psychology from the University of Buenos Aires, and an M.A. and Ph.D. in industrial and organizational psychology from the State University of New York at Albany. In 1997, he received the *Journal of Organizational Behavior* Best Paper Award for 1996 (with Charles A. Pierce and Donn Byrne). Currently, he serves as an elected member of the Executive Committee of the Human Resources Management Division of the Academy of Management and Associate Editor for *Organizational Research Method.*

Bruce J. Avolio is Professor and Director of the Center for Leadership Studies at Binghamton University. He received his Ph.D. from the University of Akron in 1982 in industrial and organizational and life-span psychology. He has published over 70 articles and book chapters on topics related to individual, team, and organizational leadership and is considered an international expert in the area of assessing and developing transformational leadership. Over the last five years, Dr. Avolio has worked with a wide range of colleagues in setting up a worldwide network of Centers for Leadership Studies. Affiliate centers to date that have been established are located in Israel, South Africa, Korea, Australia, Sweden, and New Zealand. Several new centers are planned for inauguration over the next 2 years.

Janet L. Barnes-Farrell is Associate Professor of Industrial and Organizational Psychology at the University of Connecticut. She received her Ph.D. in industrial and organizational psychology from the Pennsylvania State University. Dr. Barnes-Farrell's research interests primarily focus on problems related to the appraisal of work performance and on issues associated with aging and work. Her work has been published in the *Journal of Applied Psychology*, *Journal of Applied Social Psychology*, *Organizational Behavior and Human Decision Processes*, *Personnel Psychology*, *Psychology and Aging*, and *Work and Stress*. She currently serves on the Editorial Board of the *Journal of Applied Psychology*.

Talya N. Bauer, Ph.D., Purdue University, is Associate Professor of Organizational Behavior and Human Resource Management at Portland State University, Portland, Oregon. Her experience training, consulting, and conducting research with organizations includes work with Bristol-Meyers Squibb, NASA, Subaru-Isuzu, Hewlett-Packard, Intel, and the Los Angeles Unified School District. Her teaching and research interests include socialization, leadership, and applicant reactions to selection. She is a member of the *Journal of Applied Psychology* Editorial Board and was the Program Chair for the year 2001 Society for Industrial and Organizational Psychologist's Annual Conference in San Diego, California. Her work appears in outlets such as *Academy of Management Journal, Personnel Psychology, Journal of Applied Psychology, Research in Personnel & Human Resource Management, Group & Organization Management, Journal of Career Planning & Employment, Journal of Applied Social Psychology*, and *Journal of Business & Psychology*.

Douglas J. Brown is Assistant Professor of Industrial and Organizational Psychology at the University of Waterloo. He received his Ph.D. in industrial and organizational Psychology at the University of Akron. His research interests lie in the area of leadership and social cognitions. He has coauthored work on leadership in *Organizational Behavior and Human Decision Processes* and *The Leadership Quarterly*.

Janis A. Cannon-Bowers is Senior Research Psychologist in the Science and Technology Division of the Naval Air Warfare Center, Training Systems Division. She received her Ph.D. in 1988 in industrial and organizational psychology from the University of South Florida. Her research interests include team training and performance, crew coordination training, training effectiveness, and tactical decision making.

Jeff T. Casey is Associate Professor of Management and Policy at the State University of New York at Stony Brook, where he also holds a joint appointment in the Department of Political Science. He received his Ph.D. in 1986 in psychology from the University of Wisconsin, Madison, and has held positions as research scientist at the Massachusetts Institute of Technology and as a visiting assistant professor at the Graduate School of Business, University of Chicago. His research interests are behavioral decision making (including judgment under risk and uncertainty, and psychological models of economic behavior) and human resource management (including job performance feedback systems). He has published in such journals as *Acta Psychologica, Organizational Behavior and Human Decision Processes*, and *Management Science.*

Lisa M. Donahue is currently a doctoral candidate in industrial and organizational psychology at George Mason University. She received an M.S. in industrial and organizational psychology in 1991 from Clemson University. Lisa's research and applied work focus on improving the quality of applied human resource judgments, particularly in the area of assessment centers. She has over six years of experience directing the development of assessment procedures for the Test Development and Validation Unit, New Orleans Civil Service. Her research on applied judgments has appeared in *Journal of Social Behavior* and *Personality and Human Performance.*

Rex Dumdum is an Adjunct Professor of Management Information Systems in the School of Management and a Research Associate in the Center for Leadership Studies at Binghamton University. He received his Ph.D. in management information systems from Binghamton University in 1993. His research interests are in harnessing and integrating collective intelligence in internetworked enterprises to solve complex problems, virtual teams and leadership, electronic commerce, problem formulation in ill-structured situations, and information systems development methodologies.

Stephen M. Fiore is a Ph.D. candidate in cognitive psychology at the University of Pittsburgh Learning Research and Development Center. He is currently a Research Associate at the University of Central Florida, Team Performance Laboratory. He maintains an interdisciplinary research interest that incorporates aspects of cognitive, social, and organizational psychology in the investigation of problem solving and decision making in individuals and groups.

Susan T. Fiske, Professor of Psychology, Princeton University, previously served on the faculties of the University of Massachusetts at Amherst and Carnegie-Mellon University. A Harvard B.A. and Ph.D., she has authored over 100 journal articles and book chapters; she has edited seven books and journal special issues, including (with Gilbert & Lindzey) *The Handbook of Social Psychology* and (with Schacter & Zahn-Waxler) *The Annual Review of Psychology*. Her graduate text with Taylor, *Social Cognition* (1984; 2nd ed., 1991), defined the subfield of how people think and make sense of other people. Her federally funded social-cognition research focuses on social structure, motivation, and stereotyping, which led to expert testimony cited by the U.S. Supreme Court in the first sex discrimination case to use social science research.

Surinder Kahai is Associate Professor of Management Information Systems and a Fellow at the Center of Leadership Studies at the State University of New York at Binghamton, specializing in computer-mediated communication systems, leadership in computer-mediated contexts, and decision support systems. He earned a B.Tech in chemical engineering from the Indian Institute of Technology, an M.S. in chemical engineering from Rutgers University, and a Ph.D. in business administration from the University of Michigan. His research has been published in journals such as *Creativity Research Journal, Decision Sciences, Decision Support Systems, Journal of Applied Psychology, Personnel Psychology*, and *Small Group Research*.

Richard J. Klimoski is Professor of Industrial and Organizational Psychology and the Director of the Center for Behavioral and Cognitive Studies at George Mason University. Prior to joining the faculty at George Mason University, Richard was on the faculty of the Ohio State University. He is also a principal in the firm of GLK and Associates and has worked with a variety of organizations on such issues as human resource management systems, job-related stress, and quality of work life. His current research interests revolve around the areas of organizational control systems in the form of performance appraisal and performance feedback programs, as well as team performance. He is a past president of the Society for Industrial and Organizational Psychology and past chair of the HR Division of the Academy of Management. He is also a Fellow of the Society for Industrial/Organizational Psychology and American Psychological Society. He has served on the editorial review boards of such leading journals as *Human Resource Management Review*, *Academy of Management Journal*, and *Journal of Applied Psychology*. He served as editor of the *Academy of Management Review* from 1990 to 1993.

Kurt Kraiger is Professor of Psychology at the University of Colorado at Denver and Director of the Center for Applied Psychology. He received his Ph.D. in industrial and organizational psychology from the Ohio State University in 1983. He has published or presented over 100 papers on various topics in industrial and organizational psychology. In 1994, he received the Academy of Management's Human Resources Division Award for Best Paper (with Kevin Ford and Eduardo Salas). He has coedited a book entitled *Improving Training Effectiveness in Work Organizations*, and is currently working on two other books related to training practices. He has designed and implemented training evaluation and needs assessment programs, certification exams, competency profile systems, performance appraisal systems, and selection systems.

Robert C. Liden, Ph.D., University of Cincinnati, is Professor of Management at the University of Illinois at Chicago where he is Director of the Ph.D. Program. His research focuses on interpersonal processes as they relate to such topics as leadership, groups, and employment interviews. He has nearly 50 publications in journals such as the *Academy of Management Journal*, *Academy of Management Review*, *Journal of Applied Psychology*, *Journal of Management*, and *Personnel Psychology*. He has served on the editorial boards of the *Academy of Management Journal* and the *Journal of Management* since 1994. He was the 1999 program chair for the Academy of Management's Organizational Behavior Division, a position followed by division chair-elect (1999–2000) and division chair (2000–2001).

Manuel London is Professor and Director of the Center for Human Resource Management in the Harriman School for Management at the State University of New York at Stony Brook. He received his A.B. degree from Case Western Reserve University in philosophy and psychology and his M.A. and Ph.D. from the Ohio State University in industrial and organizational psychology. He taught at the University of Illinois at Champaign for three years. He was then a researcher and human resource manager at AT&T for 12 years before moving to Stony Brook. His books include *Self and Interpersonal Insight: How People Learn About Themselves and Others in Organizations* (published by Oxford University Press in 1995), *Job Feedback: Giving, Seeking, and Using Feedback for Performance Improvement* (published by Lawrence Erlbaum Associates in 1997), and *360-Degree Feedback: A Tool and Process for Continuous, Self-Directed Management Development* (coedited with Walter Tornow and published by Jossey-Bass in 1998).

Robert G. Lord received his Ph.D. in organizational psychology from Carnegie-Mellon University in 1975. He has been at the University of Akron since that time and is currently Professor and Chair of the Department of Psychology. He is a Fellow of the Society for Industrial and Organizational Psychology and a Fellow of the American Psychological Society. He has published extensively on topics related to social cognitions, leadership processes, leadership perceptions, and information processing, and he has published one book on this topic.

Michael K. Mount is the Henry B. Tippie Professor of Human Resource Management in the Department of Management and Organizations in the Tippie College of Business at the University of Iowa. He received his Ph.D. in industrial and organizational psychology from Iowa State University in 1977. In addition to research that investigates multisource feedback systems, Professor Mount has also conducted research that examines the relation of the Five-Factor Model personality constructs to job performance. He has published numerous articles in leading industrial and organizational psychology journals such as *Journal of Applied Psychology* and *Personnel Psychology*, and currently serves on the Editorial Board of the *Journal of Applied Psychology*. He is a Fellow in the Society for Industrial and Organizational Psychology and the American Psychological Association. He is also a Senior Scientist with the Gallup Organization.

Don Operario is a Research Psychologist at the University of California at San Francisco. He received a Ph.D. from the University of Massachusetts at Amherst in social psychology, with a minor in multicultural issues, focusing on the social context of stereotyping in race and gender relations. He took a postdoctoral fellowship at UCSF to examine the health effects of social and organizational hierarchy. His research now examines the association between stigma, social oppression, and health-related behaviors (substance use and unsafe sex), and he conducts interventions with high-risk populations.

Charles K. Parsons, Ph.D., University of Illinois, is Professor of Organizational Behavior in the DuPree College of Management at the Georgia Institute of Technology. His research interests include employment interviewing, employee socialization, the impact of performance feedback on employee motivation and performance, and employee responses to technological change. His work appears in journals such as *Academy of Management Journal, Journal of Applied Psychology, Journal of Organizational Behavior, Personnel Psychology*, and the *Journal of Occupational and Organizational Psychology*. His special teaching interests are human resource management in the legal and regulatory environment, and international human resource management. He has also performed in various administrative capacities in the college including Acting Associate Dean and Director of the Ph.D. Program.

Sumita Raghuram is Assistant Professor of Management at Fordham University, New York. She received her Ph.D. from the University of Minnesota. She has conducted research at the Copenhagen School of Business. Her research interests include virtual work, strategic and international human resource management, and workforce diversity.

Susanne P. Reilly is a consultant with Right Manus Consultants based in Stamford, Connecticut. She was formerly Vice-President, Organizational Capability at Chase Manhattan. She received her Ph.D. from Stevens Institute of Technology. Her research has been published in *Leadership Quarterly* and the *Journal of Business and Psychology*. Her current research interests deal with coaching and feedback processes.

Paul R. Sackett is Professor of Psychology at the University of Minnesota. He received his Ph.D. in industrial and organizational psychology from the Ohio State University in 1979. His research interests include personnel selection and decisions, the measurement of counterproductive behavior in the workplace, and the assessment of managerial potential. He was editor of *Personnel Psychology* and a past president of the Society for Industrial and Organizational Psychology. He has published numerous articles in such journals as the *Journal of Applied Psychology* and *Personnel Psychology*.

Eduardo Salas is Professor of Psychology at the University of Central Florida and Principal Scientist for Human Factors Research at the Institute for Simulation and Training (IST). Previously, he was a Senior Research Psychologist and Head of the Training Technology Development Branch of the Naval Air Warfare Center, Training Systems Division. He received his Ph.D. in 1984 in industrial and organizational psychology from Old Dominion University. He has coauthored over 150 journal articles and book chapters and has coedited eight books. He is on the editorial boards of *Human Factors*, *Personnel Psychology*, *Military Psychology*, *Group Dynamics*, and *Journal of Organizational Behavior*. He is currently the Series Editor for the Professional Practice Book Series and has served in numerous Society for Industrial and Organizational Psychology committees throughout the years. He is a Fellow of SIOP and the Human Factors and Ergonomics Society.

Steven E. Scullen is Assistant Professor in the College of Management at North Carolina State University. He received his Ph.D. in human resource management from the University of Iowa in 1998. His primary research interests are the measurement and management of job performance and applications of structural equations modeling to problems in human resource management. His work has appeared in *Journal of Applied Psychology*, *Personnel Psychology*, and *Organizational Research Methods*.

Valerie I. Sessa, Ph.D., is a Research Scientist and Director at the Center for Creative Leadership. Valerie's past work included codeveloping and managing a large-scale program of research in the area of executive selection. This research included an interview study of top-level executives regarding current selection practices at the very top of the organization. She codesigned and developed the Peak Selection Simulation, a multimedia simulation created to study and educate top-level leaders on how to select executives. Valerie has made many presentations on this topic, is writing book chapters and journal articles, and recently had a book published entitled *Executive Selection: Strategies for Success*. Valerie is a member of the American Psychological Association, Academy of Management, North Carolina Industrial and Organizational Psychologists, and the Society for Industrial and Organizational Psychology. She graduated from the industrial and organizational psychology doctoral program at New York University.

Nagaraj Sivasubramaniam is Assistant Professor of Organizational Behavior in the School of Management at Binghamton University where he teaches leadership, human resource management, and strategic management at the undergraduate and graduate levels. His research interests include impacts of strategic human resource management, international human resource management, leadership roles and impact in the virtual world, and the use of computer-mediated communications in organizations. Dr. Sivasubramaniam received his Ph.D. from Florida International University, Miami, Florida.

James W. Smither is a Professor in the Management Department at La Salle University. He received his Ph.D. in industrial and organizational psychology in 1985 from Stevens Institute of Technology. He is currently Associate Editor of *Personnel Psychology*. Prior to teaching at La Salle, Jim worked in corporate human resources for AT&T, and he continues to consult with many large organizations. His research and writing deal primarily with multisource feedback, coaching, and career-related development.

Zvi Strassberg holds a joint doctorate in clinical and developmental psychology from Vanderbilt University. He is Assistant Professor of Clinical Psychology in the Department of Psychology at the State University of New York at Stony Brook. His research and theoretical papers have mainly focused on the relation between cognition and social maladaptation, especially among children with aggressive behavior and their parents and peers. More recently, Dr. Strassberg's efforts have turned toward the application of cognitive-behavioral principles and practices to enhancing the job performance of individuals, groups, and organizations as a whole, through addressing the personal and interpersonal bases of effective working relationships.

Kathleen A. Tuzinski is a graduate student and Teaching Assistant in the Department of Psychology at the University of Minnesota. Her research interests include assessment center judgments, the changing nature of managerial roles, and multisource feedback. She is a coresearcher for a longitudinal study of managerial roles and for a study of the influence of relevant and irrelevant assessee characteristics on final assessment center ratings.

HOW PEOPLE EVALUATE OTHERS IN ORGANIZATIONS

I

Social Cognition and Person Perception

At the risk of oversimplification, the basic cognitive model of person perception and information processing is that people have fairly fixed views of the way things should be when they enter into interpersonal interactions. These views (schemas or prototypes) act as filters to help process large amounts of information about others' characteristics and behavior. People thereby tend to eliminate or ignore information that doesn't fit their initial views. They process information automatically whenever they can, avoid cognitive effort, and maintain consistency in their cognitive and emotional framework. When something happens out of the ordinary, they may be jogged into thinking more mindfully to capture and interpret the unusual information and reformulate their view of an individual or a group (Beach, 1990; Beach & Mitchell, 1990; London, 1995). Automatic processing, and the biases and distortions that result from it, can be avoided with various interventions, such as training and standardized data collection and processing methods.

In chapter 1, Richard Klimoski and Lisa Donahue set the foundation of theory and basic research findings for the application of person perception to how people evaluate others in organizations. They outline key person perception processes along with their antecedents and consequences from the perspective of both social cognition and applied organizational research. Person perception phenomena include cognitive, motivational, affective, interpersonal, and social processes. Social cognition provides insight into

1

practice. Organizational research offers examples of how cognitive processes operate in different types of social situations.

Klimoski and Donahue explain that the way people see and judge others is integrally tied to the social situation. Applying an input–processes–output (IPO) model, they describe outputs as the consequences of a decision for the decision maker and the person about whom the decision is made. Processes in the model are cognitive, motivational, and affective. Cognitive processes are the basis of classical person perception in social psychology. In particular, cognitive structures for social information processing (schemas and attribution processes) form heuristics to help social perceivers form judgments and make decisions. Motivational processes affect judgment, as when motives highlight the costs of being indecisive or wrong. Affective processes drive decisions that are congruent with the decision maker's mood. Important social and interpersonal factors include the history of the relationship between, and the similarity of, the decision maker and the person about whom the decision is made. Inputs include individual differences of the perceiver and target. Contextual variables include task demands, group characteristics, and features of the organizational system.

Klimoski and Donahue recognize that this IPO model is a convenient way to organize social cognitive processes. However, they go beyond this organizing framework to recognize the role of reciprocal causation and the effects of social and normative forces on person perception. They call this a "dynamic, embedded systems approach"—one that recognizes the arbitrary distinction between cause and effect and incorporates the social forces influencing person perception, such as accountability. They note that person perception cannot easily be characterized in terms of accuracy because of the contingent and volatile nature of what is being perceived. Instead, person perception should be understood in terms of the usefulness of the inferences to which it gives rise while taking into account the demands of the observer's task. These inferences are strongly influenced by the motivation and skill of the perceiver in addition to the clarity of the situation.

In short, Klimoski and Donahue set the stage for this book by showing how theory and research on person perception and social cognition offer a dynamic and rich picture of interpersonal judgment and decision making. Affect, motivation, and goals determine how person perception operates to affect decisions and behaviors. Rather than making objective, dispassionate observations, people are more likely to be ego involved in their perceptions and decisions in light of resulting personal consequences to them as well as to those about whom their decisions are made.

The second foundation chapter, by Don Operario and Susan Fiske, examines the causes and consequences of stereotypes in organizations. The authors review research on stereotyping, and offer four points about stereotypes in organizations: (a) stereotypes are elusive—they are hard to identify and even harder to control; (b) people use stereotypes to justify inequalities in organizations; (c) stereotypes influence the behaviors of both the stereotype holder and target, thus making it seem as if the stereotypes are grounded in reality; and (d) stereotypes are responsive to human intent, so they can be held in check with personal motivation and social norms.

Operario and Fiske emphasize that, although stereotypes are elusive because they are difficult to pin down definitively and even harder to control, individuals and organizations can restrain the impact of stereotypes on judgment and behavior by acknowledging their presence and potential effects. Stereotypes are automatic, category-based perceptions stemming from exaggerated beliefs that form preconceived notions about a group. They can be an adaptive, fast way to understand other people with little cognitive effort and to make judgments that are "good enough." Unfortunately, because stereotypes represent a generalization about a group, they are often used to explain bias and inequality. When people believe that stereotypes are true, they perpetuate them by attending to observations that are consistent with the stereotypes, essentially creating a self-fulfilling prophecy. The disadvantaged group comes to feel vulnerable to stereotype-based biases, which in turn amplifies the power of stereotypes. Fortunately, stereotypes are not immutable. By recognizing their subtlety and pervasiveness, personnel in organizations can create responses and norms that counter stereotypes and discourage behaviors, attitudes, and decisions that perpetuate them.

REFERENCES

Beach, L. R. (1990). *Image theory: Decision making in personal and organizational contexts*. New York: Wiley.

Beach, L. R., & Mitchell, T. R. (1990). Image theory: A behavioral theory of decision making in organizations. In B. M. Staw & L. L. Cummings (Eds.), *Research in organizational behavior* (Vol. 12, pp. 1–41), Greenwich, CT: JAI.

London, M. (1995). *Self and interpersonal insight: How people evaluate themselves and others in organizations*. New York: Oxford University Press.

1

Person Perception in Organizations: An Overview of the Field

Richard J. Klimoski
Lisa M. Donahue
George Mason University

Much of organizational behavior and processes are rooted in person perception phenomena. Person perception in organizational contexts represents motivated social judgment processes related to applied problems or issues such as Whom do I hire? Whom do I promote? Whom do I mentor? and Whom do I trust? Person perception phenomena have been addressed more or less directly both in the basic social psychological literature and in the applied personnel judgment and evaluation literature.

The primary goal of the chapter is to organize these phenomena in some meaningful way, as well as to identify their antecedents and consequences in organizational settings. As an overview, this chapter contains content similar to more traditional chapters on person perception found in social cognition texts, with an important exception. We examine person perception from the perspective of both social cognition and applied organizational research. The social cognition literature provides a theoretical perspective or "meta-theory" to produce insights into the processes underlying problems of practical importance. In a complementary way, applied organizational research provides examples of the types of interpersonal and social environments in which cognitive processes may be studied.

5

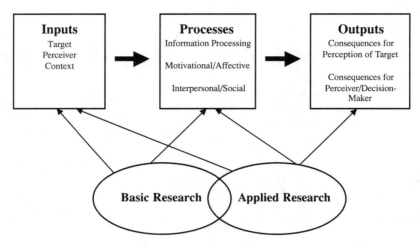

FIG. 1.1.   Input-Processes-Output (IPO) framework of person perception.

To organize the basic and applied literature and to understand when and where in work settings person perception processes are relevant, we adopt an input-processes-output (IPO) framework (see Fig. 1.1). We deviate from the traditional sequence followed in an IPO framework and start with a discussion of outputs, as our primary interest is in explaining and predicting the outcomes of person perception. We then move on to processes and, finally, inputs. Given space limitations, our discussion of person perception outcomes and inputs is cursory relative to processes. We anticipate that in subsequent chapters of this book these variables will be described in greater detail.

MAJOR THEMES

In reviewing the literature on person perception, we weave our discussion around two higher order themes. The first theme characterizes the social perceiver/decision maker as a "motivation tactician" (Fiske, 1992; Fiske, 1993; Fiske & Taylor, 1991). That is, he or she has goals for person perception and these will guide the strategies he or she uses. The second theme characterizes the social perceiver as a "coproducer" of person perception. In other words, person perception involves interaction, and the perceiver is an active participant in this interaction.

By emphasizing the coproductive nature of person perception, we accomplish the second major goal for this chapter and that is to set the analytic tone for the other chapters in this volume. Specifically, we adopt two analytic approaches consistent with the theme of coproduction. First, a dynamic and reciprocal approach is used to reflect the manner in which person perception is played out over time in social and work settings. Second, an embedded perspective is used to incorporate the idea that various levels of description (i.e., social perceiver, target, relationship, and context) affect person perception. Examples from the applied literature illustrate these analytic approaches.

WHAT IS MEANT BY "PERSON PERCEPTION PROCESSES"?

For the purposes of this chapter, we operationalize person perception phenomena as including cognitive processes, motivational and affective processes, and interpersonal and social factors. As we discuss in more detail later, this operationalization stems from the growing recognition that emotions and motivations interact with cognitive processes to influence person perception and that both interpersonal and social dynamics also play a part in the evaluation of others (see Forgas, 1995; Gollwitzer & Moskowitz, 1996; Kruglanski, 1996; Kunda, 1999).

It is important to note that when we talk about person perception, we are talking about the processes by which individuals form impressions and make inferences about other people. These impressions and inferences can be made in response to nonverbal, verbal, and interpersonal cues. As Fig. 1.2 illustrates, the behavioral cues of interest can stem from any one of a number of interactions occurring within the social context in which person perception takes place. These interactions include the target's behavior

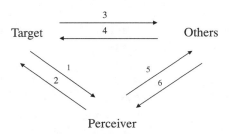

FIG. 1.2. Sources of behavioral cues from social interactions.

toward the perceiver (line 1), especially with regard to the perceiver's behavior toward the target (line 2), the target's behavior toward others (line 3), others' behavior toward the target (line 4), the perceiver's behavior toward others (line 5), especially with regard to others' behavior toward the perceiver (line 6). It is easy to see from this illustration that person perception and the interpersonal context are inextricably tied to one another.

A reasonable question regarding the processes involved in person perception is which are likely to lead to more accurate decisions and which are not. Indeed, the issue of accuracy has received considerable attention by researchers (for discussions see Funder, 1987; Kruglanski, 1989; Swann, 1984). As pointed out by Kruglanski (1989), however, ". . . as of now, no compelling analysis exist concerning the general process whereby accuracy is obtained" (p. 401). We agree that trying to identify the conditions or processes that always result in more accurate judgments is a somewhat futile endeavor. Furthermore, we think that person perception phenomena may be unsuitable to characterize in terms of accuracy, mainly because of the contingent and volatile nature of what is being perceived. Stated more simply, as a result of the dynamic and reciprocal nature of perception in social interaction, what may be accurate at one moment, may not be at the next. Instead, we suggest that the reader think of the inferences derived from person perception in terms of *appropriateness, usefulness*, or both, given the demands of the perceiver's task (see Fiske, 1992; Swann, 1984 for more on this perspective). Essentially, we are saying that applied judgements, like most human endeavors where accuracy is concerned, are strongly influenced by the motivation and capacity (skill) of the perceiver, as well as the clarity of the situation. Throughout this chapter, we discuss these factors and point out how they influence the processes and strategies used by social perceivers. In keeping with one of the chapter's major themes, we pay particular attention to motivation, indicating how perceivers can be motivated to worry about being more accurate.

OUTPUTS: APPLIED PROBLEMATICS IN ORGANIZATIONAL SETTINGS

Ultimately, applied researchers and practitioners are interested in explaining and predicting the outcomes of person perception. We characterize these outputs as applied problems and decisions, which can be further thought of as either formal or informal and as having consequences for either the target or the perceiver.

Formal decisions include those applied problematics in human resource management related to the selection, appraisal, and development of employees, whereas *informal decisions* include those related to interpersonal interactions in organizational contexts, including those relevant to phenomena such as mentoring, negotiation, conflict resolution, and multicultural relationships. Various combinations of these outcomes, such as formal decisions to promote, select, or develop an employee or informal assessments of leadership, impaired group social interaction, or a negotiation opponent's vantage point are addressed throughout the various chapters in this volume.

Before discussing the potential consequences or outcomes for the social perceiver/decision maker, it is important to identify this person. In most applied settings, this individual is typically the human resource (HR) practitioner or manager, or in some cases coworkers and teammates. In this chapter, we refer to this individual generally as the *social perceiver*. In future chapters, this person is identified more specifically.

The *consequences for the social perceiver/decision maker* are generally thought of in terms of the impact of judgments, choices, decisions, and evaluations. Also, outcomes for the perceiver can include attitudes or behaviors. Thus a perception of trustworthiness might imply less work for the manager when it comes to monitoring a subordinate's performance.

Consequences for the target can be classified in terms of *formal decisions* and *formal judgments*. Formal decisions include those made for hiring and promotion. Examples of formal judgments include those related to (a) attributes, such as those made in assessment centers and employment interviews; (b) intentions, such as those made in the service of employee development and career management; (c) performance, such as those relevant to performance assessment and appraisal; and (d) suitability, such as those relevant to promotion or training. Clearly, most individuals are strongly affected by decisions and judgments in the workplace that are derived from perceptual processes.

PROCESSES: MOVING BEYOND COGNITION

We have selected basic processes that are the most informative for understanding how person perception in work-related situations takes place. In addition, our selection was guided by the growing recognition that motivation and affect can and do affect person perception by influencing the concepts, beliefs, and rules used by perceivers in making social judgments

(Forgas, 1995; Gollwitzer & Moskowitz, 1996; Kruglanski, 1996; Kunda, 1990). Moreover, researchers now know that motivation and affect influence the mode of processing information. That is, the extent to which these processes are under the perceiver's control depends in large part on his or her goals and mood.

"Hot" Versus "Cold" Cognition

These discoveries have moved the field away from thinking about person perception as rational, information-driven processes (referred to as "cold" cognition), toward considering the influence of motivational and affective processes or "hot" cognition (Zajonc, 1980). Indeed, it is now evident that prescribed models of social judgment (e.g., Cooper, 1981; Lord, 1985) are, at best, heuristics. But because researchers were guided by these models for so long, they assumed more cognitive-based explanations for the outcomes of person perception than warranted.

This growing recognition of the distinction between "hot" and "cold" cognition in the social cognition literature has led us to include motivational and affective processes in our review of person perception phenomena relevant to understanding others in work-related contexts. Thus, our view of social perception includes cognitive, motivational, and affective processes. Because these processes are carried out in social settings, and social dynamics affect and are affected by these processes, we also consider social and interpersonal factors in our discussion.

Purposeful Person Perception

The notion that perceivers have a purpose (e.g., are motivated) reflects a shift in thinking by social cognition and person perception researchers. There is growing agreement that social perceivers select approaches to social cognition that are good enough to accomplish their goals for the setting, which for the most part involve trying to "make sense" out of another person so that they can make better choices regarding their own actions (Fiske, 1992, 1993).

Although pragmatic, person perception is still grounded in social information processing and social judgment. Thus, before addressing motivational and affective drivers, we discuss basic cognitive processes involved in person perception. We then move on to some special issues or considerations of person perception phenomena in applied contexts.

Social Information Processing

In this section, we establish some basic nomenclature by examining the social information processing involved in making social judgments and inferences. It is important to note that what we describe are basic cognitive phenomena (structures, processes, and strategies) that enable the social perceiver to form impressions and make judgments of others. Throughout our discussion of these phenomena, we point out their utility for the motivated tactician in attempting to predict others' behavior in the interest of satisfying his or her own goals.

Cognitive Structures. The structures used most often by social perceivers for everyday undertakings are schemas. Schemas are cognitive structures that represent knowledge about a concept or type of stimulus including its attributes and relations among those attributes. Schemas are used to understand people especially in situations where the social perceiver is confronted with incomplete or ambiguous information. Specifically, they allow the perceiver to "fill in the gaps" in making inferences regarding the knowledge, traits, disposition, and intentions of the target, as well as the social category to which he or she belongs. In addition, they influence other cognitive processes such as encoding, storage, and recall in a top-down fashion (Schacter, 1999; Wyer & Srull, 1994).

The schemas people use in person perception are person, role, and event (scripts) schemas. Person schemas are cognitive structures that organize one's knowledge about the traits and goals of individuals. Fiske (1993) suggested that reliance on traits is consistent with a pragmatic perspective. That is, social perceivers use traits because they enable them to make predictions about others' future behavior and to determine an appropriate interaction approach. Moreover, because of their level of abstraction, traits are more economical than behaviors. Thus, people are more likely to report traits than behaviors in describing others.

Because both social and work contexts imply roles, social perceivers in such contexts will also use role schemas in understanding others' behavior. A role schema is a cognitive structure that organizes one's knowledge about the behaviors expected of a person in a certain social position. Whereas trait schemas are more informative than behaviors, role schemas are more informative than traits (Fiske & Taylor, 1991). However, one's person and role structures are likely to interact such that trait processing occurs in-and-round roles. Evidence of this with regard to applied judgments can be found in Borman's (1987) work on personal constructs, or "folk theories."

Borman found that general dimensions such as maturity/responsibility, organization, technical proficiency, and assertive leadership were among the personal constructs included in raters' theories of effectiveness in managerial roles.

Finally, event schemas or scripts also influence social information processing. Event schemas describe the predicted or appropriate sequence of events that occur in specific situations (e.g., job interview). Because they shape one's normative expectations of behavior in social settings, deviations from scripts will draw attention. People are likely to rely heavily on such unexpected and/or inappropriate behavior when making inferences and judgments regarding others. Such would be the case when an interviewer makes an inference that a job applicant is not very interested in the position because he or she is late to the interview or is dressed too casually.

Inference (Attribution) Processes.   As suggested before, cognitive structures allow the social perceiver to make sense of the target by aiding inferences about the target on the basis of the available information. The basic process through which these inferences are made can be generally referred to as attribution. More formally, attribution is the process by which people seek to identify the causes of a target's behavior (Baron & Byrne, 2000). In so doing, individuals can gain knowledge of the target—including stable traits and dispositions and more transient intentions.

We highlight five types of inference processes that we believe to be common for most applied inference and judgment tasks. These include inferences regarding the knowledge, traits, disposition, intentions, and social category membership of the target. *Knowledge inferences* are made in situations where the perceiver needs to impute a social target's knowledge or understand what the target knows (see Nickerson, 1999, for a recent discussion). *Trait inferences* are made by the perceiver when trying to determine the target's underlying traits or qualities on the basis of the available information. *Dispositional inferences* are made in the service of understanding the target's probable patterns of behavior. Although some traits have dispositional qualities (e.g., energetic, aggressive, lazy, etc.), dispositions relate more to typical behavioral tendencies. In contrast, *intention inferences* are made by the perceiver when attempting to understand the target's more proximal, or immediate goals. Finally, *social category inferences* are made to identify and classify a target as a member of a larger social grouping (e.g., good vs. poor performers). Together, these inferences allow the pragmatic social perceiver to both make sense out of and manage his or her social world. That is, they help the perceiver to understand and predict others' behavior as well as choose his or her own behavior in an effort to facilitate interpersonal interaction.

Although people rely on the surface features (e.g., physical appearance) and behavior of the target in making attributions regarding the target's behavior, earlier inferences can also inform later ones. Thus, these inferences work together to aid the social perceiver in making sense out of the target. For instance, traits can be used to infer other traits. Such is the case when early trait inferences, called *spontaneous trait inferences*, activate *implicit personality theories* (Schneider, 1973), or beliefs about how a set of traits are interrelated, and thus produce an overall impression of the target in terms of his or her traits. But, in addition to other traits, knowledge and intentions can also assist in making trait inferences. Indeed, research has found that social perceivers often rely on the target's goals or intentions to infer traits (Borkenau, 1990; Read, Jones, & Miller, 1990). A final example of the influence of earlier inferences on later ones is when a social categorization is primed and relied on to infer levels of knowledge. This occurs when inferences are made regarding what an individual knows on the basis of an assessment of his or her race, gender, or occupation.

It is important to note that in addition to aiding subsequent inferences, earlier judgments may also interfere with them. An example of this occurs when the social context may prime or trigger a goal to categorize a target as "good" or "bad." This general impression then "engulfs" the traits associated with it, increasing their observed correlations even when their true scores do not covary. Cooper (1981) evoked such an explanation in accounting for the occurrence of halo error in applied judgments.

Ultimately, which inference(s) people make and the amount of control they exert over the inference process depend on their motives and goals in the particular judgment situation. However, in the absence of any specific information processing goals, social perceivers are likely to succumb to categorization first because social categories are easily perceived on the basis of available and obvious physical features (Brewer, 1988; Fiske & Neuberg, 1990). Although these categorizations and subsequent inferences do occur somewhat automatically (see Gilbert, Pelham, & Krull, 1988; Uleman, Newman, & Moskewitz, 1996), they can be brought under more conscious control by social perceivers (see Brewer, 1988; Fiske & Neuberg, 1990). As discussed in greater detail in the following section, the social perceiver's motives (e.g., accuracy) play a large part in determining whether the perceiver goes beyond immediate categorizations and characterizations of the target.

Cognitive Heuristics.   Thus far, we have described how the pragmatic social perceiver uses cognitive structures and inference processes to
understand others. We now consider cognitive heuristics as an additional
cognitive tool that shapes the way social perceivers form impressions of
others. Heuristics are cognitive principles and strategies that allow people
to make social judgments quickly and with less effort. Social perceivers
develop and learn to use heuristics to make judgments efficiently, especially
under conditions that may not be best suited for accuracy and thorough-
ness. More specifically, social perceivers rely on these "shortcuts" when
they lack the resources or motivation to engage in more effortful processing. However, it is important to note that heuristics do not always lead to
accurate inferences, but they may be good enough for most undertakings.

For the most part, attention has been given in the general cognition
literature to intrapersonal heuristics, including the availability heuristic, the
representativeness heuristic, and anchoring and adjustment (see Kahneman,
Solvic, & Tversky, 1982). We review these and offer some interpersonal
heuristics that we believe perceivers also use in an attempt to maintain the
predictability of their social worlds.

Intrapersonal Heuristics.   Social perceivers use the availability
heuristic whenever they make a judgment on the basis of how easily specific
types of information come to mind. The use of this heuristic may explain the
tendency of perceivers/decision makers to make judgments and evaluations
on the basis of the target's most recent behavior rather than his or her typical
performance (e.g., Farr, 1973; Highhouse & Gallo, 1997; Steiner & Rain,
1989).

The representativeness heuristic is used as a strategy when social perceivers make judgments on the basis of the extent to which something is
similar to a typical case. An example of the use of this heuristic also involves judgments of typical behavior. Specifically, the representativeness
heuristic may be used when perceivers/decision makers use a target's max-
imal job performance to make inferences regarding typical performance
(see Sackett, Zedeck, & Fogli, 1988).

Anchoring and adjustment involves using a number or value as a starting
point and then adjusting one's judgment away from this anchor. The use
of this heuristic is ubiquitous because social behavior lacks an objective
yardstick. Thus, social perceivers often anchor their judgments by relying on their own experiences, the behavior or attributes of others, or the
(relevant or irrelevant) details of the situation. This heuristic may explain
the presence of contrast effects in the interview and performance appraisal,

whereby decision makers evaluate targets relative to one another rather than some standard (see Highhouse & Gallo, 1997). Anchoring and adjustment also occurs when social perceivers use their own knowledge to anchor their inferences of what the target knows and then rely on information provided by the immediate context to make adjustments (Nickerson, 1999).

Finally, social perceivers may also use priming as a cognitive heuristic (Baron & Byrne, 2000). That is, in addition to being primed by the situational characteristics, social perceivers may also generate their own primes to assist in person perception. We already examined the notion that earlier inferences can inform later inferences. Essentially, these earlier inferences (e.g., spontaneous trait inferences and social categorization), serve as primes and affect the social perceiver's ratings of the target on other (often related) dimensions (e.g., Moskowitz & Roman, 1992).

Interpersonal Heuristics.

We propose that in addition to the intrapersonal heuristics discussed in the previous section, pragmatic social perceivers also rely on interpersonal heuristics to make inferences and to ensure a certain level of predictability in their social interactions. Like the aforementioned strategies, we believe that social perceivers use interpersonal heuristics under conditions of high cognitive load with, generally, little to no awareness. Under certain circumstances, however, the use of these heuristics may get raised to a controlled level of processing. Such would be the case when a newcomer to a team deliberately uses interpersonal heuristics to understand and predict the other members' behavior in the most quick and efficient way as possible.

We believe that the interpersonal heuristics that operate in most social judgment settings drift toward an assessment of similarities, differences, or both. That is, when making inferences about the target, the social perceiver uses as a strategy his or her assessment of how the target seems relative to others. Also, in the absence of other social agents on which to base such relative judgments, the perceiver assesses the degree to which the target is similar to or different from him or herself. Moreover, it is quite likely that, minus information to the contrary, the perceiver assumes similarity. The literature on the *false consensus effect* (e.g., Marks & Miller, 1987) and *illusion of outgroup homogeneity* (Linville, Fischer, & Salovey, 1989) provides evidence for such a bias.

Assessments of similarity and dissimilarity truly have utility for the pragmatic social perceiver. First, because of the *transference* phenomenon (Andersen & Cole, 1990), social perceivers can more easily make inferential leaps when encountering similar others (Fiske, 1993). Thus, assessments of similarity and dissimilarity can decrease the cognitive and motivational resources required for inference making, but they can also impact cognition and motivation more directly. As discussed in greater detail in the next section on motivational processes, such information provides cues to the social perceiver regarding the amount of effort to allocate to the inference task. An assessment of similarity would cue the perceiver that more systematic and effortful processing is not required, whereas an assessment of dissimilarity would indicate just the opposite.

The specific interpersonal heuristics we believe to be grounded in assessments of similarity and dissimilarity include *social categorization* and *observance of the norm of reciprocity*. We already discussed social categorization as a key inference in the process of understanding others, but a significant body of research also documents its heuristic utility (e.g., Bodenhausen, 1990, 1993; Macrae, Milne, & Bodenhausen, 1994). We believe that social categorization serves as an interpersonal heuristic by allowing the social perceiver to divide the social world into categories on the basis of similarities or differences in readily detectable (e.g., age, gender, and race) and less observable characteristics (e.g., occupation and religion). Category membership, as discussed earlier, is then used by the perceiver as the basis for making inferences and attributions regarding the target (e.g., the target is the same as or different from the perceiver or the target is the same as or different from others).

Reciprocity (i.e., the equal exchange of information or rewards) is a common normative expectation to which most social agents subscribe in the conduct of their social interactions. The *norm of reciprocity* requires that people repay others' behavior with a form of behavior that is similar. Because this expectation is so commonplace, we believe that social perceivers use its observance as an interpersonal heuristic in judging similarity and dissimilarity. For instance, the return of an equally private and personal self-disclosure by the target may be used by the perceiver in an evaluation of similarity, and in turn, attributions of trust. Failure to observe the norm of reciprocity, however, will lead to the opposite effect.

Are People Always Heuristical?   Although there is evidence that the use of schemas and heuristics is the default in social perception and judgment, the pragmatic social perceiver abandons such effort-saving strategies in favor of more systematic and controlled processing when cues from the social environment indicate that it is necessary to do so. Models of impression formation (e.g., Brewer, 1988; Fiske & Neuberg, 1990) suggest that social perceivers use a continuum of processes in forming impressions that range from more schematic to more individuating (data driven). If the perceiver interprets the available data as supporting the schema, then he or she allows it to drive inference processes. However, if a determination is made that the data contradict the schema, then the perceiver relies less on the schema and more on the data.

Motivation is also an important determinant of just how far down the continuum of impression formation processes a social perceiver will move. Otherwise stated, when a social perceiver is sufficiently motivated to do so, he or she will engage in more individuating processing. We now turn our attention to motivational processes and discuss the role of motives and goals on the manner in which individuals carry out person perception.

Motivational Processes

Given the pragmatic nature of person perception, the cognitive structures, processes, and strategies used by the motivated tactician are thought to depend on his or her motives in relationship to the situation. Two general motivational states relevant to social perception in applied contexts include those that deal with the costs of being indecisive (expectancy-oriented motives) and those that deal with the costs of being wrong (accuracy-oriented motives; see Fiske & Neuberg, 1990; Fiske & Taylor, 1991). Either of these stems from forces in the environment that motivate perceivers to seek to make accurate or "quick and dirty" decisions.

Motives That Make Salient the Costs of Being Indecisive.
In general, the costs of indecision increase whenever resources are limited. Here people will engage in more cursory, superficial processing in which "information search is curtailed, inconsistencies are ignored or seen as affirming, and snap judgments are justified" (Fiske, 1993, p. 175). According to Fiske, these quick and dirty strategies enable people to be "good enough social perceivers" and, surprisingly, allows arrival at judgments that are pretty accurate, given cognitive constraints. A number of factors can cause capacity limitations and the corresponding use of more simplified strategies (see Fiske, 1993; Kunda, 1999 for reviews). Among these factors are time pressures (Gollwitzer, 1990; Gollwitzer & Kinney, 1989), *cognitive busyness* (i.e., the current engagement in another cognitively demanding task; Gilbert, 1989; Gilbert & Hixon, 1991), anticipation of a social interaction or one's turn in this interaction (Gilbert et al., 1988; Osborne & Gilbert, 1992; Stangor & Ford, 1992), and anticipation of communication (Fiske & Taylor, 1991).

Basic research suggests that when the information processing environment reaches a certain level of difficulty, social perceivers are likely to rely on tools, such as stereotypes, in their "cognitive toolbox" (Gilbert & Hixon, 1991; Macrae et al., 1994). Indeed, evidence for the influence of cognitive busyness on the use of age-associated stereotypes in the interview has been found by Perry and colleagues (Perry & Finkelstein, 1999; Perry, Kulik, & Bourhis, 1996). As another example of this effect in applied settings, Zedeck (1986) posited that the requirement of assessors to participate in role playing may interfere with their "ability to observe as well as impact the selectivity of what is observed" (p. 275), and therefore rely on automatic or heuristic processing of social information.

Motives That Make Salient the Costs of Being Wrong. When the costs of being wrong are salient and it becomes necessary to be more accurate, perceivers/decision makers tend to exert considerably more control over social information processing. That is, when elicited, an accuracy motivate can cause them to invest more effort in the judgment task and apply strategies that are more detailed and complex (Kruglanski, 1980). Although the mere instruction to be as accurate as possible has been shown to cause perceivers to exert more effort toward and more control over information processing (Neuberg, 1989, 1994; Pavelchack, 1989), an accuracy motive is more likely to be elicited from cues from the social environment. In applied settings, such things as prevailing norms and the social structure (e.g., cooperative interdependence, status hierarchy, etc.) can increase the costs of being wrong and thus elicit an accuracy motive. Although these conditions are elaborated on in the next section on interpersonal and social processes, it is important to note that a number of them stem from the perceiver's lack of control in his or her social environment. In this regard, the social perceiver is truly pragmatic. As a result of this deprivation of control, the social perceiver will be motivated to increase the accuracy of his or her judgments in the hopes of improving the chances of satisfying personal goals (see Dépret & Fiske, 1993; Pittman & D'Agostino, 1989; Pittman & Heller, 1987).

Interaction of Motives and Goals. The foregoing might be thought of as "meta-motives" for judgments and evaluations in applied settings. There are arguably other, more immediate goals that are operating. Such a view is consistent with prevailing theoretical models of work motivation in the industrial and organizational psychology literature in which both proximal and distal goals exist for task performance in applied settings (see Kanfer, 1990; Kanfer & Ackerman, 1989). Distal goals are involved in initially deciding to allocate one's effort and cognitive resources for a particular task, but it is proximal goals that are more closely involved in the allocation of these resources throughout task completion.

The importance of goals for social behavior was recently underscored by Kenrick, Neuberg, and Cialdini (1999). As a result, these authors used goals as an organizing device for their recent social psychology text. In our view, the goals that have the greatest influence on most person perception tasks overlap to a large degree with Kenrick et al.'s and include (a) getting the task done (e.g., hiring someone), (b) preserving one's self-esteem (i.e., not looking foolish), and (c) maintaining relationships. Because of cognitive limitations, focusing on some goals may reduce the capacity to entertain others. Which of these proximal goals gain priority depends on which goals are primed by the situation or are compatible with other goals. However, some goals are chronically active because of frequent use or survival value (e.g., to protect oneself).

Depending on the situation, these goals will influence the perceiver's motives, rather than be influenced by them. Thus, these goals may often conflict with more distal, accuracy-oriented motives. This accounts for many of the judgment and evaluation errors documented in the applied literature. For instance, many rating errors in performance appraisal may actually be the result of the perceiver's consideration of the social consequences and a goal to maintain interpersonal relationships (see Longenecker, Sims, & Gioia, 1987; Wherry & Bartlett, 1982). That is, being aware of a requirement to report impressions (evaluations), the supervisor often appeared to "choose" between the benefits and social risks of finding ways to document ratings that would be extreme (e.g., the worker is very good or poor) or generating an appraisal that is somewhere in the middle—or average (i.e., the central tendency "error"). In this example, it is sometimes arguable as to just how aware the perceiver/rater is of these tradeoffs.

Similarly, invalid ratings or rating errors found in interviews, assessment centers, and performance appraisals may be accounted for by a proximal goal to "get the job done." In other words, the social perceiver may succumb to the pressure of the evaluative requirement by formulating an initial global judgment of suitability or effectiveness quickly, thus stopping short of a fully engaged assessment of the target's individual characteristics and attributes. As detailed earlier in this chapter, these global impressions frequently lead to the so-called halo error found in so many ratings. They are also implicated in *primacy effects*, or the undue influence of first impressions.

Motivation and Cognition.   Goals have been shown to influence the cognitive structures and beliefs (see Dunning, 1999), cognitive recall (Sanitioso, Kunda, & Fong, 1990), inferential processes and heuristics (Doosje, Spears, & Koomen, 1995; Pendry & Macrae, 1996; Vonk, 1999) of social perceivers, as well as the amount of effort they invest in searching for relevant beliefs and rules to apply (Ditto & Lopez, 1992; Kruglanski, 1980). In all, this research points to the conclusion that person perception processes and judgments are colored by one's motives.

Affective Processes

People's judgments and decisions regarding others will also be "heated up" by their emotions (Forgas, 1991; Kunda, 1999). That is, their structures, strategies, and modes of processing can be colored by their affective system, which consists of interpersonal evaluations, emotions, and moods. As discussed by Fiske and Taylor (1991), interpersonal evaluations and moods are affective states that are simple, long-term positive or negative feelings. Their distinction lies in whether they have a specific target: Interpersonal evaluations are in response to a specific target, whereas moods are not. In contrast, emotions are complex, relatively brief reactions involving physiological responses, subjective cognitive states, and expressive behaviors (Fiske & Taylor, 1991; Forgas, 1994).

Although there is growing agreement that an interplay exists between affect and cognition (e.g., Forgas, 1994; Isen & Baron, 1991), we limit our comments in this section to a discussion of the influence of affect on phenomena involved in person perception. In particular, we examine the manner in which mood impacts social judgments in applied settings, mainly because most of the applied research has focused in this area. In doing so, we point out the utility of moods to the social perceiver. Contrary to popular suggestions that affective states (moods and emotions) are irrational and sources of human error, we take the view that, like motives, moods have functional value (see also Kenrick et al., 1998; Zajonc, 1998). Moods alert the perceiver to changes in the environment and the need to alter current or adopt new information processing strategies (see Taylor, 1991). In this regard, we believe that moods work hand-in-hand with goals in the service of the motivated tactician. Before elaborating on these ideas, we first review some general findings of the impact of mood on people's judgments and behavior.

Mood-Congruent Social Judgment.   A great deal of research has found that a small mood manipulation (e.g., presentation of a small gift, exposure to a pleasant piece of music, etc.), can influence the cognitive processes of social perceivers (for reviews see Forgas, 1995; Schwarz & Clore, 1996). In general, this research has found evidence of mood-congruent judgment, or a match between mood and thoughts. Specifically, one's judgments of both self and others tend to be more positive when one is in a good mood and more negative when one is in a bad mood.

Mood-congruent judgments are explained as a result of mood-congruent memory (Bower, 1981, 1991). When a particular affective state is activated, it triggers cognitive categories that are similar or related to the affective state. Because this set of retrieved memories is congruent with mood, judgments tend to be congruent also. We say more about mood-congruent memory later when we discuss the mechanisms by which mood (affect) influences judgments.

Support for the mood-congruent judgment effect is found in the literature on performance appraisal and the employment interview. Whereas some researchers have examined mood, specifically, others have investigated the effects of liking as a more directed (i.e., focused on a specific person) affective state. In either case, the results point to the same conclusion: Positive moods and liking lead to more favorable evaluations of the target (e.g., Baron, 1993; Dalessio & Imada, 1984; Dipboye, 1992; Judge & Ferris, 1993; Robbins & DeNisi, 1994; Wayne & Ferris, 1990).

Mood and Cognitive Processes.   Forgas' (1995) *affect infusion model* (AIM) provides insight into just how moods and emotions influence social judgment and the manner in which people make such judgments. Specifically, Forgas posited that affect influences cognitive processes through two mechanisms. First, as illustrated by mood-congruent memory, affect serves to *prime* (trigger) similar or related (positive or negative) memories. Second, affect provides a heuristic cue to be cognitively processed along with other information about the target. Under conditions in which the social perceiver lacks the capability, motivation, or both, to engage in more effortful processing, he or she will use *affect-as-information* and look to his or her mood to inform social judgments.

Mood and the Motivated Tactician.   As suggested earlier, affect may interact with motives to help serve the purposes of the pragmatic social perceiver. Fiske and Taylor (1991) elaborated most on this notion and characterize moods and emotions as "managers of goals". Specifically, these authors suggest that emotions act as controls on cognition by alerting social perceivers to important goals. That is, emotions function as "alarm signals" that interrupt planned behavior and focus the perceiver's attention on other goals that have increased in priority (Simon, 1967, 1982). Thus, emotions serve the adaptive purpose of prioritizing goals for social perceivers, thereby allowing them to shift their goals with the changing demands of the social environment.

Interpersonal and Social Factors

Interpersonal and social realities affect many of the above cognitive, motivational, and affective phenomena previously discussed. Specifically, we expect that these interpersonal and social factors shape the motivational and affective states of the social perceiver, and in turn, the types of cognitive structures, processes, and strategies he or she uses to make sense of others. Additionally, we posit that in a reciprocal fashion, the inferences and judgments that are outcomes of these processes have further consequences for the nature and quality of the perceiver's interpersonal and social relationships.

The interpersonal and social factors that we discuss in this section can generally be classified in terms of the nature of the interpersonal relationships and the structure of the social context. With regard to interpersonal relationships, such things as the history of the relationship and the similarity between the target and the perceiver are expected to make a difference for person perception. The realities of the social context that we anticipate will influence person perception processes include (a) the degree of outcome dependence among the social agents, (b) the status, power, and hierarchical structure among the agents, and (c) the accountability of the social perceiver to other agents (see Fiske & Taylor, 1991 for a more detailed discussion of these factors.)

History and Quality of the Relationship. In general, the longer the perceiver has known the target, the more automatic and accurate social information processing and judgment become (see Fiske, 1993). In the social cognition literature, the degree of involvement between the perceiver and target is referred to as *acquaintance*. Under certain conditions, acquaintance has been shown to improve consensus, or the amount of agreement among a group of perceivers (see Kenny, 1991). It also leads to judgments that are determined more by the target than by the perceiver (Malloy & Albright, 1990). These findings can be explained by the availability of a much larger sample of behavior on which to base judgments and inferences. An example of this in the applied judgment domain comes from the assessment center literature. In general, the validity of assessors' ratings increases with opportunities to observe dimension (trait) relevant behavior (see Lievens & Klimoski, in press, for a recent review). However, evidence from the zero-contact (i.e., having zero acquaintance with the target) literature suggests that, even without the benefit of social interaction, perceivers are fairly accurate at judging others' traits (see Zebrowitz & Collins, 1997 for a review).

The quality of the relationship also has implications for social judgment. Research on ingroups versus outgroups suggests that a supervisor's evaluation of the performance of each of his or her subordinates is influenced by the quality of their dyadic relationship. Specifically, evidence exists to indicate that supervisors evaluate the performance of ingroup members more favorably than it actually is (Vecchio & Gobdel, 1984), whereas outgroup members typically receive more negative evaluations (Linville & Jones, 1980). Also, as compared to subordinates belonging to the ingroup, outgroup members often receive somewhat similar evaluations (Linville & Jones, 1980). This effect is attributed to the use of stereotypes, and thus suggests that supervisors are not as motivated to use more effortful, systematic processing for outgroup members.

Similarity of Target and Perceiver.

Similarity between the perceiver and target in terms of demographic and other characteristics often leads to perceived similarity in attitudes and values and to interpersonal attraction (Graves, 1993). Such perceived similarity presents a potential source of error in information processing. For example, perceived similarity results in the "similar to me" bias documented in the context of the employment interview (Dalessio & Imada, 1984; Graves & Powell, 1988). When interviewers perceive the applicant to be similar to them in attitudes and other characteristics, they are more likely to evaluate the applicant favorably.

However, similarity can also increase the accuracy of perceivers' judgments. As discussed by Graves (1993), similarity can smooth interaction between the target and perceiver, thus facilitating more accurate information processing. In addition, because cognitive representations of similar others are both complex (i.e., possess numerous dimensions) and accessible, perceivers' evaluations of similar others tend to be less extreme (Linville & Jones, 1980).

Outcome Dependence.

As discussed earlier, any time individuals are stripped of control, they will be more motivated to put forth effort in processing social information so that they can arrive at fairly accurate judgments that enable them to understand or predict the person's behavior on whom they rely (see Depret & Fiske, 1993, 1999). Such is the case when social perceivers are dependent on one another for achieving some mutual goal or reward. Such outcome dependency can be found among work teams that are structured to increase positive interdependence. In such situations, team members will be more motivated to predict their teammates' behavior accurately, in an effort to control or at least predict their behavior.

    Status, Power, and Hierarchy.   Also because of control deprivation, individuals of lower status or in a subordinate position will be more diligent in their information processing. As evidence of this, Snodgrass (1992) found that subordinates are more accurate in predicting how leaders evaluate them than vice versa. In addition to followers, such imbalances of status and power also have implications for low-power group members (Tjosvold, 1978; Tjosvold & Sagaria, 1978).

    Accountability.   Finally, being accountable to a third party, or having to justify a decision, also causes perceivers to process information more carefully (see Tetlock, 1991). The basic mechanism here is the same: Accountability also puts the social perceiver under someone else's control. The potential influence of accountability on individuals making a variety of human resource decisions, including those decisions that are the outcomes of interviews or performance appraisal, have been discussed in great detail by Klimoski and colleagues (Frink & Klimoski, 1998; Klimoski & Inks, 1990).

Summary

In summarizing the basic person perception-linked phenomena, we have attempted to emphasize their interrelationships, particularly highlighting the impact of motivational and social factors on social inference and judgment. Although this pragmatic approach is starting to "take hold" in the applied judgment and evaluation literature (e.g., Murphy & Cleveland, 1995), we suggest to both researchers and practitioners that our knowledge of applied judgments and decisions can be greatly increased by adopting such a perspective.

INPUTS

We now move on to the input variables that influence the previously discussed processes and phenomena, which in turn affect the outcomes of person perception. We have identified three categories of input variables—those related to (a) the individual differences of the perceiver, (b) the individual differences of the target, and (c) the context.

Individual Differences of Perceivers

The characteristics of perceivers that are likely to make a difference include those that affect the manner in which they carry out the cognitive, affective, and motivational processes involved in social perception and judgment. In our review of the literature, we have identified four major categories of individual differences that serve as perceiver "inputs" into person perception: (a) traits and other characteristics; (b) motives; (c) abilities and skills; and (d) values, beliefs, and attitudes.

Both the basic and applied literature has given considerable attention to the first three categories of perceiver inputs. First, research has identified a number of traits that influence the way in which perceivers make social judgments, including cognitive complexity (Borman, 1979; Borman & Hallam, 1991; Schneier, 1977), personality (Borman, 1979; Graves, 1993), and rating style (Borman & Hallam, 1991). We have already considered the influence of motivation, but dispositions such as a high *need to avoid closure* versus a *need for closure* have also been shown to shape the processes and strategies used by perceivers to make judgments (e.g., Ford & Kruglanski, 1995). Finally, in addition to traits and motives, the abilities and skills of perceivers have also been shown to impact the quality of their judgments (e.g., Borman & Hallam, 1991; Cardy & Kehoe, 1984; Sagie & Magnezy, 1997).

Although less attention has been given to the impact of perceivers' values, beliefs, and attitudes, research on personal theories of performance (i.e., folk theories; see Borman, 1987; Zedeck, 1986) and implicit personality theories (Lord & Foti, 1986; Lord, Foti, & DeVader, 1984) suggest that because such beliefs influence the cognitive structures that perceivers use, they too make a difference. This has also been supported in the basic literature by studies that have found that perceivers' cognitive processes are biased by their own underlying personality traits (see Rusting, 1998). In addition, these idiosyncratic theories may also impact judgments more directly. Specifically, research has also found that perceivers were more accurate in assessing traits that were relevant to them than traits that were not (Britt & Shepperd, 1999; Wright & Dawson, 1988).

Individual Differences of the Target

What information is used by social perceivers to understand and predict a target's behavior? As discussed and illustrated in Fig. 1.1, visual and vocal nonverbal, verbal, and interpersonal cues stemming from the various interactions occurring within the social context provide the "fodder" for person perception. Important visual nonverbal cues include the observable physical characteristics of targets, including their age, race, and gender (Fiske, 1993). Evidence exists that these are the core categories used in classifying others (e.g., Brewer & Lui, 1989; Hoffman & Hurst, 1990). The specific characteristics on which perceivers focus tend to be those that are most uncommon or distinctive within the social context (e.g., physically handicapped or ethnic minority; Nelson & Klutas, 2000). The role of the social context in providing another source of information regarding targets is discussed later.

Along with physical characteristics, other visual nonverbal cues (e.g., physical attractiveness, eye contact, body orientation, smiling, and gestures) and vocal nonverbal cues (e.g., pitch, speech rate, pauses, and amplitude) may be used by social perceivers to make inferences. A recent study by DeGroot and Motowidlo (1999) suggests that personal reactions toward interviewees, such as liking, trust, and attributed credibility, are the primary mechanisms by which these characteristics influence applied judgments, including interview and performance evaluations.

As noted earlier, traits are "default" target inputs, and certain traits seem to have special importance (i.e., potency) in person perception (see Osgood, Saci, & Tannenbaum, 1957). Supporting this notion is the finding that some highly observable traits, including extraversion and warmth, facilitate consensus among perceivers (e.g., Berry 1991; Kenny, Horner, Kashy, & Chu, 1992). In all, this suggests that particular traits represent central dimensions in person schema (Fiske & Taylor, 1991). Indeed, it has been argued that the "Big Five" personality dimensions may reflect the basic trait structure used to perceive and describe others (Fiske, 1993).

Another important target characteristic in applied contexts is performance, as manifested in the target's acts (e.g., work products, accomplishments, etc.) and actions (behavior). In work settings, a supervisor has the opportunity to observe the target's performance over time, so variations in performance level provide another potential behavioral cue to be processed. In general, it has been found that perceivers' judgments of current performance are influenced by past performance (e.g., Buda, 1984 cited in Sumer & Knight, 1996; Murphy, Balzer, Lockhart, & Eisenman, 1985; Smither, Reilly, & Buda, 1988; Sumer & Knight, 1996). Moreover, the sequencing and patterning of performance also seem to make a difference (Sumer & Knight, 1996).

Contextual Features (Variables)

Features of the situation also provide input for person perception. Thus, it is especially important to consider these variables when studying person perception in work settings. Unfortunately, however, these variables often receive less attention in the literature on applied judgments (Murphy & Cleveland, 1995). Here we review contextual variables that we believe influence downstream person perception processes and outcomes.

Task Demands.   We have already discussed the effects of opportunity to observe and cognitive busyness on the ability of social perceivers to effectively carry out person perception processes. In addition to these factors, the purpose of the evaluation (Dobbins, Cardy, & Truxillo, 1988; Williams, DeNisi, Blencoe, & Cafferty, 1985; Zedeck & Cascio, 1982), cost of making a poor decision (Dipboye, 1992), and pressure to make quick decisions (Dipboye, 1992), also affect social perceivers' decision processes and effectiveness. Specifically, these demands impact motivation and the amount of control social perceivers are likely to exert over information processing. For example, interviewers under pressure to make a quick decision are more likely to use heuristic processing by seeking to confirm their initial impressions about applicants (Dipboye, 1992). As an example of the opposite effect of motivation, supervisors differentiate more among ratees when ratings are gathered to develop and improve employees rather than to determine merit raises or to decide which employees to retain (Zedeck & Cascio, 1982).

Group Characteristics.   In group settings, there is opportunity for other group members to influence the judgments of a target by providing perceivers with information for comparative judgments (Ilgen & Feldman, 1983). However, comparative information can also have a biasing influence. As discussed earlier, if a target is uncommon or distinctive from the rest of the group, then he or she may be characterized in stereotypic ways by the perceiver (e.g., Nelson & Klutas, 2000).

In addition, comparative judgments by social perceivers brought on by variation in target performance may lead to contrast effects. Specifically, in groups in which there is performance variability among members, the evaluations of poor performers tend to be higher than they should be, and the evaluations of good performers are lower than warranted (Mitchell & Liden, 1982). However, these effects may not necessarily lead to inaccurate ratings. Gaugler and Rudolph (1992) found that ratings of low performing assessees were more accurate when they were evaluated in a group of dissimilar, higher performers than when they were evaluated in a group of similar, lower performers.

Systems Features.   Although the positive influence of motivation on person perception processes and outcomes has been established, few studies have directly investigated the effects of organizational rewards or punishments on applied judgments and decisions. The research that has been conducted has shown greater incentives (e.g., obtaining rewards for subordinates, avoiding interpersonal tension, etc.) for inflated evaluations than negative consequences for inaccurate evaluations (Longenecker et al., 1987). However, research by Salvemini, Reilly, and Smither (1993) provided evidence that perceivers/decision makers can adopt more accuracy-oriented approaches when offered valued rewards. Specifically, these researchers found that raters who received monetary incentives were less likely to produce biased and inaccurate ratings resulting from their knowledge of the ratees' prior performance levels.

Other aspects of applied judgment and evaluation systems may also enable social perceiver/decision makers to carry out person perception processes more effectively. Standardized procedures (Dipboye & Gaugler, 1993), observation and rating tools (DeNisi & Peters, 1996; Reilly, Henry, & Smither, 1990), and training (Dipboye & Gaugler, 1993; Schleicher, Day, Mayes, & Riggio, 1999; Woehr & Huffcutt, 1994) all have been shown to positively influence social perceivers' judgment processes and effectiveness.

TOWARD AN EMBEDDED
SYSTEMS APPROACH

Up to this point, we have chosen to characterize the nature of person perception by using an organizing framework that implies a certain "flow" or even a causal sequence. Thus inputs are thought to have consequences for cognitive, affective, motivational, and interpersonal processes, and these in turn have an impact on decisions, choices, and even relationships. However, it also should be clear by now that person perception-linked phenomena rarely unfold in such a neat, even linear fashion. The capacity to model social perception is actually quite limited precisely because of its dynamic and contingent nature. In truth, the IPO approach is just a convenient way to organize material. It would need to be modified in substantial ways if we were to make it more than a heuristic and more like a model. Specifically, we would need to consider the role of reciprocal causation (feedback and feed forward) and the impact of social and normative forces.

The Arbitrary Distinction of "Cause" and "Effect"

In many contexts involving social cognition, the perceiver is in a position to interact with others, indeed it may be the reason for being together. In such contexts, the real or anticipated interaction with another individual is quite likely to have an effect on perceptions and behavior. Such things as the following affect social cognition in the context of interpersonal interaction: (a) the importance of the interaction, (b) the clarity of expectations held for that context, (c) the behavior relative to these expectations, and (d) the nature of future interaction anticipated.

For example, most interactions of interest to the readers of this book typically involve social perception in high stakes interpersonal contexts, as in the selection interview. In such contexts, deviations from expectations take on real significance for both the applicant and the HR professional. The behavior of the applicant has great bearing on what the interviewer is perceiving and thinking and will, in turn, determine the way that the latter behaves toward the applicant. Similarly, both the applicant's own initial behavior and the impact it has on the interviewer provide feedback and shape the next bit of social exchange. When the interaction between the two is going poorly, the applicant as perceiver has to use whatever cues he or she can to diagnose just what aspect of the situation is causing the apparent difficulty—aspects of the applicant's behavior, the interviewer's interpretation, or the social dynamics between the two. In this regard, the actual and anticipated behavior of the interviewer become the stimuli for social cognition on the part of the applicant. The management of affect on a "real-time" basis in high stakes situations creates still other difficulties for the perceiver (Parkinson, 1997). That is, the perceiver's own attributions for difficulty in the interview, such as self-blame versus a conclusion that the interviewer is just "having a bad day," will present different challenges for the management of emotions.

As noted earlier, one special case where the consequences of social interaction can have major implications for person perception dynamics occurs when the individuals anticipate that they will have to work together in the future. In this case, not only would the perceiver seek to make a favorable impression, he or she, in all likelihood, would choose to interact in a way that sets up the normative expectations preferred for their interaction in the future (e.g., Heneman, Greenberger, & Anonyuo, 1989; Liden, Wayne, & Stilwell, 1993). All and all, managing this collection of motives and goals presents a formidable challenge for valid information processing.

In a related manner, the behavior linked to the perceiver's sense of the situation, can itself, transform the situation. In its classic form, this can occur because the perceiver's actions elicit the very behaviors he or she expects. This dynamic is often referred to as the "self-fulfilling prophecy" (Merton, 1948). By word or deed the perceiver makes come true (activates or encourages) those behaviors that are anticipated or expected. Such a self-fulfilling prophecy may explain why interviewees who either accurately or inaccurately expect to be unqualified may, in fact, perform less well. Specifically, for such interviewees it has been found that the interviewers ask less favorable questions, conduct shorter sessions, and "leak" negative nonverbal behaviors (Dipboye, 1982; Neuberg, 1989). Indeed, most person perception involves the coproduction of social information.

Social Forces Influencing Person Perception

The examples just discussed were designed to highlight the manner by which person perception dynamics are affected by the interaction with another individual. However, in most applied settings there are still other social forces operating.

As described earlier in this chapter, the context makes a great deal of difference relative to such things as motivation, attention, social information-processing dynamics, and memory. It also makes a big impact on the quality or validity of conclusions or decisions that flow from such phenomena. One important aspect of context yet to be detailed, however, is the actual or considered presence of others.

Social Comparison Processes.   Both normative and social forces will influence the perceiver in the context of other social perceivers.

One well-researched dynamic derives from what Festinger (1954) called "social comparison processes." In its classic form, the perceiver, in an important but ambiguous situation, tries to understand what is going on around him or her by referring to the cues being emitted by others in the same situation. In some circumstances, this is done quite automatically and quickly, as in the case of what might be considered "behavioral contagion" (Polansky, Lippitt, & Redl, 1950; Wheeler, 1966). This occurs when the perceiver senses from others a deep fear or anxiety or when the perceiver lets such fears turn into panic behavior. The presence of other social perceivers may thus affect the perceptual processes through affect and emotional states (e.g., mood).

At a more controlled level, the social perceiver looks to others in the same situation for guidance at "sense making" or "social proof" for accurate social information processing (Cialdini, 1993). For example, as a member of a panel interview, the perceiver frequently looks around to colleagues to ascertain their reactions to a candidate and calibrates assessments and behavior accordingly. Indeed, in work situations where such panel members know one another well, subtle cues such as those found in their demeanor or word choice would serve as indicators of opinion or evaluations of the candidate and affect the perceiver's own impressions accordingly.

Group Decision Making. A particular setting for such social influence is in the context of group decision making. As individuals come together to solve problems or make decisions, they are usually both the source of and the recipient of influence attempts. Certainly, such things as the issues under review and the level of motivation and knowledge of team members will govern much of what transpires in such sessions. Moreover, in the business setting, local norms will exist regarding the nature and amount of conflict that is expressed as well. Some firms are more tolerant of both cognitive (ideational) and interpersonal conflict (Jehn, 1997). All this said, it would be reasonable to expect that the perceiver would be strongly affected by social processes. Indeed, this has been amply demonstrated in research on the phenomenon of group polarization. Over many studies, it has been shown that group discussions can serve to influence members' views in either a risky or a conservative direction (see Lamm & Myers, 1978; Myers & Lamm, 1976).

It seems clear that in a discussion of any substance, the individual comes to see and interpret things differently. At times, this stems from the amount and nature of the information that gets shared (informational influence). But more often, the new way of perceiving people, actions, and so on, comes about as a result of insight regarding how others think about the topic being addressed (normative information). Thus, a person who holds a moderately unfavorable perception of a client, competitor, etcetera comes to learn in the session that others share this perspective. This would be expected to bring about a post-discussion view that is more extreme (even more negative in this example) than at the outset. In like manner, we postulate that both dynamics would operate to shape social perception.

Accountability as Social Influence

As discussed earlier, accountability forces cause the perceiver to exert greater mental (and physical) effort in the task domain of interest to a third party, commonly referred to as the "principal." However, both the timing of the knowledge of the reporting requirement and the perceiver's (agent's) view of the principal's position on issues become very important to this theory in predicting just what the perceiver does. At the risk of over-simplification, to the extent that the principal is powerful but has taken no public position on the issue at hand, research has found a tendency toward more effortful and complete information processing (Tetlock, 1983). By extension, this theory causes us to predict that under such circumstances, the perceiver would not rely on automatic processing of social information nor rely on heuristics. Instead, one would expect great diligence. In contrast, if the powerful principal has a point of view on a person or on the decision or issue to be resolved, then such care in the processing of information is less likely. In fact, the perceiver would often find it expedient to conform. Stated simply, contrary to popular views, accountability need not result in better decisions.

It seems that accountability theory would be useful in helping to model person perception and social cognitive processes in work contexts where there exist social obligations and where there is more than a communication requirement operating.

Dynamic and Embedded Approach

Throughout this chapter, we have attempted to build on and learn from the basic literature on person perception and social cognition. In doing so, we have also tried to be sensitive to the fact that the findings we have identified are often derived from studies where the context is not considered all that important. Not surprisingly then, given the goal of this book to guide HR management practices in work settings, we have regularly tried to speculate on the way that the forces in the work place could operate to affect the processes of interest. In this section, we seek to further elaborate our views of the importance of the work context.

Recent advances in both multilevel theory (Frink & Klimoski, 1998; Morgeson & Hofman, 1999) and methods (Chan, 1998; Klein & Kozlowski, 2000; Law & Wong, 1999) have made it possible for those involved in organizational studies to envision more completely what we are calling an "embedded systems" approach to modeling workplace phenomena. However, it might be useful for us to contrast (albeit briefly) traditional views to develop this point.

Historically, if researchers attempt to describe cognitive (i.e., person perception) processes in work settings, they might logically focus on looking to the individual as the unit of description and analysis. As pointed out already, much has been learned about such things as the impact of individual personality, needs and goals, and experience on such processes. Alternatively, one can look to the work team or group for explanation and causal forces. Accordingly, the role of such things as work flow among group members, group composition, and social and interpersonal dynamics in groups have also been found to have profound implications for cognitive (perceptual) processes, generally, and person perception and social judgments, in particular. Finally, there are arguments that organizational level processes (e.g., policies in action, leadership, climate, and culture) have the power to inform us also. For example, organizational climate has been frequently conceptualized as "shared perceptions" (James & James, 1989). Thus it seems that each of these levels of description and analysis have some claims to make.

Contemporary thinking, however, implies that such "cuts" at explanation and model building are flawed. It's not that researchers haven't been able to model and predict important phenomena. They can indeed do so. Yet the achievements have been modest at best when one considers the order of magnitude of effect sizes and the amount of variance accounted for. But we see important limitations to the research record for another reason. This relates to the fact that organizational researchers should be building models that have greater ecological validity.

In our use of the term, *ecological validity* means more than generalizability. There is enough reason to feel that many of our theories and findings do indeed generalize. Certainly the recent work on meta-analysis (Schmidt & Hunter, 1998) and programmatic efforts on the part of researchers who go from the field, to the lab, and back to the field (see Campbell, 1986; Driskell & Salas, 1992; Ilgen, 1986) are encouraging. But we feel this evidence is merely a harbinger of what is truly possible if researchers were to take an embedded systems approach. This is what we are advocating to those who wish to study person perception and social cognition processes that are truly relevant to the workplace.

Thus, in our view, an embedded systems approach should be used to guide research in the field. Whether in the form of field experiments or in the analysis of causal models (e.g., path analysis, structural equations modeling, etc.), the investigator would recognize and consciously include in their investigations those contextual variables at multiple levels that are theorized to affect social information processing and social judgments relevant to their applied setting or to the applied problems of interest (e.g., quality of assessment center ratings). Such research would consider and attempt to model the simultaneous effects of intraindividual, dyad, and (at least) work group or social network level forces as these impinge on person perception phenomena (e.g., Emrich, 1999; Moore, Smith, & Gonzalez, 1997). Moreover, here, we are thinking of more than just the need to account for one-way or linear dynamics. Thus an embedded systems approach would also require the study of perceptual processes as they become as much a cause as the consequence of contextual forces (Law & Wong, 1999). And this would, more often than not, have to involve longitudinal designs (Dansereau, Yammarino, & Kohles, 1999). Admittedly, this is no easy mandate to follow, but it is the path to more powerful and useful models.

Although an embedded perspective is difficult to describe verbally, it is perhaps even more challenging to portray in a diagram. In this regard, we are fortunate to have an example offered by Katz and Kahn (1978) in their treatment of role theory and role taking–making processes. Figure 1.3 reflects our adaptation of these ideas used in the service of illustrating the embedded perspective we are advocating.

In the interest of space, we do not endeavor to detail the linkages in this figure. Besides, in light of our treatment in this chapter of person perception phenomena and of the importance of the social context, the implications of each are all too obvious. However, it is worth noting the way that this figure attempts to capture the dynamic and reciprocal nature of forces affecting social perception. To this end, we again refer the reader to the social interactions that provide behavioral cues for social judgments and inferences as illustrated in Fig. 1.1. These various interactions are embedded within Fig. 1.3. Specifically, the linkages preceded by 1 represent the cues used by the perceiver in understanding the target, including the target's attributes (1A; e.g., surface features, traits, etc.), the target's relationship with the perceiver (1B; e.g., similarity, in-group vs. out-group status), and the

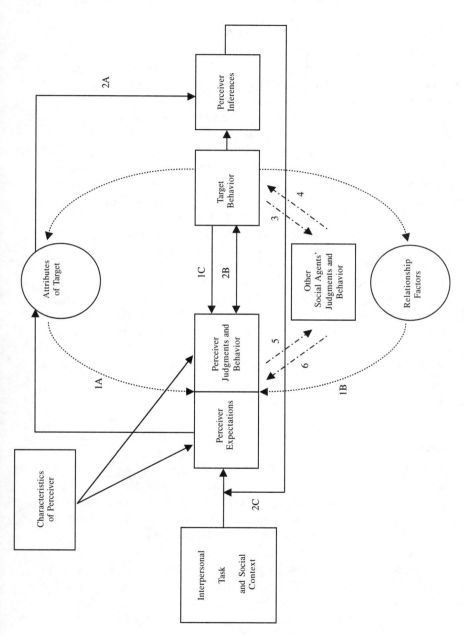

FIG. 1.3. Embedded perspective of person perception in applied contexts. Adapted from Katz & Kahn (1978). Reprinted by permission of John Wiley & Sons, Inc.

target's behavioral responses to the perceiver's initial judgments, behavior, or both (1C).

All linkages preceded by 2 represent the behavior of the perceiver in response to the target, including the perceiver's inferences made directly on the basis of the target's attributes (2A), the perceiver's inferences made indirectly through his or her interactions with the target (2B), and the perceiver's expectations resulting from earlier iterations of the inference process (2C). Furthermore linkage 2B shows that the surface features or initial behavior of the target may elicit reactions on the part of the perceiver, which in turn, bring about subsequent target behavior that provides additional cues to the perceiver on which to base target inferences.

Linkages 3 through 6 illustrate how other social agents also provide behavioral cues on which inferences can be based. Specifically, both the target's behavior toward other social agents (3) and their behavior toward the target (4) provide such information. Also, cues are given by the perceiver's behavior toward other social agents (5), and their behavior toward the perceiver (6) (i.e., "social proof").

We recommend that Fig. 1.3 (or something like it) be used as a template for those interested in modeling the social perception component embedded in applied problematics in work organizations. Alternatively, if the reader is the one responsible for dealing with such applied problems as featured in this book, then the diagram could easily serve as a diagnostic tool, serving to guide inquiry and analysis and, ultimately, inform the design of an intervention or the management of change.

CONCLUSIONS

The scientific literature dealing with person perception and social cognition that we have reviewed in this chapter presents a dynamic and complex picture of such processes. Although some of what has been uncovered recently may reinforce popular views and prevailing practices, most of what we have highlighted calls for substantial rethinking of how person perception operates to affect decisions and behavior. Most significantly, as we have pointed out, anyone interested in this area must now come to appreciate the importance of affect, motives, and goals as these influence social judgments. Although people may sometimes be dispassionate in their observations and assessments of others, it is far more likely that they will be ego involved because there are personal consequences that follow as social judgments translate to decisions or actions. Thus, we have tried to give weight to the interplay of motives with heuristical and diligent information processing. Moreover, in this chapter we have stressed the role and impact of the context for person perception, especially as the context influences the quality and nature of inferences about others. In this regard, we feel that the field is finally ready to acknowledge that person perception is as much a social as it is an individual phenomenon.

REFERENCES

Andersen, S. M., & Cole, S. W. (1990). "Do I know you?": The role of significant others in general social perception. *Journal of Personality and Social Psychology, 59*, 384–399.

Baron, R. A. (1993). Effects of interviewers' moods and applicant qualifications on ratings of job applicants. *Journal of Applied Social Psychology, 23*, 254–271.

Baron, R. A., & Byrne, D. (2000). *Social psychology* (9th ed.). Needham Heights, MA: Allyn & Bacon.

Berry, D. S. (1991). Accuracy in social perception: Contributions of facial and vocal information. *Journal of Personality and Social Psychology, 61*, 298–307.

Bodenhausen, G. V. (1990). Stereotypes as judgmental heuristics: Evidence of circadian variations in discrimination. *Psychological Science, 1*, 319–322.

Bodenhausen, G. V. (1993). Emotions, arousal, and stereotypic judgments: A heuristic model of affect and stereotyping. In D. M. Mackie & D. L. Hamilton (Eds.), *Affect, cognition, and stereotyping: Interactive processes in group perception* (pp. 13–37). San Diego, CA: Academic Press.

Borkenau, P. (1990). Traits as ideal-based and goal-derived social categories. *Journal of Personality and Social Psychology, 58*, 381–396.

Borman, W. C. (1979). Individual difference correlates of accuracy in evaluating others' performance effectiveness. *Applied Psychological Measurement, 3*, 103–115.

Borman, W. C. (1987). Personal constructs, performance schemata, and "folk theories" of subordinate effectiveness: Explorations in an Army officer sample. *Organizational Behavior and Human Decision Processes, 40*, 307–322.

Borman, W. C., & Hallam, G. L. (1991). Observation accuracy for assessors of work-sample performance: Consistency across task and individual-differences correlates. *Journal of Applied Psychology, 76*, 11–18.

Bower, G. H. (1981). Emotional mood and memory. *American Psychologist, 36*, 129–148.

Bower, G. H. (1991). Mood congruity of social judgments. In J. P. Forgas (Ed.), *Emotion and social judgments* (pp. 31–55). Oxford: Pergamon Press.

Brewer, M. B. (1988). A dual process model of impression formation. In T. K. Srull & R. S. Wyer, Jr. (Eds.), *Advances in social cognition* (Vol. 1, pp. 1–36). Hillsdale, NJ: Lawrence Erlbaum Associates.

Brewer, M. B., & Lui, L. N. (1989). The primacy of age and sex in the structure of person categories. *Social Cognition, 7*, 262–274.

Britt, T. A., & Shepperd, J. A. (1999). Trait relevance and trait assessment. *Personality and Social Psychology Review, 3*, 108–122.

Campbell, J. P. (1986). Labs, fields, and straw issues. In E. A. Locke (Ed.), *Generalizing from laboratory to field settings* (pp. 257–267). Lexington, MA: Lexington.

Cardy, R. L., & Kehoe, J. F. (1984). Rater selective attention ability and appraisal effectiveness: The effect of a cognitive style on the accuracy of differentiation among ratees. *Journal of Applied Psychology, 69*, 589–594.

Chan, D. (1998). Functional relations among constructs in the same content domain at different levels of analysis: A typology of composition models. *Journal of Applied Psychology, 83*, 234–246.

Cialdini, R. B. (1993). *Influence: Science and practice* (3rd ed.). New York: Harper Collins.

Cooper, W. H. (1981). Ubiquitous halo. *Psychological Bulletin, 90*, 218–244.

Dalessio, A., & Imada, A. S. (1984). Relationships between interview selection decisions and perceptions of applicant similarity to an ideal employee and self: A field study. *Human Relations, 37*, 67–80.

Dansereau, F., Yammarino, F. J., & Kohles, J. C. (1999). Multiple levels of analysis from a longitudinal perspective: Some implications for theory building. *Academy of Management Review, 24*, 346–357.

DeGroot, T., & Motowidlo, S. J. (1999). Why visual and vocal interview cues can affect interviewers' judgments and predict job performance. *Journal of Applied Psychology, 84*, 986–993.

DeNisi, A. S., & Peters, L. H. (1996). Organization of information in memory and the performance appraisal process: Evidence from the field. *Journal of Applied Psychology, 81*, 717–737.

Dépret, E. F., & Fiske, S. T. (1993). Social cognition and power: Some cognitive conseqences of social structure as a source of control deprivation. In G. Weary, F. Gleicher, Y. K. Marsh (Eds.), *Control motivation and social cognition* (pp. 176–202). New York: Springer-Verlag.

Dépret, E., & Fiske, S. T. (1999). Perceiving the powerful: Intriguing individuals versus threatening groups. *Journal of Experimental Social Psychology, 35*, 461–480.

Dipboye, R. L. (1982). Self-fulfilling prophecies in the selection-recruitment interview. *Academy of Management Review, 7*, 579–586.

Dipboye, R. L. (1992). *Selection interviews: Process perspectives.* Cincinnati, OH: South-Western.

Dipboye, R. L., & Gaugler, B. B. (1993). Cognitive and behavioral processes in the selection interview. In N. Schmitt, W. C. Borman, & Associates (Eds.), *Personnel selection in organizations* (pp. 135–170). San Francisco: Jossey-Bass.

Ditto, P. H., & Lopez, D. F. (1992). Motivated skepticism: Use of differential decision criteria for preferred and nonpreferred conclusions. *Journal of Personality and Social Psychology, 63*, 568–584.

Dobbins, G. H., Cardy, R. L., & Truxillo, D. M. (1988). The effects of purpose of appraisal and individual differences in stereotypes of women on sex differences in performance ratings: A laboratory and field study. *Journal of Applied Psychology, 73*, 551–558.

Doosje, B., Spears, R., & Koomen, W. (1995). When bad isn't all bad: Strategic use of sample information in generalization and stereotyping. *Journal of Personality and Social Psychology, 69*, 642–655.

Driskell, J. E., & Salas, E. (1992). Can you study real teams in contrived settings? The value of small group research to understanding teams. In R. W. Swezey & E. Salas (Eds.), *Teams: Their training and performance* (pp. 101–126). Norwood, NJ: Ablex.

Dunning, D. (1999). A newer look: Motivated social cognition and the schematic representation of social concepts. *Psychological Inquiry, 10*, 1–11.

Emrich, C. G. (1999). Context effects in leadership perception. *Personality and Social Psychology Bulletin, 25*, 991–1006.

Farr, J. L. (1973). Response requirements and primacy-recency effects in a simulated selection interview. *Journal of Applied Psychology, 57*, 228–232.

Festinger, L. (1954). A theory of social comparison processes. *Human Relations, 7*, 117–140.

Fiske, S. T. (1993). Social cognition and social perception. *Annual Review of Psychology, 44*, 155–194.

Fiske, S. T. (1992). Thinking is for doing: Portraits of social cognition from daguerreotype to laserphoto. *Journal of Personality and Social Psychology, 63*, 877–889.

Fiske, S. T., & Neuberg, S. L. (1990). A continuum of impression formation, from category-based to individuating processes: Influences of information and motivation on attention and interpretation. In M. P. Zanna (Ed.), *Advances in experimental social psychology* (Vol. 23). New York: Academic Press.

Fiske, S. T., & Taylor, S. E. (1991). *Social cognition* (2nd ed.). New York: McGraw-Hill.

Ford, T. E., & Kruglanski, A. W. (1995). Effects of epistemic motivations on the use of accessible constructs in social judgment. *Personality and Social Psychology Bulletin, 21*, 950–962.

Forgas, J. P. (1991). Affect and person perception. In J. P. Forgas (Ed.), *Emotion and social judgments* (pp. 263–290). Oxford, England: Pergamon Press.

Forgas, J. P. (1994). Sad and guilty? Affective influences on the explanation of conflict in close relationships. *Journal of Personality and Social Psychology, 66*, 56–68.

Forgas, J. P. (1995). Mood and judgment: The affect infusion model (AIM). *Psychological Bulletin, 117*, 39–66.

Frink, D. D., & Klimoski, R. J. (1998). Toward a theory of accountability in organizations and human resource management. In G. R. Ferris (Ed.), *Research in personnel and human resources management* (pp. 1–51). Greenwich, CT: JAI.

Funder, D. C. (1987). Errors and mistakes: Evaluating the accuracy of social judgement. *Psychological Bulletin, 101*, 75–90.

Gaugler, B. B., & Rudolph, A. S. (1992). The influence of assessee performance variation in assessors' judgments. *Personnel Psychology, 45*, 77–98.

Gilbert, D. T. (1989). Thinking lightly about others: Automatic components of the social inference process. In J. S. Uleman and J. A. Bargh (Eds.), *Unintended thought* (pp. 189–211). New York: Guilford.

Gilbert, D. T., & Hixon, J. G. (1991). The trouble of thinking: Activation and application of stereotypic beliefs. *Journal of Personality and Social Psychology, 60*, 509–517.

Gilbert, D. T., Pelham, B. W., & Krull, D. S. (1988). On cognitive busyness: When person perceivers meet persons perceived. *Journal of Personality and Social Psychology, 54*, 733–740.

Gollwitzer, P. M. (1990). Action phases and mind-sets. In E. T. Higgins & R. M. Sorrentino (Eds.), *Handbook of motivation and cognition: Foundations of social behavior* (Vol. 2, pp. 53–92). New York: Guilford.

Gollwitzer, P. M., & Kinney, R. F. (1989). Effects of deliberative and implemental mind-sets on illusion of control. *Journal of Personality and Social Psychology, 56*, 531–542.

Gollwitzer, P. M., & Moskowitz, G. B. (1996). Goal effects on action and cognition. In E. T. Higgins & A. W. Kruglanski (Eds.), *Social psychology: Handbook of basic principles* (pp. 361–399). New York: Guilford.

Graves, L. M. (1993). Sources of individual differences in interviewer effectiveness: A model and implications for future research. *Journal of Organizational Behavior, 14*, 349–370.

Graves, L. M., & Powell, G. N. (1988). An investigation of sex discrimination in recruiters' evaluations of actual applicants. *Journal of Applied Psychology, 73*, 20–29.

Heneman, R. L, Greenberger, D. B., & Anonyuo, C. (1989). Attributions and exchanges: The effects of interpersonal factors on the diagnosis of employee performance. *Academy of Management Journal, 32*, 466–476.

Highhouse, S., & Gallo, A. (1997). Order effects in personnel decision making. *Human Performance, 10*, 31–46.

Hoffman, C., & Hurst, N. (1990). Gender stereotypes: Perception or rationalization? *Journal of Personality and Social Psychology, 58*, 197–208.

Ilgen, D. R. (1986). Laboratory research: A question of when, not if. In E. A. Locke (Ed.), *Generalizing from laboratory to field settings* (pp. 257–267). Lexington, MA: Lexington.

Ilgen, D. R., & Feldman, J. M. (1983). Performance appraisal: A process focus. In B. M. Staw & L. L. Cummings (Eds.), *Research in organizational behavior* (Vol. 5, pp. 141–197). Greenwich, CT: JAI.

Isen, A. M., & Baron, R. A. (1991). Affect and organizational behavior. In B. M. Staw & L. L. Cummings (Eds.), *Research in organizational behavior* (Vol. 13, pp. 1–53). Greenwich, CT: JAI.

James, L. A., & James, L. R. (1989). Integrating work environment perceptions: Explorations into the measurement of meaning. *Journal of Applied Psychology, 74*, 739–751.

Jehn, K. A. (1997). Affective and cognitive conflict in work groups: Increasing performance through value-based intragroup conflict. In C. K. W. De Dreu & E. Van de Vliert (Eds.), *Using conflict in organizations* (pp. 87–100). London: Sage.

Judge, T. A., & Ferris, G. R. (1993). Social context of performance evaluation decisions. *Academy of Management Journal, 36*, 80–105.

Kahneman, D., Solvic, P., & Tversky, A. (Eds.). (1982). *Judgement under uncertainty: Heuristics and biases.* Cambridge, England: Cambridge University Press.

Kanfer, R. (1990). Motivation theory and industrial and organizational psychology. In M. D. Dunnette & L. M. Hough (Eds.), *Handbook of industrial and organizational psychology* (2nd ed., Vol. 1, pp. 75–170). Palo Alto, CA: Consulting Psychologists Press.

Kanfer, R., & Ackerman, P. L. (1989). Motivation and cognitive abilities: An integrative/aptitude treatment interaction approach to skill acquisition. *Journal of Applied Psychology, 74*, 657–690.

Katz, D., & Kahn, R. L. (1978). *The social psychology of organizations* (2nd ed.). New York: Wiley.

Kenny, D. A. (1991). A general model of consensus and accuracy in interpersonal perception. *Psychological Review, 98*, 155–163.

Kenny, D. A., Horner, C., Kashy, D. A., & Chu, L. (1992). Consensus at zero acquaintance: Replication, behavioral cues, and stability. *Journal of Personality and Social Psychology, 62*, 88–97.

Kenrick, D. T., Neuberg, S. L., and Cialdini, R. B. (1999). *Social psychology: Unraveling the mystery.* Needham Heights, MA: Allyn & Bacon.

Klein, K. J., & Kozlowski, S. W. J. (2000). Multilevel theory, research, and methods in organizations. San Francisco: Jossey-Bass.

Klimoski, R. J., & Inks, L. (1990). Accountability forces in performance appraisal. *Organizational Behavior and Human Decision Processes, 45*, 194–208.

Kruglanski, A. W. (1980). Lay epistemologic—process and contents: Another look at attribution theory. *Psychological Review, 87*, 70–87.

Kruglanski, A. W. (1989). The psychology of being "right": The problem of accuracy in social perception and cognition. *Psychological Bulletin, 106*, 395–409.

Kruglanski, A. W. (1996). Motivated social cognition: Principles of the interface. In E. T. Higgins & A.W. Kruglanski (Eds.), *Social psychology: Handbook of basic principles* (pp. 493–520). New York: Guilford.

Kunda, Z. (1999). *Social cognition: Making sense of people.* Cambridge, MA: The Mit Press.

Lamm, H., & Myers, D. G. (1978). Group-induced polarization of attitudes and behavior. In L. Berkowitz (Ed.), *Advances in experimental social psychology* (Vol. 11, 145–195). New York: Academic Press.

Law, K. S., & Wong, C. (1999). Multidimensional constructs in structural equation analysis: An illustration using job perception and job satisfaction constructs. *Journal of Management, 25*, 143–160.

Liden, R. C., Wayne, S. J., & Stilwell, D. (1993). A longitudinal study on the early development of leader-member exchanges. *Journal of Applied Psychology, 78*, 662–674.

Lievens, F., & Klimoski, R. J. (2001). Understanding the assessment center process: Where are we now? *International Review of Industrial and Organizational Psychology.*

Linville, P. W., Fischer, G. W., & Salovey, P. (1989). Perceived distributions of the characteristics of in-group and out-group members: Empirical evidence and a computer simulation. *Journal of Personality and Social Psychology, 57*, 165–188.

Linville, P. W., & Jones, E. E. (1980). Polarized appraisals of out-group members. *Journal of Personality and Social Psychology, 38*, 689–703.

Longenecker, C. O., Sims, H. P., & Gioia, D. A. (1987). Behind the mask: The politics of employee appraisal. *Academy of Management Executive, 1*, 183–193.

Lord, R. G. (1985). An information processing approach to social perception, leadership, and behavioral measurement in organizations. In B. M. Staw & L. L. Cummings (Eds.), *Research in organizational behavior* (Vol. 7, pp. 87–128). Greenwich, CT: JAI.

Lord, R. G., & Foti, R. J. (1986). Schema theories, information processing, and organizational behavior. In H. P. Sims, & D. A. Gioia (Eds.), *The thinking organization: The dynamics of organizational social cognition* (pp. 20–48). San Francisco: Jossey-Bass.

Lord, R. G., Foti, R. J., & deVader, C. (1984). A test of leadership categorization theory: Internal structure, information processing, and leadership perceptions. *Organizational Behavior and Human Decision Processes, 34*, 343–378.

Macrae, C. N., Milne, A. B., & Bodenhausen, G. V. (1994). Stereotypes as energy-saving devices: A peek inside the cognitive toolbox. *Journal of Personality and Social Psychology, 66*, 37–47.

Malloy, T. E., & Albright, L. (1990). Interpersonal perception in a social context. *Journal of Personality and Social Psychology, 58*, 419–428.

Marks, G., & Miller, N. (1987). Ten years of research on the false-consensus effect: An empirical and theoretical review. *Psychological Bulletin, 102*, 72–90.

Merton, R. K. (1948). The self-fulfilling prophecy. *Antioch Review, 8*, 193–210.

Mitchell, T. R., & Liden, R. C. (1982). The effects of social context on performance evaluations. *Organizational Behavior and Human Performance, 29*, 241–256.

Moore, S. R., Smith, S. E., & Gonzalez, R. (1997). Personality and judgment heuristics: Contextual and individual difference interactions in social judgment. *Personality and Social Psychology Bulletin, 23*, 76–83.

Morgeson, F. P., & Hofmann, D. A. (1999). The structure and function of collective constructs: Implications for multilevel research and theory development. *Academy of Management Review, 24*, 249–265.

Moskowitz, G. B., & Roman, R. J. (1992). Spontaneous trait inferences as self-generated primes: Implications for conscious social judgment. *Journal of Personality and Social Psychology, 62*, 728–738.

Murphy, K. R., Balzer, W. K., Lockhart, M. C., & Eisenman, E. J. (1985). Effect of previous performance on evaluations of present performance. *Journal of Applied Psychology, 70*, 72–84.

Murphy, K. R., & Cleveland, J. N. (1995). *Understanding performance appraisal: Social, organizational, and goal-based perspectives.* Thousand Oaks, CA: Sage.

Myers, D. G., & Lamm, H. (1976). The group polarization phenomenon. *Psychological Bulletin, 83*, 602–627.

Nelson, L. J., & Klutas, K. (2000). The distinctiveness effect in social interaction: Creation of a self-fulfilling prophecy. *Personality and Social Psychology Bulletin, 26*, 126–135.

Neuberg, S. L. (1989). The goal of forming accurate impressions during social interactions: Attenuating the impact of negative expectancies. *Journal of Personality and Social Psychology, 56*, 374–386.

Neuberg, S. L. (1994). Expectancy-confirmation processes in stereotype-tinged social encounters: The moderating role of social goals. In M. P. Zanna & J. M. Olson (Eds.), *The psychology of prejudice: The Ontario symposium*, (Vol. 7., pp. 103–130). Hillsdale, NJ: Lawrence Erlbaum Associates.

Nickerson, R. S. (1999). How we know—and sometimes misjudge—what others know: Imputing one's own knowledge to others. *Psychological Bulletin, 125*, 737–759.

Osborne, R. E., & Gilbert, D. T. (1992). The preoccupational hazards of social life. *Journal of Personality and Social Psychology, 62*, 219–228.

Parkinson, B. (1997). Untangling the appraisal-emotion connection. *Personality and Social Psychology Review, 1*, 62–79.

Pavelchack, M. A. (1989). Piecemeal and category-based evaluation: An idiographic analysis. *Journal of Personality and Social Psychology, 56*, 354–363.

Pendry, L. F., & Macrae, C. N. (1996). What the disinterested perceiver overlooks: Goal-directed social categorization. *Personality and Social Psychology Bulletin, 22*, 249–256.

Perry, E. L., & Finkelstein, L. M. (1999). Toward a broader view of age discrimination in employment-related decisions: A joint consideration of organizational factors and cognitive processes. *Human Resource Management Review, 9*, 21–49.

Perry, E. L., Kulik, C. T., & Bourhis, A. C. (1996). Moderating effects of personal and contextual factors in age discrimination. *Journal of Applied Psychology, 81*, 628–647.

Pittman, T. S., & D'Agostino, P. R. (1989). Motivation and cognition: Control deprivation and the nature of subsequent information processing. *Journal of Experimental Social Psychology, 25*, 465–480.

Pittman, T. S., & Heller, J. F. (1987). Social motivation. *Annual Review of Psychology, 38*, 461–489.

Polansky, N., Lippitt, R., & Redl, F. (1950). An investigation of behavioral contagion in groups. *Human Relations, 3*, 319–348.

Read, S. J., Jones, D. K., & Miller, L. C. (1990). Traits as goal-based categories: The importance of goals in the coherence of dispositional categories. *Journal of Personality and Social Psychology, 58*, 1048–1061.

Reilly, R. R., Henry, S., & Smither, J. W. (1990). An examination of the effects of using behavior checklists on the construct validity of assessment center dimensions. *Personnel Psychology, 43*, 71–84.

Robbins, T. L., & DeNisi, A. S. (1994). A closer look at interpersonal affect as a distinct influence on cognitive processing in performance evaluations. *Journal of Applied Psychology, 79*, 341–353.

Rusting, C. L. (1998). Personality, mood, and cognitive processing of emotional information: Three conceptual frameworks. *Psychological Bulletin, 124*, 165–196.

Sackett, P. R., Zedeck, S., & Fogli, L. (1988). Relations between measures of typical and maximum performance. *Journal of Applied Psychology, 73*, 482–486.

Sagie, A., & Magnezy, R. (1997). Assessor type, number of distinguishable categories, and assessment center construct validity. *Journal of Occupational and Organizational Psychology, 70*, 103–108.

Salvemini, N. J., Reilly, R. R., & Smither, J. W. (1993). The influence of rater motivation on assimilation effects and accuracy in performance ratings. *Organizational Behavior and Human Decision Processes, 55*, 41–60.

Sanitioso, R., Kunda, Z., & Fong, G. T. (1990). Motivated recruitment of autobiographical memories. *Journal of Personality and Social Psychology, 59*, 229–241.

Schacter, D. L. (1999). The seven sins of memory: Insights from psychology and cognitive neuroscience. *American Psychologist, 54*, 182–203.

Schleicher, D. J., Day, D. V., Mayes, B. T., & Riggio, R. E. (1999, May). *A new frame for frame-of-reference training: Enhancing the construct validity of assessment centers.* Paper presented at the annual conference of the Society for Industrial and Organizational Psychology, Atlanta, GA.

Schmidt, F. L., & Hunter, J. E. (1998). The validity and utility of selection methods in personnel psychology: Practical and theoretical implications of 85 years of research findings. *Psychological Bulletin, 124*, 262–274.

Schneider, D. J. (1973). Implicit personality theory: A review. *Psychological Bulletin, 79*, 294–309.

Schneier, C. E. (1977). Operational utility and psychometric characteristics of behavioral expectation scales: A cognitive reinterpretation. *Journal of Applied Psychology, 62*, 541–548.

Schwarz, N., & Clore, G. L. (1996). Feelings and phenomenal experience. In E. T. Higgins & A. W. Kruglanski (Eds.), *Social psychology: Handbook of basic principles* (pp. 433–465). New York: Guilford.

Simon, H. A. (1967). Motivational and emotional controls of cognition. *Psychological Review, 74*, 29–39.

Simon, H. A. (1982). Comments. In M. S. Clark, & S. T. Fiske (Eds.), *Affect and cognition: The 17th Annual Carnegie Symposium on Cognition* (pp. 333-342). Hillsdale, NJ: Erlbaum Associates.

Smither, J. W., Reilly, R. R., & Buda, R. (1988). Effects of prior performance information on ratings of present performance: Contrast versus assimilation revisited. *Journal of Applied Psychology, 73*, 487–496.

Snodgrass, S. E. (1992). Further effects of role versus gender on interpersonal sensitivity. *Journal of Personality and Social Psychology, 62*, 154–158.

Stangor, C., & Ford, T. E. (1992). Accuracy and expectancy-confirming processing orientations and the development of stereotypes and prejudice. In W. Stroebe & M. Hewstone (Eds.), *European review of social psychology* (Vol. 3, pp. 57–89). Chichester, England: Wiley.

Steiner, D. D., & Rain, J. S. (1989). Immediate and delayed primacy and recency effects in performance evaluation. *Journal of Applied Psychology, 74*, 136–142.

Sumer, H. C., & Knight, P. A. (1996). Assimilation and contrast effects in performance ratings: Effects of rating the previous performance on rating subsequent performance. *Journal of Applied Psychology, 81*, 436–442.

Swann, Jr., W. B. (1984). Quest for accuracy in person perception: A matter of pragmatics. *Psychological Review, 91*, 457–477.

Taylor, S. E. (1991). Asymmetrical effects of positive and negative events: The mobilization-minimization hypothesis. *Psychological Bulletin, 110*, 67–85.

Tetlock, P. E. (1983). Accountability and complexity of thought. *Journal of Personality and Social Psychology, 45*, 74–83.

Tetlock, P. E. (1991). An alternative metaphor in the study of judgment and choice: People as politicians. *Theory & Psychology, 1*, 451–475.

Tjosvold, D. (1978). Alternative organizations for schools and classrooms. In D. Bar-Tal & L. Saxe (Eds.), *Social psychology of education: Theory and research* (pp. 275–298). Washington, DC: Hemisphere.

Tjosvold, D., & Sagaria, S. D. (1978). Effects of relative power on cognitive perspective-taking. *Personality and Social Psychology Bulletin, 4*, 256–259.

Uleman, J. S., Newman, L. S., & Moskewitz, G. B. (1996). People as flexible interpreters: Evidence and issues from spontaneous trait inference. In M. P. Zanna (Ed.), *Advances in Experimental Social Psychology* (Vol. 28, pp. 211–279). San Diego, CA: Academic Press.

Vecchio, R. P., & Gobdel, B. C. (1984). The Vertical Dyadic Linkage Model of Leadership: Problems and prospects. *Organizational Behavior and Human Performance, 34*, 5–20.

Vonk, R. (1999). Effects of outcome dependence on correspondence bias. *Personality and Social Psychology Bulletin, 25*, 382–389.

Wayne, S. J., & Ferris, G. R. (1990). Influence tactics, affect, and exchange quality in supervisor-subordinate interactions: A laboratory experiment and field study. *Journal of Applied Psychology, 75*, 487–499.

Wheeler, L. (1966). Toward a theory of behavioral contagion. *Psychological Review, 73*, 179–192.

Wherry, R. J., & Bartlett, C. J. (1982). The control of bias in ratings: A theory of rating. *Personnel Psychology, 35*, 521–555.

Williams, K. J., DeNisi, A. S., Blencoe, A. G., & Cafferty, T. P. (1985). The role of appraisal purpose: Effects of purpose on information acquisition and utilization. *Organizational Behavior and Human Decision Processes, 35*, 314–339.

Woehr, D. J., & Huffcutt, A. I. (1994). Rater training for performance appraisal: A quantitative review. *Journal of Occupational and Organizational Psychology, 67*, 189–205.

Wright, J. C., & Dawson, V. L. (1988). Person perception and the bounded rationality of social judgment. *Journal of Personality and Social Psychology, 55*, 780–794.

Wyer, R. S., & Srull, T. K. (1994). *Handbook of social cognition* (2nd ed.). Hillsdale, NJ: Lawrence Erlbaum Associates.

Zajonc, R. B. (1980). Feeling and thinking: Preferences need no inferences. *American Psychologist, 35*, 151–175.

Zajonc, R. B. (1998). Emotions. In D. T. Gilbert & S.T. Fiske (Eds.), *The handbook of social psychology* (Vol. 1, pp. 591–632). Boston, MA: McGraw-Hill.

Zebrowitz, L. A., & Collins, M. A. (1997). Accurate social perception at zero acquaintance: The affordances of a Gibsonian approach. *Personality and Social Psychology Review, 1*, 204–223.

Zedeck, S. (1986). A process analysis of the assessment center method. In B. M. Staw & L. L. Cummings (Eds.), *Research in organizational behavior, 8*, 259–296.

Zedeck, S., & Cascio, W. F. (1982). Performance appraisal decisions as a function of rater training and purpose of the appraisal. *Journal of Applied Psychology, 67*, 752–758.

2

Causes and Consequences of Stereotypes in Organizations

Don Operario
University of California at San Francisco

Susan T. Fiske
University of Massachusetts at Amherst

At the gateway of a new millenium, as U.S. and global societies diversify in their demographic composition, understanding the causes and consequences of stereotyping has never been more important. Despite increasing contact between nations and ethnic groups, stereotypes continue to haunt communities and institutions, and the effects are particularly conspicuous in the organizational context.

Consider, for example, some recent cases in media headlines. In 1994, a group of Texaco employees filed suit against their company for racial discrimination, and hidden audiotapes revealed top company officials making racially charged remarks and conspiring to destroy documents about hiring policies. That same year, the Equal Employment Opportunity Commission sued the Mitsubishi organization (in one of the largest sexual harassment cases ever brought to trial) and alleged the company condoned a culture that was systematically hostile toward women. Within the past 5 years, a number of allegations against the Denny's Restaurant chain claimed that customers were mistreated on the basis of race; some African American customers were forced to pay before being served, and other Asian, Hispanic, and African American customers reported being turned away completely.

Psychological research on stereotyping can illuminate these and other instances of organizational misbehavior. In this chapter, we review the body of research on stereotyping and offer four points regarding the organizational manifestations. First, stereotypes have an elusive nature; they are difficult to identify and even harder to control, so their presence in organizations can be ubiquitous. Second, people can use stereotypes to explain or justify inequalities in organizations and institutions. Third, stereotypes can influence the behaviors of both the stereotype agent and target, thus making it seem as if the stereotypes are grounded in reality. Fourth, stereotypes are responsive to human intent, so they can be held in check with personal motivation and social norms created in organizations. The wealth of research on these topics suggests that stereotypes are not a thing of the past. They have evolved over time and continue to shape organizational behaviors and cultures.

STEREOTYPES ARE ELUSIVE

The word "stereotype" abounds in popular discourse. In the headlines described earlier, stereotypes arguably facilitated each injustice. But what exactly are stereotypes, and how do they work? People generally agree that stereotypes are harmful preconceptions and that they can lead to bias. Some people might add that stereotypes have some factual basis, otherwise they would disappear, and almost everybody claims that they personally try to stop stereotypes from entering their minds.

Social psychological research speaks to all three of these lay beliefs. This section overviews findings regarding the negative as well as positive effects of stereotypes, the alleged veracity of stereotypes, and people's ability to inhibit using stereotypes. From this research, we suggest that stereotypes are elusive because they are difficult to pin down definitively and to control personally. Yet individuals and organizations can restrain the impact of stereotypes on judgment and behavior by acknowledging their presence and potential effects.

The Nature of Stereotypes

The concept of the stereotype first entered social science in 1922, when journalist Walter Lippmann adopted a term used by text typesetters describing the metal stamps that represent letters. In a discussion of group conflict, Lippmann (1922) explained that people have preset images of other people based on their category memberships—their stereotypes—and these categories carry textual meaning much like printers' stamps. In a wise analysis, Lippmann posited that, aided by category stamps or stereotypes, "for the most part we do not first see and then define, we define first and then see" (p. 81).

Social psychological research has since elaborated on Lippman's theme, emphasizing the role of social categories in person perception. Categories are a fundamental tool for perceiving others. People almost instantaneously recognize others' social categories, such as their gender or race (Banaji & Hardin, 1996; Zárate & Smith, 1990), and perception ensues from the information provided by categories. They assist perceivers by conveying immediate meaning based on the category label (S. E. Taylor, 1981). Perceivers often minimize objective differences between the target and other category members (S. E. Taylor, Fiske, Etcoff, & Ruderman, 1978) and view the category as a homogenous entity (Wilder, 1984).

Category-based perception is not a malevolent process by nature. Categorization offers a speedy and adaptive means for understanding others with little effort. Cognitive energy, a limited resource, can be allocated to other demands rather than to forming detailed impressions of people in the environment (Macrae, Milne, & Bodenhausen, 1994). In a classic text, Gordon Allport (1954) summarized the functions of categories, "All categories engender meaning upon the world. Like paths in a forest, they give order to our life-space" (p. 171).

When do categories become stereotypes? Allport (1954) distinguished between (a) the basic perceptual process of categorization and (b) biased interpersonal and societal processes of stereotyping; the former reflects human nature, whereas the latter reflect social context and structure. Here, we adopt Allport's definition of the stereotype as "an exaggerated belief associated with a category. Its function is to justify (rationalize) our conduct in relation to that category" (p. 187). Stereotypes stem from categorization, but represent a fixed, static generalization about a group often as a means to explain bias and inequality.

Stereotypes, like categories, have adaptive functions. They simplify the social environment (McCann, Ostrom, Tyner, & Mitchell, 1985), expedite judgments (Dovidio, Evans, & Tyler, 1986), and free up cognitive capacity for other ongoing tasks (Bodenhausen & Wyer, 1985; Macrae, Hewstone, & Griffiths, 1993; Macrae, Milne, & Bodenhausen, 1994).

The cognitive benefits of stereotyping come with two vital costs: accuracy and fairness. Although stereotypes allow people to make quick judgments based on scant information, these judgments are not always optimal. Stereotypic judgments are often faulty (see Judd & Park, 1993, for a review). They cloud variability within a group (Mullen & Hu, 1989; Wilder, 1981), facilitate misjudgments about group members (S. E. Taylor, Fiske, Etcoff, & Ruderman, 1978), and inhibit detailed thinking about others (Sanbonmatsu, Akimoto, & Gibson, 1994; von Hippel, Jonides, Hilton, & Narayan, 1993). Moreover, stereotypes tend to favor members of the ingroup over members of the outgroup (Perdue, Dovidio, Gurtman, & Tyler, 1990), thereby placing others at a relative disadvantage. (We elaborate on these points later.)

Research indicates that stereotypes offer some functional aspects, particularly simplifying thought and judgment, but at the expense of accuracy and fairness. When people use stereotypes, they often make "good enough" judgments (Fiske, 1993b); that is, their judgments satisfy immediate personal motives. For example, screening job applicants solely on the basis of stereotypes about their educational history (e.g., universities attended and degrees held) can meet minimal (good enough) hiring criteria; large applicant pools dwindle to manageable groups, and decision makers can focus their energy on a more select pool. In this case, applicants coming from known institutions might have better employment chances (e.g., past employees from Bigshot University have been successful). But judgments based on stereotypes about social categories can yield myopic results. Using a single categorical criterion—such as education, or in other cases, gender, age, and ethnicity—blinds perceivers to other types of information and other prospective candidates.

The Truth Behind Stereotypes

To what extent do stereotypes reflect a kernel of truth? Social scientists have long debated this issue (see Lee, Jussim, & McCauley, 1995, for a recent discussion). Resolution to this debate will likely not occur soon because researchers must first address the two components of this issue: How much is a kernel? and What constitutes truth?

Researchers addressing the first question have shown that the amount and type of data necessary to verify a stereotype are difficult to establish. For example, how would one confirm or refute the stereotype that women are more emotional than men? First, researchers must decide how to measure emotionality. Then, they must decide what level of difference would matter. Significant group differences, intragroup variability, or group stability have been common criteria for gauging stereotype accuracy (Judd & Park, 1993), yet each criterion remains unconvincing. A significant group difference refers to the comparison of Group A's average score (e.g., on emotionality) relative to Group B's average score; if Group A has a statistically higher score, then researchers might conclude that Group A is more emotional. Intragroup variability measures the diversity within a group; if members of a group have very similar scores on a measure of emotionality, then their group has low variability and the group mean score better reflects each member's emotionality. Group stability reflects the consistency of the group's score over time; stable scores over time suggest the measure reflects a constant group characteristic. Indeed, different standards of confirmatory data exist (Judd & Park, 1993). In this example, researchers can gauge the average daily emotional levels of a group of women compared to group of men, or they can compare the range of emotions felt by the two groups, or they can track how consistently each group feels emotional. Differences on these indicators could reflect important group-based statistical differences, but these measure have some obvious problems: Average scores cloud variability within groups (when group members do not lie at the average) and ignore commonality between groups (when members of Group A share the same score as members of Group B). As discussed earlier, stereotypes stem from category-based generalizations, so at least a few members of the group conform to the stereotype. But to extrapolate from a few cases to corroborate the veracity of the entire stereotype is questionable (see Fiske, 1998; Judd & Park, 1993; Stangor, 1995, for more discussion).

Researchers addressing the second question have shown that "truth" is a relative concept. Some suggest that stereotypes can be deemed true when different social groups agree on their content, or when members of the stereotyped group endorse beliefs about themselves, or when objective indicators reflect the stereotype (Ottati & Lee, 1995). However, this argument overlooks the fact that stereotypes can construct reality and, effectively, determine truth (e.g., Jussim, 1991). Not only do people selectively perceive the world on the basis of their beliefs, but they act on their beliefs in ways that shape the environment (see Claire & Fiske, 1997; Snyder, 1992, for reviews). For example, by admitting members of only a certain group into one's firm or graduate program, people create a setting that confirms the abilities and success of that group relative to other groups.

Instead of considering all complexities surrounding stereotype accuracy—indeed, an impossible task—we choose to focus attention on what people actually do with their stereotypes and how their stereotypes influence themselves and others. This brings us back to a social psychological analysis of thought and behavior rather than a philosophical and political analysis of relative truth and accuracy.

The Process of Stereotyping

Stereotypes stem from category-based responses, so stereotyping represents a basic mental process. Insofar as all people categorize others on the basis of noticeable features, stereotypes bring preconceived notions to mind. However, stereotyping is not inevitable because personal motivation and social norms can facilitate more detailed perception.

Stereotypes come to mind automatically, that is, without effort or deliberative control. A body of research reveals that simply perceiving an outgroup's label (e.g., White participants seeing the word "black") can lead to stereotypic judgments (see Fiske, 1998 for a review). In a landmark study (Dovidio, Evans, & Tyler, 1986), White participants expressed biased judgments when subliminal cues presented the words "white" or "black." Participants viewed a computer screen that flashed racial categories for a few microseconds; although participants reported not seeing the words white or black, they unconsciously processed these words, as their behaviors were effected in stereotypic ways. After unconsciously encoding the word white, they were faster to respond to positive words, and after unconsciously encoding the word black, they were slower to respond to positive words (see also Banaji, Hardin, & Rothman, 1993; Devine, 1989; Fazio, Jackson, Dunton, & Williams, 1995; Lepore & Brown, 1997).

On activation of a stereotype, subsequent thoughts adhere to stereotypic beliefs. Stereotypes bias the selection and interpretation of information. When forming impressions, people attend most to stereotype-consistent information (Fiske & Neuberg, 1990). Stereotype-inconsistent information is often neglected (Bodenhausen, 1988) or, if encoded, tends to be scrutinized or rejected (Ditto & Lopez, 1992).

Sometimes stereotype-inconsistent information proves difficult to ignore. For example, after activation of the "traditional female" stereotype, perceivers might have trouble discounting the dominant and aggressive behavior of a female colleague. To resolve this tension, perceivers often construct subtypes (Weber & Crocker, 1983) that refer to organized exceptions to an overarching category, such as the subtypes "housewife" or "career woman." Because they are exceptions rather than reformulations of the rule, subtypes sustain the alleged validity of the general category stereotype (Lambert, 1995; Ramsey, Wallace, Pugh, & Lord, 1994).

Most of the stereotyping processes described here occur outside of perceivers' awareness (Banaji & Greenwald, 1995; Bargh, 1997; Devine, 1989); hence, people often deny that stereotypes bias their decisions. Moreover, the effects of stereotypes on perception are often extremely subtle by influencing attention and inference processes rather than impelling overt declarations of bias.

STEREOTYPES CAN JUSTIFY STATUS INEQUALITY

The legal cases opening this chapter demonstrate that stereotypes are not simply individual matters, but that they have institutional and systemic implications. Stereotypes derive from social relationships between groups, thus their content allegedly explains why groups inhabit their relative social standings. In organizational contexts, stereotypes derived from cultural beliefs can rationalize bias and inequality.

Dimensions of Stereotypes

What are the cultural stereotypes of women, or African Americans, or homosexuals? Responses are likely to differ depending on whom and when you ask. Social psychological studies have suggested that stereotype content is not particularly stable (Devine & Elliot, 1995). For example, stereotypes during World War II depicted Japanese Americans as threatening and dishonest, whereas contemporary stereotypes depict them as hardworking and quiet. But although the particular content of a group's stereotype may change over time, the general pattern of stereotypic attributes follows certain configurations.

Recent data suggest that stereotypes of outgroups conform to two general patterns (Fiske, Xu, Cuddy, & Glick, in press). Some groups are seen as nice or warm, but not particularly competent or smart. Categories such as housewives, people with disabilities, and elderly people currently fall into this pattern. Other groups are seen as competent and smart, but not particularly warm or social. Categories such as Asians, Jews, Black professionals, and businesswomen currently fall into this pattern. Accordingly, only one's ingroup benefits from being positive along both dimensions.

Very few social groups are viewed as both dislikable and incompetent. Instead, stereotypes tend to be ambivalent (Glick & Fiske, 1996). People might hold strong negative beliefs about certain groups, but simultaneously hold some positive beliefs as well. By balancing high likability with low competence, or viceversa, people can deny being singularly bigoted against an outgroup.

As a demonstration, consider contemporary ambivalent stereotypes of women. Stereotypes of the traditional woman depict her as warm, nurturing, family oriented, and delicate (high on the warmth dimension), but not very ambitious, intellectual, or skilled (low on the competence dimension). Overall, this stereotype blends into a positive constellation of traits (Eagly & Mladinic, 1989). But in a hiring or job scenario, this ambivalent constellation casts a negative light on women. Effective managers or leaders have male-stereotypic, not female-stereotypic, attributes (Eagly & Johnson, 1990).

The pattern of stereotypic traits stems from the outgroup's relation to the dominant majority (Fiske et al., 1999, under review). Some groups have relatively high status, whereas others have low status. Likewise, some groups have cooperative relations with the majority, whereas others have competitive relations. These variables (status and interdependence) jointly determine the content of a group's stereotypic profile. High-status groups are viewed as competent, whereas low-status groups are viewed as incompetent. Cooperative groups are viewed as likable, whereas competitive groups are viewed as dislikable. Situational context determines the effect of ambivalent stereotypes. People may prefer to work with members of competent yet asocial outgroups, but may prefer to befriend members of likable yet incompetent outgroups.

System Justification

Cultural stereotypes stem from the structural relations between groups, and they rationalize group differences in power and status. An emerging perspective in social psychology, derived from philosophy and political science, posits that stereotypes justify status quo inequalities and produce rampant cultural beliefs about the merits of various groups (Jost & Banaji, 1994; see Jost & Major, in press, for a collection of such arguments).

One striking finding emerges: People at both high and low levels of the status hierarchy tend to endorse cultural stereotypes. Stereotypes reflect existing structural relations, so people perceive them to be true. People who identify with high-status groups are likely to assert that low-status groups possess negative or undesirable traits (Pratto, Sidanius, Stallworth, & Malle, 1994; Sidanius, 1993). Even more distressing, members of low-status groups also endorse the veracity of their group's stereotypes, particularly when context legitimizes their low status (Jost, 1999). A compelling study of this effect revealed that women paid themselves less for the same type and quality of work performed by men (Jost, 1997).

Although members of disadvantaged groups might agree about their group's stereotype, they do not always personally internalize the belief. A growing body of evidence reveals that women and minorities minimize perceptions of their personal vulnerability to discrimination, although they affirm that their group as a whole is a target of discrimination (Crosby, 1984; Operario & Fiske, 1999; Operario, Fiske, & Mody, 1999; P. M. Taylor, Wright, Moghaddam, & Lalonde, 1990). This tendency stems from a desire to perceive oneself in control of important outcomes, rather than as a victim of societal bias (Ruggiero & Taylor, 1997). The implication of this self-protective strategy, however, is that targets of stereotypes are unlikely to confront the biases that challenge them, unless the setting provides ample social support to respond to their claims (Ruggiero, Taylor, & Lydon, 1997).

The matter is made worse because simply having power over another person tends to increase people's tendency to stereotype (Fiske, 1993a; Operario & Fiske, 1998). When people control the outcomes of others without being reciprocally contingent, motivation to pay close attention to subordinates diminishes (Goodwin, Gubin, Fiske, & Yzerbyt, 1999). Stereotypes allow powerful people to form good-enough impressions of subordinates, thereby conserving cognitive energy for other demands. In the organizational context, bosses tend to think much less about individual employees than vice versa (Fiske & Dépret, 1996), and when they do think about their subordinates they often do not have enough time or sufficient data to make individuating impressions.

Because stereotypes (a) stem from groups' prior relations, (b) profit from asymmetrical power dynamics, (c) justify future group relations, and (d) are consensually agreed on by high- and low-status group members, they often go unchallenged and their effects often remain undetected in institutions and organizations.

STEREOTYPES INFLUENCE BEHAVIOR

The implication throughout this chapter is that stereotypes affect more than people's thoughts and beliefs. Stereotypes influence the behaviors of both the stereotype agent and target. Behavioral effects tend to operate just as subtly as the cognitive effects noted earlier. So in many cases, stereotypes influence interpersonal interaction without people's awareness.

Behavioral Confirmation

Behavioral confirmation, also known as the self-fulfilling prophecy, refers to a process wherein perceivers cause others to confirm their preconceived biases (Merton, 1957; Snyder, 1992). Social psychology elucidates the mechanisms by which targets unknowingly enact perceiver biases. Perceivers who believe that a group possesses certain attributes (e.g., being hostile or violence prone) treat members of that group accordingly (e.g., acting defensive or aggressive; Chen & Bargh, 1997). When targets reciprocate the treatment they receive, perceivers then view their preconceptions as valid (see Claire & Fiske, 1997; Snyder, 1992, for reviews).

One well-known demonstration of this effect is the *Pygmalion in the Classroom* study (Rosenthal & Jacobson, 1968), in which researchers told teachers that a certain group of their students possessed strong academic talent, though not yet fully realized. In actuality, the group of "late academic bloomers" was randomly designated. On followup assessment, the allegedly gifted students showed enhanced performance on objective measures. Teachers ostensibly gave those students more personalized attention, positive reinforcement, and challenging work, thereby bringing to fruition their preconceptions.

Biased perceivers can unknowingly elicit confirmatory behavior through very subtle cues, such as nonverbal displays and gestures. Studies on interviewers' behaviors toward job applicants reveal how this occurs. In a classic study (Word, Zanna, & Cooper, 1974), White participants interviewed either Black or White job applicants who were actually trained research assistants. With Black applicants, participants demonstrated more defensive body posture and space, more speech errors, and allowed less time for response than with White applicants. In a follow-up study, trained research assistants interviewed White participants, and displayed either comfort or discomfort behaviors found in the previous interview session. Results indicated that the subtle, negative nonverbal gestures significantly diminished participants' interview performance (see also Chaikin, Sigler, & Derlaga, 1974; Chen & Bargh, 1997; Neuberg, 1989; Snyder, Tanke, & Berscheid, 1977).

Recent work links the automatic stereotyping research, discussed earlier, with actual behavioral outcomes. Situational variables can activate people's unconscious beliefs and motivations, which systematically direct behavior without awareness (Bargh & Barndollar, 1996). A recent study shows that nonconscious exposure to words associated with rudeness, through a sentence-scrambling technique devised by Srull and Wyer

(1979), causes people to act more rudely in later interaction; exposure to words associated with the elderly causes people to walk more slowly from the experiment room; and exposure to words associated with African Americans causes people to behave with more hostility in later interaction (Bargh, Chen, & Burrows, 1996). Other work on the automatic stereotype-behavior link reveals that when situations activate their belief systems, men who have sexist views toward women are more prone to sexually harass women in later interaction (Bargh, Raymond, Pryor, & Strack, 1995).

Stereotype Threat

In addition to unconsciously influencing interpersonal behavior, stereotypes can unconsciously make members of disadvantaged groups feel vulnerable to bias (known as *stereotype threat*). Vulnerability can undermine performance, thereby exacerbating the power of stereotypes.

Stereotype threat represents one of the most disturbing aspects of bias against disadvantaged groups. Simply knowing that one's group possesses negative stereotypes can impair performance and behavior. Experimental evidence shows that African Americans perform worse on a standardized intelligence test when informed that it measures intelligence (Steele & Aronson, 1995); when the test is not presented as a measure of intelligence, scores increase significantly. Awareness of one's negative group stereotype also diminishes academic performance for women taking math tests (Spencer, Steele, & Quinn, 1999) and for members of low socioeconomic groups (Croizet & Claire, 1998).

Thus, stereotypes need not overtly manifest themselves to hinder the outcomes of low-status group members. Awareness of the group stereotype can lead to fear of failure and confirmation of the stereotype, so group members may not try as hard or may disengage completely from a performance task (Steele, 1997). Accordingly, negative expectations about the group become self-threatening, as individuals fear their performance may affirm the accuracy of the group stereotype, and that they will be personally treated as a stereotypical group member. Studies have revealed that African American school children show lower academic identification and achievement as they advance in the school system, yet their self-esteem exceeds the more academically oriented Whites (Hare & Constenell, 1985; Osborne, 1994). So as they mature and become more aware of stereotypes about their group, African American students tend to disidentify with domains in which they are categorically expected to fall short.

Through the process of disidentification, people in general can avoid the self-esteem consequences of being negatively judged about valued domains. However, through distancing themselves from stereotype-related domains, members of disadvantaged groups in particular might indirectly confirm the veracity of the stereotype to other members of society.

CHALLENGES TO ORGANIZATIONS

Stereotypes, as illustrated in this selective research review, present multiple challenges to organizations and institutions. Access to status, resources, and employment representation have not paralleled societal increases in demographic complexity. Thus, stereotypes legitimize existing inequalities and facilitate further bias. Because of their automatic and elusive nature, stereotyping processes are not easily identifiable. Even the most well-intentioned people are prone to stereotyping others, and targets of stereotypes may have no definitive grounds for suspecting bias. Stereotypes affect the behavior of members of disadvantaged groups through direct and indirect mechanisms—through behavioral confirmation processes and performance deficits attributable to stereotype threat. These mechanisms are often subtle and unconscious, so people are often not aware when they occur. In effect, one of the greatest challenges that stereotypes pose to organizations is that they simply go unchallenged.

Over time, even minor cognitive and behavioral effects of stereotypes accrue, yielding major inequalities. A computer simulation of bias has shown that probabilities of group bias can amass, and in pyramidal organizations the chance of stereotyping at lower tiers of a hierarchy produces wide disparity at the top tiers (Martell, Lane, & Emrich, 1996). For example, minor biases in hiring or evaluating women at the lower levels of a hierarchy skew the distribution of eligibility for promotion to the next, narrower tier. In Martell et al.'s study, women were arbitrarily designated to constitute 53% of the lowest of eight organizational tiers. Even if institutional gender bias hypothetically affected only 1% of the variance in women's performance ratings, that bias would accrue such that only 35% of those promoted to the top tier would be women. Indeed, bias can diffuse upward throughout an organizational culture from seemingly miniscule biases in hiring and performance evaluation.

Organizations can counter the effects of stereotypes. Organizations must recognize the subtlety and ambivalence of modern stereotypes, creating responses specific to the needs and abilities of the 21st century (Fiske & Glick, 1995). Research shows that stereotypes, although automatically and unconsciously triggered, indeed respond to personal control (Blair & Banaji, 1996). In studies demonstrating evaluative and behavioral manifestations of prejudice, people with strong internalized values of fairness and egalitarianism did not display bias (Monteith, 1993), even when experimenters attempted to unconsciously draw forth stereotype effects (Lepore & Brown, 1997). Although experimental procedures might have been effective at activating stereotypic categories, personal standards overrode the content of societal beliefs, and people were able to act in accordance with their personal, rather than with societal, values. Social norms and standards of fairness also undermine stereotypes (Blanchard, Lilly, & Vaughn, 1991; Fiske & Von Hendy, 1992). Holding people accountable for their decisions can urge more careful, less stereotypic, thinking (Pendry & Macrae, 1996; Tetlock, 1992). People are highly unlikely to stereotype others when their own outcomes are at stake (see Fiske & Dépret, 1996, for review), so settings that underscore mutual interdependence between supervisor and subordinate, reminding them of their contingency and cooperation, can diminish stereotyping. Support systems can ameliorate the tension felt by stereotype targets and allow for confrontation of bias (Ruggiero et al., 1997).

Controlling stereotypes is not always easy. Time pressures, lack of information, and competing cognitive demands can lead even conscientious people to stereotype others without knowing it, yet personal values and choice ultimately determine whether one exerts effort to go beyond stereotypic thought (Fiske, 1989).

Hence, just because stereotypes are reflexive responses to category labels, they are not inescapable. People's thinking processes follow internalized standards and social norms, so motivations derived from the self or from the situation are equally effective at combating stereotypic biases (see Fiske, 1998, for review). This motivation hinges, however, on understanding the limitations of human judgment, recognizing when stereotypes enter the mind, and acknowledging the distinction between actual information versus stereotypic expectations.

Organizational dynamics, therefore, not only reflect the power of stereotypes, but empower stereotypes to persist. Yet through a range of mechanisms, organizational and individual intervention can mediate these effects by motivating standards of justice. Organizational interventions should capitalize on the research reviewed here, developing their strategies on the basis of theory and scientific research.

Interventions targeting individual decisions should appeal to people's internalized values of fairness, as advocated in American culture, to elicit conscientious decisions. Individual-level interventions should also hold people accountable for the decisions they make; just the perception of having to explain the basis for one's decisions can prompt nonstereotypic judgment. Making people interdependent on members of other groups for desired outcomes (e.g., through mixed-race work teams) can promote more individuated impressions and a unified spirit. Perhaps the most effective means for reducing individual-level stereotyping is by informing people how unconscious stereotyping can occur. Understanding the indirect and unconscious mechanisms by which we stereotype others is pivotal to controlling those processes.

But change is not solely an individual responsibility, as organizational actions are vital for intervention. Supervisors in organizations should acknowledge whether category-based biases in performance standards and evaluation render some groups disadvantaged in hiring or promotion. Managers should be constantly reminded about the principles of responsibility and egalitarianism, as overwhelming work demands may urge less thoughtful decision-making processes about subordinates. Institutional norms should embrace differences between people, and acknowledge and reward multiple-achievement domains: intellectual, social or interpersonal, creative, and physical talents, to name a few. Pathways of mutual interdependence between high and low levels of a hierarchy can remind management that they, too, rely on their employees for important outcomes, that employees merit individuation—not category-based judgment—because of their unique contributions to the organization. Finally, objective third parties should occasionally monitor organizations, interviewing people at every level of the hierarchy to assess whether overt and covert biases resulting from stereotypes permeate the organizational culture.

ACKNOWLEDGEMENTS

Don Operario, Department of Medicine, University of California, San Francisco; Susan T. Fiske, Department of Psychology, University of Massachusetts at Amherst.

Research was supported by grants from the National Institute of Mental Health (MH15742, MH19391, and MH41801) and the National Science Foundation (9421480).

Correspondence should be sent to Don Operario, Center for AIDS Prevention Studies, University of California, 1388 Sutter Street, Suite 605, San Francisco, CA 94109. Electronic mail may be sent to Doperario@psg.ucsf.edu.

REFERENCES

Allport, G. W. (1954). *The nature of prejudice*. Reading, MA: Addison-Wesley.

Banaji, M. R., & Greenwald, A. G. (1995). Implicit gender stereotyping in judgments of fame. *Journal of Personality and Social Psychology, 68*, 181–198.

Banaji, M. R., & Hardin, C. (1996). Automatic stereotyping. *Psychological Science, 7*, 136–141.

Banaji, M. R., Hardin, C., & Rothman, A. J. (1993). Implicit stereotyping in person judgment. *Journal of Personality and Social Psychology, 65*, 272–281.

Bargh, J. A. (1997). The automaticity of everyday life. In R. S. Wyer, Jr. (Ed.), *Advances in social cognition* (Vol. 10, pp. 1–61). Mahwah, NJ: Lawrence Erlbaum Associates.

Bargh, J. A., & Barndollar, K. (1996). Automaticity in action: The unconscious as repository of chronic goals and motives. In P. Gollwitzer & J. A. Bargh (Eds.), *The psychology of action: Linking cognition and motivation to behavior* (pp. 457–481). New York: Guilford.

Bargh, J. A., Chen, M., & Burrows, L. (1996). Automaticity of social behavior: Direct effects of trait construct and stereotype activation in action. *Journal of Personality and Social Psychology, 71*, 230–244.

Bargh, J. A., Raymond, P., Pryor, J. B., & Strack, F. (1995). Attractiveness of the underling: An automatic power→sex association and its consequences for sexual harassment and aggression. *Journal of Personality and Social Psychology, 68*, 768–781.

Blair, I. V., & Banaji, M. R. (1996). Automatic and controlled processes in stereotyping priming. *Journal of Personality and Social Psychology, 70*, 1126–1141.

Blanchard, F. A., Lilly, T., & Vaughn, L. A. (1991). Reducing the expression of racial prejudice. *Psychological Science, 2*, 101–105.

Bodenhausen, G. V. (1988). Stereotypic biases in social decision making and memory: Testing process models for stereotype use. *Journal of Personality and Social Psychology, 55*, 726–737.

Bodenhausen, G. V., & Wyer, R. S., Jr. (1985). Effects of stereotypes on decision-making and information-processing strategies. *Journal of Personality and Social Psychology, 48*, 267–282.

Chaikin, A. L., Sigler, E., & Derlaga, V. J. (1974). Nonverbal mediators of teacher expectancy effects. *Journal of Personality and Social Psychology, 71*, 262–275.

Chen, M., & Bargh, J. A. (1997). Nonconscious behavioral confirmation processes: The self-fulfilling consequences of automatic stereotype activation. *Journal of Experimental Social Psychology, 33*, 541–560.

Claire, T., & Fiske, S. T. (1997). A systemic view of behavioral confirmation: Counterpoint to the individualist view. In C. Sedikides, J. Schopler, & C. Insko (Eds.), *Intergroup cognition and intergroup behavior* (pp. 205–231). Mahwah, NJ: Lawrence Erlbaum Associates.

Croizet, J. C., & Claire, T. (1998). Extending the concept of stereotype threat to social class: The intellectual underperformance of students from low socioeconomic backgrounds. *Personality and Social Psychology Bulletin, 24*, 588–594.

Crosby, F. (1984). The denial of personal discrimination. *American Behavioral Scientist, 27*, 371–386.

Devine, P. G. (1989). Stereotypes and prejudice: Their automatic and controlled components. *Journal of Personality and Social Psychology, 17*, 44–50.

Devine, P. G., & Elliot, A. J. (1995). Are racial stereotypes really fading? The Princeton trilogy revisited. *Personality and Social Psychology Bulletin, 21*, 1139–1150.

Ditto, P. H., & Lopez, D. F. (1992). Motivated skepticism: Use of differential decision criteria for preferred and nonpreferred conclusions. *Journal of Personality and Social Psychology, 63*, 568–584.

Dovidio, J. F., Evans, N., & Tyler, R. B. (1986). Racial stereotypes: The contents of their cognitive representations. *Journal of Experimental Social Psychology, 22*, 22–37.

Eagly, A. H., & Johnson, B. T. (1990). Gender and leadership style: A meta-analysis. *Psychological Bulletin, 108*, 233–256.

Eagly, A. H., & Mladinic, A. (1989). Gender stereotypes and attitudes toward women and men. *Personality and Social Psychology Bulletin, 15*, 543–558.

Fazio, R. H., Jackson, J. R., Dunton, B. C., & Williams, C. J. (1995). Variability in automatic activation as an unobtrusive measure of racial attitudes: A bona fide pipeline? *Journal of Personality and Social Psychology, 69*, 1013–1027.

Fiske, S. T. (1989). Examining the role of intent: Toward understanding its role in stereotyping and prejudice. In J. S. Uleman & J. A. Bargh (Eds.), *Unintended thought* (pp. 253–283). New York: Guilford.

Fiske, S. T., & Glick, P. (1995). Controlling other people: The impact of power on stereotyping. *American Psychologist, 48*, 621–628.

Fiske, S. T. (1993b). Social cognition and social perception. In M. R. Rosenzweig & L. W. Porter (Eds.), *Annual review of psychology* (Vol. 44, pp. 155–194). Palo Alto, CA: Annual Reviews.

Fiske, S. T. (1998). Stereotyping, prejudice, and discrimination. In D. T. Gilbert, S. T. Fiske, & G. Lindzey (Eds.), *The handbook of social psychology* (Vol. 2, pp. 357–411). Boston: McGraw-Hill.

Fiske, S. T., & Dépret, E. (1996). Control, interdependence, and power: Understanding social cognition in its social context. In W. Stroebe & M. Hewstone (Eds.), *European review of social psychology* (Vol. 7, pp. 31–61). New York: Wiley.

Fiske, S. T., & Neuberg, S. L. (1990). A continuum model of impression formation, from category-based to individuating processes: Influence as a function of information, motivation, and attention. In M. P. Zanna (Ed.), *Advances in experimental social psychology* (Vol. 23, pp. 1–108). San Diego, CA: Academic Press.

Fiske, S. T., & Von Hendy, H. M. (1992). Personality feedback and situational norms can control stereotyping processes. *Journal of Personality and Social Psychology, 62*, 577–596.

Fiske, S. T., Xu, J., Cuddy, A. J. C., & Glick, P. (1999). Respect versus liking: Status and interdependence underlie ambivalent stereotypes. *Journal of Social Issues.*

Glick, P., & Fiske, S. T. (1996). The Ambivalent Sexism Inventory: Differentiating hostile and benevolent sexism. *Journal of Personality and Social Psychology, 70*, 491–512.

Goodwin, S. A., Gubin, A., Fiske, S. T., & Yzerbyt, V. (2000). Power can bias impression formation: Stereotyping subordinates by default and by design. *Group Processes and Intergroup Relations.*

Hare, B. R., & Costenell, L. A. (1985). No place to run, no place to hide: Comparative status and future prospects of Black boys. In M. B. Spencer, G. K. Brookins, & W. Allen (Eds.), *Beginnings: The social and affective development of Black children* (pp. 201–214). Hillsdale, NJ: Lawrence Erlbaum Associates.

Jost, J. T. (1997). An experimental replication of the depressed-entitlement effect among women. *Psychology of Women Quarterly, 21*, 387–393.

Jost, J. T. (1999). *Perceived legitimacy as an implicit and explicit moderator of ingroup and outgroup favoritism among members of low-status groups.* Unpublished manuscript, Stanford University.

Jost, J. T., & Banaji, M. R. (1994). The role of stereotyping in system justification and the production of false consciousness. *British Journal of Social Psychology, 33*, 1–27.

Judd, C. M., & Park, B. (1993). Definition and assessment of accuracy in social stereotypes. *Psychological Review, 100*, 109–128.

Jussim, L. (1991). Social perception and social reality: A reflection-construction model. *Psychological Review, 98*, 54–73.

Lambert, A. J. (1995). Stereotypes and social judgments: The consequences of group variability. *Journal of Personality and Social Psychology, 68*, 388–403.

Lee, Y., Jussim, L., & McCauley, C. R. (Eds.). (1995). *Stereotype accuracy.* Washington, DC: American Psychological Association.

Lepore, L., & Brown, R. (1997). Category and stereotype activation: Is prejudice inevitable? *Journal of Personality and Social Psychology, 72*, 275–287.

Lippmann, W. (1922). *Public opinion.* New York: Harcourt Brace.

Macrae, C. N., Hewstone, M., & Griffiths, R. G. (1993). Processing load and memory for sterotype-based information. *European Journal of Social Psychology, 28*, 319–325.

Macrae, C. N., Milne, A. B., & Bodenhausen, G. V. (1994). Stereotypes as energy-saving devices: A peek inside the cognitive toolbox. *Journal of Personality and Social Psychology, 66*, 37–47.

Martell, R. F., Lane, D. M., & Emrich, C. (1996). Male-female differences: A computer simulation. *American Psychologist, 51*, 157–158.

McCann, C. D., Ostrom, T. M., Tyner, L. K., & Mitchell, M. L. (1985). Person perception in heterogeneous groups. *Journal of Personality and Social Psychology, 49*, 1449–1459.

Merton, R. K. (1957). *Social theory and social structure*. New York: The Free Press.

Monteith, M. J. (1993). Self-regulation of prejudiced responses: Implications for progress in prejudice-reduction efforts. *Journal of Personality and Social Psychology, 65*, 469–485.

Neuberg, S. L. (1989). The goal of forming accurate impressions during social interaction: Attenuating the impact of negative expectancies. *Journal of Personality and Social Psychology, 56*, 374–386.

Operario, D., & Fiske, S. T. (1999a). *Ethnic identity moderates perceptions of prejudice: Judgments of personal versus group and subtle versus blatant discrimination*. Unpublished manuscript, University of California at San Francisco.

Operario, D., & Fiske, S. T. (1999b). *Gender identity moderates perceptions of discrimination against women*. Unpublished manuscript, University of California at San Francisco.

Osborne, J. (1994). Academics, self-esteem, and race: A look at the underlying assumption of the disidentification hypothesis. *Personality and Social Psychology Bulletin, 21*, 449–455.

Ottati, V., & Lee, Y. (1995). Accuracy: A neglected component of stereotype research. In Y. Lee, L. Jussim, & C. R. McCauley (Eds.), *Stereotype accuracy: Toward appreciating group differences* (pp. 29–59). Washington, DC: American Psychological Association.

Pendry, L. F., & Macrae, C. N. (1996). What the disinterested perceiver overlooks: Goal-directed social categorization. *Personality and Social Psychology Bulletin, 22*, 249–256.

Perdue, C. W., Dovidio, J. F., Gurtman, M. B., & Tyler, R. B. (1990). Us and them: Social categorization and the process of intergroup bias. *Journal of Personality and Social Psychology, 59*, 475–486.

Pratto, F., Sidanius, J., Stallworth, L. M., & Malle, B. F. (1994). Social dominance orientation: A personality variable predicting social and political attitudes. *Journal of Personality and Social Psychology, 67*, 741–763.

Ramsey, S. L., Wallace, D. S., Pugh, M. A., & Lord, C. G. (1994). The role of subtypes in attitudes toward superordinate social categories. *British Journal of Social Psychology, 33*, 387–403.

Rosenthal, R., & Jacobson, L. F. (1968). *Pygmalion in the classroom*. New York: Holt, Rinehart & Winston.

Ruggiero, K. M., & Taylor, D. M. (1997). Why minority group members perceive or do not perceive the discrimination that confronts them: The role of self-esteem and perceived control. *Journal of Personality and Social Psychology, 72*, 373–389.

Ruggiero, K. M., Taylor, D. M., & Lydon, J. E. (1997). How disadvantaged group members cope with discrimination when they perceive that social support is available. *Journal of Applied Social Psychology, 27*, 1581–1600.

Sanbonmatsu, D. M., Akimoto, S. A., & Gibson, B. D. (1994). Stereotype-based blocking in social explanation. *Personality and Social Psychology Bulletin, 20*, 71–81.

Sidanius, J. (1993). The psychology of group conflict and the dynamics of oppression: A social dominance perspective. In W. McGuire & S. Iyengar (Eds.), *Current approaches to political psychology*. Durham, NC: Duke University Press.

Snyder, M. (1992). Motivational foundations of behavioral confirmation. In M. P. Zanna (Ed.), *Advances in experimental social psychology* (Vol. 25, pp. 67–114). San Diego, CA: Academic Press.

Snyder, M., Tanke, E. D., & Berscheid, E. (1977). Social perception and interpersonal behavior: On the self-fulfilling nature of social stereotypes. *Journal of Personality and Social Psychology, 35*, 656–666.

Spencer, S. J., Steele, C. M., & Quinn, D. M. (1999). Stereotype threat and women's math performance. *Journal of Experimental Social Psychology, 35*, 4–28.

Stangor, C. (1995). Content and application inaccuracy in social stereotyping. In Y. Lee, L. Jussim, & C. R. McCauley (Eds.), *Stereotype accuracy: Toward appreciating group differences* (pp. 275–292). Washington, DC: American Psychological Association.

Steele, C. M. (1997). A threat in the air: How stereotypes shape intellectual identity and performance. *American Psychologist, 52*, 613–629.

Steele, C. M., & Aronson, J. (1995). Stereotype vulnerability and the intellectual test performance of African-Americans. *Journal of Personality and Social Psychology, 69*, 797–811.

Taylor, D. M., Wright, S. C., Moghaddam, F. M., & Lalonde, R. N. (1990). The personal/group discrepancy: Perceiving my group, but not myself, to be a target for discrimination. *Personality and Social Psychology Bulletin, 16*, 254–262.

Taylor, S. E. (1981). A categorization approach to stereotyping. In D. L. Hamilton (Ed.), *Cognitive processes in stereotyping and intergroup behavior* (pp. 83–115). Hillsdale, NJ: Lawrence Erlbaum Associates.

Taylor, S. E., Fiske, S. T., Etcoff, N. L., & Ruderman, A. J. (1978). Categorical and contextual bases of person memory and stereotyping. *Journal of Personality and Social Psychology, 36*, 778–793.

Tetlock, P. E. (1992). The impact of accountability on judgment and choice: Toward a social contingency model. In M. P. Zanna (Ed.), *Advances in experimental social psychology* (Vol. 23, pp. 331–376). San Diego, CA: Academic Press.

von Hippel, W., Jonides, J., Hilton, J. L., & Narayan, S. (1993). Inhibitory effect of schematic processing on perceptual encoding. *Journal of Personality and Social Psychology, 64*, 921–935.

Weber, R., & Crocker, J. (1983). Cognitive processes in the revision of stereotypic beliefs. *Journal of Personality and Social Psychology, 45*, 961–977.

Wilder, D. A. (1981). Perceiving persons as a group: Categorization and intergroup relations. In D. L. Hamilton (Ed.), *Cognitive processes in stereotyping and intergroup behavior* (pp. 213–258). Hillsdale, NJ: Lawrence Erlbaum Associates.

Wilder, D. A. (1984). Predictions of belief homogeneity and similarity following social categorization. *British Journal of Social Psychology, 23*, 323–333.

Word, C. O., Zanna, M. P., & Cooper, J. (1974). The nonverbal mediation of self-fulfilling prophecies in interracial interaction. *Journal of Experimental Social Psychology, 10*, 109–120.

Zárate, M. A., & Smith, E. R. (1990). Person categorization and stereotyping. *Social Cognition, 8*, 161–185.

II

Selection

Charles Parsons, Robert Liden, and Talya Bauer, in chapter 3, begin this section by examining person perception in the employment interview. The most common selection process used by organizations, the interview, involves the active and passive exchange of verbal and nonverbal information influenced by the participants' schemas and information processing capabilities and biases. This chapter considers the perspectives of both the interviewer and the applicant. The interviewer's goal is to evaluate the applicant and make a decision (accept, reject, or consider further). The applicant's goal is to evaluate the organization, in part on the basis of the impression made by the interviewer. Parsons, Liden, and Bauer explain that the interviewer and applicant come to the interview with a number of cognitions already formed, such as goals and expectations for the interview and conceptions of the type of person sought and the nature of the job. The interview itself is a reciprocal interchange and processing of information (cognitions and feelings based on observations and experiences), ultimately leading to judgments formed by both parties.

Chapter 3 first considers the interviewer's perception, then the applicant's perspective, and finally the reciprocal interactions. In the process, the authors review (a) research on demographic stereotyping; (b) how nonjob-related applicant characteristics (e.g., gender, weight, and age) affect impressions; (c) the extent to which participants distort information to confirm expectations; (d) accuracy goals; (e) how experience influences the use of irrelevant factors; and (f) the effects of interview structure on avoidance of information processing biases and distortions, information from other sources, and perceived fairness.

Valerie Sessa begins chapter 4 with the reminder that executive selection is often not a systematic process, but one that is fraught with the potential for personal biases, organizational politics, search team dynamics, and inaccurate judgments and decisions. Unlike selection of lower level personnel (which is likely to be based on job analysis, validated tests, and structured interviews), executive selection is more individualistic because each job is unique and the process for identifying and selecting candidates is likely to be unique. Although executive assessments may be used, with reports on candidates commissioned from recruitment firms and psychologists, person-perception and social-cognition processes are very likely to influence candidate search and evaluation. In the absence of scientifically based personnel selection principles, executive selections are likely to be plagued by errors or biases in person perception.

Sessa's chapter presents a framework for executive selection. She demonstrates how person perception affects the selection process. She then describes the differences in choosing between internal and external candidates. Finally, she offers suggestions for developing research programs on executive selection and improving practice using principles derived from an understanding of person perception. The chapter is based on interviews with almost 500 executives in the top three levels of organizations (CEOs and two levels down). The interviewees were asked about a selection decision in which they had personally participated in the past few years. Half of the sample were asked about a selection that turned out to be a success; the other half were asked about a selection that turned out to be a failure. The research points out that person-perception processes enter into each element of the executive selection decision, for instance: using salient but irrelevant characteristics of candidates to categorize them, using nonpredictive descriptions of job performance leading to unrealistic or inaccurate expectations, and ignoring summary data. Despite these and other person-perception biases, such as rater leniency, halo effects, and restriction of range, executives tend to be extremely confident in the quality of their own judgments, even when data indicate that they are incorrect. These biases act as information filters. Moreover, internal and external candidates are likely to be perceived very differently. For instance, external executives are perceived more favorably during the selection process but once in the position are less likely to be seen as successful. This may be because there is less negative information available about external candidates. However, external candidates know less about the organization and so may have a more difficult time once on the job. Also, internal and external candidates may be chosen for different reasons. External candidates may be favored when the company needs a new vision, whereas internal candidates may be favored when the organization is already in a state of change and an executive who has specific experience or background with the company is needed, or there is a desire for stability. In addition, selectors receive information from different sources when evaluating internal and external candidates. Selection committees rely on interviews, résumés, and references for evaluating external candidates, and performance appraisals, succession plans, and subordinate reviews for evaluating internal candidates.

Sessa concludes with some recommendations for research, for example: study executive selection systematically, gain a better understanding of the differences between selection at higher levels versus lower levels in the organization and what impact this has on the selection process, and test the effects of applying rigorous selection methods. She also offers ideas for practice, such as using teams with a variety of members to make the selection decision. Team members who are affected by the decision in different ways may use different criteria for including and excluding potential candidates. They will likely broaden the pool of candidates under consideration. Increasing the variety of candidates in the applicant pool is a way of ensuring that a wide array of candidate characteristics are considered.

The assessment center is another major instance of interpersonal judgment in measuring people's (usually managers') performance and using the measurements to make predictions about them. This process was designed to take person perception into account. The technique calls for judgments of performance under controlled conditions, such as standard exercises, well-defined performance dimensions, and multiple, trained raters. In chapter 5, Paul Sackett and Kathleen Tuzinski review the literature on assessment center ratings. They describe how assessment center content and rating procedures have been redesigned to produce a clear and reliable set of performance factors. In examining research on assessor judgments, they clarify how assessors attend to and process behavioral information in an assessment center.

In the traditional assessment center, dimension ratings are made after all exercises have been completed and there has been a group discussion among the raters. Another method sometimes used is rating dimensions immediately after each exercise, before the group discussion. The group discussion is held in order to determine if consensus can be reached on final dimensions ratings. Assessment centers attempt to measure aspects of performance that are evident in a set of simulations or exercises that are representative of the job. However, the relationships among the different dimensions within exercises are higher than the relationships between the same dimensions across exercises. This seems to reflect a natural tendency for raters to think more in terms of overall exercise performance than in terms of dimensions. This may occur because exercise-based schema, rather than dimension-based schema, are more readily available and easier to apply. Behavioral checklists, rater training, and the use of fewer dimensions are some of the methods engaged to overcome this phenomenon. However, exercise bias remains despite these interventions.

Because raters in assessment centers do not make finely differentiated dimensional judgments, assessment centers can be designed to take advantage of this fact. Different exercises measure effectiveness in a variety of important roles, such as negotiator, counselor, fact finder, or persuader. Scoring should then be exercise based, with assessors reaching agreement on performance in each exercise. The dimensions within each exercise would be exercise specific, and hence quite narrow in scope. The resulting dimensions would not be aggregated across exercises. Sackett and Tuzinski point out that this method is not intended to weaken or eliminate exercise factors, but instead is a way to build on the tendency of raters to evaluate their effectiveness relative to the specific role that dominates the exercise. The resulting measures need to be validated by correlating them with measures of performance on the same role outside the assessment center, for instance, multisource survey ratings or supervisory performance ratings.

3

Person Perception in Employment Interviews

Charles K. Parsons
Georgia Institute of Technology

Robert C. Liden
University of Illinois–Chicago

Talya N. Bauer
Portland State University

Employment interviews are the most common employee selection procedure. An applicant may receive numerous interviews with a single employer. The interview provides a setting for the exchange of information between applicant and employer on which evaluation and decisions are reached. Although the face-to-face interview is probably most common, other alternatives are certainly gaining popularity (video based, telephone, etc.). Because of the importance and frequency of employment interviews, a great deal of research has been conducted on the accuracy of interviewer judgments of applicants and the process through which interviewers reach decisions about applicants. More recently, there has been an increasing interest in applicant reactions to employment interviews and other aspects of employee recruitment.

One of the common threads underlying interviews is their interpersonal nature. As an interpersonal event, the interview creates a behavioral setting that engages the various parties in person-perception and social-cognition processes. Information is sought through verbal requests, and both verbal and nonverbal behavior are interpreted. Information processing can be highly active or very passive. The interviewer is expected to form an evaluation about the applicant, and this evaluation will formally affect the applicant's status (e.g., denied employment, given a job, or still under consideration). Similarly, the applicant's interpretation of the interview will likely influence his or her impression of the interviewer and the organization under consideration. This impression will play a role in deciding whether to accept a job if offered as well as inform further job search activity. Underlying this brief descriptive process are the interviewer's and applicant's cognitive processes that influence what information is sought and how it is interpreted. The interview setting has been a popular one for studying person perception and social cognition. We provide an overview of the research and how it fits into the theoretical models described in this book's introductory chapters. Recommendations for practice and future research efforts are provided.

As an employee selection procedure, there has traditionally been an interest in the validity of the interview. Early reviews of interview research focused on this perspective and concluded that the validity is typically quite low (Mayfield, 1964; Ulrich & Trumbo, 1965; Wagner, 1949). More recent reviews have distinguished between unstructured and structured interviews and have concluded that the criterion-related validity for interviews with little structure remains low (meta-analysis, $r = .20$), whereas criterion-related validity is substantially higher for more highly structured interviews (meta-analysis, $r = .57$; Huffcutt & Arthur, 1994). The concept of interview structure is more fully summarized later in this chapter. However, in spite of providing much better procedural guidelines for the design and conduct of interviews, this research emphasis on predictive validity tends to ignore the underlying cognitive processes that may influence the accuracy of interviewer decisions.

Early research on the interview process by Springbett (1958) and Webster (1964) suggests that there were numerous cognitive and behavioral biases underlying how interviewers conducted interviews and interpreted applicant behavior. Springbett and Webster suggested that interviewers gave too much weight to negative information, made decisions early in the interview, and made decisions based on the comparison of the applicant to an ideal candidate. These decision "heuristics" were inferred from the research as opposed to studied directly. Subsequent to this early work, interest in better understanding the cognitive and behavioral aspects of the interview process has escalated. Though most of this research has focused on the interviewer, the applicant's perspective has received more attention.

In this chapter, we organize relevant contemporary research around the framework that appears in Fig. 3.1. In this figure, we propose that

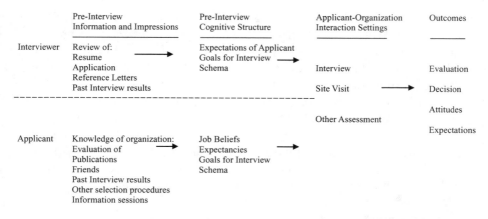

FIG. 3.1. Framework for existing research on person perception and social cognition in employment interviews.

interviewers and applicants each arrive at the interview with preinterview information and impressions from many sources. These impressions are combined with other preinterview cognitive variables, such as goals for the interview, expectations, and so on that will affect how verbal and non-verbal information is perceived during the interview. During the actual interview, the behavioral, cognitive, and affective reactions of the two parties have reciprocal causality, that is, interviewer behavior affects applicant behavior through the impact on cognition and perception constructs; this, in turn, will affect interviewer behavior through cognitive and perception constructs. Ultimately, both parties form relevant judgments and make decisions that result in interview outcomes. We structure chapter 3 by first addressing the interviewer's perspective, followed by the applicant's perspective, and subsequently the reciprocal personal interactions that occur during the interview. Finally, we discuss the implications of these research results for both future research on person perception and social cognition as well as the practice of employment interviewing.

THE INTERVIEWER'S PERSPECTIVE

Researchers have explored a number of factors for their possible effects on the preinterview perceptions of applicants and the processing of information about applicants. Liden and Parsons (1989) proposed that interviewers' preinterview impressions of applicants might be influenced by individual characteristics such as sex, race, age, or ethnic background. Dipboye and Gaugler (1993) developed a process model of the way interviewers process information and make decisions concerning interviewees. In their model, both interviewer and interviewee knowedge, skills, and abilities (KSAs) are depicted as merging during the interview to influence perceptions of one another. The interviewer compares his or her cognitive representation of the job with information gathered about the interviewee to form initial expectations. Phillips and Dipboye (1989) conducted a field study involving 34 interviewers and 161 applicants in a large financial services company. They found that interviewer preinterview impressions were based on an application form including extensive background information and standardized test scores for numerical ability and knowledge of economics.

In summary, the research on impression formation and interviews shows that preinterview impressions based on paper credentials and the physical characteristics of applicants influence the postinterview impressions held by interviewers. Moreover, this effect may also hold once the applicant enters the organization. Schoorman (1988) showed that managers who had a hand in hiring a subordinate gave that subordinate a higher rating in subsequent performance reviews than did other organizational members who did not participate in the hiring process for that subordinate. This may imply that supervisors who have favorable impressions of newcomers (based on their work experience and perceived marketability) before they enter the organization, might behave toward them as if they were higher performers and therefore give them more support and recognition once within the organization. In the next section, we more fully delineate the cognitive constructs underlying the person-perception and social-cognition processes of the interviewer during the employment interview.

Preinterview Cognitive Structure

In addition to the preinterview impressions formed from application information, references, and so on, a number of other cognitive variables are considered relevant at the point of the initiation of the interview. These variables continue to play a role in the actual search for and processing of information during the interview. For now, we introduce them as part of the preinterview cognitive structure. The employment interview is heavily laden with expectations concerning socially accepted behavior. Logically, interviewer schemas should play a major role in perception and information processing during the interview. However, research in this area usually adopts the concepts of stereotypes, expectations, and goals.

Stereotypes.   Though there is no agreement on the definition of stereotype, in general, it means that a perceiver uses category-based processing of information about the "target." Once a target is categorized, the perceiver uses category membership to make inferences about the target. In employment interviewing, the concept of stereotyping is often associated with age, race, gender, and disability bias although other features of individuals (e.g., obesity) are also subject to stereotyping and negative bias. In the context of the interview, negative stereotyping (e.g., perceiving an applicant as a member of a category that has negative implications for competence and qualifications) can cause an interviewer to reach unjustified, unfavorable conclusions about individual applicant competence and job qualifications. This is because the perceiver may not be motivated to attend to differentiating features of the individual in either the search for additional information about the individual, or appropriate "weighting" of such information in forming overall judgments. Over the years, the research on demographic stereotyping and interview outcomes has been of great interest because of the legal implications of such effects under Title VII of the 1964 Civil Rights Act, the Americans with Disabilities Act, and the Age Discrimination in Employment Act. Roehling, Campion, and Arvey (1999) reviewed the research on demographic bias on judgments of applicant competence and qualifications. They concluded that, although both research and theory suggest a multitude of additional factors that determine whether an interview is likely to allow demographic characteristics to bias judgment, the weight of the evidence is that such bias does occur and thus deserves further study. In a separate review on weight-based discrimination, Roehling (1999) concluded that negative stereotypes of overweight individuals, though not necessarily having legal ramifications, were common.

One approach to studying the impact of stereotypes is presented in the research by Pingitore, Dugoni, Tindale, and Spring (1994). In that study, professional actors followed the same script in a simulated interview, but their weight was manipulated by adding prostheses to produce the appearance of moderate obesity (i.e., 20% heavier than the average-weight applicant). Participants in the study rated the applicant's personal disposition along a set of 16 adjective pairs (productive–nonproductive, attractive–unattractive, etc.). Pingitore et al. found that applicant weight accounted for 20% of the variance in the perceived dispositions of the applicants. Thus, the issue of appearing overweight does lead to negative inferences about other aspects of the individual.

An alternative approach for assessing the degree to which individuals hold certain stereotypes was demonstrated by Gallois, Callan, and Palmer

(1992). The researchers used the Sex-Role Stereotyping Questionnaire (SRSQ) to measure the extent to which interviewers held traditional sex-role stereotypes. They asked the interviewer to first think of a typical young adult male and describe him by using 41 bipolar adjective items. Then they asked the interviewer to think of a typical young adult female and, using the same format, describe her. A difference score between the two cumulative ratings was computed and represented the strength of the stereotype held by the interviewer. Gallois et al. found that sex-role stereotyping impacted the evaluations of applicants who displayed aggressive behavior and applicants who displayed nonassertive behavior, but not assertive applicants.

When considering the role of stereotyping processes in person perception in the interview and how it ultimately affects judgments of applicant competence and qualifications, one must also consider how the interviewer contrasts perceptions of the applicant with some "standard." Early research on interviewing (e.g., Webster, 1964) suggests that interviewers hold an image of an "ideal applicant" that serves as the standard for contrasting actual applicant characteristics in evaluation. Sources of information on the ideal applicant may come from past interviewer experience, job analysis, generalized impressions of "good employees," perhaps the image of self as ideal, and so on. In simple terms, the interviewer's impressions of the applicant are influenced by category-based perceptions (stereotypes) and these impressions are contrasted to the ideal-applicant category. As the degree of difference between these categories increases, the applicant is viewed more negatively (Van Vianen and Willemsen, 1992).

Expectations.   Probably the most often studied cognitive variable in employment interviews is that of initial impressions and expectations for the applicant and how these impressions and expectations influence both the search for and interpretation of applicant information during the actual interview. The earlier section on preinterview information and impressions reviewed research on how interviewers often have access to information about the applicant prior to actually meeting the applicant (e.g., application blank, prior interviewer notes, letters of recommendation, etc.). The extent to which this prior information creates an impression and related expectations about the applicant determines the interviewer's inclination to engage in interview conduct (e.g., questions, demeanor, other nonverbal behavior) that influences both applicant behavior (verbal and nonverbal) and interpretation of what is perceived (Dipboye, 1982). This creates the classic "self-fulfilling prophecy" described by Merton (1948) as the applicant provides information that is interpreted as confirming the interviewer's initial expectation.

Of particular importance for interview research is a study by Snyder and Swann (1978) indicating that the nature of interviewer questions might be based on intentions to document initial expectations. That is, interviewers ask questions that elicit answers most likely to confirm their preinterview beliefs. Although the Snyder and Swann study did not involve employment interviews, Dipboye (1982) and Sackett (1982) contended that the phenomenon uncovered by these researchers might generalize to the employment interview setting. In four separate experiments (two of which used professional recruiters as participants), Sackett found no supporting evidence to replicate Snyder and Swann's results for employment interview situations. Similarly, little support for confirmatory questioning strategies was found by McDonald and Hakel (1985). However, subsequent research provided evidence indicating that interviewers' questions were influenced by their preinterview impressions of the applicants (Binning, Goldstein, Garcia, & Scattaregia, 1988; Dougherty, Turban, & Callender, 1994; Macon & Dipboye, 1988). In two of these investigations, it was found that the types and numbers of interviewers' questions were biased to confirm preinterview impressions (Binning et al., 1988; Dougherty et al., 1994). In a sample of actual interviews, Dougherty et al. found that the preinterview impressions of interviewers were related to confirmatory behaviors by the interviewers during the interview. When interviewers formed a positive impression of the interviewees, they asked questions designed to confirm their expectations. In general, they treated applicants in a more favorable way, attempting to provide them with their best opportunity to succeed in the interview. Dougherty and Turban (1999) concluded that the reason for such inconsistent results may be that participants in the earlier studies were asked to select questions from a list, whereas in the later studies interviewers were asked to generate their own interview questions. The inconsistent initial results and later identification of a moderating variable to possibly explain the inconsistencies in results parallel the overall findings in the self-fulfilling prophecy literature (Madon, Jussim, & Eccles, 1997).

Beyond behavioral confirmation effects, it has also been suggested that interviewers will cognitively distort interview information about the applicant in order to confirm initial expectations. Smith, Neuberg, Judice, and Biesanz (1997) found this effect in a mock interview experiment by having both the interviewers and independent raters, who were not subject to the expectation manipulation, evaluate applicant behavior. Then, by using structural equation modeling, Smith et al. showed that a significant direct effect remains for interviewer expectations on interviewer evaluation of applicant behavior after accounting for the independent rater evaluation of applicant behavior. Springbett (1958) suggested that negative initial impressions would be less subject to change than positive initial impressions. Macan and Dipboye (1990) found the opposite effect in their research. In both studies, the authors speculated that the relative costs of different decision errors may influence the weighting of interview information in the final decision.

Interviewer Goals.   It has been long recognized that employment interviews may serve multiple functions, such as selecting the best applicants and "selling" these applicants on the desirability of the recruiting organization, and that interviewer behavior would vary as a function of his or her primary goal. This was one explanation offered for why interviewers tend to spend more time talking to applicants for whom they have formed a positive early impression. The "selection" goal has been met, and the interviewers are selling the applicant on the positive aspects of the job and organization to meet the "recruiting" goal. These may be referred to as *organizational goals*. It is often felt that these multiple goals influence the conduct of the interview as well as how interview information is processed. Some researchers have suggested that there may be multiple social goals including "getting to know" the target and "getting along with" the target (Leyens, Dardenne, & Fiske, 1998). Finally, it has also been suggested that the interviewer as perceiver will be influenced by the specific goals concerning the processing of information and evaluation of the applicant. We label these *cognitive goals*. As mentioned in chapter 1 of this book, Fiske (1993) has argued that perception is a motivated activity and that judgments are accurate within the context of current purposes. Recent interview research has examined the impact of interviewer goals both as direct effects on conduct and evaluation as well as a variable that might interact with initial interviewer expectations such that initial expectation might have less impact on interview outcomes under certain goal conditions.

Judice and Neuberg (1998) contrasted interviews conducted under a confirmation goal condition to interviews conducted under an accuracy goal condition. In the accuracy condition, the interviewers asked applicants more novel questions (exploring new topics) than did the confirmation condition interviewers. The confirmation condition interviewers asked more expansion questions (expanding on existing topics) than did the accuracy condition interviewers. In addition, the goals interacted with initial expectations such that the negative expectation–confirmation goal led to the fewest questions, whereas the most questions were asked under the accuracy goal–negative expectations condition. Interestingly, interviewer demeanor was best under the negative expectation–confirmation goal condition, which the authors interpreted to mean the interviewer felt that there was something socially wrong with holding an explicit confirmation goal thus they compensated by being most pleasant to the applicant.

The Role of Individual Differences

Interviewer characteristics have also been proposed to influence perceptions of applicants. Graves (1993) proposed that interviewer experience, demographic characteristics, cognitive abilities, and personality characteristics all have a bearing on the way in which interviewers process information about applicants. Graves argued that increased interviewer experience results in more complex cognitive schemas that allow the interviewers to reach judgments about applicants more quickly than is true for less experienced interviewers. It has also been suggested, however, that interviewers are more likely to make judgments on the basis of irrelevant factors (such as age or sex) when they process information quickly by relying on "peripheral" thought processes (Forret & Turban, 1996; Harris, 1989). These authors applied Petty and Cacioppo's (1986) Elaboration Likelihood Model (ELM) as a framework for investigating interviewer information processing. Forret and Turban contended that interviewers will reach more accurate judgments of applicants when they engage in much elaboration or thought in processing information about applicants. It is possible, of course, that Graves' and Forret and Turban's arguments are not necessarily contradictory. The complex cognitive structures of experienced interviewers may not allow for categorization of applicants solely on irrelevant factors such as demographic background.

It appears that the similarity between interviewer and interviewee influences the interviewer's initial impressions of the applicant. Similarity on demographic characteristics (Frank & Hackman, 1975; cf. Graves & Powell, 1996), attitudes (Baskett, 1973; Peters & Terborg, 1975), and experience (Wade & Kinicki, 1997) have been shown to be related to interviewer liking of the applicant as well as subsequent hiring decision. A concern with judgments of applicants based on similarity to the interviewer is that they will not be fair (Graves, 1993; Motowidlo, 1986).

Effects of Interview Structure on Interviewer Judgments

Although there are numerous ways that structure can be introduced in the design of interviews (Campion, Palmer, & Campion, 1997), all share the common characteristic of introducing some degree of control in the format used for conducting the interview. Ideally, structured interviews are developed by formulating questions on the basis of a job analysis, asking all interviewees precisely the same questions, and using anchored rating scales for scoring the responses (Campion, Pursell, & Brown, 1988). Empirical evidence, summarized in several meta-analyses has provided overwhelming support for structured over unstructured formats (Huffcutt & Arthur, 1994; McDaniel, Whetzel, Schmidt, & Mauer, 1994). Despite this convincing evidence, the reason for the effect has not been empirically established (Maurer, Sue-Chan, & Latham, 1999). One explanation, of particular relevance to social cognition and person perception, is that highly structured interview formats reduce the amount of bias that enters the interviewer's decision-making process (Dipboye, 1994). Because of the requirement to ask questions exactly as written, interviewers are not able to ask questions in such a way as to potentially bias interviewee responses. Thus, the biasing effects of selecting questions, wording questions, or both, to highlight negative qualities of an interviewee would be avoided (cf. Binning et al., 1988). Also, interviewers within a structured context are not "allowed" to ask additional questions not contained in the interview protocol. The use of anchored rating scales (rather than subjective summaries of interviews) further limits the degree to which biases will enter into the evaluation of the interviewee.

Despite the clear evidence in support of structured interviewing techniques, the vast majority of employment interviews continue to use unstructured formats (Dipboye, 1994). It appears that a combination of political, cultural, and personal reasons steer organizations away from the use of structured interview formats. Even when structured interviews are used, over time they tend to become more and more unstructured. Dipboye (1994) argued that it may be best to reach a compromise between structured and unstructured methods. For example, interviewers may use a set of structured questions, but then be permitted to ask probing questions. Such an approach might accomplish higher validities than purely unstructured interviews, but at the same time provide interviewers with the autonomy to tailor each interview to each interviewee.

In summary to this point, we have provided an overview of the primary cognitive and person-perception constructs that have been studied in employment interviewing research from the interviewer's perspective. We view this topic as a continuing interest to researchers in social psychology as well as management. Given the importance of the interview to effective organizational selection systems and the potential for training and other interventions to improve interviewing, we expect this research literature to continue to develop.

THE APPLICANT'S PERSPECTIVE

The next section covers constructs relevant to the applicant's perspective on the interview and other related topics. The applicant regards the interview and interviewer as sources of information about positive and negative aspects of the employing organization. The frame of reference is both broader (e.g., what would it be like to work in this organization) and possibly having a longer time frame (e.g., evaluating the long-range potential of the employment opportunity). The applicant also reacts to pre-employment hiring procedures, such as interviews, when forming impressions of the organization. The applicant, therefore, faces the dual challenge of managing self-presentation and processing information relevant to forming an impression of the organization. Because of this somewhat different focus, research in this area has had less direct application of person-perception and social-cognitive theory. We overview the theories that are invoked as well as the relevant research and provide some suggestions for further investigations in this area.

Organizational Selection Systems

Recruiting, selecting, and hiring new employees is a costly and time-consuming process (Rynes & Boudreau, 1986). It is estimated that one third of a new hire's annual salary is spent on recruiting efforts alone (Spencer, as cited in Recruiting Trends, 1986), and that the selection methods used can have huge financial consequences (Schmidt, Hunter, Outerbridge, & Trattner, 1986). It is in an organization's best interest to attract applicants and have their top choice accept their offer.

As Barber, Hollenbeck, Tower, and Phillips (1994) pointed out, the interview serves two distinct purposes. First, it serves as a selection device that helps to identify and select the "best" applicants. Second, it serves as a recruitment device. The interview is often the first contact that an applicant has with members of the organization. Recruiting events are salient indicators of what life within the organization will be like and recruiting events represent important interpersonal and work-related contact prior to job choice. It has been proposed that because job choice takes place under conditions of imperfect information, all recruitment experiences (not just the interview) frequently serve as signals of unobservable organizational characteristics (Rynes, Heneman, & Schwab, 1980; Rynes & Miller, 1983).

For example, in their qualitative study of recruiting, Rynes, Bretz, and Gerhart (1991) found that consistent with signaling theory (Spence, 1973;

1974), recruits interpreted a wide variety of recruiting experiences (e.g., recruiter competence, the sex composition of interview panels, and recruitment delays) as symbolic of broader organizational characteristics. These early interactions or signals (Rynes & Barber, 1990) may greatly influence applicant expectations about the organization.

Recruitment experiences seem to have stronger signaling value when organizational representatives are in the same functional area as the applicant and when experiences occur during the site visit as opposed to the campus interview (Rynes et al., 1991). Thus, person-job and person-organization fit may be related to recruiting because accurate signals may lead recruits to base their job choice decisions on valid information, whereas poor, unclear signals may decrease a recruit's ability to accurately assess their fit or congruence with the job and organization (Fisher, Ilgen, & Hoyer, 1979). Unfortunately, recruitment research has not tended to be longitudinal and has rarely followed recruits throughout the hiring process, so it is presently unclear to what extent this occurs and the relative role the interview plays during that process.

Applicant's Preinterview Information and Impressions

As noted previously, applicant's reactions to the interview and the interviewer will often be generalized to impressions about the employer. In addition, it appears that preinterview impressions of the organization and the job influence behavior toward and perceptions of the interviewer (see Fig. 3.1). Research on applicant decision making has suggested that applicant preinterview beliefs about the organization have a much stronger impact on accepting a job offer than does the interviewer during the recruitment interview (cf. Rynes, 1991). However, the impact of preinterview beliefs on behavior during the interview and subsequent decision making has rarely been studied. In Fig. 3.1, we characterize the applicant's cognitive structure as consisting of job beliefs, expectancies, and goals. Job beliefs are the perceived attributes of the job and organization and thought to influence job offer acceptance. Expectancies are an applicant's belief about the likelihood of receiving a job offer and are thought to influence the motivation to pursue the job. Goals are the general and proximal targets that direct allocation of attention and effort during the interview.

During the interview, the applicant has two general goals: to convey a positive impression of his or her competencies and to gather information about the employer. In attempting to convey a positive image, the applicant may engage in *impression management behaviors*, which can consist of *entitlements, enhancements*, and *self-promotion*. Entitlements are verbal claims of responsibility for some positive events. Enhancements are statements that are intended to persuade the interviewer that the applicant has some positive quality. Self-promotion is the use of statements meant to persuade the interviewer that the applicant has some specific quality that the interviewer is looking for. Impression management behavior during the interview is a somewhat risky endeavor for the applicant because it may not lead to positive impressions by the interviewer (Baron, 1986; Kacmar, Delery, & Ferris, 1992).

Research on why some applicants engage in more impression management behavior than others is needed. Recent research by Delery and Kacmar (1998) did not provide much support for the role of classic individual differences, such as locus of control and self-esteem. However, these authors suggested that future research might consider the applicant's perception that the interviewer might be susceptible to impression management, perhaps on the basis of the interviewer's age, experience, and so on. Stevens (1997) found that preinterview job beliefs and expectancies influenced impression management as applicants appeared to provide both more self-presentation and other enhancement when they liked the organization and when they thought a job offer was likely. Applicants were also less likely to ask questions that were more likely to yield negative information about the organization. Stevens also found that preinterview impressions were related to the perception of the interviewer even after controlling for actual interviewer behavior.

The impact of proximal applicant goals has been dramatically demonstrated in research on the self-fulfilling prophecy hypotheses. As described earlier, the basic idea is that interviewers form an expectation based on preinterview (or early interview) information and this expectation influences the questions they ask applicants as well as their interpretations of applicant responses. However, this line of reasoning assumes that the applicant is a passive participant. Some applicants may be determined to provide favorable information about themselves in spite of negatively constraining questions posed by the interviewer. This is the basic idea behind impression management. Smith et al. (1997) conducted an elaborate study in which interviewers had their expectations manipulated and applicants had their behavioral style manipulated through instructions to be either deferential (e.g., let the interviewer set the tone) or nondeferential (e.g., make sure the desired impression is presented). The nondeferential applicants did significantly better than the deferential applicants in overcoming the negative expectations of the interviewer. What is even more interesting is that in a second interview each applicant faced an interviewer with the opposite expectations. Therefore an applicant who had faced interviewer-questioning behavior motivated by a negative expectation, now faced interviewer-questioning behavior motivated by a positive expectation. In the second interview, the deferential applicants were more highly influenced by the first interviewer's expectations than those of the second interviewer. That is, their behavioral pattern in the second interview had been strongly influenced by their experience in the first interview. The nondeferential applicants' performance was not influenced by their experience in the first interview. These findings raise a host of interesting questions about the intervening cognitive variables that explain the carry over effect of the first interview for applicants who had the goal of "going with the flow." Did they lower their expectations for performance? Had their locus of control over who causes success or nonsuccess in the interview shifted to an external cause of the interviewer?

Applicants also have schemas or assumptions about expected behavioral patterns during the course of the interview. Shaw (1983, as cited in Jablin, Miller, & Sias, 1999) found that applicants tended to assume that (a) the interviewer's major responsibility was to listen to and acknowledge their qualifications, (b) any applicant questions should be viewed as appropriate and responded to accordingly, and (c) the major responsibility of the applicant was to express his or her qualifications and feelings. When the first assumption was violated (e.g., the interviewer did not express an interest in the applicant's qualifications), the applicant became quiet and didn't elaborate further. This effect seems consistent with the findings of Smith et al. (1997) whereby applicants who were deferential to the interviewer behaved in a manner that reinforced the interviewer's preinterview expectations. Further research on applicant interview schemas would be useful.

Applicant Reactions to Selection Systems

Applicant decision making subsequent to the employment interview is influenced, in part, by what occurs during the interview. Much of the research in the area of applicant reactions to interviews and other selection procedures has been based on the organizational justice literature (e.g., Greenberg, 1993). *Procedural justice* refers to the perceived fairness of the methods used to make organizational decisions (Folger & Greenberg, 1985). Such justice perceptions are then related to attitudes toward organizations (Lind & Tyler, 1988). The underlying logic is that applicants perceive a hiring process as more fair to the extent that the selection procedures seem fair. *Distributive justice* refers to the perceived fairness of outcomes of decisions. Organizations have the ability to influence procedural justice. Thus, procedural justice is an important aspect of reactions that applicants have to organizational selection systems.

Research in this area has been largely driven by Gilliland's (1993) model of applicant reactions to selection systems. It includes ten procedural justice rules that are intended to affect the perceived fairness of an organization's selection process. These justice rules fall under three broad categories. The *formal characteristics* category includes job relatedness, chance to perform, reconsideration opportunity, and consistency. Under the *explanation* grouping is feedback, information known, and openness. Within the *interpersonal treatment* domain is treatment at the test site, two-way communication, and propriety of questions. These rules are theorized to influence perceptions of overall fairness of a given selection process and other outcomes.

Studies of applicant reactions and associated outcomes have tended to support Gilliland's (1993) model (e.g., Bauer, Maertz, Dolen, & Campion, 1998; Cropanzano & Konovsky, 1995; Macan, Avedon, Paese, & Smith, 1994; Smither, Reilly, Millsap, Pearlman, & Stoffey, 1993; Truxillo & Bauer, 1999). In addition, it has also been shown that applicants tend to favor procedures that are seen as job related (e.g., Ployhart & Ryan, 1997; Rynes, 1993; Rynes & Connerley, 1993; Smither et al., 1993; Steiner & Gilliland, 1996). In general, interviews are rated as "fair" when compared to other selection methods (e.g., Smither et al., 1993; Steiner & Gilliland, 1996). Gilliland and Steiner (1999) have proposed that different interview formats (i.e., structured, formal, etc.) may influence applicant reactions to them. Clearly, administration consistency should be perceived as higher in structured interviews, but little research has been conducted that tests these propositions.

Kohn and Dipboye (1998) investigated some of these propositions with two experiments. In the first study, participants were given transcripts of interviews and found that individuals actually perceived unstructured interviews as more fair overall. This was especially true when they were given only limited information about the job. Surprisingly, in the second experiment, they found participants preferred interviews low on job relevance, high on voice, and low on standardization. This may be attributed to the nature of their undergraduate sample as these students may have less job experience and therefore prefer less structured questions. Clearly, more research is needed in the area of applicant reactions to interview formats.

Research on applicant reactions to recruiters and interviewers shows that, at least at the point at which data are collected, treatment by interviewers matters to applicants (e.g., Powell, 1991; Rynes, Bretz, et al., 1991). Gilliland (1995) interviewed former graduates who had recently undergone extensive recruiting experiences and who had accepted a job offer. A majority of the critical incidences reported to him regarding fairness during selection related to interviews (104 vs. 34 for ability tests, 18 for work samples, and 16 for integrity tests). Most (37%) of the incidents related to the treatment received by the applicants during the interviews. Again, more research is needed to understand how all ten of the procedural justice rules outlined by Gilliland (1993) relate to applicant perceptions of the organization.

Applicant Individual Differences in Interview Behavior

Limited work has been conducted on applicant individual differences in behavior during interviews. Delery and Kacmar (1998) hypothesized that applicant self-monitoring, self-esteem, locus of control, age, and training would all be related to applicant impression-management behavior. They found, however, very limited relationships. Only self-esteem and locus of control were related to one aspect of impression management, entitlement. Interviewer characteristics were more strongly related with four of the five predicting at least one aspect of interviewer impression-management behavior. Similarly, Barber et al. (1994) proposed that applicants with high self-monitoring, high cognitive ability, and low trait anxiety would experience less stress during interviews than other applicants. They supported this proposition as all of these individual differences were related to better information acquisition and performance during the interviews.

Site Visits

Because much of the previous research on applicant reactions to interviews has occurred during initial campus interviews, the lack of impact of interviewers on applicant job beliefs and expectancies may be attributed, in part, to the highly ritualized conduct of these interviews. However, if the applicant is recommended by the interviewer, then the next step is often the site visit, which can be thought of as an extensive interview that is used during later stages of the selection process where more lengthy, in-depth discussions with coworkers and supervisors are conducted. These interviews are often used to determine who among the finalists will be chosen for a job (Eder, Kacmar, & Ferris, 1989).

Site visits typically involve one of the most significant face-to-face information sharing situations that occur during recruitment and selection. They are often a good opportunity for applicants and their potential supervisors to form impressions about each other before job applicants begin their first day on the job, and they can be seen as an intensive series of interviews.

Pre-entry interaction is not unusual. Prior to entry, many of the supervisor–newcomer dyads will engage in formal and informal interviewing. Approximately 86% of all companies surveyed require some sort of an interview with an immediate supervisor before hiring a professional or technical worker. Applicants to managerial positions were interviewed by an immediate supervisor by 77% of the companies surveyed (Bureau of National Affairs, Inc., 1988). It is apparent that most recruits interact with their future supervisors prior to entering their hiring organizations.

This early interaction may influence their later working relationship and thus the newcomer's adjustment process (Rynes, 1991). Because interviews bring new members into face-to-face contact with the organization and with potential coworkers, site visits should be helpful in preparing the person for early encounters within the organization (Dipboye, 1992). During the site visit, the recruit begins to learn more about the climate, norms, and expectations of the organization, future coworkers, and their future supervisor. The more time that is spent with supervisors, the more the supervisor and newcomer should be influenced as their expectations are forming.

Very little research has been done that involves site visits (for an exception see Taylor & Bergmann, 1987). A site visit is a more in-depth interviewing and information trading part of recruiting (Milkovich & Boudreau, 1991). Recruits who make it to this stage in the recruitment process have usually passed initial résumé screenings and interviews.

Information Sources During Recruitment

Fisher et al. (1979) found that recruits rated information from insiders (e.g., potential supervisors and coworkers) as more trustworthy than recruiters. In addition, Fink, Bauer, and Campion (1994) found that meeting potential supervisors increased ratings of attractiveness toward the hiring organization following site visits. In their longitudinal study of site visits, they found that meeting with potential coworkers and supervisors was important to recruits. "Meeting the person who would be my boss really influenced my job choice. I can't wait to start my job." "One of the people in the department that would be at one level above me took me on a tour of the city which was really great." Meeting a variety of people was also looked upon favorably. People felt that having a lot of time to interact and ask questions allowed them to get the "real" story about working in that organization. Thus, it seems that at least at the self-report level, information source does influence newcomer reactions.

In summary, much of the research regarding applicant behavior during recruiting and interviews has tended to focus on how the information provided to applicants (both what and how) affects their impressions of the organization and the likelihood of accepting a job. More research is needed to determine the interrelationship among the constructs studied thus far as well as additional factors that might make a difference to applicants during interviews and throughout the recruiting process.

Applicant performance in interviews also needs further research especially in the areas that emphasize the role of schemas, goals, and expectations. The impression management stream of research has provided a conceptualization of proactive applicant behavior, but more research is needed on the cognitive and perceptual underpinnings of the tactics that applicants use to manage their impressions. Also, it would seem that the frequent use of college students as research participants should be supplemented by research using both less educated and more experienced applicants. The elaboration of information sought in the interview and the presentation of self during the interview might be related to education and experience. Furthermore, some concepts that were mentioned in chapter 1 of this book might be fruitful research topics. For example, research on "affect" and its impact on perception and cognition would be interesting.

Interviewer-Applicant Interaction

Though it is obvious that employment interviews are characterized by verbal and nonverbal interactions between people, little research has actually studied cognitive and person-perception processes as central to this interaction. The communications research has studied the sequencing of communication exchanges (e.g., Jablin, Miller, & Sias, 1999), but does not engage the cognitive constructs alluded to in Fig. 3.1. To provide some basis for future research, we would like to briefly describe a framework proposed by Patterson (1994). In this framework, the individuals (interviewer and applicant) are assumed to arrive at the interview with goals, interpersonal expectancies, affect, and dispositions (similar to our Fig. 3.1). These characteristics then affect both the action schemas and cognitive resources available to each. The interaction that occurs between the two then requires attention and effort toward both decoding the other's behavior as well as encoding one's own behavior. As either the interviewer or applicant engages the other, cognitive resources will be diverted to either the decoding or encoding process depending on the individual's personality, goals, and so on. For example, an anxious, introverted person (the actor) trying to show that he or she has good social skills might divert substantial cognitive resources to managing his or her behavior (encoding), but at the expense of more accurately decoding the partner's behavior. Fewer resources available for decoding may lead to more errors of inference in the decoding because of reliance on category-based processing, heuristics, or other cognitive processes that are less resource intense. The partner may then be viewing a stream of behavior from which inferences about traits and dispositions are made. The partner's tendency to use an active or passive information processing approach to this information will depend on his or her available resources for decoding the behavior. That is, the partner's personality, goals, behavioral scripts, etcetera will influence the processing of the information and the impression formed at any particular point in the interview.

The potential richness of cognitive models such as Patterson's (1994) provides new avenues for research in employment interviewing. Research methods would require the measurement of both cognitive and behavioral variables as they emerge over time. One could adopt the framework of Patterson to study topics like impression management in the interview.

CONCLUSION

In summary, research on employment interviewing has been influenced by models of social-cognitive and person-perception processes. However, our review of the recent research in several different literatures yielded a somewhat restricted set of variables under consideration when compared to the comprehensive treatment of the topic in chapter 1 of this book. Furthermore, there is virtually no research that tries to test social-cognitive models of sequential interviewer–applicant interactions. Part of the explanation may be the applied nature of the problem. Most people who study employment interviews are interested in the outcomes of the process (e.g., decisions, perceived fairness, etc.) and may work with simplified models of the process that seem to be good enough for potentially improving the process in order to yield better decisions and greater satisfaction with the process by the involved individuals. This pragmatic approach has yielded a good deal of progress in the area of structured interviewing for improving the predictive validity of the employment interview but less insight on the applicant's perspective. There would seem to be rich opportunities for new knowledge in all of these areas.

ACKNOWLEDGEMENTS

Correspondence concerning this chapter should be addressed to Charles K. Parsons, DuPree College of Management, Georgia Institute of Technology, 755 Ferst Drive, Atlanta, Georgia 30332. Electronic mail may be sent to charles.parsons@mgt.gatech.edu.

REFERENCES

Barber, A. E., Hollenbeck, J. R., Tower, S. L., & Phillips, J. M. (1994). The effects of interview focus on recruitment effectiveness: A field experiment. *Journal of Applied Psychology, 79*, 886–896.

Baron, R. A. (1986). Self-presentation in job interviews: When there can be "too much of a good thing." *Journal of Applied Social Psychology, 16*, 16–28.

Baskett, G. D. (1973). Interviewer decisions as determined by competency and attitude similarity. *Journal of Applied Psychology, 57*, 343–345.

Bauer, T. N., Maertz, C. P., Dolen, M. R., & Campion, M. A. (1998). A longitudinal assessment of applicant reactions to an employment test. *Journal of Applied Psychology, 83*, 892-903.

Binning, J. F., Goldstein, M. A., Garcia, M. F., & Scattaregia, J. H. (1988). Effects of preinterview impressions on questioning strategies in same- and opposite-sex employment interviews. *Journal of Applied Psychology, 73*, 30–37.

Bureau of National Affairs, Inc. (1988). *Recruiting and selection procedures* (PPFS No. 146). Washington, DC.

Campion, M. A., Palmer, D. K., & Campion, J. E. (1997). A review of structure in the selection interview. *Personnel Psychology, 50*, 655–702.

Campion, M. A., Pursell, E. D., & Brown, B. K. (1988). Structured interviewing: Raising the psychometric properties of the employment interview. *Personnel Psychology, 41*, 25–42.

Cropanzano, R., & Konovsky, M. A. (1995). Resolving the justice dilemma by improving the outcomes: The case of employee drug screening. *Journal of Business & Psychology, 10*, 221–243.

Delery, J. E., & Kacmar, K. M. (1998). The influence of applicant and interviewer characteristics on the use of impression management. *Journal of Applied Social Psychology, 28*, 1649–1669.

Dipboye, R. L (1982). Self-fulfilling prophecies in the selection interview. *Academy of Management Review, 7*, 579–586.

Dipboye, R. L. (1992). *Selection interviews: Process perspectives.* Cincinnati, OH: South-Western.

Dipboye, R. L. (1994). Structured and unstructured selection interviews: Beyond the job-fit model. In K. M. Rowland & G. R. Ferris (Eds.), *Research in Personnel and Human Resources Management,* (Vol 12, pp. 79–123). Greenwich, CT: JAI Press.

Dipboye, R. L., & Gaugler, B. B. (1993). Cognitive and behavioral processes in the selection interview. In N. Schmitt & W. C. Borman (Eds.), *Personnel selection in organizations* (pp. 135–171). San Francisco: Jossey-Bass.

Dougherty, T. W., & Turban, D. B. (1999). Behavior confirmation of interviewer expectations. In R. W. Eder & M. M. Harris (Eds.), *The employment interview handbook* (pp. 217–228). Thousand Oaks, CA: Sage.

Dougherty, T. W., Turban, D. B., & Callender, J. C. (1994). Confirming first impressions in the employment interview: A field study of interviewer behavior. *Journal of Applied Psychology, 79,* 659–665.

Eder, R. W., Kacmar, K. M., & Ferris, G. R. (1989). Employment interview research: History and synthesis. In R. W. Eder & G. R. Ferris (Eds.), *The employment interview: Theory, research, and practice* (pp. 17–42). Newbury Park, CA: Sage.

Fink, L. S., Bauer, T. N., & Campion, M. A. (1994). Job candidates' views of site visits: Site visits do make a difference. *Journal of Career Planning and Employment, 54,* 32–38.

Fisher, C. D., Ilgen, D. R., & Hoyer, W. D. (1979). Source credibility, information favorability, and job offer acceptance. *Academy of Management Journal, 22,* 94–103.

Fiske, S. T. (1993). Social cognition and social perception. In M. R. Rosenzweig & L. M. Porter (Eds.), *Annual review of psychology* (Vol. 44, pp. 155–194). Palo Alto, CA: Annual Reviews.

Folger, R., & Greenberg, J. (1985). Procedural justice: An interpretive analysis of personnel systems. In K. M. Rowland & G. R. Ferris (Eds.), *Research in personnel and human resources management,* (Vol. 3, pp. 141–183). Greenwich, CT: JAI Press, Inc.

Forret, M. L., & Turban, D. B. (1996). Implications of the elaboration likelihood model for interviewer decision processes. *Journal of Business and Psychology, 10,* 115–128.

Frank, L. L., & Hackman, J. R. (1975). Effects of interviewer-interviewee similarity on interviewer objectivity in college admissions interviews. *Journal of Applied Psychology, 60,* 356–360.

Gallois, C., Callan, V. J., & Palmer, J. A. (1992). The influence of applicant communication style and interviewer characteristics on hiring decisions. *Journal of Applied Social Psychology, 22,* 1041–1060.

Gilliland, S. W. (1993). The perceived fairness of selection systems: An organizational justice perspective. *Academy of Management Review, 18,* 694–734.

Gilliland, S. W. (1995). Fairness from the applicant's perspective: Reactions to employee selection procedures. *International Journal of Selection and Assessment, 3,* 11–19.

Gilliland, S. W., & Steiner, D. D. (1999). Applicant reactions. In R. W. Eder & M. M. Harris (Eds.), *The employment interview handbook* (pp. 69–82). Thousand Oaks, CA: Sage.

Graves, L. M. (1993). Sources of individual differences in interviewer effectiveness: Model and implications for future research. *Journal of Organizational Behavior, 14,* 349–370.

Graves, L. M., & Powell, G. N. (1996). Sex similarity, quality of the employment interview, and recruiters' evaluations of actual applicants. *Journal of Occupational and Organizational Psychology, 69,* 243–261.

Greenberg, J. (1993). The social side of fairness: Interpersonal and informational classes of organizational justice. In R. Cropanzano (Ed.), *Justice in the workplace: Approaching fairness in human resource management* (pp. 79–103). Hillsdale, NJ: Lawrence Erlbaum Associates.

Harris, M. M. (1989). Reconsidering the employment interview: A review of recent literature and suggestions for future research. *Personnel Psychology, 42,* 691–726.

Huffcutt, A. I., & Arthur, W., Jr. (1994). Hunter and Hunter (1984) revisited: Interview validity for entry-level jobs. *Journal of Applied Psychology, 79,* 184–190.

Jablin, F. M., Miller, V. D., & Sias, P. M. (1999). Communication and interaction processes. In R. W. Eder & M. M. Harris (Eds.), *The employment interview handbook* (pp. 297–320). Thousand Oaks, CA: Sage.

Judice, T. N., & Neuberg, S. L. (1998). When interviewers desire to confirm negative expectations: Self-fulfilling prophecies and inflated applicant self-perception. *Basic and Applied Social Psychology, 20,* 175–190.

Kacmar, K. M., Delery, J. E., & Ferris, G. R. (1992). Differential effectiveness of applicant impression management tactics on employment interview decisions. *Journal of Applied Social Psychology, 22,* 1250–1272.

Kohn, L. S., & Dipboye, R. L. (1998). The effects of interview structure on recruiting outcomes. *Journal of Applied Social Psychology, 28*, 821–843.

Leyens, J. P., Dardenne, B., & Fiske, S. T. (1998). Why and under what circumstances is a hypothesis-consistent testing strategy preferred in interviews. *British Journal of Social Psychology, 37*, 259–274.

Liden, R. C., & Parsons, C. K. (1989). Understanding interpersonal behavior in the employment interview: A reciprocal interaction analysis. In R. W. Eder & G. R. Ferris (Eds.), *The employment interview: Theory, research, and practice* (pp. 219–232). Newbury Park, CA: Sage.

Lind, E. A., & Tyler, T. R. (1988). *The social psychology of procedural justice.* New York: Plenum.

Macan, T. H., Avedon, M. J., Paese, M., & Smith, D. E. (1994). The effects of applicants' reactions to cognitive ability tests and an assessment center. *Personnel Psychology, 47*, 715–738.

Macon, T. M., & Dipboye, R. L. (1988). The effects of interviewers' initial impressions on information gathering. *Organizational Behavior and Human Decision Processes, 42*, 364–387.

Macon, T. M., & Dipboye, R. L. (1990). The relationship of preinterview impressions to selection and recruitment outcomes. *Personnel Psychology, 43*, 745–768.

Madon, S., Jussim, L., & Eccles, J. (1997). In search of the powerful self-fulfilling prophecy. *Journal of Personality and Social Psychology, 72*, 791–809.

Maurer, S. D., Sue-Chan, C., & Latham, G. P. (1999). The situational interview. In R. W. Eder & M. M. Harris (Eds.), *The employment interview handbook* (pp. 159–177). Thousand Oaks, CA: Sage.

Mayfield, E. C. (1964). The selection interview: A re-evaluation of published research. *Personnel Psychology, 17*, 239–260.

McDaniel, M. A., Whetzel, D. L., Schmidt, F. L., & Mauer, S. D. (1994). The validity of employment interviews: A comprehensive review and meta-analysis. *Journal of Applied Psychology, 79*, 599–616.

McDonald, T., & Hakel, M. D. (1985). Effects of applicant race, sex, suitability, and answers on interviewers' questioning strategy and ratings. *Personnel Psychology, 38*, 321–334.

Merton, R. K. (1948). The self-fulfilling prophecy. *Antioch Review, 8*, 193–210.

Milkovich, G. T., & Boudreau, J. W. (1991). *Human resource management.* Boston: Richard D. Irwin.

Motowidlo, S. J. (1986). Information processing in personnel decisions. *Research in Personnel and Human Resource Management, 4*, 1–44.

Patterson, M. L. (1994). Interaction behavior and person perception: An integrative approach. *Small Group Research, 25*, 172–188.

Peters, L. H., & Terborg, J. R. (1975). The effects of temporal placement of unfavorable information and of attitude similarity on personnel selection decisions. *Organizational Behavior and Human Performance, 13*, 279–293.

Petty, R. E., & Cacioppo, J. T. (1986). The elaboration likelihood model of persuasion. *Advances in Experimental Social Psychology, 19*, 123–205.

Phillips, A., & Dipboye, R. L. (1989). Correlational tests of predictions from a process model of the interview. *Journal of Applied Psychology, 74*, 41–52.

Pingitore, R., Dugoni, B. L., Tindale, R. S., & Spring, B. (1994). Bias against overweight job applicants in a simulated employment interview. *Journal of Applied Psychology, 79*, 909–917.

Ployhart, R. E., & Ryan, A. M. (1997). Toward an explanation of applicant reactions: An examination of organizational justice and attribution frameworks. *Organizational Behavior & Human Decision Processes, 72(3)*, 308–335.

Powell, G. N. (1991). Applicant reactions to the initial employment interview: Exploring theoretical and methodological issues. *Personnel Psychology, 44*, 67–83.

Powell, G. N. (1996). Recruiters' and applicants' awareness of the other party's postinterview evaluations. *Psychological Reports, 79*, 1363–1369.

Recruiting trends. (1986, April). *Resource* (newsletter of the American Society for Personnel Administration), p. 7.

Roehling, M. V. (1999). Weight-based discrimination in employment: Psychological and legal aspects. *Personnel Psychology, 52*, 969–1016.

Roehling, M. V., Campion, J. E., & Arvey, R. D. (1999). Unfair discrimination issues. In R. W. Eder and M. M. Harris (Eds.), *The employment interview handbook* (pp. 49–67). Thousand Oaks, CA: Sage.

Rynes, S. L. (1991). Recruitment choice, job choice, and post-hire consequences: A call for new research directions. In M. D. Dunnette (Ed.), *Handbook of industrial and organizational psychology* (2nd ed., pp. 399–444). Palo Alto, CA: Consulting Psychologists.

Rynes, S. L. (1993). When recruitment fails to attract: Individual expectations meet organizational realities in recruitment. In H. Schuler, J. L. Farr and M. Smith (Eds.), *Personnel selection and assessment: Individual and organizational perspectives* (pp. 27–40). Hillsdale, NJ: Lawrence Erlbaum Associates.

Rynes, S. L., & Barber, A. E. (1990). Applicant attraction strategies: An organizational perspective. *Academy of Management Review, 15*, 286–310.

Rynes, S. L., & Boudreau, J. W. (1986). College recruiting in large organizations: Practice, evaluation, and research implications. *Personnel Psychology, 39*, 729–757.

Rynes, S. L., Bretz, R. D., & Gerhart, B. (1991). The importance of recruitment in job choice: A different way of looking. *Personnel Psychology, 44*, 487–521.

Rynes, S. L., & Connerley, M. L. (1993). Applicant reactions to alternative selection procedures. *Journal of Business & Psychology, 7*, 261–277.

Rynes, S. L., Heneman, H. G., III, & Schwab, D. P. (1980). Individual reactions to organizational recruiting: A review. *Personnel Psychology, 39*, 529–542.

Rynes, S. L., & Miller, H. E. (1983). Recruiter and job influences on candidates for employment. *Journal of Applied Psychology, 68*, 147–154.

Sackett, P. R. (1982). The interviewer as hypothesis tester: The effects of impressions of an applicant on interviewer questioning strategy. *Personnel Psychology, 35*, 789–804.

Schmidt, F. L., Hunter, J. E., Outerbridge, A. N., & Trattner, M. H. (1986). The economic impact of job selection methods on size, productivity, and payroll costs of the federal work force: An empirically based demonstration. *Personnel Psychology, 39*, 1–29.

Schoorman, F. D. (1988). Escalation bias in performance appraisals: An unintended consequence of supervisor participation in hiring decisions. *Journal of Applied Psychology, 73*, 58–62.

Smith, D. M., Neuberg, S. L., Judice, T. N., & Biesanz, J. C. (1997). Target complicity in the confirmation and disconfirmation of erroneous perceiver expectations: Immediate and longer term implications. *Journal of Personality and Social Psychology, 73*, 974–991.

Smither, J. W., Reilly, R. R., Millsap, R. E., Pearlman, K., & Stoffey, R. W. (1993). Applicant reactions to selection procedures. *Personnel Psychology, 46*, 49–76.

Snyder, M., & Swann, W. (1978). Hypothesis-testing processes in social interaction. *Journal of Personality and Social Psychology, 36*, 1202–1212.

Spence, M. (1973). Job market signaling. *Quarterly Journal of Economics, 87*, 355–374.

Spence, M. (1974). Competitive and optimal responses to signals: An analysis of efficiency and distribution. *Journal of Economic Theory, 7*, 296–332.

Springbett, B. M. (1958). Factors affecting the final decisions in the employment interview. *Canadian Journal of Psychology, 12*, 13–22.

Steiner, D. D., & Gilliland, S. W. (1996). Fairness reactions to personnel selection techniques in France and the United States. *Journal of Applied Psychology, 81*, 134–141.

Stevens, C. K. (1997). Effects of preinterview beliefs on applicants' reactions to campus interviews. *Academy of Management Journal, 40*, 947–966.

Taylor, M. S., & Bergmann, T. J. (1987). Organizational recruitment activities and applicants' reactions to different stages of the recruitment process. *Personnel Psychology, 40*, 261–285.

Truxillo, D. M., & Bauer, T. N. (1999). Applicant reactions to test score banding: Three field examples. *Journal of Applied Psychology, 84*, 322–340.

Ulrich, L., & Trumbo, D. (1965). The selection interview since 1949. *Psychological Bulletin, 63*, 100–116.

Van Vianen, A. E. M., & Willemsen, T. M. (1992). The employment interview: The role of sex stereotypes in the evaluation of male and female job applicants in the Netherlands. *Journal of Applied Social Psychology, 22*, 471–491.

Wade, K. J., & Kinicki, A. J. (1997). Subjective applicant qualifications and interpersonal attraction as mediators within a process model of interview selection decisions. *Journal of Vocational Behavior, 50*, 23–40.

Wagner, R. (1949). The employment interview: A critical review. *Personnel Psychology, 2*, 17–46.

Webster, E. C. (1964). *Decision making in the employment interview.* Montreal Canada: McGill University, Industrial Relations Centre.

4

Executive Promotion and Selection

Valerie I. Sessa
Center for Creative Leadership, Greensboro, North Carolina

Top executives acknowledge that one of their more important duties is selecting other top-level executives, and there is some evidence that suggests doing this well enhances the chance that organizations will be successful (e.g., Martell & Carroll, 1995). Interestingly, corporate executives rarely access one major source of learning to help with these selections—that of industrial and organizational psychologists who have been studying, learning, and providing information regarding selection processes since the build-up of the armed forces in World War II (DeVries, 1993; Hogan, Curphy, & Hogan, 1994). Instead, personal biases predominate (Lamb, 1987). Additionally, there is an indication that industrial and organizational psychologists who assist in executive selection do not use their own validated techniques to a great extent (see Clark, 1992; Ryan & Sackett, 1987).

However, one of the functions of scientifically based personnel selection principles is to improve the accuracy of personnel selection by using carefully constructed, rational methods that overcome the natural human biases in person perception. Conducting job analyses, deriving worker requirements, measuring worker requirements, establishing the validity, reliability, and usefulness of the selection procedure, and (especially since the late 1960s), statistically ensuring freedom from bias, are aimed at objectifying data and controlling decision processes such that selectors are able to choose the best person for the position with less reliance on biased person perception.

Despite these efforts, biases still exist—even when scientifically based personnel selection principles are used. The person or persons involved in making a selection bring their own perspectives to the decision (*Principles for the Validation and Use of Personnel Selection Procedures*, 1987, p. 12). When scientifically based personnel selection principles are removed (as is the case in executive selection), unless other principles take their place, selections return to being based on individual judgment or group decisions plagued by errors or biases in person perception. This may be one reason for the high failure rates of executives at the very top of today's organizations—with estimates of failure ranging from 27% (Sessa, Kaiser, Taylor, & Campbell, 1998) to as high as 75% (Hogan, Raskin, & Fazzini, 1990). Indeed, in early 2000, CEOs were leaving their organizations at a rate of 5 per day (Jones, 2000).

This chapter describes a general framework for executive selection into the top three levels of the organization (CEO and two levels down), demonstrates how person perception affects the selection process within this framework, and uses one example to show where person perception is having a salient effect: choosing between internal and external candidates.

This chapter is derived primarily from an interview study in a larger program of research conducted at the Center for Creative Leadership (see Sessa et al., 1998). In this study, begun in fall 1993, almost 500 executives in the top three levels of organizations (CEOs and two levels down) were asked about an executive selection in which they had personally participated in the past few years. Approximately half the executives in the sample were asked to discuss a selection that turned out to be a success, the executives in the other half of the sample were asked to discuss a selection that turned out to be a failure. The executives were asked why this selection was labeled a success or a failure and then asked very detailed questions about the selection processes used for that particular executive. They were also asked some general questions about selection in their companies overall.

Most of the executives in the sample were white males (94% and 90%, respectively), with an average age of 46 (ranging from 28 to 63); 34% were CEOs, 59% were in the second level, and 6% were in the third level down. Participants were predominantly in for-profit organizations (83%), although some came from large nonprofits and large government institutions. Executives were drawn from companies of all sizes: 30% from companies employing 50,000 or more; 28% from companies of 10,000 to 49,000; 29% from companies of 1,000 to 9,999; and 13% from companies of less than 1,000 employees.

OUTLINING THE EXECUTIVE SELECTION PROCESS

This section briefly describes a general framework of executive selection. This framework delineates the general content of selection to allow a better understanding of where and how person perception impacts this process.

Executive selection is more than just putting a candidate into a position. It is an entire process that includes (a) conducting an organizational needs assessment, defining (b) job requirements and (c) candidate requirements, (d) identifying candidate pools, (e) doing the matching process, (f) managing the executive once on board, and, finally, (g) evaluating the executive's performance and organizational outcomes (Sessa et al., 1998). (See Fig. 4.1.) A description of the framework elements follows.

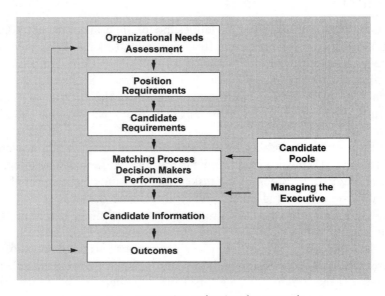

FIG. 4.1. Executive selection framework.

Organizational Needs Assessment

Organizational context has an impact on selection at the top (see for example, Sessa & Campbell, 1997). One of the first steps in the executive selection process is to conduct an organizational needs assessment to define and assess the work environment in terms of the characteristics of the organization. An organizational assessment can include an examination of the internal environment (e.g., strategy, climate, changes, strengths, needs, and short- and long-term goals) and the external environment (e.g., industry ranking, market, competition, regulatory environment, future trends, and political instabilities).

However, selectors involved in high-level selection processes do not spend much effort gaining an understanding of the needs of organizations. In the interview study, selectors listed on average 2.47 ($SD = 1.29$) organizational needs that they considered during a particular selection. These needs included: sustaining the organization (63.2%), growth of the organization (20.7%), turnaround situations (20.4%), start-ups (18.9%), cultural or strategic changes (17.6%), and restructurings (16.7%). Ninety-four percent of the needs mentioned were internal to the organization; very few participants mentioned needs concerning the external environment.

Position Requirements

Outlining position requirements defines the job in terms of the activities or tasks performed. One can derive from this what it means to be successful in the position and what the predictors of that success are. Unfortunately, outlining position requirements within the top three levels of the organization is problematic—separating the "job" from the "person in the job" is difficult (Sackett & Arvey, 1993), as is defining exactly what "success" means (Akkerman, 1993).

In the interview study, selectors reported that they listed, on average, 3.76 ($SD = 2.03$) position requirements. These requirements included: creating strategy (47%); identifying tasks specific to the department (41.7%); managing or supervising others (37%); improving business or productivity (30.8%); charting new directions (27.4%); building, maintaining, or participating in teams (26.4%); and creating a vision (19.0%). When one considers the complexity of today's organizations and the responsibilities inherent in high-level positions, it appears that those who make selection decisions at the top do not do an in-depth consideration of either the organization or the position. Because of the lack of attention paid to these factors, executive selectors may be using "cognitive heuristics" to make sense of what is needed.[1] (See Klimoski & Donahue, chapter 1.)

Candidate Requirements

The next step in the framework is to infer from the position requirements and the organizational needs assessment the behaviors, knowledge, skills, abilities, and characteristics that executives need to be competent both in terms of the position and the organization (Gupta, 1992; Van Clieaf, 1992).

Selectors in the interview study mentioned, on average, 6.7 ($SD = 3.7$) candidate requirements that they look for in candidates. These requirements include: specific functional backgrounds (62.0%), managerial skills (42.6%), interpersonal skills (39.2%), communication skills (36.7%), technical knowledge (35.4%), leadership skills (32.9%), team skills (30.7%), specific task skills (23.5%), experience in a particular field (23.2%), specific degrees (22.0%), experience in a particular industry (21.0%), specific business experience (20.4%), ethics (17.9%), company knowledge (17.2%), energy or drive (16.6%), strategic planning skills (16.3%), fit with culture (16.0%), intelligence (15.7%), creativity or innovation (15.0%), and flexibility or adaptability (14.7%).

Candidate Pools

Recruitment for a position can occur either internally or externally. Who is being recruited at the top executive levels? The interview data show that selected executives were predominately middle-aged, white males. Both recent reviews of the executive selection literature (Sessa & Campbell, 1997) and the interview study suggest that the executive level candidate pools from which selected executives were drawn in the 1990s are also still predominately middle-aged, white males. In the interview study the selected executives were drawn from pools that contained, on average, 2.4 other executives ($SD = 1.89$, with a range of 0 to 12). Additionally, as discussed in detail later in this chapter, candidates are increasingly being brought in from outside of the organization as opposed to promoted or selected from within.

---

[1]It is difficult to determine whether executives rely on cognitive heuristics in this situation (a) because they rely on these heuristics in general to make decisions at the top, (b) because they do not have or perceive they do not have the time to engage in a thorough assessment (i.e., "cognitive busyness"), or (c) because they do not realize the importance of this step.

The Matching Process

The matching process—assessing fit between the candidates and the position—is the heart of the framework. Decisionmakers assess available candidates in terms of what they bring to the organization and match them to organization, job, and candidate requirements. At the top level, the match appears to be more subjective than matches at the lower levels. Corporate executives do not use personnel selection tools to get information about job candidates. Reviews of the literature (DeVries, 1993) and the interview study show that top-level selectors rely, for the most part, on interviews, references, and résumés—some of the least reliable methods for selection. Interestingly, even psychologists who conduct individual assessments of managerial candidates for corporate clients are likely to use similar subjective judgments, although they do report a greater likelihood of considering scores on ability tests and personality tests in their judgments (Ryan & Sackett, 1987, 1998).

One main concept that executives do say that they use is *fit* (43.6% mentioned fit in the interview study). Many executives are hard-pressed to articulate what exactly fit is, but "they know it when they see it." Other reasons for selecting one candidate over others include: business experience or knowledge (36.1%), track record (27.9%), technical expertise (18.7%), interpersonal (26.2%) and other characteristics or style (16.4%), they are already acquainted to the selectors (22.3%), insufficient experience (25.5%) or lack of fit with the job or the organization (16.7%) among other candidates, and they were the only candidate seriously considered for the position (23.5%).

Managing the Executive

Research demonstrates that it can take an executive up to $2\frac{1}{2}$ years to master the position (Gabarro, 1987), suggesting that the selection does not stop when the final decision is made and the offer accepted (see Hall, 1995). How the executive is introduced to the organization and how the organization is introduced to the executive are also part of the process.

Despite the fact that it may take a lengthy time for executives to master a position, executives receive little training or preparatory support (31%) and receive little support from those higher in the organization (23%) once in their new position. Executives are evaluated right away (within the first 5 months in the new position) on their relationships and how they are performing or "doing" their job. They are usually given a grace period of about 5 months before they are evaluated on bottom-line organizational results.

Performance and Outcomes

This is what ultimately defines success on the job and validates the selection process. As one moves up the organizational hierarchy, job scope (breadth and number of units), scale (internal complexity, diversity, and ambiguity), and accountability broaden considerably, especially for the CEO job (Bentz, 1987; Rock, 1977). Because of this complexity, measuring success in the job as one moves up the hierarchy is increasingly difficult to define.

How are executives defined as successful? Selectors in the interview study mentioned that executives are evaluated in three areas: performance, relationships, and bottom-line organizational results. What discriminated between successful and unsuccessful executives? We found that relationships with subordinates and producing tangible organizational outcomes were the two domains most clearly related to the selected executives' success (see Sessa et al., 1998).

PERSON PERCEPTION PROCESSES

This section focuses on the decision makers or "social perceivers" (see Klimoski & Donahue, chapter 1) in the selection process. The decision makers responsible for selection at the top are different from the decision makers responsible for selection in the lower levels of the organization. At the lower levels, decisions are often guided with the help of people in the human resources department who know about formal selection procedures, what selection tools are available, and how to use both. Indeed, the human resource department may actually conduct the selection process, developing and administering selection tests. Within the upper levels, the social perceiver or perceivers are an individual (either acting alone or consulting with others), or a group of higher level executives including the boss and peers of the boss of the open position, the CEO, and the chair of the board of directors. These selectors may know little about the formal aspects of selection. For example, in the interview study, 21% of the executives originally interviewed had not participated in the selection process of a high-level executive. Additionally, only 35.7% of the selections involved human resource professionals and only 36.9% of the selections involved search firm professionals. Furthermore, as described earlier in this chapter, the selectors do not rely on sophisticated selection techniques that have been developed to ensure reliability, validity, and usefulness of measurement. As a result of this particularly complex situation, affect, personal values, beliefs, and expectations can become more influential than objective criteria in the development of the candidate pool and the final choice of an executive.

Ruderman and Ohlott (1990) suggested that there are four main biases in person perception that have the greatest potential to influence the selection processes of high-level executives. These biases center on who is chosen for inclusion in the candidate pool and how to evaluate those candidates: the way the evaluation questions are framed for deciding whom to include in the candidate pool; use of salient but irrelevant candidate characteristics for categorization; use of nonpredictive descriptions of job performance leading to unrealistic or inaccurate expectations; and exclusion of summary data and inclusion of concrete, vivid information.

Whom to Consider

The first bias Ruderman and Ohlott (1990) described is in the creation of the candidate pool and has to do with whether the selectors use an inclusion or exclusion bias. With an inclusion bias, only those executives who are perceived as clearly good candidates for a position are added to or included in the candidate pool. With an exclusion bias, executives are removed or rejected from the candidate pool after they are perceived as clearly unlikely to be good candidates for a position. Those who report they eliminate people from consideration (exclusion) recommend more candidates for a particular position than those who report they recommend individuals (inclusion) for employment (Ryan & Sackett, 1987). The difference in size of the candidate pools is attributable to the inclusion or exclusion of candidates in the middle range, those that could be good candidates given more time or development. Those using an inclusion bias do not consider those in the middle range, whereas those using an exclusion bias retain them for consideration. The data from the interview study suggest that executives may rely more heavily on an inclusion bias because of the small average number of candidates within the candidate pools. This bias may serve to limit who is considered as a candidate for a high-level position.

Categorizing Candidates

It is a natural human tendency for humans to put others into groups, types, jobs, or other slots using their own schemas and stereotypes (see Operario & Fiske, chapter 2). Schemas are useful shortcuts that help simplify and manage complex information. However, they have a downside as well. When asked to judge others, people tend to use readily available information rather than exhaustively searching through their memories for all information. Typically, the information that is readily available is consistent with their schema. In the case of selection, executives are working with two sets of schemas: their schema of what it takes to perform well in a particular position and the schemas they develop for each candidate in the candidate pool. During the selection process, executives attempt to match their schema for each candidate to their schema for an ideal candidate and select the candidate who best matches the ideal. As reported earlier in this chapter, the data from the interview study suggest that selectors do not spend much time analyzing the organization and the position, making it difficult to determine what criteria executives do use to develop the requirements they need in a candidate. Without using organization needs and position requirements, high-level executives may rely on their own implicit theories of what it takes to succeed as an executive in their organization.

What may happen in this instance is that executives who differ from the ideal on irrelevant criteria (for example, race, gender, age, physical appearance, functional or educational background, or other personal characteristics that have not been shown to affect performance) may be overlooked unless there is a conscious effort to include them. Again, the data from the interview study suggest that candidate pools contain "traditional" executive candidates who are for the most part middle-aged, white males.

Using Nonpredictive Descriptions of Job Performance

Dazzling accomplishments in one role (whether a position or some sort of unvalidated selection test) do not guarantee success in another role. Unfortunately, past job performance that is irrelevant to future challenges is often used as a predictor of success (Sorcher, 1985). This tendency to make predictions based on information without considering its predictability is known as *insensitivity to predictability* (Tversky & Kahneman, 1974). This insensitivity systematically introduces bias into the process because the selection decision is made on the basis of information about candidates that does not predict their future capabilities or success on the new job. For example, an executive who turns around a failing business unit may fail at maintaining and expanding an already successful unit.

Summary Versus Vivid Descriptions

This bias exists when executives evaluate candidates by relying on their own personal experiences with candidates or the verbal recommendations of others rather than written summaries of performance. For example, when given an array of information about a candidate (i.e., interviews, personnel files, search firm reports, references, and résumés), typically executives choose first to look at and spend most of their time viewing interviews (Deal, Sessa, & Taylor, 1999)

This bias, like others, serves as a natural way to simplify a complex situation. It is made further salient by noting the finding that data reported in summary forms from interviews or assessments are often not seen as credible by executive decision makers (Hall, 1986). Thus, judgments of executive characteristics may be based on the approval or disapproval of one or a few executives who may observe the candidate only once and in a high-pressure, high-visibility, or atypical situation (e.g., a job interview).

Despite these person perception biases and others (e.g., rater leniency, halo effects, and restriction of range), executives, like other humans, possess an "illusion of validity," that is, they are extremely confident in the quality of their own judgments—even in the face of data that suggest they are incorrect (Lichenstein, Fischoff, & Philips, 1982). Use of groups during the selection process may help temper this illusion of validity but not correct it. In the interview study, individual selection decisions were the least likely to be successful (35.5% success rate) and were significantly less successful than the most frequently successful group consensus decisions (55.1% successful). Of the consultative decisions, 48.6% were successful, which was not significantly different than individual or group decisions.

INTERNAL PROMOTION
AND EXTERNAL SELECTION

Up to this point, I have discussed a general executive selection framework and have suggested that this process needs to be considered through the eyes of the selectors. The next section outlines a situation where executive person perception filters are particularly salient—selecting among a pool containing both internal and external candidates.

This scenario is particularly relevant to consider because companies are increasingly selecting executives from the outside. Nearly one third of the CEOs at the top of 1,000 public companies are outsiders (Byrne, Reingold, & Melcher, 1997; Heller, 1997) compared to about 9% three decades ago. Similarly, the executives interviewed in the interview study estimated that 41% of their hires (most one and two levels down) are external. This number is slightly higher than estimates reported elsewhere (for example, Byrne et al., 1997; Heller, 1997) but everyone reports a consistent trend of hiring high-level executives from outside the firm.

Additionally, when executives consider both internal candidates and external candidates during selection, they tend to select the external executive over the internal executive. Selectors who say that they specifically want to hire someone from within the organization do so 93% of the time and those who say that they specifically want to bring someone new into the organization hire an external candidate 95% of the time. But when selectors are open to considering both internal and external candidates, they choose an external candidate 75% of the time! This finding suggests that top-level executives may be biased toward choosing external candidates over internal candidates.

However, external hires are less likely to be seen as successful compared to internal hires, once in the position. In the interview study, when asked to estimate the internal and external selection failure rates in their own organizations, executives estimated that their failure rate for internal hires was 24% whereas their failure rate for external hires was 35%! Once on the job, external executives were over twice as likely to be fired when they demonstrated poor performance compared to internal hires (who were more likely to be demoted or otherwise moved aside for poor performance). A recent study looking at the ascension of executives into the position of president reports similar findings. Specifically, nearly two thirds of new presidents hired from outside the organization had left their companies within 4 years compared with 38% of those promoted from within (Ciampa & Watkins, 1999).

For some reason, external executives appear more favorable during the selection process but once in the position are less likely to be perceived as successful. There are three interrelated explanations for this seeming paradox: First, selectors choose insiders or outsiders on the basis of different perceptions of the organization and its needs; second, selection processes differ for internal and external candidates such that external executives appear more favorable in terms of qualifications than internal ones; and third, external hires are treated the same as internal hires once on the job but they are evaluated differently.

Organizations Choose Internal and External Candidates for Different Reasons

The manner in which top-level executives perceive and define their organization affects their preference for internal or external candidates. In the interview study, when the organization needs and position requirements included such things as introducing new technology, new business start-ups, and general need to develop employees within the organization, selectors more often turn to the outside to select a candidate. Not surprisingly, internal executives are more likely to be selected for a position as a developmental challenge for that executive.

Start-ups and developing staff deserve an extra mention. When confronted with a new business start-up or the need to develop employees, although selectors show a marked preference for candidates from outside the organization, these hires are much less likely to succeed in the position than candidates hired from inside the organization. For start-ups, 62.5% of the internal hires are successful versus 33.3% of the external hires. For developing staff, 50% of the internal hires are successful versus 30.8% of the external hires.

Selectors also tend to choose internal candidates or external candidates depending on particular candidate requirements they perceive are needed. When selectors define the candidate requirements to include company knowledge, product knowledge, and intelligence, they are more likely to select an insider. When they need an intensive background in a particular industry, a specific business experience, and managerial skills, organizations are more likely to select an outsider.

The information reported above suggests that when top-level executives define the organization as being in a state of change (e.g., through start-ups, new technology, improving their own staff), they perceive that they need to bring in an executive with specific background, experience, and skills (e.g., background in a particular industry, specific business experience, or managerial skills) that they do not have available on staff. External executives are brought in to fill the need, yet it is evident that external hires are not likely to be successful.[2]

By contrast, when top-level executives perceive the organization's state as more stable, executives redefine the situation from one of selection, or "What can this candidate offer to the position?" to one of development, or "What can this position do for this executive?" That is, they tend to define the position as a developmental one and as needing someone who is intimately familiar with the organization. In such cases, the selectors are likely to have a discussion regarding how this position can stretch or develop employees.

---

[2]It is important to note that the organizational needs that favor external hires pose significantly troublesome challenges. It is difficult to determine if these executives are not successful because they were external hires or because the job itself is harder.

Differing Selection Processes

During the actual selection process, the contexts for internal and external executives differ. When evaluating external executives, selection committees are also trying to "sell" their organization and position, and thus have the motivation to present themselves (whom the selected candidate will be working with), the organization, and the position in a favorable manner. On the other hand, when evaluating internal executives, selection committees have less need to sell and greater need to "reward" an internal executive for past performance. Thus, executive search committees have different motivations that may influence their perceptions of the candidates at the outset of the process.

Within these differing contexts (sell vs. reward), the selection tools used with internal candidates differ from those used with external candidates. This practice leads to drawing and using different information to make decisions on these two sets of candidates.

Use of Selection Tools.

Selectors receive information from different sources when evaluating internal and external candidates. When considering external executives, selection committees rely more heavily on interviews, résumés, and references—although these three tools are used to collect information on both internal and external candidates. External searches are more likely to involve search firms to get information about candidates. For internal candidates, the selectors are more likely to supplement interviews, résumés, and references with performance appraisals, succession plans, and subordinate reviews.

External candidates can control the information in résumés and interviews and, to some extent, search firms and references. Thus, not only is information gathered from more limited places on external candidates but also the information can be biased to more likely include positive information and to less likely include negative information. Information gathered on internal candidates (using performance appraisals, succession plans, and reviews, as well as information gained informally) may be more balanced in terms of strengths and development needs.

Seeking and Using Information.

Because of the different tools used to gather information, different types of information are gained on candidates. For example, one selector in the interview study said this about an unsuccessful external hire, "The internal candidate was excluded on the basis of weak leadership skills. But externals were not assessed on leadership skills."

The reason the executive is ultimately chosen from the pool of candidates differs between internal and external candidates in several areas. External executives are brought in when they have something that the organization specifically needs, that is, they are more often chosen for their business expertise, other specific knowledge and skills, and technical expertise. They are also often chosen because other candidates in the pool demonstrated a lack of specific skills needed (e.g., communication skills). They are chosen for their interpersonal characteristics. Also, external candidates are more often selected from the candidate pool because of their perceived fit to the organization's culture. Internal executives are more often chosen because of their track record of success within the organization. They are selected because they are known entities and have demonstrated enough merit to qualify them for additional development.

In sum, because of differing contexts and the selection tools used, selectors perceive, gain, and use different information on internal and external candidates. For external executives, they are selling the job, and they gain less information on external candidates. But the information they do have may be biased toward the positive (resulting in an exchange of positive information). Selectors are more evaluative of internal candidates and gain more (and more balanced) information about them. Because of the difference in the amount and type of information gained, selectors perceive external candidates to be better matches to their schema of an ideal candidate.

Treatment and Evaluation Once in the Position

According to the reports of the interviewees, there are no differences in the way hires from outside the organization are managed once in the position compared to those who are hired internally—even though outsiders are often brought in to aid the organization as part of a change effort. Interestingly, internals, who are often promoted for their own development, are also not likely to receive any sort of support in the position. Less than one third of the new hires receive training or other preparatory support before taking the position. Less than one fourth receive support from superiors, and executives other than superiors were rarely mentioned as providing support.

There are differences in the way external hires and internal hires are judged in the first 5 months in the position. External hires are less likely than internal hires to be judged on organizational results (83% of the external executives were not evaluated on their results during their first 5 months, whereas 65% of the internal executives were not evaluated during this period) and their relationships (50% of the external executives were not evaluated on their relationships during their first 5 months, whereas 18% of the internal executives were not evaluated during this period). However, despite the lack of support indicated in the previous section, external hires are more likely to be judged more harshly than internal hires in terms of their actual performance. That is, they received more negative evaluations (29% vs. 12%) and fewer positive evaluations (54% vs. 71%). External executives are judged on how they do their jobs, and often judged harshly, almost immediately after accepting the position.

There are also differences in evaluations of strengths and weaknesses of internal and external hires. Externally hired executives are more likely to be seen as having strengths in the technical expertise needed to accomplish the position requirements than internal hires. This makes sense because external hires are specifically hired for their skills, whereas internal hires are expected to develop their skills. However, despite the fact that interpersonal skills were a criterion used in their selection, external hires are seen as having problems with their peers.

Internally hired executives are more likely to be seen as having specific knowledge, skills, abilities, characteristics, and values needed for the position as compared to externally hired executives. They are also seen as generally getting along with all others. Thus, despite being hired for developmental reasons, internal hires fared better and are seen as having the skills needed for the position.

External hires are hired to be perfect and punished for not being so. Internal hires are believed to be flawed and in need of development. When they perform, they are not expected to be perfect.

SUMMARY

Filling a high-level executive position is a difficult task. High-level positions are complex and have bottom-line impact on organizational results. Highly qualified executives are scarce (Chambers, Foulon, Handfield-Jones, Hankin, & Michaels, III, 1998). Principles of selection and sophisticated selection tools developed within lower levels of the organization do not easily translate into helpful tools for executive searches and may be dismissed as irrelevant. Those tools developed for higher level positions (e.g., individual assessment, see Jeanneret & Silzer, 1998) are not commonplace although use is growing. Executives are accustomed to being considered experts in decision making and may not consider the expertise of those trained in selection processes. Instead, high-level executives resort to simple selection processes, succumbing to an illusion of validity of their decision-making processes despite relying heavily on biases, schemas, stereotypes, and other cognitive simplification processes. This selection process, in part, serves to explain the current high levels of failure at the top of today's organizations.

Selection experts need to provide principles of selection specifically targeted to high-level selection processes that help executives in a simple and noninvasive manner.

Implications for Research

Study Executive Selection.   Executive selection is worthy of systematic study in its own right (e.g., Beatty & Zajac, 1987; Hollenbeck, 1994). Although some of what is known about selection (among industrial and organizational psychologists) can be extrapolated to this level, much more is necessary to learn, both on a formal selection basis and an informal person perception basis using a variety of research methodologies.

Explore Other Ways Person Perception Impacts Executive Selection and How to Regulate It.   Despite the availability of a variety of selection methods, executives continue to rely heavily on interviews, references, and résumés. Instead of concentrating on new and more valid selection methods, perhaps there is a need to shift emphasis to why executives choose the methods they do and on communicating how to improve and supplement these methods. The key here may be to show executives how to draw information from the sources they use based on the predictors needed. For example, there has been a great deal of research on using structured questions and behavioral examples to improve the validity and reliability of selection interviews (see Borman, Hanson, & Hedge, 1997, for review). Yet executives do not find these techniques comfortable (Mabey & Iles, 1991) and continue to use interviews in an idiosyncratic fashion (Graves & Karren, 1996). Perhaps an applied area of research could determine "how" to use them comfortably.

Communicate What Is Known About Selection.   Executives do not have access to selection procedures. Data reported here demonstrate that human resource executives are only included in the decision making one third of the time. Industrial and organizational psychologists need to disseminate research about selection to these executives in easily accessible forms. One suggestion is to combine what is known into current executive language around "competencies." Properly defined and determined on the basis of job and organization analyses, competencies can be seen as "predictors."

Implications for Practice

Use Teams With a Variety of Members to Make the Selection Decision. As shown earlier in this chapter, teams make better selection choices than individuals. Team members may use different criteria for including and excluding potential candidates, thus broadening the candidates considered. They may call into question each other's biases, schemas, and stereotypes. Finally, as the different team members interact with the candidates, they may each develop different "vivid" descriptions of the candidates that, as a team, need to be defined into a summary that all can agree on.

Use a Holistic, Context-Rich Look at the Corporation and the Position and Connect it With Candidate Requirements. Spending time and effort discussing the organization, position, and candidate requirements does two things during the selection process. First, candidate requirements will more likely be based on specific organizational needs and will less likely be based on implicit theories of successful executives. Second, through discussion, the selection committee members can develop similar or related views of the ideal candidate requirements.

Consider a Variety of Candidates in the Available Pool. The presence of nontraditional candidates may develop a perception of accountability to a greater authority (the legal environment) and thus may force selectors to more carefully objectify and consider the assumptions, biases, stereotypes, and schemas inherent in their own decision making processes—regardless of the candidate chosen.

Consciously Decide What Information Is Needed on Each Candidate and How to Best Attain That Information. Up-front discussion regarding what to look for in candidates may help to form schemas that are made more on the basis of position information and less on the basis of information that is not job relevant. Task-based accomplishments can be ascertained by carefully asking for them in interviews and by looking for specific experiences on résumés. But it may be difficult to assess such particular needs as interpersonal characteristics and values using these tools. These qualifications may be better assessed through carefully worded questions to references and, if needed, through experts trained in assessment.

Use the Same People and the Same Information Sources to Get Information on, and Make Decisions About, All Candidates. For example, if a search firm is used to find external candidates, the firm should also be used to assess potential internal candidates. This does not mean that one should not use performance appraisals, succession plans, and subordinate reviews when considering an internal candidate. But one must realize that this information provides a different picture of internal candidates.

Combine the Development and Selection Paradigms for Both Internal and External Candidates. Assess both what the candidate can do for the organization as well as what the organization must do to support and develop the candidate. Do not overestimate the capabilities of external executives. Conversely, do not underestimate the capabilities of the firm's own executives.

Evaluate Executives According to the Original Criteria Used to Hire Them. This allows one to gain an understanding of the selection processes: What went well? What could be improved the next time? Did the individual who was selected do as well as expected? If not, what factors in the context and the selection process could have yielded a better environment and the information to make a better decision?

REFERENCES

Akkerman, A. E. (1993). Criteria and individual assessment. In M. Smith and I. T. Robertson (Eds.), *Advances in selection and assessment*. New York: Wiley.

Beatty, R. P., & Zajac, E. J. (1987). CEO change and firm performance in large corporations: Succession effects and manager effects. *Strategic Management Journal, 8*, 305–317.

Bentz, V. J. (1987). *Explorations of scope and scale: The critical determinant of high-level executive effectiveness* (Rep. No. 31). Greensboro, NC: Center for Creative Leadership.

Borman, W. C., Hanson, M. A., & Hedge, J. W. (1997). Personnel selection. *Annual Review of Psychology, 48*, 299–337.

Byrne, J. A., Reingold, J., & Melcher, R. A. (1997, August 11). Wanted: A few good CEOs. *Business Week*, pp. 64–70.

Chambers, E. G., Foulon, M., Handfield-Jones, H., Hankin, S. M., & Michaels, III, E. G. (1998). The war for talent. *The McKinsey Quarterly, 3*, 44–57.

Ciampa, D., & Watkins, M. (1999). *Right from the start: Taking charge in a new leadership role.* Boston: Harvard Business School Press.

Clark, T. (1992). Selection methods used by executive search consultancies in four European countries: A survey and critique. *International Journal of Selection and Assessment, 1*, 41–49.

Deal, J. J., Sessa, V. I., & Taylor, J. (1999). *Choosing Executives: A research report on the peak selection simulation.* Greensboro, NC: Center for Creative Leadership.

DeVries, D. L. (1993). Executive selection: A look at what we know and what we need to know (Rep. No. 321). Greensboro, NC: Center for Creative Leadership.

Gabarro, J. J. (1987). *The dynamics of taking charge.* Boston: Harvard Business School Press.

Graves, L. M., & Karren, R. J. (1996). The employee selection interview: A fresh look at an old problem. *Human Resource Management, 35*, 163–180.

Gupta, A. (1992). Executive selection: A strategic perspective. *Human Resource Planning, 15*(1), 47–61.

Hall, D. T. (1986). Dilemmas in linking succession planning to individual executive learning. *Human Resource Management, 25*, 235–265.

Hall, D. T. (1995). Executive careers and learning: Aligning selection, strategy, and development. *Human Resource Planning, 18*, 14–23.

Heller, R. (1997, October). Outsiders' inside track to the top. *Management Today*, 21.

Hogan, R., Curphy, G. J., & Hogan, J. (1994). What we know about leadership: Effectiveness and personality. *American Psychologist, 49*, 493–504.

Hogan, R., Raskin, R., & Fazzini, D. (1990). The dark side of charisma. In K. E. Clark & M. B. Clark (Eds.), *Measures of leadership.* West Orange, NJ: Leadership Library of America.

Hollenbeck, G. P. (1994). *CEO selection: A street-smart review* (Rep. No. 164). Greensboro, NC: Center for Creative Leadership.

Jeanneret, R., & Silzer, R. F. (1998). *Individual psychological assessment: Predicting behavior in organizational settings.* San Francisco: Jossey-Bass.

Jones, D. (2000, February 29). Overwhelmed CEOs leaving in droves. *USA Today*, sec B, p. 1.

Lamb, R. B. (1987, April). CEOs for this season. *Across the Board, 24*, 34–41.

Lichenstein, S., Fischoff, B., & Philips, L. D. (1982). Calibration of probabilities: The state of the art. In D. Kahneman, P. Slovic, & A. Tverksy (Eds.), *Judgment under uncertainty: Heuristics and biases* (pp. 306–334). New York: Cambridge University Press.

Mabey, C., & Iles, P. (1991). HRM from the other side of the fence. *Personnel Management, 23*, 50–53.

Martell, K., & Carroll, S. J. (1995). Which executive human resource management practices for the top management team are associated with higher firm performance? *Human Resource Management, 34*, 497–512.

Principles for the Validation and Use of Personnel Selection Procedures, 3rd ed., College Park, MD, Society for Industrial and Organizational Psychology, 1987.

Rock, R. H. (1977). *The chief executive officer: Managing the human resources of the large diversified industrial company.* Lexington, MA: Heath.

Ruderman, M. N., & Ohlott, P. J. (1990). *Traps and pitfalls in the judgment of executive potential* (Rep. No. 141). Greensboro, NC: Center for Creative Leadership.

Ryan, A. M., & Sackett, P. R. (1987). A survey of individual assessment practice by I/O psychologists. *Personnel Psychology, 40*, 455–488.

Ryan, A. M., & Sackett, P. R. (1998). Individual assessment: The research base. In R. Jeanneret & R. Silzer (Eds.) *Individual psychological assessment: Predicting behavior in organizational settings.* San Francisco: Jossey-Bass.

Sackett, P. R., & Arvey, R. D. (1993). Selection in small *N* settings. In N. Schmitt & W. C. Borman (Eds.), *Personnel selection in organizations*. San Francisco: Jossey-Bass.

Sessa, V. I., & Campbell, R. J. (1997). *Selection at the top: An annotated bibliography* (Rep. No. 333). Greensboro, NC: Center for Creative Leadership.

Sessa, V. I., Kaiser, R., Taylor, J. K., & Campbell, R. J. (1998). *Executive selection: A research report on what works and what doesn't* (Rep. No. 179). Greensboro, NC: Center for Creative Leadership.

Sorcher, M. (1985). *Predicting executive success*. New York: Wiley.

Tversky, A., & Kahneman, D. (1974, September 27). Judgment under uncertainty: Heuristics and biases. *Science, 185,* 1124–1131.

Van Clieaf, M. S. (1992). Strategy and structure follow people: Improving organizational performance through effective executive search. *Human Resource Planning, 15,* 33–46.

5

The Role of Dimensions and Exercises in Assessment Center Judgments

Paul R. Sackett and Kathleen A. Tuzinski
University of Minnesota

Assessment centers present a fascinating dilemma for those wishing to understand the processes underlying assessor ratings. There is a gap between the espoused theory of how assessment centers operate and the findings of an extensive body of research on assessment ratings that has been the focus of much theorizing and considerable empirical research. The espoused theory is that assessment centers are organized around a set of dimensions (e.g., attributes such as leadership, organizing and planning, and decision making). Opportunities to observe dimension-relevant behavior are possible through the use of multiple exercises (e.g., in-basket, leaderless group discussion, and oral presentation). The various dimensions are rated in each exercise, resulting in a dimension-by-exercise matrix of ratings. Observations relevant to a given dimension across various exercises are then integrated to form an overall evaluation of a candidate's standing on that dimension. Finally, dimension ratings are integrated to form an overall evaluation of each candidate.

This espoused theory emphasizes dimensions, with exercises serving as vehicles for the observation of dimension-relevant behavior. However, when dimension-by-exercise rating matrices are examined, the typical finding is that exercises dominate: Ratings of all the dimensions in a given exercise are highly correlated. In contrast, ratings of any given dimension across exercises show lower correlations. In factor analytic terms, the factors underlying assessment center ratings reflect exercises rather than dimensions. Since the early report by Sackett and Dreher (1982), this finding that exercises rather than dimensions are the major source of variance in ratings has been replicated repeatedly, and various attempts to modify assessment procedures in order to reverse this finding have been undertaken. This chapter presents a review of the literature on the dominance of exercise factors in assessment ratings, the various explanations offered for this phenomenon, and the literature on attempts to modify assessment center content or rating procedures in hopes of producing stronger evidence for a dimension-based factor structure. We hope that a reexamination of previous research on assessor judgments will help clarify how assessors attend to and process behavioral information in an assessment center.

A BRIEF INTRODUCTION
TO ASSESSMENT CENTERS

An assessment center is an evaluative setting in which the behavior of a group of candidates is observed and evaluated on multiple dimensions by a number of trained observers while the candidates engage in various exercises designed to provide a platform for the display of job-relevant behaviors. The prototypical job is managerial in nature, though assessment centers are used for a wide variety of jobs. Rather than a place or location, the assessment center is a technique. It can operate anywhere: at the home company, or at a hotel, convention center, or offices of an external consulting firm. It often varies in length, commonly from a half day to 3 days. It can be modified to suit the individual needs of any organization and can be tailored for almost any purpose: selection or promotion, early identification of managerial talent, employee development, or diagnosis of training needs. Clearly, assessment centers are characterized more by their diversity than homogeneity, leading most scholars to agree that a "typical" assessment center does not exist (Gaugler, Rosenthal, Thornton, & Bentson, 1987; Spychalski, Quinones, Gaugler, & Pohley, 1997; Thornton, 1992).

One characteristic of the assessment center is that multiple, trained assessors observe the participants in the exercises and rate their behavior on relevant performance dimensions. Because a large number of participants often go through the center at one time, any single assessor commonly observes only one or two of the exercises and relies on the other assessors for behavioral descriptions of candidate behavior in the other exercises. For this reason, a group discussion is held to ensure that all assessors have the most complete information on each participant before assigning dimension ratings. In the traditional assessment center, dimension ratings are not assigned until all exercises have been completed and a group discussion has taken place (often referred to as the *within-dimension* approach to rating). However, many assessment centers have adopted the practice of rating dimensions immediately after each exercise, before the group discussion (often referred to as the *within-exercise* approach to rating). The latter practice is controversial and has brought some criticism from assessment center traditionalists. After the dimension ratings have been assigned by the individual assessors, a group consensus meeting is held for the purpose of coming up with final dimension ratings for each participant. Final dimension ratings should represent how well the participant did for each dimension across all exercises. In addition to the final dimension ratings, an overall assessment rating (OAR), reflecting overall performance across the final dimension ratings, is produced by group consensus.

Research has consistently demonstrated that assessment centers do very well in predicting future success in management. The predictive validity of the OAR has been demonstrated in a number of different contexts for a variety of criteria: salary progress (Bray & Grant, 1966); organizational level attained (Hinrichs, 1978); increases in responsibility (Wollowick & McNamara, 1969); sales (Bray & Campbell, 1968); and military officer training (Borman, 1982). In a meta-analytic review of 50 assessment center studies, Gaugler et al. (1987) found, for four categories of criteria (ratings of job performance, potential, performance in training, and career advancement), that 90% of assessment centers produce predictive validity coefficients above .15 (after correcting for sampling error, range restriction, and criterion unreliability).

Subsequent to this meta-analysis, the literature on the predictive validity of assessment centers has often cited Gaugler et al.'s (1987) overall corrected mean validity coefficient of .37 as the predictive validity of the assessment center method. However, in doing the meta-analysis, they found that accounting for statistical artifacts did not explain much of the variance among the validity coefficients, and a large percentage of variance (46%) was left unaccounted for. This finding raises an important point about the predictive validity of assessment centers: Because of the variations in their purpose, design, implementation, and criteria, assessment centers differ greatly in their ability to predict future outcomes. When one considers the extreme heterogeneity that characterizes the assessment center method (Guion, 1998), the meaning of a single validity coefficient for something as unstandardized as the assessment center method is questionable. We endorse the consistent presentation of both a corrected mean and standard deviation when summarizing meta-analytic results.

CONSTRUCTS UNDERLYING ASSESSMENT CENTER RATINGS

The traditional explanation for how assessment centers work is that stable personal qualities (dimensions) are measured through a set of situations representative of the target job (exercises). Sackett and Dreher (1982) argued that in order to accept the dimension-centered view of the judgment process underlying assessment ratings, the dimensions must be stable enough across exercises to demonstrate cross-situational consistency (convergent validity), yet be distinguishable enough from other dimensions within the same exercise so that there is differentiation among them (discriminant validity). They noted assessment centers that use the within-exercise rating method produce a set of ratings that can be conceptualized and analyzed as a multitrait–multimethod (MTMM) matrix, with dimensions as the traits and exercises as the methods.

In a MTMM matrix, there are three types of correlations: (a) monotrait–heteromethod (MT–HM), or same dimension across all exercises; (b) heterotrait–monomethod (HT–MM), or different dimensions within the same exercise; and (c) heterotrait–heteromethod (HT–HM), or different dimensions from different exercises. Evidence for dimensions as the constructs underlying assessor judgments is suggested whenever the MT–HM correlations are higher than either the HT–MM or HT–HM correlations.

Sackett and Dreher (1982), and the many subsequent researchers who have examined similar assessment center data, have typically used either or both of two analytic techniques for examining such a matrix: factor analytic techniques or the decomposition of a MTMM matrix for purposes of comparing convergent and discriminant validity. Both modes of investigation are based on the same fundamental insight: If dimensions are at the heart of how information about candidates is organized and stored by the assessors, then the strongest pattern of correlations in the MTMM matrix should be among ratings of the same dimension across exercises. This should be manifested in a finding of dimension factors rather than exercise factors and in a finding of high within-dimension convergence and high within-exercise divergence in the MTMM matrix.

Factor analyses of assessment centers, however, have consistently produced greater evidence for exercise rather than dimension factors (Bycio, Alvares, & Hahn, 1987; Chan, 1996; Fleenor, 1996; Kleinmann, Kuptsch, & Köller, 1996; Kudisch, Ladd, & Dobbins, 1997; Robertson, Gratton, & Sharpley, 1987; Russell, 1987; Sackett & Dreher, 1982; Sackett & Harris, 1988; Schneider & Schmitt, 1992), thus calling into question the traditional explanation for how assessment centers work. Exercise factors persist despite efforts to increase construct validity by modifying the scoring procedure (Harris, Becker, & Smith, 1993; Silverman, Dalessio, Woods, & Johnson, 1986), using behavioral checklists (Donahue, Truxillo, Cornwell, & Gerrity, 1997), or having assessors reconceptualize dimensions as managerial functions (Joyce, Thayer, & Pond, 1994). Some studies have been successful in at least obtaining a mix of both exercise and dimension factors (Arthur, Woehr, & Maldegan, 2000; Bycio et al., 1987; Donahue et al., 1997; Kleinmann et al., 1996; Kudisch et al., 1997; Sackett & Harris, 1988; Schneider & Schmitt, 1992); however, none have been successful in eliminating exercise factors. We are aware of only one study that has achieved stronger dimension than exercise effects (i.e., Arthur et al., 2000). These findings are disconcerting because they contradict the espoused theory of assessment centers and underscore a need for elucidating the types of schemas invoked as assessors observe and rate candidates in an assessment center.

Table 5.1 is a summary of the average correlations from MTMM matrices of previous construct validity studies that are grouped into two categories. The first category involves analyses of existing assessment centers, whereas the second category involves the intentional modification of one or more features of the assessment center process with the explicit goal of obtaining stronger convergent and discriminant validity evidence. None of the convergent validity coefficients in the unmodified assessment centers are larger than their corresponding discriminant validity coefficients. The average convergent validity coefficient is .25, whereas the average discriminant validity coefficient is .58. Of those studies reporting HT–HM coefficients, the average is .21. When different dimensions from separate exercises correlate this highly, pervasive halo error is indicated (Sackett & Dreher, 1982). The findings for unmodified centers listed in Table 5.1, in addition to factor analytic findings, suggest that assessors tend to categorize behavior in terms of exercises, not dimensions. Replications of these findings

TABLE 5.1

Average MTMM Correlations From Validity Studies: Unmodified and Modified
Assessment Centers

		Correlations		
	N	*Convergent Validity MT–HM*	*Discriminant Validity HT–MM*	*HT–HM*
Unmodified Centers				
Sackett & Dreher (1982)				
Organization A	86	.07	.64	.06
Organization B	311	.11	.40	.07
Organization C	162	.51	.65	.45
Bycio et al. (1987)	1,170	.36	.75	NR
Robertson et al. (1987)				
Organization 1	41	.28	.64	NR
Organization 2	48	.26	.66	NR
Organization 3	84	.23	.60	NR
Organization 4	49	.11	.49	NR
Russell (1987)	75	.25	.53	.19
Chan (1996)	46	.07	.71	NR
Fleenor (1996)	73–101	.22	.42	.16
Kleinmann & Köller (1997)	70	.44	.63	.37
Kudisch et al. (1997)	138	.29	.41	.16
Modified Centers[a]				
Silverman et al. (1986)				
Within-exercise scoring	45	.37	.68	.31
Within-dimension scoring	45	.54	.65	.44
Harris et al. (1993)				
Within-exercise scoring	237	.32	.42	NR
Within-dimension scoring	556	.33	.41	NR
Arthur et al. (2000)[b]				
Within-dimension scoring	149	.60	.39	NR
Reilly et al. (1990)				
Graphic rating scales	120	.24	.47	NR
Behavioral checklist	235	.43	.41	NR
Donahue et al. (1997)				
Graphic rating scales	188	.32	.30	.61
Behavioral checklist	188	.25	.24	.40
Schliecher et al. (1999)				
Limited assessor training	63	.48	.74	.46
FOR training	63	.34	.66	.28

(Continued)

TABLE 5.1

(Continued)

		Correlations		
	N	*Convergent Validity MT–HM*	*Discriminant Validity HT–MM*	*HT–HM*
Gaugler & Thornton (1989)				
3 dimensions	37	.83	.89	.83
6 dimensions	40	.80	.85	.77
9 dimensions	34	.70	.83	.69
Kleinmann et al. (1996)				
Nontransparent dimensions	59	.30	.60	.30
Transparent dimensions	60	.35	.61	.37
Joyce et al. (1994)				
Dimensions as attributes	75	.22	.44	.21
Dimensions as managerial functions	77	.10	.29	.07

Note. Unmodified centers are those studies that have examined existing assessment centers without implementing a modification. [a] For those studies that included an unmodified center as a control, the modified assessment center is always listed second. [b] Only a modified center was reported in this study. HT–HM = heterotrait–heteromethod; HT–MM = heterotrait–monomethod; MT–HM = monotrait–heteromethod; MTMM = multitrait–multimethod; NR = not reported.

demonstrate that they are not simply a result of atypical organizations or assessment centers. Using confirmatory factor analysis (CFA), Sackett and Harris (1988) demonstrated that the models that fit best were composed of either strictly exercise factors or some mixture of both exercise and dimension factors. When the "construct-validity problem" of assessment centers became accepted as a real phenomenon, researchers began to modify various aspects of the assessment center observation and rating process in hopes of producing a pattern of ratings more consistent with the dimension-based theory of assessor judgments.

A line of inquiry that frequently occurs in response to Sackett and Dreher's findings questions the construct validity of the dimensional view of assessment centers; it is characterized as, "Sackett and Dreher assert that assessment centers lack construct validity." This is a misstatement. A better characterization would be, "Sackett and Dreher assert that evidence is lacking for the position that the constructs measured by assessment centers are those intended by their designers." Assessment ratings clearly do reflect constructs; at issue is whether the traditional explanation of what constructs assessment centers measure is the correct one. This misunderstanding is reflected in recent writings asserting a paradox based on the unitarian view of validity and the model of the relationships between construct-, content-, and criterion-related validity. According to Arthur et al. (2000), because assessment centers have demonstrated both content- and criterion-related validity, it would follow under the unitarian view of validity that they should also display construct validity. Any belief that assessment centers can have the first two types of validity without the third would be inconsistent with this view. We see no paradox here: Assessment centers do not "lack construct validity," but rather lack clear consensus as to the constructs they do assess. The unitarian perspective on validity does not argue that it is necessary that different forms of validity evidence converge; it is certainly possible to design a measure that representatively samples job content and predicts a criterion of interest but is assigned what is later proven to be an incorrect construct label. Rather, the unitarian perspective is that all lines of evidence contribute to an overall understanding of the meaning of a score and of the inferences that can be drawn from that score. (See *Standards for Educational and Psychological Testing*, American Educational Research Association [AERA], American Psychological Association [APA], & National Council on Management and Education [NCME], 1999.)

ATTEMPTS TO IMPROVE CONVERGENT AND DISCRIMINANT VALIDITY

Researchers have proposed a number of different hypotheses to explain why the convergent and discriminant validity of assessment center ratings is so low. These findings seem to indicate a natural tendency for assessors to think more in terms of overall exercise performance than in terms of dimensions. One reason for this tendency is perhaps that an exercise-based rather than dimension-based schema is more readily available and easier to use. The majority of studies focusing on improving convergent and discriminant validity are in some way attempts to help assessors use a schema more similar to that intended by the assessment center designer— one based on dimensions. The studies differ in the mechanism to influence the way assessors store and report information about the candidates. The studies reviewed here have modified the following features of assessment centers: scoring procedure, method for recording behavior, assessor training, and dimensions. The second category (modified centers) in Table 5.1 summarizes the average correlations of these studies.

Scoring Procedure

Recall that there are two fundamentally different rating approaches in assessment centers. In the within-exercise approach, dimension ratings are made immediately after each exercise, whereas in the within-dimension approach, ratings are not made until after the assessor group discussion. Only the within-exercise approach permits an examination of convergent and discriminant validity, as it is the only method that produces dimension ratings for each exercise. One argument put forward to explain the dominance of exercise factors is that it is merely an artifact of the within-exercise rating method; it forces assessors to think in terms of exercises because ratings are assigned after each exercise. In other words, assessors would naturally use a more dimension-based schema, if it wasn't for the within-exercise method forcing them to think in terms of exercises. To think in terms of dimensions, assessors should use the within-dimension method.

Silverman et al. (1986) compared the MTMM matrix correlations obtained from the within-exercise and within-dimension scoring methods. Because the within-dimension method does not produce exercise-specific ratings, the procedure was modified to add another step after the final dimension ratings were obtained; the assessors went back to the exercises and rated all of the dimensions within each. These ratings were compared to the within-exercise ratings that had already been assigned on completion of each exercise.

As seen in the table, the mean convergent validity coefficient was higher in the within-dimension condition (.54 vs. .37) but the discriminant validities stayed about the same. Note that the discriminant validity coefficients were still larger than the convergent validity coefficients. Furthermore, the correlations between different dimensions from different exercises (HT–HM) actually increased from the old method to the new, possibly signifying an increase in halo (Sackett & Dreher, 1982). In the presence of halo, an increase in the convergent validity coefficient must be interpreted with caution.

Harris et al. (1993) replicated this study with a modification to the within-dimension scoring procedure. They were concerned with Silverman et al.'s (1986) decision to have the assessors assign exercise-specific dimension ratings after they assigned across-exercise final dimension ratings. This could be an alternative explanation for the higher convergent validity in the within-dimension method. Harris and colleagues changed the within-dimension scoring procedure by having the exercise-specific dimension ratings assigned before the final dimension ratings. Unlike Silverman and colleagues, they found almost no difference in the convergent and discriminant validity coefficients between the two methods.

Arthur et al. (2000), following the within-dimension approach used by Harris et al. (1993), is the only study to report higher convergent than discriminant validity coefficients. The cause of this departure from the typical pattern of findings is unclear. One suggested explanation is that 51% of the assessors were psychologists. It has been demonstrated that psychologists, in comparison to managers, make better assessors (Gaugler et al., 1987; Sagie & Magnezy, 1997). Using CFA, Sagie and Magnezy modeled the ratings of managers and psychologists and found that psychologists used all of the dimensions, whereas the managers used only two out of five. It is important to note that a large number of assessment centers in research and practice use managers as assessors almost exclusively. Caution and further research is needed, as one cannot determine whether the use of psychologists or some other feature is responsible for these findings.

Method for Recording Behavior

Because the cognitive demands placed on assessors are a concern, researchers have identified behavioral checklists as one possible way for reducing these demands. Behavioral checklists are lists of behaviors grouped by dimension that can be checked as they are observed during an exercise. Two studies that have used behavioral checklists to address the problem of low construct validity are listed in the table (Donahue et al., 1997; Reilly, Henry, & Smither, 1990). It appears that behavioral checklists did improve discriminant validity slightly; the coefficients decreased by .06 in both studies. In addition, both studies were able to narrow the gap between the discriminant and convergent coefficients—an improvement over most previous studies. However, Donahue and her colleagues also conducted a CFA and found that the best-fitting model for the behavioral checklist was still composed of both dimension and exercise factors. At this point the evidence is not very strong for the utility of behavioral checklists but they seem to be a promising technique for reducing cognitive complexity.

Rater Training

Because managers tend to have their own idiosyncratic theories about personality, some form of rater training is usually needed. Despite training, managers report difficulties in thinking of candidates in terms of dimensions

(Lowry, 1995). Frame-of-reference (FOR) training has shown some success in the area of performance appraisal. FOR training in assessment centers brings individual perceptions into a common frame of reference by focusing on the dimensions themselves and their corresponding behaviors. Schliecher, Day, Mayes, and Riggio (1999) designed an assessment center with a 90-min. FOR training segment and found a decrease in both discriminant validity coefficients (HT–MM and HT–HM). However, the discriminant coefficient still remained higher than the convergent coefficient (r = .66 and .34, respectively). The decrease in the convergent coefficient from r = .48 to .34, might indicate a decrease in halo—a conclusion that is supported by a decrease in the HT–HM correlation (Schliecher et al., 1999). Still, the FOR training was not effective enough to reverse the pattern of coefficients. Before drawing any conclusions about the effectiveness of FOR, it is important to note that regardless of the type of training program, 90 min. might not be sufficient time to equip a nonpsychologist rater with the background and skills to make distinctions among dimensions and the appropriate inferences from behavior to personal attributes.

Changing the Number and Nature of the Dimensions

The issue of cognitive demands placed on raters is a recurring concern. Three features of assessment center dimensions that researchers have targeted are: (a) the number of dimensions; (b) the transparency of the dimensions; and (c) the nature of the constructs that they represent.

Number of Dimensions.   The average number of dimensions in a survey of over 200 organizations was 11 (see Gaugler, Bentson, & Pohey, as cited in Thornton, 1992). Some researchers have questioned whether it is cognitively possible for trained assessors to consider more than three to six dimensions when categorizing behavior. Studies that regressed the OAR on the individual dimensions indicated that assessors reduce information down to only a few dimensions—sometimes even a single factor (Russell, 1985; Sackett & Hakel, 1979; Sagie & Magnezy, 1997; Shore, Thornton, & Shore, 1990).

In a laboratory study, Gaugler & Thornton (1989) designed an assessment center so that assessors would categorize behavior into either three, six, or nine dimensions. The correlations in the second category of Table 5.1 are striking because they are all very high. In fact, for all three conditions, the convergent MT–HM correlations are just about equal to the HT–HM correlations. This pattern of correlations indicates pervasive halo, which makes interpretation difficult and begs for follow-up studies on the issue of dimension number.

Transparency of Dimensions.   Transparency refers to the extent to which participants can identify the appropriate behavior that is called for in each exercise (Kleinmann, 1993; Kleinmann et al., 1996). Low construct validity may be partially due to the candidates' inability to see demands for similar behavior across exercises. Explaining to the participants the behavioral demands in each exercise is one way of helping them to see consistency across exercises. For example, a leadership dimension can be made transparent to a candidate by describing leadership behavior and the exercises in which leadership will be assessed. Having knowledge of the behavior required in each exercise, the candidate should show more consistency. High consistency in relevant behaviors to the dimensions assessed should result in higher levels of both convergent and discriminant validity. As seen in the table, convergent validity was slightly better in the transparency condition (.30 vs. .35). However, discriminant validity did not improve (.60 vs. .61), and the HT–HM correlations actually increased slightly from .30 to .37, indicating a larger presence of halo error in the transparency condition.

The Nature of the Dimensions.   The nature of the dimensions in an assessment center requires that assessors make inferences about personal attributes from behavior. Some researchers have suggested dispensing with the inferences and focusing on the effectiveness of behavior in the context of the specific exercise being evaluated. The central focus of assessment centers would shift from internal personal attributes to effectiveness in specific situations. This suggestion has been made numerous times under various guises: managerial roles (Sackett & Dreher, 1982); work samples (Robertson et al., 1987; Silverman et al., 1986); role congruency (Russell, 1987; Russell & Domm, 1995); and task-specific assessment centers (Lowry, 1995). Admittedly, different labels could reflect slightly different intentions but all have been described as alternatives to trait- or person-centered ratings.

Joyce et al. (1994) created a task-based assessment center by reconceptualizing attribute-based dimensions as managerial functions. Managerial functions focus only on the actual content and structure of the work. Two examples of managerial functions used in this study were Handling

Information and Recruiting/Selecting. Their task-based assessment center consisted of seven managerial functions measured by four exercises and was compared to a traditional attribute-based assessment center. As shown in the table, despite the general reduction in the magnitude of the three types of coefficients, the relationship between the convergent and discriminant validity coefficients generally remained consistent and indicated no real improvement in the construct validity.

Subsequent to this study, some researchers have suggested Joyce et al. (1994) refutes the assertion that attribute-based assessments should be replaced by task-based assessments (Howard, 1997). However, it can be argued that the way in which Joyce and colleagues operationalized their task-based assessment as managerial functions was a cosmetic rather than substantial change because multiple dimensions were still observed and rated within each exercise. In addition some of their functions, such as Establishing Effective Work-Group Relationships, do not seem to require any less inferences about personal attributes than their person-centered dimension called Sensitivity, which they defined as, "using actions that indicate a consideration of the feelings and needs of others" (p. 112). There is yet to be a study treating the exercises themselves as tasks.

IS THE DOMINANCE OF EXERCISE FACTORS A PROBLEM?

The work reviewed in the previous section addressed the issue of "Can the problem of the dominance of exercise factors be fixed?" Here we turn to a discussion of conceptual perspectives that question whether the dominance of exercise factors is, in fact, a problem in need of fixing. Howard (1997) offers a thorough and thoughtful summary of a variety of such perspectives. Howard is a strong supporter of the within-dimension rating method, and she observes that the issue of the dominance of exercise factors can only be studied when the within-exercise rating method is used. She suggests that the commonly observed pattern of convergent and discriminant validity evidence is an artifact of the within-exercise rating method and that this pattern of evidence is not, in fact, a threat to assessment center validity.

One set of arguments deals with the pattern of convergent validity evidence. Howard (1997) notes that there are a variety of reasons why high convergence of dimension ratings across exercises should not be expected. First, exercises are not intended as parallel forms, and ratings of a given dimension across exercises are not intended as parallel measures. Dimensions are complex and multifaceted, and each exercise in which a dimension is evaluated is intended as a source of information about only some facets of a dimension. Second, exercises vary in the degree to which they provide opportunities for a candidate to exhibit dimension-relevant behavior. In fact, assessment centers that use the within-exercise rating method differ in the number of dimensions rated in each exercise. Some limit the dimensions rated in an exercise to those for which the exercise is a particularly rich source of information, whereas others obtain a rating of each dimension in each exercise. The latter would be expected to contribute to low convergence because some exercises are of limited relevance for some dimensions. A dimension rating in any given exercise may provide an unreliable estimate of the candidate's standing on the dimension and thus contribute to low convergence of dimension ratings across exercises. Third, MTMM matrix analysis treats each rating as an equally informative piece of information about a candidate's overall standing on a dimension. In fact, as noted previously, there are marked differences in the amount and quality of dimension-relevant information provided by the various exercises. Ideally, well-trained assessors know this and attend differentially to different exercises when making an overall dimension rating. Thus, low convergence may not indicate a failure to assess overall dimension performance appropriately.

Another set of arguments deals with the discriminant validity evidence. The key observation is that all ratings in a given exercise are made by a single assessor, with different assessors responsible for different exercises. Thus, when focusing on ratings of a given dimension across exercises, each rating is made by a different assessor; whereas when focusing on the set of dimension ratings made within an exercise, each rating is made by the same assessor. This stacks the deck in favor of obtaining high correlations within an exercise. The thought experiment of interest would be to see what would happen if either (a) a single assessor rated a candidate in all exercises, or (b) a unique assessor rated each dimension within an exercise. Howard (1997) believes that because within-exercise ratings are not independent, the independence assumption needed for the analysis of MTMM matrices is violated, and thus the MTMM analyses are not informative. She says, "Perhaps it is time to conclude that traditional construct validation techniques are inappropriate for assessment centers" (p. 27).

We acknowledge the value of many of the points summarized by Howard, though we do not share the conclusion she draws from them. We agree that low convergence of dimension ratings across exercises in and of itself is not proof that final dimension ratings do not measure the intended constructs.

We agree that within-exercise ratings of various dimensions made by one rater would be expected to produce higher correlations than would within-exercise ratings made by a different rater for each dimension. We note, though, that interrater reliabilities of about .70 have been reported for ratings of dimensions within an exercise (Huck, 1977). This value can be used to attenuate the discriminant validity values in Table 5.1 to provide an estimate of what the values would have been had independent assessors been used to rate each dimension within an exercise. This is done by multiplying the tabled values by .83 (the square root of .70). Even with attenuation, the discriminant validity values remain high.

We disagree with the conclusion that traditional construct validation techniques are inappropriate for assessment centers. A distinction we wish to make is one between viewing the analysis of MTMM matrices as providing useful and important insights into issues of the constructs underlying assessor judgments (a view we support) versus viewing such analyses as the sole basis for conclusions about construct validity (a view we do not support). Howard makes a persuasive case that it is possible that the overall dimension ratings in a given assessment center measure the intended dimensions well despite low convergence of dimension ratings across exercises and low differentiation among dimensions within an exercise. But evidence in support of this possibility is needed. Such evidence would take the form of external evidence of construct validity (e.g., evidence that overall dimension ratings produce patterns of convergent and discriminant validity with independent measures of the dimensions). Thornton, Tziner, Dahan, Clevenger, and Meir (1997) note that there is a dearth of such information and offer some generally supportive evidence for one assessment center using test scores and independent one-on-one assessments by psychologists. That center used the within-dimension rating method; similar evidence from centers using the within-exercise method would be very useful.

Although we agree that MTMM matrix analysis is not probative as to the construct validity of overall dimension ratings, we do find such analysis quite informative. We note that the patterns of MTMM matrix data vary substantially across centers. We highlight three prototypical patterns. In all three, there is low discrimination of dimension ratings within individual exercises. The first is a finding of zero or near-zero convergence of dimension ratings across exercises. We find this pattern particularly disconcerting—it is hard to argue that an overall dimension rating is meaningful without shared variance among the various exercise-specific ratings of the dimension. The second is a finding of a moderate degree of convergence of dimension ratings across exercises. It is in such situations that evidence for both dimension and exercise factors is found. The third is a finding of high correlation among all ratings, within and across exercises, and including HT–HM correlations. This is another pattern of great concern, suggesting a strong, global halo effect with little to no differentiation across either dimensions or exercises. We view examination of MTMM matrices as a useful diagnostic device for identifying the pattern of ratings characterizing a particular assessment center.

CONCLUSIONS

The persistent finding of strong exercise factors in the analysis of assessor ratings indicates that when a single assessor is asked to observe candidate performance in an exercise and then rate the candidate on a number of dimensions, the resulting ratings are highly influenced by a common factor. We believe that this factor reflects an overall evaluation of candidate effectiveness in the exercise. The persistence of exercise factors despite interventions such as the use of behavioral checklists, assessor training, and reductions in the number of dimensions to be rated in an exercise suggests that assessors do not make finely differentiated dimensional judgments.

This suggests an alternative possibility for assessment center design. If assessor judgments focus naturally on effectiveness of exercise performance, then one might design assessment centers in a manner consistent with this focus. Sackett and Dreher (1984) offered the suggestion that assessment centers might be conceptualized as a series of exercises designed to assess effectiveness in a variety of important job roles, such as negotiator, counselor, fact finder, and persuader, among many others. Building on taxonomies of managerial roles, they envisioned the use of job analytic procedures designed to identify the key managerial roles for the target job and the design of exercises to elicit behaviors reflecting performance in these roles. Scoring would be exercise-oriented with assessors reaching agreement as to effectiveness of performance in each exercise. Dimension labels could be used as guides to documenting and categorizing behavior within an exercise and as aides in giving feedback on effective and ineffective aspects of exercise performance. The dimension labels would be narrower and some might be exercise specific; no attempt to aggregate dimensional ratings across exercises would be made.

It is our sense that this suggestion has been misconstrued by some. Several studies have attempted to conceptualize exercises as simulations of job tasks or roles but have obtained dimension ratings within each task and investigated whether conceptualizing exercises in this fashion results in a change in patterns of convergent and discriminant validity (Joyce et al., 1994). The Sackett and Dreher proposal, however, was not intended as a suggestion toward a method for weakening or eliminating exercise factors; rather, it was a suggestion for an assessment center design that builds on the tendency of assessors to evaluate the effectiveness of exercise performance. The proposal renders the issue of convergent and discriminant validity moot, as it does not posit dimensions as characteristics to be aggregated across exercises. In that respect, it is parallel to the suggestion that the within-exercise rating method be abandoned in favor of the within-dimension method; neither the within-dimension rating method or the Sackett and Dreher exercise scoring proposal would result in data amenable to MTMM matrix analysis. An evaluation of the merits of these scoring methods would rest on other forms of evidence, such as correlations with external measures.

In summary, we have reviewed the now extensive body of evidence documenting the dominance of exercise factors in the postexercise judgments made by assessors and suggested that this reflects a pervasive tendency for an evaluation of overall effectiveness of exercise performance to influence ratings of individual dimensions. We have reviewed the growing body of literature on attempts to modify various aspects of the assessment center process in hopes of reducing or eliminating these exercise factors. The persistence of exercise factors is, we argue, further evidence of the pervasiveness of this tendency toward an evaluation of overall effectiveness. We have reviewed conceptual arguments that question whether this pattern of findings is, in fact, a threat to the traditional dimension-centered view of the assessment judgment process. Although persuasive arguments can be made that it remains possible for overall dimensions ratings to reflect their intended constructs despite these recurring pattern of convergent and discriminant validity data, evidence consistent with this possibility is limited to date. Competing suggestions have been offered in response to the convergent and discriminant validity data, both of which eliminate postexercise dimension ratings. One is to use within-dimension scoring, consistent with the original AT&T model; the other is to aggregate evaluations of effectiveness of exercise performance. We view continuing to pursue the merits of these different suggestions as a worthwhile, though difficult, endeavor. The criterion-related validity evidence for assessment centers indicates that although mean validity is substantial, so is unexplained variability across studies. Variations in the assessor judgment process are among the possible contributors to this variability.

REFERENCES

Arthur, W., Woehr, D., & Maldegan, R. (2000). Convergent and discriminant validity of assessment center dimensions: A conceptual and empirical re-examination of the assessment center construct-related validity paradox. *Journal of Management, 26*, 813–835.

American Educational Research Association, American Psychological Association, & National Council on Management and Education (1999). *Standards for educational and psychological testing.* Washington, DC: American Educational Research Association.

Borman, W. C. (1982). Validity of behavioral assessment for predicting military recruiter performance. *Journal of Applied Psychology, 74*, 957–963.

Bray, D. W., & Campbell, R. J. (1968). Selection of salesmen by means of an assessment center. *Journal of Applied Psychology, 52*, 36–41.

Bray, D. W., & Grant, D. L. (1966). The assessment center in the measurement of potential for business management. *Psychological Monographs, 80*, 1–27.

Bycio, P., Alvares, K. M., & Hahn, J. (1987). Situational specificity in assessment center ratings: A confirmatory factor analysis. *Journal of Applied Psychology, 72*, 463–474.

Chan, D. (1996). Criterion and construct validation of an assessment center. *Journal of Occupational and Organizational Psychology, 69*, 167–182.

Donahue, L. M., Truxillo, D. M., Cornwell, J. M., & Gerrity, M. J. (1997). Assessment center construct validity and behavioral checklists: Some additional findings. *Journal of Social Behavior and Personality, 12*, 85–108.

Fleenor, J. W. (1996). Constructs and developmental assessment centers: Further troubling empirical findings. *Journal of Business and Psychology, 10*, 319–335.

Gaugler, B. B., Rosenthal, D. B., Thornton, G. C., & Bentson, C. (1987). Meta-analysis of assessment center validity. *Journal of Applied Psychology, 72*, 493–511.

Gaugler, B. B., & Thornton, G. C. (1989). Number of assessment center dimensions as a determinant of assessor accuracy. *Journal of Applied Psychology, 74*, 611–618.

Guion, R. M. (1998). *Assessment, measurement, and prediction for personnel decisions.* Mahwah, NJ: Lawrence Erlbaum Associates.

Harris, M. M., Becker, A. S., & Smith, D. E. (1993). Does the assessment center scoring method affect the cross-situational consistency of ratings? *Journal of Applied Psychology, 78*, 675–678.

Hinrichs, J. R. (1978). An eight-year follow-up of a management assessment center. *Journal of Applied Psychology, 63*, 596–601.

Howard, A. (1997). A reassessment of assessment centers: Challenges for the 21st century. *Journal of Social Behavior and Personality, 12*, 13–52.

Huck, J. R. (1977). The research base. In J. L. Moses & W. C. Byham (Eds.), *Applying the assessment center method.* Elmsford, New York: Pergamon.

Joyce, L. W., Thayer, P. W., & Pond, S. B. (1994). Managerial functions: An alternative to traditional assessment center dimensions? *Personnel Psychology, 47*, 109–121.

Kleinmann, M. (1993). Are rating dimensions in assessment centers transparent for participants? Consequences for criterion and construct validity. *Journal of Applied Psychology, 78*, 988–993.

Kleinmann, M., & Köller, O. (1997). Construct validity of assessment centers: Appropriate use of confirmatory factor analysis and suitable construction principles. *Journal of Social Behavior and Personality, 12*, 65–84.

Kleinmann, M., Kuptsch, C., & Köller, O. (1996). Transparency: A necessary requirement for the construct validity of assessment centers. *Applied Psychology: An International Review, 45*, 67–84.

Kudisch, J. D., Ladd, R. T., & Dobbins, G. H. (1997). New evidence on the construct validity of diagnostic assessment centers: The findings may not be so troubling after all. *Journal of Social Behavior and Personality, 12*, 129–144.

Lowry, P. E. (1995). The assessment center process: Assessing leadership in the public sector. *Public Personnel Management, 24*, 443–449.

Reilly, R. R., Henry, S., & Smither, J. W. (1990). An examination of the effects of using behavioral checklists on the construct validity of assessment center ratings. *Personnel Psychology, 43,* 71–84.

Robertson, I., Gratton, L., & Sharpley, D. (1987). The psychometric properties and design of managerial assessment centres: Dimensions into exercises won't go. *Journal of Occupational and Organizational Psychology, 60,* 187–195.

Russell, C. J. (1985). Individual decision processes in an assessment center. *Journal of Applied Psychology, 70,* 737–746.

Russell, C. J. (1987). Person characteristics versus role congruency explanations for assessment center ratings. *Academy of Management Journal, 30,* 817–826.

Russell, C. J., & Domm, D. R. (1995). Two field tests of an explanation of assessment centre validity. *Journal of Occupational and Organizational Psychology, 68,* 25–47.

Sackett, P. R., & Dreher, G. F. (1982). Constructs and assessment center dimensions: Some troubling empirical findings. *Journal of Applied Psychology, 67,* 401–410.

Sackett, P. R., & Dreher, G. F. (1984). Situation specificity of behavior and assessment center validation strategies: A rejoinder to Neidig and Neidig. *Journal of Applied Psychology, 69,* 187–190.

Sackett, P. R., & Hakel, M. D. (1979). Temporal stability and individual differences in using assessment information to form overall ratings. *Organizational Behavior and Human Performance, 23,* 120–137.

Sackett, P. R., & Harris, M. M. (1988). A further examination of the constructs underlying assessment center ratings. *Journal of Business and Psychology, 3,* 214–229.

Sagie, A., & Magnezy, R. (1997). Assessor type, number of distinguishable dimension categories, and assessment centre construct validity. *Journal of Occupational and Organizational Psychology, 70,* 103–108.

Schliecher, D. J., Day, D. V., Mayes, B. T., & Riggio, R. E. (1999, April). *A new frame of reference for Frame of Reference Training: Enhancing the construct validity of assessment centers.* Paper presented at the Fourteenth Annual Conference for the Society for Industrial and Organizational Psychology, Atlanta, GA.

Schneider, J. R., & Schmitt, N. (1992). An exercise design approach to understanding assessment center dimension and exercise constructs. *Journal of Applied Psychology, 77,* 32–41.

Shore, T. H., Thornton, G. C., & Shore, L. M. (1990). Construct validity of two categories of assessment center dimension ratings. *Personnel Psychology, 43,* 101–116.

Silverman, W. H., Dalessio, A., Woods, S. B., & Johnson, R. L. (1986). Influence of assessment center methods on assessors' ratings. *Personnel Psychology, 39,* 565–578.

Spychalski, A. C., Quinones, M. A., Gaugler, B. B., & Pohley, K. (1997). A survey of assessment center practices in organizations in the United States. *Personnel Psychology, 50,* 71–90.

Thornton, G. C. (1992). *Assessment centers in human resource management.* Reading, MA: Addison-Wesley.

Thornton, G. C., Tziner, A., Dahan, M., Clevenger, J. P., & Meir, E. (1997). Construct validity of assessment center judgments: Analyses of the behavioral reporting method. *Journal of Social Behavior and Personality, 12,* 109–128.

Wollowick, H. B., & McNamara, W. J. (1969). Relationship of the component of an assessment center to management success. *Journal of Applied Psychology, 53,* 348–352.

III

Appraisal

The two chapters in this section on appraisal examine how person perception influences judgments of others' job performance. In chapter 6, Janet Barnes-Farrell provides a comprehensive overview of the influence of person perception on performance appraisal. She outlines the primary cognitive tasks that form the underpinnings of performance measurement, highlights social cognition processes that guide judgments and ratings of worker performance effectiveness, and identifies features of performance appraisal situations that affect the nature and difficulty of appraisal tasks. For example, she explains how social stereotypes, categorization, and attribution processes affect appraisals. The chapter concludes with challenges in designing performance appraisal methods that reduce the effects of irrelevant information and biases and increase appraisal accuracy and value. This is made more complicated by changing organizational environments, such as such flatter organizations and geographically dispersed units.

Chapter 7 examines an appraisal method that has become increasingly popular in organizations: multisource feedback (MSF) surveys (i.e., 360-degree feedback). Ratings may be obtained from bosses, peers, subordinates, customers, and self-ratings so that all perspectives may be available. Sometimes this is limited to upward feedback from subordinates. This technique has become popular because it recognizes that input about performance cannot be limited to the supervisor's perspective and that other viewpoints are needed for a complete picture. This is especially the case because the manager's job has become increasingly complex with the advent of new technology, geographically dispersed work groups, and multiple components of the managerial role. MSF surveys provide a rich source of information to influence behavior change and performance improvement. The results may be used for both development purposes (i.e., to give managers feedback to help guide their development) and for administration (to make pay and job assignment decisions based on the results). In this chapter, Michael Mount and Steven Scullen examine how person perception and social cognition influence the ratings process and the use of the ratings. In particular, their chapter covers five major areas: (a) a brief overview of MSF practices; (b) how person perception and interpersonal judgment research facilitate our understanding of the factors that influence performance ratings; (c) a review of research on the psychometric properties of MSF ratings, such as mean levels of ratings and interrater agreement; (d) the results of recent research on the underlying structure of performance ratings to determine what MSF ratings actually measure; and (e) a discussion of the implications of the research results for the application of MSF ratings.

Mount and Scullen note that the performance rating process requires raters to process and remember a substantial amount of information. Person perception processes allow raters to form cognitive frameworks (schemas or prototypes) to guide the processing of social information. Schemas reduce the cognitive demands of the rating process, allowing raters to easily categorize, weigh, and average bits of information to form an overall impression. Employees develop schemas of what they expect from their supervisors, peers, subordinates, and customers. These prototypes may be based on implicit personality theories and stereotypes, and they affect the way people attend to, encode, store, and retrieve information about others. Regarding the psychometric nature of multisource ratings, Mount and Scullen's review of research reveals that on average, self-ratings tend to be higher than ratings from bosses, peers, or subordinates but mean differences among the latter three sources are relatively small. Whether recipients of MSF change their behavior and improve their performance as a result of the feedback depends, in part, on whether the raters and ratees are held accountable for the information provided and the use of that information to bring about positive change.

Mount and Scullen show that performance ratings may be influenced by ratee general performance, ratee dimensional performance, idiosyncratic rater effects, rater perspective effects, and random measurement error. Their research shows that rater bias is very large and accounts for the most variance in ratings. Within this category, the idiosyncratic component is the most important determinant of the ratings. The second component, perspective effects, is smaller than the idiosyncratic component. Idiosyncratic effects, such as halo (the perception of one performance dimension influencing the perception of other performance dimensions), do not necessarily contaminate ratings with irrelevant information. Rather, they may represent one rater's viewpoint. This information may be especially useful in suggesting directions for development even if the information shouldn't be used to draw general conclusions about the ratee's performance. Because raters don't agree much with one another, caution must be used in generalizing results from one rater to another. Mount and Scullen support the common practice in MSF programs of aggregating ratings within role (e.g., reporting the average peer rating, the average subordinate rating, etc.) because these ratings capture components that are unique to the role of the rater and different from other perspectives.

6

Performance Appraisal: Person Perception Processes and Challenges

Janet L. Barnes-Farrell
University of Connecticut

Whether it occurs as an informal process or as part of an elaborate formal performance management system, the evaluation of worker performance by supervisors and others in the work environment is an integral part of work life. Clearly, the success of an organization depends, in part, on the effectiveness with which organizational members carry out their work responsibilities. Formal evaluations of the contributions of individual workers provide important information that can guide decisions and actions aimed at increasing organizational effectiveness. In addition, the interdependent nature of worker, coworker, and supervisor work roles provides a natural incentive for supervisors and coworkers to be sensitive to the performance of other workers because it may have implications for their own ability to accomplish work and reap organizational rewards. Thus, informal appraisal of worker performance is likely to occur on a continuing basis, even in the absence of formal performance appraisal systems.

Performance appraisal can be conceptualized as incorporating two related, but distinguishable, phases. The initial phase, performance measurement, includes processes that culminate in informal and formal evaluations of work performance. Performance measurement comprises both private judgments about work performance and formal assessments of worker performance effectiveness; the latter generally take the form of ratings or narrative comments about worker performance that are recorded as part of a formal performance appraisal system. The second phase includes the ensuing impact of those evaluations on organizational decisions, on appraiser interactions with those they evaluate, on worker reactions to performance appraisal, and on work behaviors. Several important issues relevant to the "aftermath" of performance measurement (e.g., feedback, coaching, and development) are discussed in other chapters of this book and will not be addressed here.

This chapter focuses on the performance measurement phase of performance appraisal, with an emphasis on the ways that person perception and social cognition processes relate to the problem of arriving at high-quality judgments and ratings about the work effectiveness of others. My goals are threefold: (a) to outline the primary cognitive tasks that form the underpinnings of performance measurement; (b) to highlight social cognition processes that guide judgments and ratings of worker performance effectiveness; and (c) to identify important features of performance appraisal situations that affect the nature and difficulty of appraisal tasks.

IS PERSON PERCEPTION AN APPROPRIATE VEHICLE FOR UNDERSTANDING PERFORMANCE APPRAISAL?

The argument that person perception and social cognition processes are relevant to performance appraisal and the quality of performance measurements is not a new one (cf., DeNisi, Cafferty, & Meglino, 1984; Ilgen, Barnes-Farrell, & McKellin, 1993; Ilgen & Feldman, 1983; Landy & Farr, 1980). Performance appraisal maps readily onto the input-process-output (IPO) framework suggested by Klimoski and Donahue in chapter 1 of this book. In order to understand performance appraisal as an organizational application of person perception, it may be helpful to translate some critical features of their framework into the context of performance appraisal.

Cast in terms of the conceptual framework outlined by Klimoski and Donahue (2000), the *social perceiver* in performance appraisal situations is the rater/appraiser responsible for evaluating worker performance. Typically, the person who is expected to take on the task of performance measurement is a worker's direct supervisor or manager. Increasingly, however, organizations have begun to call upon peers and team members to provide evaluations of their coworkers' performance and contributions to work-group functioning. Furthermore, organizations that use performance appraisal as the basis for discussions about worker skill development often call on employees to engage in self-evaluation of performance. Organizations that choose to emphasize the accountability of their managers to the effective management and development of those they supervise may ask subordinates to provide judgments about aspects of their managers' performance. Thus, the task of performance evaluation is by no means one that is limited to managers and supervisors.

The *social target*, in turn, is the worker whose performance is being evaluated. As implied by the description of social perceivers, the target is generally in a role subordinate to the perceiver but may also be a supervisor (in the case of upward evaluations), a coworker or team member (in the case of peer evaluations), or the worker (in the case of self-evaluations).

There are a number of *consequences for the perceiver* that are particularly relevant to performance measurement situations. For example, appraisers are likely to consider the extent to which their judgments and judgment strategies: (a) allow them to carry out tasks more efficiently; (b) imply the need for additional monitoring of performance; (c) provide them with the ability to avoid unpleasant interactions; and (d) allow them to maintain a positive self-image. Because judgments and judgment strategies frequently enhance some outcomes at the expense of others, the importance of each of these consequences to perceivers has implications for the strategies they use as they address the problem of making and communicating evaluations of target performance.

Primary *consequences for the target* are performance ratings and written comments that formally document a worker's performance effectiveness, as well as informal evaluations that affect the continuing quality of interpersonal relationships between perceiver and target. In addition, there are a host of potential secondary consequences for the target that emanate from the way performance measurements are used by managers and organizations. These range from personal attitudes and behavioral responses to organizational rewards and punishments.

In summary, performance appraisal relies heavily on the ability and willingness of a social perceiver (the appraiser) to make interpersonal judgments about the qualities and capabilities of a social target (the worker), based on social, behavioral, and physical cues available to the perceiver. Furthermore, those judgments have consequences for the perceiver, the target, and the nature of their social relationship.

Accomplishing Performance Measurement: Appraisers' Tasks

To make useful, accurate judgments of work effectiveness, appraisers must tackle a number of cognitively demanding tasks. These can be characterized as three collections of tasks that appraisers carry out as they develop judgments about worker performance: information gathering, information storage, and information retrieval.

Information Gathering. This includes direct observation of worker behaviors and collecting information from alternative sources when direct observation is not feasible. Keep in mind that information gathering may be done in an active, systematic fashion, or as is often the case, may occur in a relatively haphazard way. Much information that appraisers have at their disposal is acquired passively: It is "encountered" during regular interactions with workers or through unsolicited comments and reports from others. When information is gathered in this way, the opportunity exists for relevant information to be overlooked, or for some behaviors and information to receive undue attention. Thus, information gathering tasks reflect the need to identify and attend to relevant information, the need to recognize and screen out "noise" relative to the task of measuring worker performance, and the need to seek additional information when appropriate. As noted later, these needs may conflict with other tasks and goals of the perceiver.

Information Storage. These tasks include organizing information into meaningful categories, integrating information with previous knowledge about the worker, and storing information in ways that will allow the perceiver to access it at a later point in time. Storage tasks largely reflect two important features of performance appraisal: (a) the memory-based nature of performance appraisal; and (b) the need to efficiently "sort out" out the bits and pieces of information that one acquires about workers during daily interactions with them in a way that allows later use of that information or integration with an emerging interpersonal perception of the worker's skills, capabilities, and motivation.

Information Retrieval. These tasks include the recall of general and specific information about workers and judgments and comparison of worker information with organizational standards for performance. These tasks are particularly pertinent to formal performance appraisal because formal performance measurement generally requires appraisers to reflect on information and informal evaluations of the worker that have accumulated over a fairly long period of time and may require appraisers to document their evaluations with specific instances of performance that illustrate or elaborate on the evaluation.

KEY PERSON PERCEPTION PROCESSES

Each of the classes of tasks identified previously represents a cognitive challenge to those who appraise work performance. Interpersonal perception processes affect the way we handle those challenges. Several social cognition processes have particular significance for performance appraisal. The functions each of these processes serve and critical issues that they raise for accurate performance measurement are described further.

Selective Attention

These processes guide perceivers in filtering information as it is encountered. They primarily reflect responses to human information processing limitations and the need or preference to devote cognitive resources to other tasks. The functional value of selective attention processes resides in their ability to focus attention on relevant social targets or relevant behavior while ignoring information that represents noise relative to the appraiser's information processing goals.

Because information that is ignored cannot affect performance measurements and information that is attended to has the potential to have great impact on performance measurements, the critical question with respect to performance appraisal is: What is considered relevant? This is primarily a function of the appraiser's knowledge of the task at hand and the appraiser's goals. An appraiser's familiarity with job requirements and behaviors that reflect effective and ineffective performance guide him or her in identifying behaviors and cues that are relevant to the task of performance measurement; selective attention processes then focus attention on those features of a worker's behavior. Unfamiliarity with or confusion about the behaviors that are relevant to performance can lead raters to focus on nonrelevant aspects of a worker's behavior or cues (e.g., age) that are unrelated to performance effectiveness. Likewise, appraisers' particular information processing goals (e.g., identification of performance problems vs. recognition of potential to advance in the organization) allow them to discriminate between signal and noise relative to their goals. The goal of identifying performance problems signals alertness to negative information. Furthermore, it is likely to direct additional attention to the behavior of particular workers who have a history of performance problems, while relegating competent performers to the status of background noise. Alternatively, the goal of identifying "stars" signifies that appraisers should monitor the environment for positive information.

Schema-Based Processing

This represents a vehicle for interpreting information and organizing information in meaningful ways. As a framework for organizing, interpreting, and retrieving information, schema-based processing affects the kind and amount of information gathering appraisers engage in (i.e., it guides attention and signals when appraisers have sufficient information to move on to other tasks or other targets), the classification of targets and behaviors for future reference, and the quality of information that appraisers recall.

Schemas, which are organized around prototypical instances of a particular category (e.g., outstanding performer), may be elaborate or minimal and are subject to modification as perceivers learn about their environment and their social targets (Fiske, 1993). For example, as appraisers develop an understanding of "effective performance," their schemas regarding effective performance are revised; similarly, schemas that represent individual workers are gradually revised as managers become better acquainted with their subordinates. Furthermore, features of the interpersonal environment (e.g., appraiser characteristics, goals, and moods) affect the relative accessibility of different categories and their associated schema. This means that information may be interpreted and stored differently as a function of which schema is invoked in a particular situation (Wyer & Srull, 1994).

The functional value of schema-based processing is that it allows appraisers to interpret target behavior quickly and efficiently by matching features of target behavior to salient features of a schema. When there is reasonable correspondence between observed behavior and an available schema, the target's behavior can be interpreted readily without the need for additional monitoring or cognitive effort. Difficulties in matching the characteristics of observed behavior with available schemas signal the need for a more careful consideration of the target's behavior. This may trigger additional information gathering, revision of current schemas, or attribution processes that can assist in "sensemaking." Difficulties in arriving at ready interpretation of behaviors also tend to increase the extent to which particular targets and behaviors are memorable, and this has implications for the outcome of recall and evaluation tasks.

Social Stereotypes

These are closely related to schema-based processing in the sense that they provide a vehicle for drawing inferences on the basis of limited information. Readily observed cues such as gender or age can be used to access a wealth of expectations about other features of the target. In particular, stereotypes are likely to influence information gathering and information storage when (a) social targets are readily identified as members of a group for which the perceiver has developed stereotypic expectations, (b) there are competing demands on the appraiser's time, and (c) the consequences of failing to gather complete information are minor relative to other consequences of interest to the perceiver. It should be noted that invoking stereotypes and other cognitive shortcuts is not necessarily a bad thing. Stereotypes allow one to make reasonable estimates about unobserved behavior—which is exactly the task that many overloaded appraisers face. Furthermore, although stereotypes that reflect beliefs about a social group will necessarily contain inaccuracies with respect to descriptions of individuals, there is considerable evidence that many social stereotypes represent a very reasonable "starting" point for estimating the characteristics and behaviors of individuals who belong to the social group that the stereotype represents (Lee, Jussim, & McCauley, 1995; Madon, et al., 1998). Moreover, perceivers rarely ignore individuating information when it is provided to them. As such, the most reasonable response to concerns about the influence of stereotypes on appraisals is to (a) design situations that minimize the need to rely on cognitive shortcuts and (b) actively encourage appraisers to seek individuating information.

Social Categorization

This is the process of recognizing distinctions among social targets and using those distinctions to classify targets as members of a group (i.e., classifying others as similar or dissimilar to oneself). The functional value of social categorization is that it allows simplification of the social world by dividing it into groups of individuals who can be seen and treated as relatively similar to one another. Social categorization also has implications for other person perception processes, including attentional processes and stereotyping. For example, perceivers are more likely to rely on stereotypes to help them draw inferences about social targets who are classified as "different" from themselves along some salient dimension (e.g., age, gender, and values; Koltuv, 1962).

Attribution Processes

In contrast to the cognitive efficiency provided by schema-based processing and stereotyping, attribution processes are more controlled, effortful processes that reflect an attempt to understand the causes of behaviors that are not easily categorized or interpreted. In the context of performance appraisal, examples of attribution processes include the use of cognitive heuristics (e.g., availability and representativeness heuristics) to draw inferences about "ownership" for success and failure and to draw inferences about worker ability and motivation. These kinds of inferences are particularly pertinent to performance appraisal because work accomplishments represent a combination of worker contributions and work-system contributions. Appraisers must diagnose the extent to which work accomplishments can be traced to the capabilities and efforts of workers versus the enhancing or hindering effect of the work environment (Carson, Cardy, & Dobbins, 1991). Attribution processes provide strategies to do just that.

Other Person Perception Processes

A number of other person perception processes have been linked to performance judgments as well. These include *framing* and *priming* (processes that reflect the impact of expectations on attention to information in the environment and encourage perceivers to interpret information in a manner consistent with their expectation); *anchoring* and *adjustment* (calibration processes that help perceivers interpret new information in light of previous information); and *contrast* and *assimilation* (processes that increase or decrease the perceived similarity between social objects).

THE APPRAISAL CONTEXT: SPECIAL FEATURES OF PERFORMANCE MEASUREMENT

The significance of each of the processes noted previously depends, to a large extent, on the context in which appraisers are expected to carry out the tasks that were described. Performance appraisal takes place under conditions that include significant time constraints and competing demands that limit an appraiser's ability to devote attention to the task at hand. Furthermore, appraisers are not uninvolved independent observers—they are (often) supervisors or (less often) coworkers who have ongoing social interactions with the individuals they appraise. They have prior expectations about the competencies and motivation of individual workers, beliefs about the way appraisal information will be used, and concerns about the impact of appraisals on their ability to maintain effective working relationships. These features create particular challenges for the ability and willingness of raters to carry out the tasks involved in performance measurement. Important aspects of the terrain of performance appraisal in organizational settings are outlined, with consideration given to the kinds of person perception processes and strategies they invoke.

Time Constraints

Above all, it should be recognized that appraisal almost always takes place in an environment that includes significant competing demands on an appraiser's time and attention. Bluntly stated, many managers experience significant work overload; they simply don't have time to get everything done. Furthermore, the consequences of devoting less time to the appraisal process are often less salient than the consequences of devoting less time to other work responsibilities. Thus, many appraisers have real constraints on their time that create situations where they are not able to devote large blocks of time to appraisal tasks, and they are not willing to reallocate precious time to these tasks because there are few incentives (and many disincentives) to do so. As a result, there may be considerable pressure to use judgment strategies that minimize the amount of time an appraiser devotes to appraisal tasks. The use of social categorization, stereotypes, and schema-based processing are natural consequences of the need to be efficient.

The practical problem for those who design and implement appraisal systems is to recognize how to save time without sacrificing the quality of performance measurement. This is a recurring theme for which there are no simple solutions. However, two points are worth noting before going further. First, organizations must recognize that choosing to spend time on performance appraisal tasks always comes at a cost. They must ensure that there is an appropriate payoff. In other words, they must develop cultures and reward systems that encourage appraisers to reallocate their time and mental energies to accurate performance measurement. Second, it is reassuring to remember that cognitive simplification strategies can be quite functional; they do not always lead to declines in the quality of performance measurement. The key is to help appraisers recognize when it is important to engage in more effortful strategies and encourage them to do so when it is appropriate.

Multiple Targets

Appraisal frequently requires the evaluation of multiple targets. Managers designated to formally assess worker performance often have so many formal direct reports that it is not feasible to engage in elaborate, systematic observation of all workers' performance. Instead, they must develop satisficing strategies. They may rely heavily on a few cues that are then supplemented by information drawn from stereotypes. Another way of handling this problem is by devoting more attention to some targets than others. Managers may choose to focus their observational efforts on those workers who appear to have performance difficulties; alternatively, they may choose to focus most of their observational resources on the identification of talent.

Efficient judgment strategies that allow a rater to spend more time on some targets than others are one possible outgrowth of this situation. This has particular significance for the way appraisers manage information gathering tasks. Selective attention, schema-based processing, and reliance on social stereotypes all represent vehicles for managing this problem. Each of these processes provide appraisers with tools for gathering "just enough" information to draw reasonable inferences about workers' performance effectiveness. The challenge for appraisers is to ensure that such cognitive efficiencies do not lead them to overlook important information or to give short shrift to monitoring the performance of particular workers whom they consider to be "known quantities." In this regard, devices that systematically structure observational opportunities and observational goals for all workers can assist appraisers in recognizing deficiencies and disparities in information gathering for members of large work groups.

In addition to the obvious time considerations required by the assessment of multiple targets, a context is created in which evaluation of one worker's performance cannot be divorced from perceptions of other workers in the group. This can lead to the development of evaluation strategies that emphasize comparisons among workers rather than comparisons between workers and organizational standards. Furthermore, individual appraisers may adopt strategies that minimize apparent differences among work-group members (e.g., for purposes of encouraging cooperation) or strategies that emphasize differences among work-group members (e.g., for purposes of encouraging competition and rewarding outstanding performance).

Practitioners who design formal performance appraisal systems should give careful thought to these issues. When the performance of other work-group members serves as a comparison standard during performance measurement, those measurements are only meaningful in the context of that work group. If the primary concern is measurement of performance relative to some organizational standards, such internal calibration effects may create problems. For example, in high-performing work groups, workers whose performance level is at odds with the rest of the group will be at a decided disadvantage. The contributions of workers who exhibit perfectly adequate performance relative to organizational standards are likely to be undervalued (Mitchell & Liden, 1982). The performance of other workers will tend to shift the "standard" for competent performance upwards. Furthermore, the target worker's performance will be perceptually contrasted with the exemplary contributions of other work-group members, distorting measurements of his or her performance further downward. Similarly, workers who perform competently in the context of a relatively inept work group will likely benefit from the contrast between their distinctively higher performance levels and that of other work-group members (the so-called "frog pond" effect). These problems can be minimized by designing measurement instruments that provide clear, unambiguous examples of performance that reflect organizational standards. In addition, appraisers can be encouraged to structure the process of performance measurement so that it mitigates these effects. For example, if the goal is to find ways of minimizing comparisons with others workers (in the interest of focusing on comparison with organizational standards), appraisers may be advised to evaluate all aspects of a worker's performance before moving on to the next worker rather than evaluating all workers with respect to each area of performance in turn.

Insufficient Information

Appraisers are often required to carry out performance measurement tasks in the relative absence of relevant information. This may occur for a variety of reasons, many of them structural. For example, in team-based organizations, managers are often required to evaluate the performance of individual team members, although their jobs may be structured so that team members interact only rarely with the individual who has formal responsibility for evaluations. As a result, the appraiser may only see the products of a team's work efforts, with little opportunity to observe the contributions of individual team members to those products. When appraisers must carry out performance measurement tasks in an information-scarce context, cognitive strategies that allow them to draw inferences on the basis of limited information are likely to emerge. For example, easily observable cues such as gender or age may be used to classify targets in ways that allow an appraiser to draw on stereotypes about members of that social group as the basis for extrapolating to unobserved classes of behavior and performance. Note that although the processes that are invoked for information-scarce environments are similar to those invoked in the interest of cognitive efficiency, there is an important distinction to be made between the two situations. In one case, appraisers are unwilling to invest the time necessary to gather additional information; in the other case, appraisers do not have the opportunity to observe relevant information. Thus, they have different implications for practitioners concerned with designing effective performance measurement systems.

The trend toward geographically dispersed work groups, virtual teams, and telework is likely to increase the prominence of this feature of performance appraisal because they reduce opportunities for direct observation. Direct observation in these emerging work environments is generally limited to brief, infrequent contacts. Unless direct observation is supplemented with information from other sources, appraisers are forced to rely on prior experiences, stereotypic expectations, or inferences drawn from the quality and quantity of work products. Some creative solutions include taking advantage of technological innovations to increase observational opportunities, systematically gathering information from indirect sources (e.g., coworkers), and developing monitoring systems that rely on worker self-reports. However, it is important to be aware of the fact that information drawn from other sources may be treated differently when appraisers integrate what they have learned about a worker into an evaluation. For example, information based on direct observation has a greater influence on evaluations than information provided by others (Golden & Barnes-Farrell, 1999) and information provided from computerized performance monitoring systems is processed differently than visual data (Kulik & Ambrose, 1993).

Information Overload

Ironically, appraisal situations are also frequently characterized by an over-abundance of information. Appraisers are simply not equipped to process the volume of information they encounter in a typical work day. Of course, much of this information is not relevant to the task at hand. Selective attention processes and schema-based processing provide a means of responding to this problem. As pointed out earlier in the discussion of selective attention processes, the key here is the need to be able to distinguish between relevant and nonrelevant information. The design of performance measurement instruments and rater training programs can explicitly address this issue by clarifying what behaviors appraisers should direct their attention to.

Uneven Information

Some appraiser–target relationships have a fairly long history, whereas others represent fairly brief acquaintances; furthermore, the quality of the relationship between an appraiser and a target affects the appraiser's choice to spend time with the target or to spend time monitoring the performance of the target, and the target's choice to "share" information with the appraiser. Moreover, some aspects of worker performance are more readily observed than others. For these reasons, appraisers generally have more information at their disposal about some workers than others and more information about some performance domains than others.

Stereotypes, schemas, and expectations all guide the evaluation process in these situations. As in the case of insufficient information, these processes are a means of making inferential leaps from the known to the unknown.

Memory Demands

In the case of formal performance appraisal systems, appraisers are generally expected to measure performance that has taken place during a window of time that often ranges from 6 months to 1 year. Thus, the memory demands associated with performance appraisal are substantial; they create particular challenges for information storage tasks and information retrieval tasks.

For information storage, the challenge is to develop strategies for classifying people and information in ways that will allow them to be recalled in a relatively intact fashion. As described earlier, prototypes and schemas form the classificatory schemes that are used to encode and store information about workers' behaviors and performance. Thus, the richness and relevance of appraisers' schemas are important because they include information about specific expected behavioral tendencies; when there is a close match between targets and the categories to which they are assigned, it will be possible to reconstruct reasonably accurate representations of the behavioral observations that gave rise to a particular evaluation.

Appraiser strategies and appraisal system design features that provide cues and assistance in accurately recalling relevant information increase the likelihood that performance ratings will reflect a representative sample of worker behaviors. For example, frame-of-reference (FOR) rater training helps appraisers to develop schemas that accurately represent organizationally important aspects of work performance, rather than relying on idiosyncratic ideas about performance standards and the behaviors that signify them (Woehr & Huffcutt, 1994). Similarly, performance evaluation instruments that include specific examples of the kinds of behaviors relevant to different performance requirements can cue the recall of information in that domain. In addition, tools such as behavior diaries provide timely records of appraisers' observations that can lessen memory demands when they are called on to provide performance measurements at a later point in time.

Time-Based Aspects of Target Performance

Performance appraisal reflects the evaluation of patterns of behaviors that unfold over time. This implies that appraisers have a task that is more complex than simply diagnosing the level of performance a worker exhibits. In addition, appraisers track and evaluate patterns of performance over time. They must cope with the problems of distinguishing among typical, average, and maximum performance; recognizing and interpreting the meaning of variability in worker performance; and interpreting the meaning of systematic patterns of increasing or decreasing performance.

These are important issues because different patterns of performance lead to different evaluations and different inferences about worker capabilities and motivation. There are at least two important person perception processes that are relevant to this problem. First, attribution processes are invoked as appraisers try to make sense of patterns of performance. Stable patterns of performance are generally evaluated more positively than variable patterns of performance (DeNisi & Stevens, 1981). On the other hand, variability in performance also leads to inferences about the potential for higher performance in the future. Thus, a worker whose pattern of performance is fairly erratic, ranging from substandard to truly exceptional, may be diagnosed as an underachiever with high potential but low motivation.

Second, the manner in which performance information is initially processed has implications for the recognition of patterns. On-line evaluation processes that encourage raters to immediately process behavioral observations in terms of their evaluative implications tend to produce an evaluation of work performance that is reinforced or revised by new information that is acquired. This would tend to minimize recognition of patterns of performance because new information is simply integrated into a revised diagnosis of the worker's performance level. In contrast, appraisal systems that are designed to encourage raters to focus on observing behaviors while "suspending judgment" provide conditions that are more likely to allow patterns of behavior to be recognized. In practice, this may be difficult to achieve because work environments appear to provide natural encouragement for evaluative processing of most behavioral information (Martin & Klimoski, 1990). The matter is further complicated because prior evaluations of performance also affect the kind of information to which appraisers attend, so they may ignore new information about a worker's performance unless it is sufficiently discrepant from their current assessment that it warrants investigation.

The design of appraisal systems can directly incorporate features that assist appraisers with the problem of systematically recognizing and responding to patterns of worker performance. For example, measurement systems like the Distributional Measurement system developed by Kane (1986) directly incorporate vehicles for measuring both the level and the variability in performance. In addition, tools for recording relevant instances of performance can be introduced as a way of helping appraisers to track and recognize patterns of performance as they unfold. For example, behavior diaries (cf. DeNisi, Robbins, & Cafferty, 1989) provide a record of appraiser observations regarding critical employee behaviors. Unfortunately, behavior diaries and similar monitoring techniques may be difficult to implement effectively because of their cumbersome, time consuming nature. Technological innovations such as on-line diaries, electronic performance monitoring techniques, and computerized databases of worker self-reports provide the potential to help managers collect and manage this information in a fairly efficient way.

Multiple Goals

Performance appraisal systems are almost always designed with multiple purposes in mind (Cleveland, Murphy, & Williams, 1989). Commonly, organizations invest in formal performance appraisal systems in the hope that they will be able to use performance measurements to make interpersonal distinctions among workers that can be used as input to compensation decisions. They also propose to use the appraisal system to identify individual workers' areas of performance strengths and weaknesses, which will serve as the basis for developmental feedback and performance coaching. Although it sounds like an efficient use of organizational resources, in fact this creates real dilemmas for appraisers. Information and strategies that effectively meet the measurement goal of rank ordering workers are somewhat different from strategies that assist appraisers in accurately assessing the strengths and weaknesses of individual workers. Furthermore, appraisers bring personal goals and motives to the appraisal situation that may conflict with organizational goals for performance measurement. They may be much more concerned with minimizing the time devoted to the appraisal process, maintaining harmonious working relationships, or minimizing legal and political liabilities than they are with the quality and accuracy of interpersonal judgments. Their choice of judgment strategies will be highly influenced by personal motives that may be at odds with the goal of accurate interpersonal judgments.

Social Interaction

Performance appraisal always takes place in the context of existing social relationships. These include the relationship between supervisor and subordinate and relationships among group members. Appraisers generally have more information available about those with whom they have high-quality relationships and those with whom they have long-standing relationships. In addition, the nature of social relationships generates affect associated with the target; this affects the kind of information that appraisers attend to and their interpretation of that information by priming them to anticipate, and be more sensitive to, positive or negative information.

It is also important not to overlook the impact of rater concerns about maintaining the quality of social relationships. This creates pressure to focus on positive information, particularly during information gathering and information recall tasks. It also encourages perceptual processes that minimize distinctions among work group members.

Political Context

As Longenecker, Sims, & Gioia (1987) pointed out, performance appraisal can have powerful political overtones. Murphy and Cleveland (1995) argued that the organizational and political context of performance appraisal is likely to exert a stronger influence on performance ratings than appraiser capabilities and limitations do. In particular, accurate measurement may have low utility in light of the political environment. For example, if accurate measurement is at odds with an organizational culture of minimizing any differences between employees, strong norms to ignore individual differences will override appraisers' capabilities to recognize those differences. Similarly, managers will find it in their best interests to manipulate performance measurements upward if it allows them to retain workers who perform critical functions for them.

Individual Differences Among Perceivers

Appraisers differ with respect to their skills and motivation to carry out the tasks of performance appraisal. Those who see accurate appraisal as consistent with their own personal goals are more willing to invest the time, cognitive effort, and emotional expense to carry out appraisal tasks in an effortful way. This is relevant to the influence of stereotypes and other tools for simplifying the interpersonal judgment process. Appraisers who are highly invested in the goal of accurate performance measurement will be more willing to seek out individuating information about workers, rather than relying on the "quick and dirty" inference process that is provided by stereotypes.

Other appraiser characteristics also affect the manner in which they carry out the social cognition tasks associated with appraisal. Of particular note are the effects of affective states, which have begun to receive additional attention. Most people are familiar with the admonition to avoid the boss when he or she is in a rotten mood. The implication is that appraiser affect serves as a prime that influences attention and interpretation of information; the appraiser will selectively attend to negative information (selective attention) and will interpret information in the worst possible light (framing). More subtle effects observed for mood states include the impact of depressive states on the extent to which information is processed and on self-serving attribution biases in appraisal (Greenberg, Pyszczynski, Burling, & Tibbs, 1992; Reich & Weary, 1998).

WHAT DOES THE FUTURE BODE FOR THE DESIGN OF EFFECTIVE APPRAISAL SYSTEMS?

Some of the challenges that appraisers face represent relatively fixed aspects of performance appraisal—they simply come with the territory. Certainly, the problem of encouraging appraisers to be systematic and effortful without introducing yet more demands on their limited time resources will continue to represent an important theme for those responsible for designing and implementing performance measurement systems. In addition, several emerging features in work environments are likely to have particular ramifications for tasks and features that have been outlined in this chapter.

Changing demographics are creating a workforce in which supervisors and work-group members may have little common background on which to draw when making inferences, amplifying the potential role of stereotypes in appraisal. The emergence of flatter organizations creates reporting structures that dramatically increase the number of workers a manager has responsibility for appraising, which will exacerbate the multiple target problem for appraisers. In addition, the emphasis on teamwork that has begun to dominate many organizations provides incentives to de-emphasize intragroup differences and emphasize interpersonal functioning. It also introduces the new challenge of considering how to manage the basic tasks of performance appraisal when the appraisal target is the collective efforts, capabilities, and contributions of a team. Other new work arrangements such as telecommuting, virtual teams, and dispersed work groups of various kinds continue to proliferate; the difficulties that these raise for gathering relevant information about workers will require significant attention. Finally, advances in information technology offer unique opportunities to design innovative tools in support of appraisers' efforts to provide high-quality measurements of worker performance monitoring.

REFERENCES

Carson, K., Cardy, R., & Dobbins, G. (1991). Performance appraisal as effective management or deadly management disease: Two initial empirical investigations. *Group and Organization Studies, 16*, 143–159.

Cleveland, J., Murphy, K., & Williams, R. (1989). Multiple uses of performance appraisal: Prevalence and correlates. *Journal of Applied Psychology, 74*, 130–135.

DeNisi, A., Cafferty, T., & Meglino, B. (1984). A cognitive view of the performance appraisal process: A model and research propositions. *Organizational Behavior and Human Performance, 33*, 360–396.

DeNisi, A., Robbins, T., & Cafferty, T. (1989). Organization of information used for performance appraisals: Role of diary keeping. *Journal of Applied Psychology, 74*, 124–129.

DeNisi, A., & Stevens, G. (1981). Profiles of performance, performance evaluations, and personnel decisions. *Academy of Management Journal, 24*, 592–602.

Fiske, S. T. (1993). Social cognition and social perception. *Annual Review of Psychology, 44*, 155–194.

Golden, T., & Barnes-Farrell, J. (1999, April). *Relative influence of direct and indirect observations on performance ratings*. Poster session presented at the 14th annual conference of the Society for Industrial and Organizational Psychology, Atlanta, GA.

Greenberg, J., Pyszczynski, T., Burling, J., & Tibbs, K. (1992). Depression, self-focused attention, and the self-serving attributional bias. *Personality and Individual Differences, 13*, 959–965.

Ilgen, D. R., Barnes-Farrell, J. L., & McKellin, D. (1993). Performance appraisal process research in the 1980's: What has it contributed to appraisals in use? *Organizational Behavior and Human Decision Processes, 54,* 321–368.

Ilgen, D. R., & Feldman, J. (1983). Performance appraisal: A process approach. In B. M. Staw (Ed.), *Research in organization behavior* (Vol. 2). Greenwich, CT: JAI.

Kane, J. S. (1986). Performance distribution assessment. In R. Berk (Ed.), *The state of art in performance assessment.* Baltimore, MD: Johns Hopkins University Press.

Klimoski, R., & Donahue, L. (2000). Person perception: An overview of the field. In M. London (Ed.), *How people evaluate others in organizations: Person perception and interpersonal judgment in Industrial-Organizational psychology.* Mahwah, NJ: Lawrence Erlbaum Associates.

Koltuv, B. (1962). Some characteristics of intrajudge trait intercorrelations. *Psychological Monographs, 76* (33, Whole No. 552).

Kulik, C., & Ambrose, M. (1993). Category-based and feature-based processes in performance appraisal: Integrating visual and computerized sources of performance data. *Journal of Applied Psychology, 78,* 821–830.

Landy, F., & Farr, J. (1980). Performance rating. *Psychological Bulletin, 87,* 72–107.

Lee, Y-T, Jussim, L. J., & McCauley, C. R. (Eds.). (1995). *Stereotype accuracy: Toward appreciating group differences.* Washington, DC: American Psychological Association.

Longenecker, C., Sims, H., & Gioia, D. (1987). Behind the mask: The politics of employee appraisal. *Academy of Management Executive, 1,* 183–193.

Madon, S., Jussim, L., Keiper, S., Eccles, J., Smith, A., & Palumbo, P. (1998). The accuracy and power of sex, social class, and ethnic stereotypes: A naturalistic study in person perception. *Personality and Social Psychology Bulletin, 24,* 1304–1318.

Martin, S., & Klimoski, R. (1990). Use of verbal protocols to trace cognitions associated with self- and supervisor evaluations of performance. *Organizational Behavior and Human Decision Processes, 46,* 135–154.

Mitchell, T., & Liden, R. (1982). The effects of social context on performance evaluations. *Organizational Behavior and Human Performance, 29,* 241–256.

Murphy, K., & Cleveland, J. (1995). *Understanding performance appraisal: Social, organizational, and goal-based perspectives.* Thousand Oaks, CA: Sage.

Reich, D. A., & Weary, G. (1998). Depressives' future-even schemas and the social inference process. *Journal of Personality and Social Psychology, 74,* 1133–1145.

Woehr, D. J., & Huffcutt, A. (1994). Rater training for performance appraisal: A quantitative review. *Journal of Occupational and Organizational Psychology, 67,* 189–205.

Wyer, R., & Srull, T. (1994). *Handbook of social cognition* (2nd ed.). Hillsdale, NJ: Erlbaum.

7

Multisource Feedback Ratings: What Do They Really Measure?

Michael K. Mount
University of Iowa

Steven E. Scullen
North Carolina State University

Performance ratings are subjective judgments made about another person's performance. They are the most frequently used measure of individuals' performance in organizations. They are also the most frequently used criteria by industrial and organizational (I/O) psychologists in research studies. Although hundreds of studies over the past 50 years have investigated the properties of performance ratings, there is incomplete understanding of and numerous misconceptions about what performance ratings actually measure. In recent years, this issue has become more critical in view of the increased popularity of multisource feedback (MSF) systems. Relatively little is known about the properties of ratings from nontraditional sources such as subordinates, peers, and customers. The lack of understanding of what performance ratings actually measure has hindered both research and practice in I/O psychology.

The major purpose of this chapter is to examine what multisource (i.e., boss, peer, and subordinate) performance ratings actually measure. There are five major sections. The first provides a brief overview of MSF practices and establishes the context in which MSF ratings occur. The second discusses how person perception and interpersonal judgment research can facilitate understanding of the factors that influence performance ratings. The third reviews research that has examined the basic psychometric properties of MSF ratings, such as mean levels of ratings and interrater agreement. The fourth, and major section, discusses the results of recent research that has examined the latent structure of performance ratings. This section focuses specifically on the question of what MSF ratings actually measure. The fifth discusses the implications for research and practice pertaining to the use of MSF ratings.

WHAT IS MSF?

The term MSF refers to situations in which surveys are used to gather performance information from more than one rater perspective and, in most cases, from multiple raters within each perspective. The perspectives that are most commonly used in MSF systems are bosses, peers, subordinates, and self (although customers, internal or external, may also be included). Upward feedback (from subordinates only) and 360-degree feedback (from bosses, peers, subordinates, and possibly customers) are specific types of MSF. Other terms that are used more or less interchangeably in the literature are multirater feedback or multirater assessment.

MSF has become an important part of performance management systems in recent years, with most of the larger firms in the United States either already using it, or at least contemplating such use (London & Smither, 1995; Romano, 1994). In most cases, MSF is intended to promote managers' self-development by communicating to them how others in the workplace perceive their performance in areas that are important to the organization (London & Smither, 1995). That is, most MSF programs focus on developmental rather than administrative objectives.

Multiple perspectives are believed to be particularly valuable for development because each type of rater has different kinds of interactions with the manager; thus, each can contribute valid performance information that is unique to raters from that perspective. Some (e.g., London & Tornow, 1998) have argued that because today's workplace is characterized by flattened organizational structures and team-based work, it is especially important to supplement the supervisor's views on performance with feedback from nontraditional sources (i.e., peers, subordinates, and customers). This process is believed to generate a more complete picture of a ratee's overall performance than any of the perspectives could provide alone (Borman, 1991; Tornow, 1993).

PERSON PERCEPTION RESEARCH AND MSF RATINGS

The performance rating process requires raters to process and remember a great deal of information. To facilitate this process, raters construct schemas or cognitive frameworks to organize and guide the processing of social information. Schemas develop gradually over raters' lifetimes through interactions with the environment and reflect the unique ways that raters attend to, encode, store, and retrieve information about others. They are believed to differ along different classes of stimuli. For example, schemas that refer to the different social roles of individuals are called prototypes, such as the role of a basketball coach or the role of a flight attendant. Those that refer to the way others' personalities are conceptualized are called implicit personality theories. Schemas that refer to different categories of people are called stereotypes.

Schemas provide a useful framework for discussing what performance ratings actually measure. In general, schemas serve an important function by reducing the cognitive demands of the process, thereby achieving a sort of cognitive economy. This is especially important when ratings are assigned because raters are required to process enormous amounts of information, often concerning multiple ratees, and extending over a lengthy time period. Information processing is further complicated by the fact that much of the performance information may be contradictory, ambiguous, or both. Consider a subordinate who is asked to make a rating as part of an MSF system. She or he is faced with the task of integrating many small pieces of information about the boss into a unified impression. This may be the first time the subordinate has been asked to make ratings of this kind. Further, he or she may not have received any training prior to making the ratings and may not have any role-prescribed norms available to judge the appropriateness of his or her ratings. In addition, he or she may feel intimidated or uncomfortable about rating the boss, even though assurances have been made that the ratings are confidential and anonymous.

What is really known about how a rater in these circumstances goes about assigning ratings to his or her boss? Person perception research indicates that raters probably use a combination of methods to assign ratings but most likely the bits of information are weighted and then averaged to form an overall impression. Typically, the information is sorted along two dimensions, positive–negative and social–intellectual, although many others may be used. Over time the subordinate has developed a role schema for bosses that consists of prototypes, implicit personality theories, and stereotypes. In turn, these schemas influence the way he or she attends to, encodes, stores, and retrieves information about "bosses" in general, and his or her current boss in particular. For example, if the rater's boss schema is characterized by the label of neurotic, then the rater will remember information about the boss that is consistent with moody, irritable, nervous, and stress-prone people. On the other hand, if the schema could be characterized by the label of conscientiousness, then the rater will remember information about the ratee that is consistent with hardworking, dependable, efficient, and prudent people.

In the context of MSF ratings, there are two characteristics of raters that are especially relevant to the formulation of schemas and, subsequently, to the ratings that are assigned. One is the rater's organizational perspective (e.g., whether the person is a subordinate, peer, or boss), and the other is the rater's unique individual perspective (separate and distinct from the organizational perspective). This distinction is important because individuals assign ratings that are consistent with their unique schema. Because ratings can capture both the actual performance of the ratee and the rater's unique rating tendencies, it is important to first understand the nature of the rater's schema in order to understand how it influences performance ratings. In the paragraphs that follow, we review previous research that has quantified the major factors that influence performance ratings and relate these findings to person perception research.

WHAT ARE THE PSYCHOMETRIC CHARACTERISTICS OF MSF RATINGS?

Although MSF ratings are now being used extensively, "it is clear that this is an area in which practice is well ahead of theory and empirical research" (London & Smither, 1995, p. 807). In the last several years, however, considerable research has been directed toward developing that theoretical and empirical base. In this section, we examine the psychometric properties of MSF ratings: mean differences across sources, interrater reliabilities (within sources), and correlations between different sources. Then we review findings concerning the effectiveness of MSF in terms of performance improvement.

Do Mean Levels of Ratings Differ?

From the perspective of person perception and MSF research, if there are differences across rater perspectives in the level of ratings assigned, then it could mean that raters from different perspectives attend to different behaviors of ratees and assign ratings differently as a result. Alternatively, it could mean that they attend to the same behaviors of ratees but they evaluate them more positively or negatively, depending on their unique schema. Note that even though raters could differ in the absolute level of the ratings they assign when rating multiple attributes of a ratee, they might still agree in their rank ordering of those attributes for the ratee.

Harris and Schaubroeck (1988) compared mean levels of ratings made by bosses, peers, and self-raters. Although none of the mean differences across those three sources was statistically significant, their meta-analysis suggested that self-ratings are highest, followed by peer ratings, and then boss ratings. Specific findings in their study were that self-ratings were higher than boss ratings ($d = .70$), self-ratings were higher than peer ratings ($d = .28$), and peer ratings were higher than boss ratings ($d = .23$).

Unfortunately, subordinate ratings were not included in the Harris and Schaubroeck (1988) meta-analysis. Conway and Huffcutt (1997) included subordinate ratings in their more recent meta-analysis of the psychometric properties of MSF but they did not examine mean differences. Therefore, one must turn to large-scale primary studies to examine the means of subordinate ratings relative to ratings from other sources. One study (Scullen, Mount, & Sytsma, 1996) involving over 2,200 managers indicates that subordinate ratings are generally comparable to both peer ratings and boss ratings but are lower than self-ratings. Scullen et al. found that there was a tendency on some dimensions for subordinate ratings to be slightly higher than either peer or boss ratings. A similar study by Tsui (1983) yielded generally similar results. Tsui found, however, that some subordinate ratings were slightly lower than boss ratings.

Overall, research supports the conclusion that, on average, self-ratings tend to be higher than ratings from bosses, peers, or subordinates but mean differences among the latter three sources are relatively small.

How Much Do Raters From the Same Perspective Agree?

Differences in correlational agreement for raters from the same (e.g., two bosses or two peers) or different (e.g., a boss and a peer or a subordinate and a boss) perspectives provide information about whether ratees (or attributes of ratees) are rank ordered the same way. From the perspective of person perception research, high agreement among raters when rating an attribute of a ratee suggests that raters are attending to, encoding, storing, and retrieving information about others in similar ways. Note that this does not imply that the judgments are accurate, only that they are similar. Nor does it imply that the level of ratings assigned is the same. It is possible that two raters have rank ordered attributes of the ratee in similar ways but differ in the absolute level of the ratings (i.e., there are mean differences across raters).

Conway and Huffcutt (1997) found that within-source interrater reliabilities are lower for management jobs than for nonmanagement jobs. The average interrater reliabilities of boss ratings were .44 and .54 for management and nonmanagement jobs, respectively. The corresponding reliabilities for peer ratings were .36 and .39. For subordinate ratings, the average interrater reliability was .30 for management jobs. They could not compute subordinate interrater reliability for nonmanagement jobs because nonmanagers typically do not have subordinates. The reliability figures reported by Conway and Huffcutt are consistent with findings from Viswesvaran, Ones, and Schmidt (1996). The Viswesvaran et al. meta-analysis of reliabilities yielded mean interrater reliability estimates of .52 for boss ratings and .42 for peer ratings.

A smaller primary study based on a generalizability theory analysis yielded interrater reliability (actually generalizability) estimates of .38 for boss ratings, .26 for peer ratings, and .25 for subordinate ratings (Greguras & Robie, 1998). The Greguras and Robie reliability estimates are clearly lower than those from Conway and Huffcutt (1997) for managers but they are very similar to the estimates of interrater reliability in Scullen et al. (1996). Greguras and Robie argued that differences in rating purpose may be responsible for the differences in the estimated reliabilities. Both the Greguras and Robie and the Scullen et al. estimates of interrater reliability were computed from ratings that had been made for developmental purposes only. The Conway and Huffcutt meta-analysis was different in that it was not limited to developmental ratings. They included studies in which ratings had been made for administrative purposes as well. Thus, it is possible that the reliabilities of developmental ratings are different from the reliabilities of ratings that have administrative consequences.

In all of the studies reported above, boss ratings were found to be more reliable than either peer or subordinate ratings. Reliabilities for peer and subordinate ratings appear to be approximately equal, especially when used for developmental purposes.

How Much Do Ratings From Different Perspectives Agree?

The Harris and Schaubroeck (1988) and Conway and Huffcutt (1997) meta-analyses both indicate that self-ratings do not correlate highly with ratings from the other sources. Self-ratings correlated at approximately .20 with each of the other sources in both studies (corrected correlations for self-ratings ranged from .29 to .36). The highest intersource correlation in both studies was between boss ratings and peer ratings. Estimates of the observed correlation (corrected correlations in parentheses) between boss and peer ratings were .32 (.80) in Conway and Huffcutt and .48 (.62) in Harris and Schaubroeck. Harris and Schaubroeck did not estimate the correlations between subordinate ratings and ratings from the other sources but the Conway and Huffcutt estimates were: subordinate–boss, .22 (.57); subordinate–peer, .22 (.66); and subordinate–self, .14 (.26).

Does Performance Improve After MSF?

One of the fundamental assumptions behind MSF programs is that managers will be able and willing to use the feedback they receive from others to improve their performance. Research has shown, however, that this does not always happen. Kluger and DeNisi's (1996) meta-analysis indicates that in about one out of three situations in which feedback is provided, performance actually declines. Research has begun to reveal the nature of the factors that influence the extent to which MSF results in real and lasting improvements in performance.

Much of the evidence concerning whether managers improve their performance after receiving feedback has examined the effects of upward feedback. That evidence suggests that two factors are associated with improved performance. One is the initial level of self-ratings relative to ratings from others. The other concerns how individuals and organizations use the performance information gathered in MSF.

Several studies have shown that it is overraters (those who rate their performance higher than others do) who improve the most after receiving feedback (Atwater, Rouse, & Fischthal, 1995; Johnson & Ferstl, 1999; Smither et al., 1995; Walker & Smither, 1999). It is believed that significant discrepancies between one's view of his or her performance and others' views of that performance can be powerful motivation for change (London & Tornow, 1998).

At the same time, however, it is interesting to note that in the Smither et al. (1995) and Reilly, Smither, and Vasilopolous (1996) studies, overraters tended to improve regardless of whether they got individualized feedback. In both of those studies, managers received feedback that was specific to their own individual performance only if it had been rated by at least three subordinates. Managers whose performance had been rated by less than three subordinates received feedback only about the performance of managers in general. Reilly et al. speculated that the reason why performance improved in the managers who received only generalized feedback was that the feedback instrument called their attention to behaviors that are valued by the organization, and cited laboratory evidence (Dominick, Reilly, & McGourty, 1996) supporting that contention.

A more important question about performance improvement is whether it is sustainable. Some of the earlier studies (e.g., Smither et al., 1995) examined changes in performance over a period of a few months. Reilly et al. (1996) extended the Smither et al. study to 2.5 years and found that performance improvements were sustained over the longer time period. Walker and Smither (1999) followed performance for 5 years and also found that improvement was maintained. Thus, it appears to be true that MSF can lead to performance improvement (as measured by increased subordinate ratings) that is sustainable for at least several years.

A second key variable in improving performance involves how performance information is generated and then used. London, Smither, and Adsit (1997) argued that MSF systems are more effective if they are designed to hold both ratees and raters accountable. They believe that ratees should not just be given feedback but they should also be expected to act on it. They also argued that raters should be accountable for bringing about positive change. They suggested, for example, that subordinates or peers participate in designing items for the performance survey. Then, after feedback is delivered, managers should conduct follow-up discussions with their raters to clarify the feedback and discuss specific suggestions for the manager's development plan. In support of that view, Walker and Smither (1999) found that subordinate ratings of performance were particularly likely to improve over a 5-year period if the manager held post-feedback sessions of that type.

There is other evidence suggesting that many raters, and especially subordinates, are uncomfortable with being held accountable for their ratings. Antonioni (1994) found that because of fear of retaliation, subordinate raters prefer to rate anonymously. Other research (London, Wohlers, & Gallagher, cited in London et al., 1997) has shown that subordinates indicate they would rate more favorably if their ratings were identified than if they were anonymous.

In sum, the research literature suggests that MSF can have a positive and long-lasting impact on job performance, especially in those ratees who overestimate their performance (when compared to the views of other raters). The relative advantages of individualized and generalized feedback are still unclear, however. Similarly, research has not yet determined the most effective level of accountability, especially for subordinates who are called upon to rate their bosses.

WHAT DO MSF RATINGS ACTUALLY MEASURE?

We have discussed the general practice of MSF, the role of schemas in the rating process, the basic psychometric characteristics of MSF ratings, and whether behavior changes as a consequence of MSF ratings. But a fundamental question about MSF ratings remains unaddressed. What do MSF ratings actually measure?

Because MSF ratings are made by multiple raters from multiple perspectives on multiple traits, they provide a rich source of information that can be used to understand the factors that influence performance ratings. Researchers can use MSF ratings to compute multitrait–multirater (MTMR) matrices, a form of the multitrait–multimethod matrix (MTMM; Campbell & Fiske, 1959). The MTMR matrix can then be submitted to confirmatory factor analysis (CFA), through which performance (trait) effects on the observed ratings can be separated from rater (method) effects and the effects of random measurement error. Several CFA models have been proposed for this general purpose (e.g., Kenny, 1979; Widaman, 1985). More complex models can also be used to further partition the performance and rater effects into subcomponents. With the appropriate CFA model, the researcher can estimate the relative magnitudes of the effects of multiple influences on observed ratings. Ultimately, this information can be used to understand what MSF ratings actually measure. In the next section, we discuss recent research that has examined these issues and their implications.

Three Broad Factors That Influence Performance Ratings

Generally speaking, there are three broad factors that influence performance ratings: the ratee's actual job performance, the rater's biases in the perception and recall of that performance, and measurement error (Wherry & Bartlett, 1982). Ratee job performance consists of two components, the ratee's general level of job performance and the ratee's performance on specific dimensions of the job. General performance refers to the ratee's overall level of performance, all performance dimensions considered. In our view, general job performance is reflected in any variance that is common to all ratings of performance (i.e., to ratings of all performance dimensions and by all raters). This conception of general performance is related to the concept of true halo (Cooper, 1981) in that both refer to correlations across all performance dimensions. True halo results in correlations in actual performance across performance dimensions. Some degree of true halo is to be expected because many of the antecedents of performance (e.g., mental ability and conscientiousness) are similar across the various dimensions. To the extent that ratings validly represent true job performance, a corresponding general performance factor should be present in ratings.

We define the second component, dimensional performance, in terms of deviations from the ratee's general level of performance (i.e., as residuals). Dimensional performance levels must be considered because a ratee's performance is not the same on all dimensions (e.g., performance on technical skills may differ from performance on human relations skills). Further, the level of performance on dimensions such as technical or administrative skills may differ from general performance. As we have defined them, actual performance on a particular dimension is the sum of the general performance and dimensional performance components.

Rater biases consist of two components, the rater's idiosyncratic tendencies and the rater's organizational perspective. Although there are several types of idiosyncratic rating variance, it is halo that is most often associated with this category. Halo refers to the effects of a rater's overall impression of an employee's performance on ratings of different dimensions, and is widely thought to be a major influence on performance ratings. Because halo is often used as a "catch-all" phrase for different types of idiosyncratic rating effects, it has been used inconsistently by researchers and practitioners. Other types of effects (e.g., differences in leniency) are also likely to be present in any situation in which multiple raters are present. Therefore, it would be erroneous to call this effect halo error. Consequently, we use the term idiosyncratic rater effects to include all of the effects associated with individual raters.

The second rater bias component, the rater's organizational perspective (self, subordinate, peer, or boss), may influence performance ratings for two primary reasons (Borman, 1997). First, raters from different organizational perspectives might observe different samples of the ratee's performance. Second, raters from different perspectives might observe the same aspects of performance but attach different weights to them. Previous research has provided evidence that perspective effects exist but their precise magnitude relative to other effects was not examined (Mount, Judge, Scullen, Sytsma, & Hezlett, 1998). Although perspective-related components are typically thought of as a part of rater bias, one could argue that such effects capture real differences in the behaviors that are observed. If so, then these components might capture actual performance of the ratee, rather than rater bias. This point is discussed further.

Random measurement error refers to unsystematic variance in performance ratings. It is important to understand the magnitude of such errors because random measurement error limits the extent to which measurements are reliable, and that, in turn, limits the validity of inferences made from those measurements.

Research Investigating the Latent Structure of MSF Ratings

Our previous research with M. Goff (Scullen, Mount, & Goff, in press) examined the magnitude of these five components (ratee general performance, ratee dimensional performance, idiosyncratic rater effects, rater perspective effects, and random measurement error) using two large MSF data sets ($n > 2000$ in both cases). Each data set contained seven ratings for each manager: a self-rating and ratings made by two bosses, two peers, and two subordinates. All ratings were made for developmental purposes. Three theoretically important dimensions of managerial performance were used: administrative (e.g., planning, organizing, and assigning to tasks), human (e.g., working with and through people to accomplish objectives), and technical (e.g., knowledge of relevant methods and techniques in the

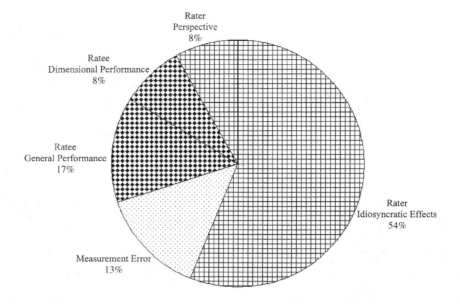

Ratee performance consists of General and Dimensional Performance.

Rater bias consists of Idiosyncratic Effects and Perspective Effects.

Note: Results are averaged across perspectives and dimensions for the MSP and Profilor data sets

FIG. 7.1. Percentage of observed ratings variance associated with the five categories of effects. Results are averaged across perspectives and dimensions for the MSP and Profilor data sets. From "Understanding the Latent Structure of Job Performance Ratings," by S. E. Scullen, M. K. Mount, and M. Goff, in press, Journal of Applied Psychology. Copyright by Reprinted with permission.

functional area). Results obtained from these data have numerous implications for understanding what MSF ratings actually measure and also have numerous implications for person perception research. Consequently, we discuss the major findings based on the average effects across the two data sets.

Scullen et al. (in press) estimated the magnitudes of the five components (general and dimensional performance, idiosyncratic and perspective bias, and random measurement error) using CFA. Although details of the results varied somewhat between the two data sets, both supported the same general conclusions. Fig. 7.1 summarizes the results for the five components averaged across rating perspectives and performance dimensions for the two data sets. The magnitude of the five components is expressed in terms

TABLE 7.1

Percentage of Observed Rating Variance Associated With Five Categories
of Effects for Boss, Peer, and Subordinate Ratings

Categories of Effect	Perspective			
	Boss	*Peer*	*Sub*	*Mean*
Rater bias effects				
Idiosyncratic effects (halo error)	47	58	57	54
Organization perspective	10	0	15	8
Total	57	58	72	62
Ratee performance effects				
General performance	19	21	10	17
Dimensional performance	11	8	5	8
Total	30	29	15	25
Measurement error	13	14	13	13

of percentages of variance accounted for in the observed ratings. Table 7.1 illustrates each of these effects for three rater perspectives (boss, peer, and subordinate), and is discussed further.

First, from both a practical and theoretical perspective it is important to know how much of the variance in performance ratings is systematic. The amount of systematic variance influences whether performance ratings are reliable or repeatable, which in turn influences whether valid inferences can be drawn from the ratings. Figure 7.1 shows that the amount of measurement error is relatively small (13%), which means that approximately 87% of the observed rating variance is systematic. Table 7.1 shows that the results were approximately the same for all rating perspectives. Thus, it can be concluded that most of what MSF ratings capture is systematic and reliable, which is a necessary step in establishing the validity of the ratings.

Figure 7.1 also shows that the rater bias category is very large and accounts for the largest amount of variance (62%, averaged across perspectives). Within this category the idiosyncratic component was the largest by far, accounting for approximately half (54%) of the total rating variance when averaged across boss, peer, and subordinate ratings. The second component, perspective effects, was smaller than the idiosyncratic component, accounting for 8% of the rating variance when averaged across perspectives.

Figure 7.1 also shows the magnitude of the ratee performance components (i.e., the sum of general and dimensional variance). They were relatively small compared to rater bias effects, accounting for a total of 25% of the total rating variance on average. Of the two types of performance effects, the general performance component (17%) was larger than the dimensional component (8%) when averaged across perspectives. Thus, of the portion of ratings that is associated with the ratee's performance, most is associated with the ratee's general, underlying performance rather than with specific, dimensional performance.

Table 7.1 provides a specific analysis of the magnitude of the effects for the boss, peer, and subordinate perspectives (averaged across data sets). Generally speaking, the results were similar across perspectives (with several notable exceptions that are discussed later). For example, the amount of systematic variance in the ratings was approximately the same for the three perspectives (86–87%).

From the perspective of person perception research, it is particularly noteworthy that the rater bias effects were the largest, by far, for each perspective. They were substantially larger than the ratee performance effects. Within the rater bias category, idiosyncratic rater effects accounted for the largest amount of variance in ratings, ranging from 47% for boss ratings to 58% for peer ratings. Person perception research shows that raters formulate schemas to cope with the cognitive demands of the rating process. That is, in an attempt to organize and process social information, raters develop their own relatively unique ways of attending to, encoding, storing, and retrieving information. The large idiosyncratic effect observed is consistent with the conceptualization of cognitive schemas as being largely unique to each individual rater. Clearly, however, it is not accurate to say that schemas are totally unique to an individual rater. The results described above indicate that a meaningful portion (25%) of what ratings capture is the performance of the ratee. Because performance was defined as that portion of the ratings that was shared by other raters, it suggests that raters' cognitive schemas overlap to a moderate degree.

The amount of ratings variance accounted for by general performance was substantially larger than the amount accounted for by dimensional performance for each of the rater perspectives. The general performance component captures variance that is common to all judgments made by all raters of a ratee's performance but that is not associated with performance on any specific dimension. The finding that the general performance effects dominate dimensional performance effects has implications for person perception research. It suggests that when performance information is processed by raters (regardless of perspective), it occurs at a level that is more general than specific along an evaluative (positive–negative) dimension. In short, raters tend to evaluate others on a global dimension that reflects the person's overall level of performance. Also, after accounting for overall performance, there is little ratings variance associated with dimensional performance.

One result that differed across perspectives was the magnitude of the effect associated with organizational perspective. Meaningful effects were observed for subordinate (15%) and boss ratings (10%) but not for peer ratings (0%). This means that boss and subordinate raters attend to, encode, store, and retrieve social information about a ratee in ways that may be unique to raters from the same perspective. There is no evidence that this is true of peer raters.

WHAT ARE THE IMPLICATIONS FOR RESEARCH AND PRACTICE?

A basic assumption of MSF ratings and other performance ratings is that they should capture the performance of the person being rated. This statement is so obviously true that it hardly seems worth mentioning. However, the Scullen et al. (in press) results show that only about 25% of the variance in MSF ratings reflects ratee performance. Although this amount is meaningful and useful, it is relatively small compared to that represented by the idiosyncratic tendencies of individual raters (54%). The fact that the idiosyncratic effects alone are more than twice as large as the effects associated with the ratee's performance (on average) is cause for alarm.

Performance ratings should also capture the specific performance dimension rated. This statement, too, seems so obviously true as to be meaningless. However, Fig. 7.1 and Table 7.1 show that only a small portion (8%) of the ratings variance reflects ratee performance on the particular dimension being rated. In fact, of the portion of ratings that reflect performance, the general performance effects are more than twice as large for each perspective as the effects associated with the specific dimensions. Given the Scullen et al. (in press) definition of specific performance as deviations from general performance, the relatively small amount of variance accounted for by specific performance has two possible explanations. One is that individual ratees exhibit little true variation in their performance across dimensions. The other explanation is that ratee performance does vary substantially across dimensions, but raters do not attend to or recall those deviations.

In the first case, relatively small dimensional components would correctly reflect the minor performance deviations across dimensions. In the latter case, however, small dimensional components would represent rater errors in perception, storage, or recall of performance information.

The finding that rater biases exert a strong influence on observed ratings is not new. What is new, however, is the knowledge of how large these effects are both in an absolute sense and relative to other effects, such as general and dimensional performance. This information provides a more complete understanding of what performance ratings actually capture. Although it is implicitly assumed that performance ratings measure the performance of the ratee, in reality most of what is being measured by MSF ratings (regardless of perspective) is the unique rating tendencies of the rater. Thus, MSF ratings reveal more about the rater than they do about the ratee. These findings have numerous implications for theory and practice in I/O psychology. They also have implications for person perception research and social judgment research.

Advantages of MSF Systems

In view of the finding that the largest influence on performance ratings is the idiosyncratic rating tendencies of raters a legitimate question to ask is, "What use can be made of a single rater's rating?" The answer is that it depends on the purpose of the ratings. It is common practice to treat idiosyncratic (e.g., halo) effects as rater bias; that is, as information that contaminates ratings with irrelevant information. But if the purpose of the rating is to provide developmental feedback to the ratee, then such effects may not represent bias per se but instead may reflect useful information that represents a single rater's viewpoint. A well-known axiom in psychology is that individuals act according to the truth as they believe it to be. In order for a ratee to improve his or her effectiveness in working with another, he or she must first understand how the other person perceives him or her. Individual ratings represent the "truth" as that rater perceives it; whether the ratings are accurate in the traditional sense is irrelevant for this purpose. That is, each rater's ratings contain valuable information that the ratee can use to try to better understand how the rater interacts with him or her.

On the other hand, the large idiosyncratic component in the ratings indicates that caution must be used in generalizing results from one rater to those of another because raters do not agree much with each other. Thus, if the purpose of the ratings is to make employment decisions, the use

TABLE 7.2
Ratee Performance, Rater Bias, and Measurement Error as Function of the
Number and Type of Raters for the Technical Skills Dimension

Rater Perspective	Ratee Performance		Rater Bias		Measurement Error	
	1 Rater	2 Raters	1 Rater	2 Raters	1 Rater	2 Raters
Boss	.31	.45	.48	.40	.21	.15
Peer	.31	.47	.45	.34	.24	.19
Subordinate	.17	.26	.64	.60	.19	.14
Boss, peer, and subordinate	.51	.68	.35	.23	.14	.09

of a single rater's rating—whether it is a boss, peer, or subordinate—is ill
advised. In this context, the primary benefit of MSF systems is that multiple
raters' ratings can be used to "average out" idiosyncratic rating variance,
thereby increasing the proportion of performance variance in the ratings. In
general, if ratings are averaged across $\underline{n}$ raters, each of the error components
is divided by $\underline{n}$, while the true variance components remain unchanged
(Cronbach, Gleser, Nanda, & Rajaratnam, 1972). This effectively increases
the proportion of observed variance that is true variance.

Table 7.2 provides an illustration using one data set, the Management
Skills Profile (Sevy, Olson, McGuire, Frazier, & Paajanen, 1985), for the
technical skills dimension from Scullen et al. (in press). The benefits of
using two raters compared to one are shown for ratee performance effects
(general plus dimensional performance), rater bias effects (idiosyncratic
and perspective effects), and measurement error. As a practical matter, in
most MSF systems results for a single rater's rating would be provided to
a ratee only for boss ratings. (We provide the data for a single peer and
a single subordinate rating for comparative purposes.) Typically, results
would be shown for a perspective only if there were two or more ratings
for that perspective. The last cell entry shows the effects when one or two
raters each from boss, peer, and subordinate perspectives (six raters total)
are used jointly.

The advantages of using multiple raters are readily apparent. For each
perspective, the use of two raters increases the amount of ratee performance
captured by the ratings by about 50%. For example, the amount of performance variance that is captured by the use of two boss ratings increases

from 31% to 45%. Further, the amount of rater bias and measurement error decreases significantly. For example, the amount of rater bias captured by the two bosses' ratings decreases from 48% to 40%. The last row entry in the table shows that if one boss, one peer, and one subordinate rating are used jointly, the amount of ratee performance accounted for increases to 51%. That is, approximately half of the rating variance accounted for is associated with ratee performance when one boss, peer, and subordinate rating are used jointly. This is substantially larger than the effects for a single rater from any perspective (which ranged from 17% to 31%), and somewhat larger than the effects for two raters from any perspective (which ranged from .26% to .47%).

Table 7.2 also shows that when two boss, two peer, and two subordinate ratings are used together, the effects are even more pronounced. The amount of ratee performance variance accounted for by the six ratings increases to 68%. This is a realistic example because it is common practice in MSF systems for ratees to be rated by two or more raters from each perspective (or some variant of this). Finally, although not shown in the table, the magnitude of the effects using another realistic scenario consisting of one boss, three peers, and three subordinates (seven raters total) would be: ratee performance, 68%; rater bias, 24%; and random error, 8%. These results are very similar to those reported in Table 7.2 for the joint use of two bosses, two peers, and two subordinates. In both examples, approximately two thirds of the ratings variance is associated with ratee performance.

Although the results presented here are for one dimension (technical skills), we have conducted additional analyses that demonstrate similar results for other dimensions. In summary, it is clear that a significant advantage of MSF rating systems is that averaging across several raters significantly increases the amount of ratee performance accounted for while reducing the effects of rater bias and random error.

Other Issues in MSF Ratings

One practical issue is how to treat the variance associated with the rater's perspective. Scullen et al. (in press) found a small, but meaningful, perspective effect associated with boss ratings and subordinate ratings but not for peer ratings. These findings have implications for the way that multisource ratings are aggregated and reported to ratees. They support the common practice in MSF programs of aggregating ratings made by bosses and ratings made by subordinates, as these ratings have been shown to capture something unique to that perspective and different from other perspectives.

Despite the fact that the peer perspective does not appear to be unique, we believe that peers are an important source of ratings information. First, peer ratings capture meaningful amounts of performance variance. This in itself makes them valuable. Second, peers are a good source of ratings because of their numbers. As we discussed earlier, it is beneficial to have a large number of raters because the greater the number of raters, the more performance variance that is captured.

A different but related issue is whether perspective-related effects represent rater bias or ratee performance. An argument can be made that variance in ratings that is shared by raters from one perspective but not by raters from another perspective represents a perspective bias. However, if raters from a particular perspective rate differently because they observe different aspects of the ratee's performance, then perspective effects might capture actual ratee performance that is observed by raters from that perspective only. For example, managers may have qualitatively and quantitatively different types of interactions with their subordinates than they do with their bosses. Consequently, differences in the ratings from the two perspectives may reflect true differences in the performance each has observed. If so, then the perspective-related variance components would represent valid performance information, and not perspective-related biases. Accordingly, perspective-related variance should be added to the general and dimensional performance variance to fully account for performance-related variation in ratings.

Using the data presented in Fig. 7.1, the percentage of variance associated with actual ratee performance would increase from 22% (general plus dimensional performance) to 30% when perspective related variance is included. It should be noted that these results vary by perspective. Significantly, there would be no incremental gain in the amount of performance-related variance captured by peer ratings because they exhibited no perspective-related variance.

One issue of interest to organizations and to ratees in MSF systems is whether ratings from some perspectives are more valid than others. We are using validity here to refer to the portion of rating variance that is associated with ratee performance (i.e., the greater the percentage of ratee performance captured by the ratings, the higher the validity of the ratings). Considering the Scullen et al. (in press) data as a whole, it appears that boss ratings are the most valid, although this conclusion is tempered by the way performance is defined. As Table 7.1 shows, when general and dimensional performance effects are combined, boss and peer ratings account for more ratee performance (30% and 29%, respectively) than do subordinate ratings (15%). In this sense, boss and peer ratings are equally valid, as they capture approximately equal amounts of ratee performance. However, if perspective-related variance is included as part of actual performance, then boss ratings would be judged as most valid because they capture the most performance-related variance (40%, compared to 29% for peers, and 30% for subordinates). At the same time, boss ratings are the least idiosyncratic (47%, compared to 58% for peers, and 57% for subordinate ratings). When defined in this way, these results indicate that boss ratings are the most valid overall.

SUMMARY

In summary, performance ratings are the most frequently used measure of employee performance in organizations. They are also the most frequently used criterion by I/O psychologists in research studies. Therefore, it is important that I/O psychologists and practitioners understand what performance ratings actually measure, as this dictates how performance ratings are interpreted and, ultimately, how they can and should be used. This is particularly important given the enormous popularity of MSF ratings in recent years because relatively little is known about the properties of ratings from nontraditional rating sources. The research reviewed illustrates that MSF ratings do measure ratee performance as intended, although the amount of performance-related variance is only moderate and differs by rater perspective.

More important perhaps, results show that what MSF ratings measure is largely the idiosyncratic rating tendencies of the rater. Whether idiosyncratic rater effects should be interpreted as undesirable rater bias depends on the purpose of the ratings. If the purpose is developmental feedback, then such effects can be interpreted as meaningful information that represents the rater's unique perceptions of the individual. On the other hand, if the purpose is to use ratings to make personnel decisions, then the value of MSF ratings is that multiple ratings can be averaged, which will result in a better understanding of the performance level of the individual.

Person perception research shows that raters formulate schemas and assign ratings in a way that is consistent with these schemas. The results of our previous research show that idiosyncratic rating tendencies have a large effect on performance ratings. This suggests that raters' cognitive schemas are largely unique and overlap only modestly with those of other raters. In order to increase the validity of performance ratings in MSF systems or any other rating situation, the amount of idiosyncratic rating error must be reduced. Because these effects are likely a function of raters' schemas, it is imperative that I/O psychologists understand more about how and why raters form their unique schemas. Research that investigates how to train raters to formulate schemas that facilitate attending to, encoding, storing, and retrieving performance-related information would be useful in efforts to increase the validity of ratings.

ACKNOWLEDGEMENTS

Michael K. Mount, Tippie College of Business, University of Iowa; Steven E. Scullen, College of Management, North Carolina State University.

Correspondence concerning this chapter should be sent to Michael K. Mount, Tippie College of Business, University of Iowa, Iowa City, Iowa 52242. Electronic mail may be sent to michael-mount@uiowa.edu.

REFERENCES

Antonioni, D. (1994). The effects of feedback accountability on upward appraisal ratings. *Personnel Psychology, 47*, 349–356.

Atwater, L., Rouse, P., & Fischthal, A. (1995). The influence of upward feedback on self- and follower ratings of leadership. *Personnel Psychology, 48*, 35–59.

Borman, W. C. (1991). Job behavior, performance, and effectiveness. In M. D. Dunnette & L. M. Hough (Eds.), *Handbook of industrial and organizational psychology*, (Vol. 2, pp. 271–326). Palo Alto, CA: Consulting Psychologists Press.

Borman, W. C. (1997). 360° ratings: An analysis of assumptions and a research agenda for evaluating their validity. *Human Resource Management Review, 7*, 299–315.

Campbell, D. T., & Fiske, P. W. (1959). Convergent and discriminant validation by the multitrait-multimethod matrix. *Psychological Bulletin, 56*, 81–105.

Conway, J. M., & Huffcutt, A. I. (1997). Psychometric properties of multisource performance ratings: A meta-analysis of subordinate, supervisor, peer, and self-ratings. *Human Performance, 10*, 331–360.

Cooper, W. H. (1981). Ubiquitous halo. *Psychological Bulletin, 90*, 218–244.

Cronbach, L. J., Gleser, G. C., Nanda, H., & Rajaratnam, N. (1972). *The dependability of behavioral measurements: Theory of generalizability for scores and profiles*. New York: Wiley.

Dominick, P. A., Reilly, R. R., McGourty, J. M. (1996, April). *Changing team behaviors through peer feedback: Does what they say really matter?* Paper presented at the 11th annual meeting of the Society for Industrial and Organizational Psychology, San Diego, CA.

Greguras, G. J., & Robie, C. (1998). A new look at within-source interrater reliability of 360-degree feedback ratings. *Journal of Applied Psychology, 83*, 960–968.

Harris, M. M., & Schaubroeck, J. (1988). A meta-analysis of self-supervisor, self-peer, and peer-supervisor ratings. *Personnel Psychology, 41*, 43–62.

Johnson, J. W., & Ferstl, K. L. (1999). The effects of interrater and self–other agreement on performance improvement following upward feedback. *Personnel Psychology, 52*, 271–303.

Kenny, D. A. (1979). *Correlation and causality*. New York: Wiley.

Kluger, A. N., & DeNisi, A. (1996). The effects of feedback interventions on performance: A historical review, a meta-analysis, and a preliminary feedback intervention theory. *Psychological Bulletin, 119*, 254–284.

London, M., & Smither, J. W. (1995). Can multi-source feedback change perceptions of goal accomplishment, self-evaluations, and performance-related outcomes? Theory-based applications and directions for research. *Personnel Psychology, 48*, 803–839.

London, M., Smither, J. W., & Adsit, D. J. (1997). Accountability: The Achilles heel of multi-source feedback. *Group & Organization Management, 22*, 162–184.

London, M., & Tornow, W. W. (1998). Introduction: 360-degree feedback—more than a tool! In M. London & W. W. Tornow (Eds.), *Maximizing the value of 360-degree feedback*, (pp. 1–8). Greensboro, NC: Center for Creative Leadership.

Mount, M. K., Judge, T. A., Scullen, S. E., Sytsma, M. R., & Hezlett, S. A. (1998). Trait, rater, and level effects in 360-degree performance ratings. *Personnel Psychology, 51*, 557–576.

Reilly, R. R., Smither, J. W., & Vasilopoulos, N. L. (1996). A longitudinal study of upward feedback. *Personnel Psychology, 49*, 599–612.

Romano, C. (1994). Conquering the fear of feedback. *HR Focus, 71*, 9–19.

Scullen, S. E., Mount, M. K., & Goff, M. (in press). Understanding the latent structure of job performance ratings. *Journal of Applied Psychology*.

Scullen, S. E., Mount, M. K., & Sytsma, M. R. (1996). *Comparisons of self, peer, direct report, and boss ratings of managers' performance*. Paper presented at the 11th annual meeting of the Society for Industrial and Organizational Psychology, San Diego, CA.

Sevy, B.A., Olson, R. D., McGuire, D. P., Frazier, M. E., & Paajanen, G. (1985). *Managerial skills profile technical manual*. Minneapolis, MN: Personnel Decisions.

Smither, J. W., London, M., Vasilopoulos, N. L., Reilly, R. R., Millsap, R. E., & Salvemini, N. (1995). An examination of the effects of an upward feedback program over time. *Personnel Psychology, 48*, 1–34.

Tornow, W. W. (1993). Perceptions or reality: Is multi-perspective measurement a means or an end? *Human Resources Management, 32*, 221–230.

Tsui, A. S. (1983). *Qualities of judgmental ratings by four rater sources*. East Lansing, MI: National Center for Research on Teacher Learning. (ERIC Document Reproduction Service No. ED 237 913).

Viswesvaran, C., Ones, D. S., & Schmidt, F. L. (1996). Comparative analysis of the reliability of job performance ratings. *Journal of Applied Psychology, 81*, 557–574.

Walker, A. G., & Smither, J. W. (1999). A five-year study of upward feedback: What managers do with their results matters. *Personnel Psychology, 52*, 393–423.

Wherry, R. J., Sr., & Bartlett, C. J. (1982). The control of bias in ratings: A theory of ratings. *Personnel Psychology, 35*, 521–551.

Widaman, F. F. (1985). Hierarchically rested covariance structure models for multitrait-multimethod data. *Applied Psychological Measurement, 9*, 1–26.

IV

Developmental Processes

Person perception is important in understanding assessments that contribute to developmental processes. These include the conceptualization and perception of leadership, evaluating career dynamics, coaching for development, and assessing and intervening with problem employees.

Leadership is usually thought of in terms of how a manager's or executive's traits and associated behavior affect subordinates' behavior and performance. Subordinates, peers, and others are often called on to evaluate their supervisor's performance and assess their leadership capabilities, for instance, in the form of upward and multisource (360-degree) ratings. As such, how observers conceptualize leadership, and how this conceptualization influences their observations and evaluations of the leader, are important to understanding the components of leadership. In chapter 8 on person perception and leadership, Douglas Brown and Robert Lord argue that leadership needs to be understood not just in terms of the effects of leadership traits and behaviors on subordinates' performance ("first order" theories of leadership) but also in terms of subordinates' cognitive process, their antecedents (e.g., subordinates' schemas and affect, environmental conditions, leader behavior and characteristics, and performance outcomes), and their effects on behavioral ratings. Moreover, subordinates' cognitions mediate the effects of leader behaviors on subordinates' motivation, cognition, affect, and performance. That is, how subordinates categorize and interpret leadership influences how they react to it.

Specifically, Brown and Lord suggest that subordinates' categorization of leadership and their sense-making processes determine the influence that leaders exert over their subordinates and the formal judgments subordinates make when they are asked to rate their supervisor's leadership behaviors and characteristics. As such, leadership needs to be understood in terms of information processing and a social-cognitive perspective. Brown and Lord review the cognitive and information processing mechanisms that underlie subordinate leadership categorization. They argue that it is not leadership traits in and of themselves that affect performance outcomes but rather how these traits and behaviors are perceived by followers that lead to these outcomes. When one ignores cognitive processes, one misses a key element of leadership. In other words, leadership, such as charisma and transformational qualities, is in the eye of the beholder as much as the leader.

Brown and Lord discuss how subordinates' knowledge of leadership categories develops through day-to-day experiences. People develop large knowledge structures about leadership, and these structures are widely shared and understood. However, leadership schemas or prototypes vary with context (e.g., business, military, and education) and organizational level (executive, middle, and lower management). They also vary with national culture, task type, and gender. In addition, a leader's characteristics prime perceptual categories that are used by subordinates in making sense of the leader's behaviors. As a result, there are variations in how leadership is conceptualized depending on the perceivers' experiences over time, their needs and goals, and the task or situation.

In addition to understanding subordinates' cognitive processes, it is also important to understand leaders' cognitions in terms of how they view the situation and others' reactions to them. Leaders adjust their behavior depending on the situational demands. The idea of standardized assessment of leadership skills or capabilities may be more a convenient fiction than reality, and appropriate leadership is highly variable from time to time and place to place. Leaders need to recognize environmental and social cues that convey differences in their subordinates' needs and expectations as well as demands of the task at the moment. Leaders need self-monitoring skills and social intelligence to discern these requirements. Indeed, these cognitive processes may be more critical for leadership than any specific pattern of leadership traits or behaviors.

In chapter 9, Kurt Kraiger and Herman Aguinis examine how supervisors assess subordinates' learning and development needs, career motivation, and progress. Specifically, they consider the processes by which supervisors and others evaluate employees' learning and developmental needs, make decisions affecting their career motivation or expectations for training, and track their progress through training. They discuss interpersonal perception and evaluation factors affecting training success at three stages: pretraining, during training, and post-training. For each stage, they identify and define person perception constructs that affect judgments of capabilities and accomplishments, which in turn, will affect employee learning and development. They argue that a failure to account for cognitive heuristics involved in needs assessment and training design phases may result in either faulty decisions about the need for training or undermine trainee self-efficacy and motivation to learn. They recommend that errors in judgment can be avoided by (a) making training analysts and course designers aware of the possible deleterious effects of these attribution errors, (b) encouraging them to challenge statements of causality made by supervisors or incumbents (e.g., asking for supporting documentation), and (c) showing trainers how to anticipate and correct for the impact of these evaluations on employee attitudes.

Coaching is a leadership development method that has become highly popular. Firms hire external coaches to assist their top leaders in obtaining, understanding, and applying performance feedback. Also, organizations expect managers at all levels to coach the people who report to them. Coaching helps managers use available feedback to enhance their self-knowledge and adjust their behavior to increase their effectiveness. In chapter 10, James Smither and Susanne Reilly highlight the elements of person perception that affect the coaching process. They organize this chapter around a five-stage model of effective coaching: (a) establishing the coaching relationship, (b) assessment, (c) goal setting and development planning, (d) implementation, and (e) evaluating progress and the coaching relationship.

Establishing the coaching relationship requires understanding how schemas shape attributions, motives for self-knowledge, impression management tactics, and the role of liking and reciprocity in compliance and persuasion. Assessment involves the influence of the coach's schemas, correspondent inferences (the tendency to underestimate the power of situations compared to dispositions), self-deception and inflated self-views, and receptivity to feedback when knowing that a coach is looking at performance data. Goal setting is affected by principles of goal and control theories, implementation intentions, and an orientation toward maximizing positive outcomes (promotion focus) versus negative outcomes (prevention focus). Implementation is affected by self-efficacy, self-fulfilling prophecies, irrational persistence, and self-handicapping. Finally, evaluating progress is affected by the individual's tendency to slot feedback into a specific self-schema and the extent to which the individual has a broad conceptualization versus a narrow conceptualization of possible self. In light of the person perception and social psychological phenomena related to the different stages of coaching, Smither and Reilly review how coaches can understand and manage employees' expectations about the coaching experience, help employees become comfortable with heightened self-awareness, and help them minimize their biases and illusions.

In the section's final chapter, Zvi Strassberg writes about issues of person perception in dealing with problem employees—in particular, people who behave aggressively in the workplace. In doing so, he examines the role of social cognition in the origins and remediation of interpersonal difficulties. He proposes a model that provides a comprehensive understanding of social cognitive functioning, describes the cognitive mechanisms of social competence versus interpersonal difficulties (emphasizing aggression), and shows how the model can be used to facilitate positive behavioral change. Strassberg draws on theory and research from contemporary clinical psychology to provide a basis for understanding, assessing, and intervening in problems of social maladjustment. He applies a social information processing model to understanding interpersonal skills and difficulties in the workplace. He then discusses the model's use in planning and implementing interventions for social maladjustment with a meaningful case example. Next he suggests applications of the model to the demands placed on professionals concerned with education, training, coaching, and counseling within organizations.

Strassberg's social information processing model for dealing with problem employees begins with social cues that influence people's motivation and how they process information. Processing steps include encoding and interpreting information, formulating goals and responses, and taking action. These steps are influenced by the actors' (e.g., supervisor's and subordinates') motivation and cognitive shemas about themselves, others, and the situation, as well as by scripts (beliefs) about the way problems are, or should be, solved. Processing deficits and biases are likely from aggressive individuals. These include limited searching for information, negative distortions, negative attributions about others' intentions, personalizing feedback, behavior repertoires limited to aggression, low self-efficacy for competent behavior (or, conversely, the belief that aggression is the only response that works), and deficiency in assertion skills that lead to consensus and cooperation. Workplace applications and interventions to facilitate problem resolution include executive coaching, training, and organizational support (e.g., having a human resource professional "on-call" for consultation to deal with glitches in implementing therapeutic strategies or provide positive feedback for behavioral change).

8

Leadership and Perceiver Cognition: Moving Beyond First Order Constructs

Douglas J. Brown
University of Waterloo

Robert G. Lord
University of Akron

Leadership has been a central concern for industrial and organizational psychology since its inception. This is because both common sense theories (Calder, 1977; Pfeffer, 1977) and careful empirical analyses (e.g., Day & Lord, 1988; Oeth, 1996; Thomas, 1988) show that leadership can have a substantial impact on organizational performance. Consequently, the assessment of qualities or behaviors of leaders has been a continuing interest of researchers, in part, because it is viewed as a means to understand a leader's impact on organizational performance. Leadership assessment is also a continuing process performed by organizational members as they seek to understand their social and political context and who is likely to exert influence or affect organizational performance. This informal, intuitive assessment of leadership has immediate practical consequences for organizational members. It is the basis of social power (Hollander & Offerman, 1990), and it influences the amount of discretion accorded a leader (Hambrick & Finklestein, 1987).

Common sense assessments of leadership by organizational members also are implicit in many of the formal mechanisms that are used for assessing leadership. Perhaps the most common means of assessing leaders is to ask other organizational members to evaluate leadership capabilities or to rate specific leadership behaviors. Such ratings are also the predominant type of data used by social scientists in trying to understand how leaders impact on organizational performance. In short, the informal assessment of leadership qualities and behaviors is a central element underlying informal organizational politics and influence, formal leadership assessment practices, and scientific research in leadership.

Although these leader focused concerns have sustained interest in informal assessment of leadership, social cognitive researchers have investigated the perceptual processes that actually produce leadership perceptions. Dominating this literature has been a focus on understanding the variance in leadership that is attributable to aspects of leadership targets (e.g., behavior or traits). Although leader qualities are clearly important for understanding leadership (Lord, Brown, & Harvey, in press), the social-cognitive processes of subordinates and observers are also important. Because leadership ultimately involves the behaviors, traits, and characteristics of leaders as these are interpreted by observers (Calder, 1977; Hollander, 1992; Lord & Maher, 1991), the scientific study of leadership requires sensitivity to perceiver's information processing and not simply to a leader's characteristics and actions.

Unfortunately, most popular and contemporary approaches to leadership have not explicitly considered the role of person perception processes. Rather, leadership research and practice primarily has concentrated on creating behavioral rating tools, for example, the Multifactor Leadership Questionnaire (MLQ; Bass, 1985) and the Leader Behavior Description Questionnaire (LBDQ; Stogdill, 1963), and describing the traits and behaviors thought to underlie effective leadership. Such approaches may be problematic for the scientific advancement of leadership. In fact, little appears to have changed in this literature since Calder (1977) critiqued researchers for focusing on first order constructs (common sense views of leadership) to the neglect of second order constructs (constructs grounded in scientific theory). That is, leadership researchers have primarily defined leadership in terms of easily observable behaviors (e.g., communicating a vision) and their direct impact on outcomes, rather than in terms of underlying processes and mechanisms (e.g., why or how does vision influence subordinates) that are derived from scientific theory. Thus, although current popular approaches to leadership have expanded the descriptive scope of leadership behaviors (e.g., LBDQ to the MLQ) and have cataloged behavior-outcome relationships, this approach has not greatly advanced our understanding of the underlying process that would explain how one individual can exert influence over individuals, groups, and organizations. Attributional theories of leadership (Martinko & Gardner, 1987) and social or social-cognitive research on leadership (Lord & Maher, 1991; Meindl, 1995) have addressed this issue, and are thus the focus of this chapter.

Here we suggest that subordinate categorization of leaders and subordinate sense-making processes represent core mechanisms that can be used to understand both the influence that leaders exert over their subordinates during informal day-to-day interactions, as well as the formal leadership judgments that are made by raters. The categorization of a target as a leader by subordinates can impact both the influence that a leader can have over his or her subordinates (Lord & Smith, 1999), as well as more formal assessments of leadership (Murphy & Cleveland, 1995). Ultimately, leadership is a well-learned social category that is applied and used by social actors to guide their interactions with their environments and make judgments about fellow organizational actors.

Because leadership is applicable in most social interactions (i.e., leadership emerges in most groups), humans have developed highly elaborate, well-learned, and contextually driven leadership knowledge structures. In many respects, leadership knowledge is expertly applied by humans (Lord & Maher, 1990), allowing them to quickly and efficiently (i.e., with little effort) transform the superficial surface features of their social or physical environments into deeper meaning structures. For example, data indicate that leadership is ascribed to individuals with higher verbal participation rates (e.g., Stein & Heller, 1979), individuals who are visually salient (e.g., Phillips & Lord, 1981), and individuals who sit at the head of a jury table (e.g., Bray, Struckman-Johnson, Osborne, McFarlane, & Scott, 1978). Although such disparate factors may not appear to have much in common, the deeper meaning suggested by all of these behaviors is dominance, which is a key dimension of the underlying structure of perceivers' leadership prototypes (Lord, Foti, & De Vader, 1984). In this chapter, we suggest that advancement in scholarly thinking about leadership will benefit from the integration of the second order constructs that underlie expert human information processing with a social-cognitive perspective on leadership.

In presenting our thesis we address three issues. First, we consider whether leadership can be divorced from subordinate information processing and categorization, and through two examples we show that an understanding of rater's information processing is necessary, even in areas that have not formally incorporated such processes. Following this issue, we review the basic cognitive and information processing mechanisms that underlie subordinate leadership categorization mechanisms. In particular, we discuss the content of leadership knowledge and the processes that are relevant to its application. Finally, we discuss the advantages of approaching leadership from a cognitive perspective both in terms of application and in terms of building leadership knowledge and theory.

A CASE FOR SUBORDINATE INFORMATION PROCESSING IN THE STUDY OF LEADERSHIP

Questionnaires

By far the largest volume of leadership work has used behavioral questionnaires, which are both convenient and reflect common sense theories that leader actions directly impact on organizational outcomes. Although these evaluations have taken different surface forms (e.g., LBDQ and MLQ), the basic procedures and assumptions that underlie the use of these tools has remained relatively static across time. In the case of both the LBDQ and MLQ, extensive pilot work was conducted to capture the behaviors that underlie leadership. From this larger set of items, factor analyses were used to isolate a smaller set of constructs. For example, in the case of the MLQ a larger set of transformational leadership behaviors was reduced to four broad behavioral dimensions (e.g., Individual Consideration, Intellectual Stimulation, Inspirational Motivation, and Idealized Influence), whereas research on the LBDQ has typically focused on two broad dimensions (e.g., Initiating Structure and Consideration). In both cases, the dominant method for generating leader behavior measurement is through observer ratings, typically subordinates, of the degree to which a leadership target engages in specific behaviors. Finally, in both cases the predominant theoretical approach has been to build theories relating these behavioral dimensions to organizational outcomes like subordinate performance or satisfaction.

Because the theoretical foundation of both perspectives is rooted within a behavioral approach to leadership (e.g., leadership effects are the result of leader behavior), little attention has been paid to understanding the subordinate information processing that underlies responses to these questionnaires. Yet, work within both literatures suggests that questionnaire responses may be highly influenced by individual rater's information processing

(Avolio & Yammarino, 1990; Phillips & Lord, 1981; Yammarino & Dubinsky, 1994). For example, in a series of studies using Within and Between Analysis (WABA), Yammarino and his colleagues examined the degree to which responses to the MLQ reflect individual, dyadic, or group level effects. In all cases, little support was found for dyadic or group level effects, which would be consistent with a behavioral approach; however, strong evidence was found for individual level effects, which suggests substantial rater effects. From such results, Yammarino and Dubinsky (1994) concluded that transformational leadership, as assessed by the MLQ, may exist, "in the eye of the beholder" (p. 805).

An implication of the Yammarino and Dubinsky (1994) research is that the actual behavior of a leader only partially explains the variance in questionnaire ratings and that a full understanding of these ratings requires an examination of the cognitive and affective processes of raters (Hall & Lord, 1995). In fact, Bass and Avolio (1989) found that individual responses to the MLQ items are related to the prototypicality ratings of items by raters. Consistent with these findings, considerable research on questionnaire-based descriptions of leadership behavior indicates that perceivers who rated fictitious leaders yielded the same factor structure for questionnaires as perceivers who rated their own supervisor (Eden & Leviatan, 1975; Rush, Thomas, & Lord, 1977). This research suggests that questionnaire ratings reflect both the implicit theories of raters as well as the actual behaviors of leaders. Further, it suggests that first order constructs—leadership dimensions—may be more dependent on ratee cognitive constructs than leader behavioral tendencies.

In addition to "cold" cognitive categorization processes, recent work also suggests that the "hot" affective classification of a leadership target may be important for understanding questionnaire-based ratings, particularly those related to transformational and charismatic leadership (Brown & Keeping, 1999; Lewter & Lord, 1992). For example, exploratory analyses by Lewter and Lord indicated that rater liking predicts MLQ ratings independently of the actual behaviors exhibited by a leadership target. Similarly, Brown and Keeping found that, on average, liking accounted for 31% of the variance in rater's responses to MLQ items. Such results are not surprising when it is realized that an early stage in impression formation is the development of an overall affective evaluation of a target (Srull & Wyer, 1989) and that mental representations include both affective and cognitive components (Edwards, 1990). In fact, research by James and James (1989) suggests that a higher order hedonic factor may underlie rater's responses to questionnaire items, and that this overall affective factor may account for the relationships that have been found among organizational questionnaires.

Trait-Based Perspectives

Often, leadership potential has been assessed with personality and trait-based measures. This work has ranged from Miner's (1978) examinations of an individual's motivation to lead to work on the trait-based correlates of leadership. In much of the trait-based literature, strong relationships have been found between individual difference measures and leadership (Hogan, Curphy, & Hogan, 1994). For example, a meta-analysis of the trait literature (Lord, De Vader & Alliger, 1986) shows strong and consistent associations among traits such as intelligence, dominance, masculine orientations, and leadership emergence (with corrected correlations of traits with leadership emergence being as high as .50). Subsequent research has extended the wide variety of traits associated with leadership to include traits associated with behavioral flexibility, such as self-monitoring ability (Zaccaro, Foti, & Kenny, 1991). Finally, recent research suggests that instead of concentrating on single traits, investigators should focus on personality patterns (Smith & Foti, 1998). The work of Smith and Foti indicates that a pattern of high dominance, high general self-efficacy, and high intelligence is strongly associated with leadership emergence.

Although the trait literature appears to suggest that leadership originates from a leader, an alternative, information processing interpretation of these data is equally plausible. Hollander and Julian (1969), for example, noted that traits in and of themselves do not influence organizational and group outcomes, rather it is the traits or patterns of traits as they are perceived by followers that lead to these outcomes. Consistent with this idea, Operario and Fiske (chapter 2 of this volume) review social psychological findings that demonstrate how perceiver categorization of individual targets can substantially impact a perceiver's behaviors and thoughts with respect to that target (e.g., Chen & Bargh, 1997; Snyder, Tanke, & Berscheid, 1977). Simply put, a subordinate's perceptual categorization of environmental stimuli (e.g., their supervisor), serves as a constraint on a subordinate's actions. In fact, some authors have gone so far as to suggest that perceptions and actions share a representational system (Dijksterhuis & van Knippenberg, 1998). Humans must quickly and dynamically translate environmental perceptions into behavior, thoughts, and feelings, which is facilitated by a common representational system for perceptions and behavior. Just as the categorization of a dangerous object in the environment increases an individual's ability to flee, the categorization of a supervisor as a leader increases compliance by subordinates. The reverse process operates as well. A leader's perception of a subordinate's ability affects their behavior with respect to that subordinate (Eden, 1992).

Overall, the position just outlined suggests that leadership work that focuses strictly on traits as the cause of leadership misspecifies the underlying process by ignoring an important component. In order to fully comprehend the influence of leaders, it is necessary to explore the cognitive categorization mechanisms of perceivers. Furthermore, such categorization mechanisms may be equally applicable for understanding the influence of leadership behavior on organizational outcomes. As work by Uleman, Newman, and Moskewitz (1996) and Gilbert (1989) indicates, behavior is quickly and automatically encoded in terms of trait categories by perceivers, as traits are the currency of social interaction and perception. Thus, it may be that leadership behavior has its primary influence on subordinates through the activation of trait perceptions which are used to categorize an individual as a leader or nonleader (Cantor & Mischel, 1979; Lord & Maher, 1991). Once applied to a target, a leadership category can constrain a subordinate's access to target related knowledge structures that, in turn, serve as the proximal determinants of action, thought, and feeling (e.g., Baldwin, 1992; Lord, Brown, & Freiberg, 1999).

Importantly, our position suggests that attempts that are focused on isolating precise leadership behaviors or traits fail to recognize that leadership is the result of social-cognitive processes within followers (Lord & Maher, 1991). Figure 8.1 illustrates the differences between traditional leadership models that focus on first order constructs displayed in panel a (i.e., behavioral descriptions), and those that focus on second order constructs displayed in panel b (i.e., perceiver perceptual and psychological processes). As indicated in this figure, first order theories suggest that leadership stems simply from the traits and behaviors of leadership that have been isolated through behavioral observations, whereas the foundation of second order theories is based on a thorough understanding of subordinate perceptual and sense-making processes (labeled subordinate cognition in Fig. 8.1).

Interestingly, recent work that has emerged in the transformational/ charismatic leadership literature is consonant with our social-cognitive perspective. Much of this work has converged toward a paradigm that emphasizes leader behavior and follower effects (Conger, 1999), yet this work also recognizes the importance of follower values, identities, and attributional processes. For example, Gardner and Avolio (1998) suggested that charismatic leadership can be considered from a dramaturgical perspective

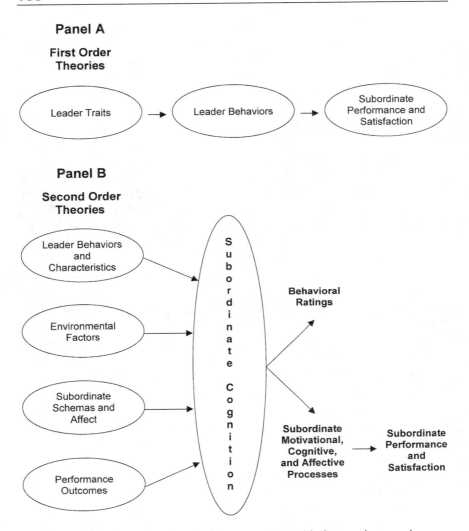

FIG. 8.1. Modeling leadership processes with first and second order factors.

that, "demonstrates the centrality of identification processes to the attribution of charismatic leadership" (p. 35). Their work suggests that charisma develops through a dynamic and integrative process in which cognitive, motivational, affective, and social contagion processes link leader and follower self-systems while producing attributions of charismatic qualities to leaders.

Summary

As our discussion thus far highlights, whether one is interested in the ratings assigned to leaders or understanding how leaders influence subordinates, information processing mechanisms are a key consideration. The centrality of information processing is not surprising given that humans are expert person perception processors who quickly translate and map the surface structure (e.g., behaviors and situations) of their social environments into deeper meaning structures (categories, traits, etc.) to form coherent, context specific interpretive frames of their social environments.

On the basis of the previous discussion, three questions become important for understanding the social-cognitive foundation of leadership. First, if leadership is based on a knowledge structure that is used by perceivers, what is the content of this knowledge structure? (See Lord et al., 1984; Offerman, Kennedy, & Wirtz, 1994.) Second, if leadership involves the application of a well-learned knowledge structure, then can one use what one knows about other knowledge structures to understand when leadership will be applied by social perceivers? (See Higgins & Brendl, 1995.) Third, if leadership involves perceivers using a previously learned knowledge structure to form coherent interpretations of their environments, then how are these categories dynamically adjusted to fit the current need or identities of the social actor and his or her current context? (See Hanges, Lord, & Dickson, 2000; Lord et al., in press; Lord, Brown, Harvey, & Hall, 2000.) We address each of these questions in the following section.

LEADERSHIP AS A KNOWLEDGE STRUCTURE

Content of Leadership Knowledge

According to Lord and Maher (1991), detailed leadership knowledge categories develop through day-to-day experiences within groups. Initially, environmental exemplars form the basis of an individual's leadership knowledge. With repeated exposure and experience with leaders, however, perceivers extract deeper and more abstract leadership knowledge structures (e.g., Klein, Loftus, Trafton, & Fuhrman, 1992; Sherman, 1996; Sherman & Klein, 1994). Consistent with this idea, Matthews, Lord, and Walker (1990) found that young children make their leadership judgments on the basis of exemplars, whereas older children's leadership judgments are based on abstract prototypes. These abstract knowledge structures, in turn, can be used by perceivers to quickly translate behavior into a deeper meaning by categorizing a target's behavior in terms of leadership.

Work that has examined the content of leadership knowledge structures suggests that individuals' leadership categories are broad, multidimensional cognitive structures (Offerman et al., 1994). In the most comprehensive assessment of leadership knowledge structures, Offerman and her colleagues had multiple samples generate and rate items that were associated with leadership. Their results suggest that leadership knowledge structures are composed of eight broad dimensions: sensitivity, dedication, tyranny, charisma, attractiveness, masculinity, intelligence, and strength. Moreover, these factors were invariant across sex groupings and across descriptions of a "leader," and "effective leader" or a "supervisor" stimulus conditions.

Although superficially Offerman et al.'s (1994) results might suggest that leadership can be characterized as a single, multidimensional knowledge structure, the reader is reminded that expert knowledge is domain specific and is learned through domain relevant experience (Chi, Glaser, & Farr, 1988). Offerman et al.'s work pertained to a single context—business. However, the complexity of modern life provides exposure to leaders in multiple domains, which suggests leadership knowledge will be organized into knowledge structures specific to multiple domains. Accordingly, leadership prototypes have been found to vary across contexts (Lord et al., 1984) and hierarchical levels (Baumgardner, Lord, & Foti, 1990). Recent work has also suggested that leadership knowledge may vary with culture (Den Hartog, House, Hanges, & Ruiz-Quintanilla, 1999; Gerstner & Day, 1994; O'Connell, Lord, & O'Connell, 1990). The cultural differences in leadership knowledge may be a particularly important distinction for leadership practitioners to understand given the globalization of many activities (e.g., business, finance, politics, and military activities). Shaw (1990) suggested that one cause of failure for expatriate managers may be because their definitions of leadership do not match that of their followers.

Undoubtably the most comprehensive assessment of cross-cultural differences in leadership prototypes comes from the work of Robert House and his GLOBE partners. In a study involving 15,022 middle managers from 60 different societies and cultures, Den Hartog et al. (1999) examined the extent to which 112 leadership items were seen as, "impeding or facilitating usually effective leadership" (p. 235). They predicted that items indicative of charismatic leadership qualities would be universally endorsed but they allowed for the possibility that the expression of these qualities could vary across culture.

Results supported both of these expectations. Three of their six secondary factors (charismatic/value based, team oriented, and participative) were prototypical of outstanding leadership in all cultures. Similarly, several sets of items were universally endorsed. Many items (35) were also found to vary substantially across culture, and these included several items associated with charismatic/transformational leadership, such as enthusiastic, compassionate, sensitive, unique, and risk taking. Further, qualitative analyses from many countries (Mexico, China, the Netherlands, and Australia) showed that the expression of charismatic qualities varied across culture.

If we conceptualize specific attributes and the translation of these attributes into perceived leadership qualities as reflecting surface structures, then surface structures did indeed show substantial cross-cultural variability. However, more fundamental aspects of leadership, such as charismatic/value oriented, team oriented, or participative leadership, were universally seen as beneficial. These secondary factors are more removed from actual behaviors and can be considered to reflect deep-structure properties of leadership. Though universally endorsed, we should stress that such properties reflect inferences by perceivers that may be affected by many factors in addition to qualities of leaders (situational factors, perceiver needs, goals and recent experience, perceptual salience, etc.). Deep structures are individual interpretations or meanings constructed by perceivers.

The preceding discussion highlights both that humans possess large well-developed knowledge structures regarding leadership and that these knowledge structures are widely shared and understood. Although the content of leadership knowledge is important, this information does not indicate when leadership knowledge will be applied. In fact, research in other domains suggests that it is important to understand the processes that underlie category application and activation and not simply category content. As noted by Lepore and Brown (1997), different aspects of category knowledge (e.g., positive vs. negative elements) are activated for high versus low prejudiced individuals, a finding that has been substantiated by other researchers (e.g., Wittenbrink, Judd, & Park, 1997). Results such as these suggest that a cognitively based understanding of leadership cannot simply focus on knowledge structure content, as has been the case in much previous work. Instead, a cognitively based theory requires an understanding of the processes and mechanism through which leadership categories become activated.

When is a Leader Category Used?

If leadership is a social category (as we have previously outlined), which is used by humans to make sense of their social environments, then the principles that dictate the application of other knowledge structures are applicable to the leadership literature. Here we suggest that there are two basic processes that underlie whether a particular category will be used. First, knowledge must be accessible to be used. Generally speaking, accessible knowledge guides thought and directs behavior. Second, and related to the first point, a category must have functional value within a given context. For example, an individual's knowledge of chess configurations has little functional value when playing checkers. We discuss each of these principles in the following section.

Leadership Category Accessibility.
Knowledge accessibility refers to an individual's preparedness to use a particular knowledge structure (Higgins & Brendl, 1995). Because humans possess much more knowledge then can be applied at any given point in time, category (schema, prototype, or trait) use is heavily dependent on accessibility. This general principle is so robust for understanding human information processing that it has been demonstrated across a wide range of literatures (the self literature, Markus & Wurf, 1987; the attitudes literature, Fazio & Williams, 1986; the impression formation literature, Higgins, Rholes, & Jones, 1977; and the personality literature, Mischel & Shoda, 1995). Moreover, accessibility has been found to be important not only for understanding perceptual processes but also for understanding human action (Bargh & Chartrand, 1999). Clearly, knowledge accessibility is a basic process that should be an important consideration in any domain that contains a human information processing component (e.g., action, thought, or affect). Two factors that dictate category accessibility and use in the leadership literature are whether a category has been environmentally primed and whether an individual is chronically prepared to use a particular category (Bargh, 1994).

Human information processors activate knowledge when an impasse is encountered and a solution is not immediately available (Newell, 1990). This suggests that leadership knowledge is activated within individuals when it has functional value for addressing current environmental concerns. Given that leaders are expected to provide direction and produce good performance outcomes, we anticipate that perceivers who are faced with ambiguity and poor performance will access their leadership knowledge when searching for remedies. Recent work is consistent with this idea. For example, Meindl (1995) stressed that leadership is a social construction process of perceivers and that crisis accentuates the attribution of causality to leaders. Extending this line of research, Emrich (1999) found that crisis contexts unconsciously activate leadership schema in perceivers. Using a simulated selection task, she found greater false recall of leadership behaviors for applicants for managerial jobs when they were expected to manage units in crisis as compared to tranquil situations. This difference in recalled behavior occurred even though the information provided about the managerial applicants was exactly the same in the crisis and tranquil conditions. In short, this literature suggests that environmental contexts activate leadership knowledge as an interpretive framework for social actors (see Fig. 8.1, panel b). Moreover, Emrich's results highlight that perceivers need not be consciously aware that knowledge structures have been activated (Bargh, 1994).

In addition to the environment, individual differences in chronic accessibility exist between individuals, leading to differences in individual's preparedness to use knowledge structures such as leadership. Because individuals do not analyze all possible categories (e.g., traits, schemas, or scripts) before applying one in a given context, the categories that come to mind quickest are utilized. Therefore, individuals with a highly accessible leadership category (e.g., leadership self-schematics) would be anticipated to chronically utilize a leadership category (Smith, Brown, Lord, & Engle, 1998). One factor that substantially affects the accessibility of a category is whether it is self-relevant. Because self-relevant information is highly elaborated (Banaji & Prentice, 1994) and it serves as a referent for many of our decisions regarding others (e.g., Dunning & Hayes, 1996), it tends to be accessed quickly in a wide variety of situations. Therefore, individuals who are schematic (Markus, 1977) with regard to leadership may be chronically primed to use leadership categories.

Applicability of Knowledge. In addition to the activation of a knowledge structure, knowledge must be applicable if it is to be used in a given context. Because leadership is a category that is applied to individuals, this category should only be used when perceivers see people as important causes of organizational events. Therefore, external attributions of behavior will undermine leadership attributions. A large number of experimental studies show that when participants are given information indicating positive group outcomes, leadership perceptions are increased; when participants are given information regarding poor group outcomes, leadership perceptions are diminished (see Lord, 1985, for a review). However, these performance-cue effects are greater when perceivers used person rather than script schema (Murphy & Jones, 1993) and when they attribute causality to leaders rather than external factors (Maurer & Lord, 1991; Phillips & Lord, 1981).

Clearly, these results suggest that leadership is a potentially relevant knowledge structure when behavior is attributable to human actors. Extending this line of thinking, we anticipate that individual differences in the tendency to make internal versus external attributions will influence the application of a leadership category. Some examples of individual difference factors that may have an impact include: internal versus external locus of control (Weiner, 1985), entity versus incremental theories of performance (Gervey, Chiu, Hong, & Dweck, 1999), and cultural differences (Choi, Nisbett, & Norenzayan, 1999; Menon, Morris, Chiu, & Hong, 1999).

Dynamic Aspects of Leadership Structures

Thus far, our presentation of the cognitive basis of leadership has treated category prototypes as relatively fixed perceptual structures. However, the notion that categories are fixed memory structures has been criticized by Barsalou (1983), who demonstrated that categories can be constructed on-the-fly. Lord et al. (2000) argued that the distinctions among various leadership categories are too numerous and too context sensitive to assume that they all represent different fixed-memory structures that are learned through extensive experience. They noted that studies have shown that leadership prototypes vary with context (e.g., business, military, and education), hierarchical level (upper or lower level management), national culture, task type, and gender. Further, it has also been suggested by Hall and Lord (1995) that leader characteristics can prime different perceptual categories in followers.

In total, this work suggests that a more flexible means of generating context specific categories is needed. Building on developments in cognitive science, Lord et al. (in press) argued that prototypes are generated by preconscious, subsymbolic information processing architectures (connectionist architectures) that can operate in parallel to create a context-sensitive, interpretive structure on-the-fly. Because such architectures operate in parallel, they are well suited to integrate many sources of information very rapidly, typically in less than half a second.

Connectionist architectures use networks of simple processing units that continuously integrate information from input sources and pass the resulting activation (or inhibition) on to connected (output) units. In such networks, the meaning created by an activated pattern depends both on the nature of the inputs (i.e., context) and the strength of connections among units (i.e., weights that incorporate past learning). Because such networks construct meaning based on the activation of an entire network, they provide

Contextual Constraints

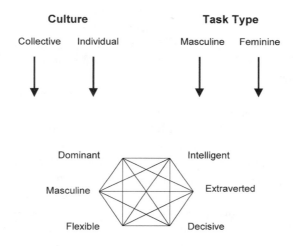

Perceiver's Leadership Schema

FIG. 8.2. An example of a connectionist model.

excellent representations of pattern recognition (categorization) processes. Smith and Foti's (1998) work described earlier shows the importance of patterns in leadership categorizations. Interestingly, connectionist networks allow for both stability, which arises from connections among units that change slowly, and for flexibility, which results from different patterns in input activation, that can change with context.

A simple example of a connectionist architecture, that is applicable to leadership is depicted in Fig. 8.2. Captured in this figure, and expressed in our previous discussion, are the two aspects of connectionist models that allow for the dynamic, situation specific creation of a leadership category by perceivers. First, there are basic elements of leadership knowledge. This refers to the content of leadership knowledge (e.g., traits) that we discussed earlier in this chapter; this is depicted in the bottom portion of the figure. Importantly, the connections between these elements vary in their strength, such that some elements serve as a strong activation source (or inhibition) for some elements (e.g., dominant and masculine) but are more weakly connected to others (e.g., dominant and flexible). Second, the context also serves as an important source of activation for different aspects of leadership schema. In Fig. 8.2, for example, aspects of a culture (e.g., collectivistic vs.

individualistic) and the task context (e.g., masculine job vs. feminine job) are taken into account in parallel by perceivers to activate or inhibit different elements of a perceiver's leadership schema. For example, in feminine task environments, flexibility and extroversion may be strongly activated by context, whereas in masculine task environments, masculinity and dominance may be strongly activated by context. Interestingly, when multiple contextual factors (e.g., gender type of task and culture) are taken into account at once, hybrid cognitive structures are created that are based on all contextual sources and the strength of connections between basic content units (Hanges et al., 2000; Lord & Brown, 2000; Smith & DeCoster, 1998).

An implication of connectionist thinking is that category prototypes should exhibit both variations across individuals (or cultures) based on experience (e.g., differing connections between elements), and variations within individuals as both their internal context (needs and goals) and external context (tasks or situations) change. These multiple contextual factors in turn will combine to form understandable prototypes. For example (see Fig. 8.2), a feminine task environment when combined with a collectivist cultural environment will be assimilated through connectionist processes to activate a strong communal leadership prototype. Alternatively, a masculine task environment when combined with an individualistic culture will be assimilated through connectionist processes to activate a strong agentic leadership prototype. Clearly, connectionist models can account for the contingent nature of leadership (Lord et al., 2000).

Moreover, connectionist models also provide a robust, general cognitive foundation on which to build an understanding of leadership behavior and follower perception. Leadership behavior, like other behaviors, is the result of perceiving situations, relating situational perceptions to accumulated knowledge, and then using scripts to guide the production of situationally appropriate behavior (Wofford & Goodwin, 1994). Thus, a critical step in script activation is a leader's perceptual interpretation of the current context. By dynamically and instantaneously integrating multiple environmental features, connectionist models can explain how leaders adapt their behavior on a moment-to-moment basis. Clearly, an advantage of approaching leadership from a connectionist perspective is that the same basic mechanisms can explain how perceivers' prototypes and leaders' behavioral scripts can be fluid and contextually sensitive, yet at the same time be coherent and consistent over time when context is stable.

A connectionist model has important implications when applied to leadership assessment. First, it implies that the knowledge structures used by perceivers to create a deeper meaning for leadership are likely to be very context specific. To some extent, leaders must also adjust on-the-fly to context specific meanings. The notion of a "standardized" assessment of leadership skills or capacities may be simply a convenient fiction, in that appropriate leadership is highly variable. Second, what may be most critical for leaders is the ability to recognize environmental and social cues that convey differences in context. Thus, self-monitoring skills (Zaccaro et al., 1991), social intelligence (Zaccaro, Gilbert, Thor, & Mumford, 1991), and meta-cognitive processes pertaining to how one is perceived by others (Malloy and Janowski, 1992) may be more critical to effective leadership than any specific pattern of traits or learned leadership behaviors. This possibility certainly warrants extensive research in the future.

CONCLUSION

Historically, leadership researchers have focused on first order constructs (e.g., behaviors) and neglected the second order constructs (e.g., processes) that may underlie leadership (Calder, 1977). In this chapter, we suggested that the foundations of a comprehensive theory of leadership requires researchers to understand the social-cognitive processes of organizational actors. Both the formal leadership evaluations that are made of leaders (e.g., questionnaires) and the process through which leaders impact their subordinates appear to have a social-cognitive foundation. Moreover, general social-cognitive principles may serve as the foundation from which to understand a leaders' actions (Lord et al., 2000). Thus, social-cognition and sense-making processes provide a robust psychological foundation on which to understand leadership.

This is, however, only one possible way to understanding leadership. We are not suggesting that researchers seeking to develop second order rather than common sense theories of leadership can only rely on cognitive science for second order constructs. In fact, there are many second order constructs that can serve as the foundation of a scientific theory of leadership. For example, recent work suggests that leadership theories can be founded on an understanding of the self-structures of subordinates, leaders, or both (Lord et al., 1999; Shamir, House, & Arthur, 1993). This approach is becoming central to our understanding of charismatic leadership (Conger, 1999). In addition, although they have not yet been used to understand leadership processes, theories of emotion (Izard, 1991; Lazarus, 1991) or attachment (Bowlby, 1969) might also provide useful constructs for developing second order leadership theories.

Our focus on subordinate cognitive processes may have a number of interesting implications for practitioners. Unlike first order theories, which imply that one should select leaders with specific qualities or attempt to intervene by training leadership behavior, the type of second order theories we describe imply that effective leadership requires feedback from and adjustments to subordinates. If leadership is critically dependent on subordinate cognitive processes, as we argue, then the development of effective leadership necessitates coupling leadership with feedback processes that are sensitive to follower cognitions (e.g., 360-degree feedback systems). In fact, Atwater, Roush, and Fischthal (1995) found that after receiving feedback from followers, leadership ratings improved. Our perspective also suggests that, in a more general sense, leadership practice might benefit from a "reverse engineering" perspective. That is, second order scientific constructs can be used to work backwards from complex organizational or social processes to understand the potential role of leaders and points of leverage in these processes for practitioners. First order theories of leadership essentially work forward from leader traits and behaviors, which may be a much less effective means to understand organizational phenomena.

REFERENCES

Atwater, L., Roush, P., & Fischthal, A. (1995). The influence of upward feedback on self- and follower ratings of leadership. *Personnel Psychology, 48*, 35–59.

Avolio, B. J., & Yammarino, F. J. (1990). Operationalizing charismatic leadership using a level of analysis framework. *Leadership Quarterly, 1*, 193–208.

Baldwin, B. W. (1992). Relational schemas and the processing of social information. *Psychological Bulletin, 112*, 461–484.

Banaji, M. R., & Prentice, D. A. (1994). The self in social contexts. *Annual Review of Psychology, 45*, 297–332.

Bargh, J. A. (1994). The four horsemen of automaticity: Awareness, intention, efficiency, and control in social cognition. In R. S. Wyer & T. K. Srull (Eds.), *Handbook of social cognition*. Hillsdale, NJ: Lawrence Erlbaum Associates.

Bargh, J. A., & Chartrand, T. (1999). The unbearable automaticity of being. *American Psychologist, 54*, 462–479.

Barsalou, L. W. (1983). Ad hoc categories. *Memory and Cognition, 11*, 211–227.

Bass, B. M. (1985). *Leadership and performance beyond expectations*. New York: The Free Press.

Bass, B. M., & Avolio, B. J. (1989). Potential biases in leadership measures: How prototypes, leniency, and general satisfaction relate to ratings and rankings of transformational and transactional leadership constructs. *Educational and Psychological Measurement, 49*, 509–527.

Baumgardner, T. L., Lord, R. G., & Forti, J. C. (1990). *A prescription for aspiring leaders: Implications of expert–novice schema differences and alternative leadership categorization models*. Unpublished manuscript, University of Akron, Ohio.

Bowlby, J. (1969). *Attachment and loss: Vol. 1. Attachment*. New York: Basic Books.

Bray, R. M., Struckman-Johnson, C., Osborne, M., McFarlane, J., & Scott, J. (1978). The effects of defendant status on decisions of student and community juries. *Social Psychology, 41*, 256–260.

Brown, D. J., & Keeping, L. M. (1999). *Examining the role of affect in transformational leadership.* Manuscript submitted for publication.

Calder, B. J. (1977). An attribution theory of leadership. In B. M. Staw and G. R. Salancik (Eds.), *New directions in organizational behavior* (pp. 179–204). Chicago: St. Clair Press.

Cantor, N., & Mischel, W. (1979). Prototypes in person perception. In L. Berkowitz (Ed.), *Advances in experimental social psychology.* New York: Academic Press.

Chen, M., & Bargh, J. A. (1997). Consequences of automatic evaluation: Immediate behavioral predispositions to approach or avoid the stimulus. *Personality and Social Psychology Bulletin, 25*, 215–224.

Chi, M. T. H., Glaser, R., & Farr, M. J. (1988). *The nature of expertise.* Hillsdale, N. J.: Lawrence Erlbaum Associates.

Choi, I., Nisbett, R. E., & Norenzayan, A. (1999). Causal attribution across cultures: Variations and universality. *Psychological Bulletin, 125*, 47–63.

Conger, J. A. (1999). Charismatic and transformational leadership in organizations: An insider's perspective on these developing streams of research. *Leadership Quarterly, 10*, 145–180.

Day, D. V., & Lord, R. G. (1988). Executive leadership and organizational performance: Suggestions for a new theory and methodology. *Journal of Management, 14*, 111–122.

Den Hartog, D. N., House, R. J., Hanges, P. J., & Ruiz-Quintanilla (1999). Culture specific and cross-culturally generalizable implicit leadership theories: Are the attributes of charismatic/transformational leadership universally endorsed? *Leadership Quarterly, 10*, 219–258.

Dijksterhuis, A., & van Knippenberg, A. (1998). The relation between perception and behavior, or how to win a game of Trivial Pursuit. *Journal of Personality and Social Psychology, 74*, 865–877.

Dunning, D., & Hayes, A. F. (1996). Evidence for egocentric comparison in social judgment. *Journal of Personality and Social Psychology, 73*, 459–469.

Eden, D. (1992). Leadership and expectations: Pygmalion effects and other self-fulfilling prophecies in organizations. *Leadership Quarterly, 3*, 271–305.

Eden, D., & Leviatan, U. (1975). Implicit leadership theory as a determinant of the factor structure underlying supervisory behavior scales. *Journal of Applied Psychology, 60*, 736–741.

Edwards, K. (1990). The interplay of affect and cognition in attitude formation and change. *Journal of Personality and Social Psychology, 59*, 202–216.

Emrich, C. G. (1999). Context effects in leadership perceptions. *Personality and Social Psychology Bulletin, 25*, 991–1006.

Fazio, R. H., & Williams, C. J. (1986). Attitude accessibility as a moderator of the attitude perception and attitude behavior relations: An investigation of the 1984 presidential election. *Journal of Personality and Social Psychology, 51*, 505–514.

Gardner, W., & Avolio, B. J. (1998). The charismatic relationship: A dramaturgical perspective. *Academy of Management Review, 23*, 32–58.

Gerstner, C. R., & Day, D. V. (1994). Cross-cultural comparison of leadership prototypes. *Leadership Quarterly, 2*, 121–134.

Gervey, B. M., Chiu, C., Hong, Y., & Dweck, C. S. (1999). Differential use of person information in decisions about guilt versus innocence: The role of implicit theories. *Personality and Social Psychology Bulletin, 25*, 17–27.

Gilbert, D. T. (1989). Thinking lightly about others: Automatic components of the social inference process. In J. S. Uleman & J. A. Bargh (Eds.), *Unintended thought.* New York: Guilford, 189–211.

Hall, R. J., & Lord, R. G. (1995). Multi-level information-processing explanations of followers' leadership perceptions. *Leadership Quarterly, 6*, 265–287.

Hambrick, D. C., & Finkelstein, S. (1987). Managerial discretion: A bridge between polar views of organizational outcomes. In B. M. Staw and L. L. Cummings (Eds.), *Research in organizational behavior* (Vol. 9). Greenwich, CT: JAI.

Hanges, P. J., Lord, R. G. & Dickson, M. W. (2000). An information-processing perspective on leadership and culture: A case for connectionist architecture. *Applied Psychology: An International Review, 49*, 133–161.

Higgins, E. T., & Brendl, C. M. (1995). Accessibility and applicability: Some activation rules influencing judgment. *Journal of Experimental Social Psychology, 31*, 218–243.

Higgins, E. T., Rholes, W. S., & Jones, C. R. (1977). Category accessibility and impression formation. *Journal of Experimental Social Psychology, 13*, 141–154.

Hogan, R., Curphy, G. J., & Hogan, J. (1994). What we know about leadership effectiveness and personality. *American Psychologist, 49*, 493–504.

Hollander, E. P., (1992). Leadership, followership, self, and others. *Leadership Quarterly, 3*, 43–55.

Hollander, E. P., & Julian, J. W. (1969). Contemporary trends in the analysis of leadership processes. *Psychological Bulletin, 71*, 387–397.

Hollander, E. P., & Offerman, L. R. (1990). Power and leadership in organizations: Relationships in transition. *American Psychologist, 45*, 179–189.

Izard, C. E. (1991). *The psychology of emotions*. New York: Plenum.

James, L., & James, L. R. (1989). Integrating work environment perceptions: Explorations in the measurement of meaning. *Journal of Applied Psychology, 74*, 739–751.

Klein, S. B., Loftus, J., Trafton, J. G., & Fuhrman, R. W. (1992). Use of exemplars and abstractions in trait judgments: A model of trait knowledge about the self and others. *Journal of Personality and Social Psychology, 63*, 739–753.

Lazarus, R. S. (1991). *Emotion and adaptation*. New York: Oxford University Press.

Lewter, J., & Lord, R. G. (1992, August). *Affect and the multifactor leadership questionnaire: A replication and extension*. Paper presented at the Academy of Management Convention, Las Vegas, NV.

Lepore, L., & Brown, R. (1997). Category and stereotype activation: Is prejudice inevitable? *Journal of Personality and Social Psychology, 72*, 275–287.

Lord, R. G. (1985). An information processing approach to social perceptions, leadership, and behavioral measurement in organizations. In B. M. Staw & L. L. Cummings (Eds.), *Research in organizational behavior* (Vol. 7, pp. 87–128). Greenwich, CT: JAI.

Lord, R. G., & Brown, D. J. (2000). *Leadership, values, and subordinate self-concepts*. Unpublished manuscript, University of Akron, Ohio.

Lord, R. G., Brown, D. J., & Freiberg, S. J. (1999). Understanding the dynamics of leadership: The role of follower self-concepts in the leader/follower relationship. *Organizational Behavior and Human Decision Processes, 78*, 167–203.

Lord, R. G., Brown, D. J., & Harvey, J. L. (in press). System constraints on leadership perceptions, behavior and influence: An example of connectionist level processes. In M. A. Hogg & R. S. Tindale (Eds.), *Blackwell handbook of social psychology, Vol. 3: Group processes*. Oxford, England: Blackwell.

Lord, R. G., Brown, D. J., Harvey, J. L., & Hall, R. J. (2000). *Contextual constraints on prototype generation and their multilevel consequences for leadership perception*. Manuscript submitted for publication.

Lord, R. G., De Vader, C. L., & Alliger, G. (1986). A meta-analysis of the relation between personality traits and leadership perceptions: An application of validity generalization procedures. *Journal of Applied Psychology, 71*, 402–410.

Lord, R. G., Foti, R. J., & De Vader, C. L. (1984). A test of leadership categorization theory: Internal structure, information processing, and leadership perceptions. *Organizational Behavior and Human Performance, 34*, 343–378.

Lord, R. G., & Maher, K. J. (1990). Alternative information processing models and their implications for theory, research, and practice. *Academy of Management Review, 15*, 9–28.

Lord, R. G., & Maher, K. J. (1991). *Leadership and information processing*. Boston: Routledge.

Lord, R. G., & Smith, W. G. (1999). Leadership and the changing nature of work performance. In D. R. Ilgen & E. D. Pulakos (Eds.), *The changing nature of work performance: Implications for staffing, personnel decisions, and development.* San Francisco, Jossey-Bass.

Malloy, T. E., & Janowski, C. L. (1992) Perceptions and meta-perceptions of leadership: Components, accuracy, and dispositional correlates. *Personality and Social Psychology Bulletin, 18,* 700–709.

Markus, H. R. (1977). Self-schema and processing information about the self. *Journal of Personality and Social Psychology, 35,* 63–78.

Markus, H. R., & Wurf, E. (1987). The dynamic self-concept: A social psychological perspective. *Annual Review of Psychology, 38,* 299–337.

Martinko, M. J., & Gardner, W. L. (1987). The leader/member attribution process. *Academy of Management Review, 12,* 235–249.

Matthews, A. M., Lord, R. G., & Walker, J. B. (1990). *The development of leadership perceptions in children.* Unpublished manuscript, University of Akron, Ohio.

Maurer, T. J., & Lord, R. G. (1991). An exploration of cognitive demands in group interaction as a moderator of information processing variables in perception of leadership. *Journal of Applied Social Psychology, 21,* 821–840.

Meindl, J. R. (1995). The romance of leadership as a follower-centric theory: A social constructionist approach. *Leadership Quarterly, 6,* 329–341.

Menon, T., Morris, M. W., Chiu, C., & Hong, Y. (1999). Culture and the construal of agency: Attribution to individual versus group dispositions. *Journal of Personality and Social Psychology, 76,* 701–717.

Miner, J. B. (1978). Twenty years of research on role motivation theory of managerial effectiveness. *Personnel Psychology, 31,* 739–760.

Mischel, W., & Shoda, Y. (1995). A cognitive-affective system theory of personality: Reconceptualizing situations, dispositions, dynamics, and invariance in personality structure. *Psychological Review, 102,* 246–268.

Murphy, K. R., & Cleveland, J. N. (1995). *Understanding performance appraisal.* Thousand Oaks, CA: Sage.

Murphy, M. R., & Jones, A. P. (1993). The influence of performance cues and observational focus on performance rating accuracy. *Journal of Applied Social Psychology, 23,* 1523–1545.

Newell, A. (1990). *Unified theories of cognition.* Cambridge, MA: Harvard University Press.

O'Connell, M. S., Lord, R. G., & O'Connell, M. K. (1990, August). *An empirical comparison of Japanese and American leadership prototypes: Implications for overseas assignment of managers.* Paper presented at Academy of Management Convention, San Francisco, CA.

Oeth, C. (1996). *Leadership in the National Football League.* Unpublished doctoral dissertation, University of Akron, Ohio.

Offermann, L. R., Kennedy, J. K., Jr., & Wirtz, P. W. (1994). Implicit leadership theories: Content, structure, and generalizability. *Leadership Quarterly, 5,* 43–58.

Operario, D., & Fiske, S. T. (2000). Causes and consequences of stereotypes in organizations. In M. London (Ed.), *How people evaluate others in organizations: Person perception and interpersonal judgment in Industrial-Organizational psychology.*

Pfeffer, J. (1977). The ambiguity of leadership. *Academy of Management Review, 2,* 104–112.

Phillips, J. S., & Lord, R. G. (1981). Causal attributions and perceptions of leadership. *Organizational Behavior and Human Performance, 28,* 143–163.

Rush, M. C., Thomas, J. C., & Lord, R. G. (1977). Implicit leadership theory: A potential threat to the internal validity of leader behavior questionnaires. *Organizational Behavior and Human Performance, 20,* 93–110.

Shaw, J. B. (1990). A cognitive categorization model for the study of intercultural management. *Academy of Management Review, 15,* 626–645.

Shamir, B., House, R. J., & Arthur, M. B. (1993). The motivational effects of charismatic leadership: A self-concept based theory. *Organizational Science, 4,* 577–594.

Sherman, J. W. (1996). Development and mental representation of stereotypes. *Journal of Personality and Social Psychology, 70*, 1126–1141.

Sherman, J. W., & Klein, S. B. (1994). Development and representation of personality impressions. *Journal of Personality and Social Psychology, 67*, 972–983.

Smith, E. R., & DeCoster, J. (1998). Knowledge acquisition, accessibility, and use in person perception and stereotyping: Simulation with a recurrent connectionist network. *Journal of Personality and Social Psychology, 74*, 21–35.

Smith, J. A., & Foti, R. J. (1998). A pattern approach to the study of leader emergence. *Leadership Quarterly, 9*, 147–160.

Smith, W. G., Brown, D. J., Lord, R. G., & Engle, E. M. (1998). *Leadership self-schema and their effects on leadership perceptions.* Manuscript submitted for publication.

Snyder, M., Tanke, E. D., & Berscheid, E. (1977). Social perception and interpersonal behavior: On the self-fulfilling nature of social stereotypes. *Journal of Personality and Social Psychology, 35*, 656–666.

Srull, T. K., & Wyer, R. S., Jr. (1989). Person memory and judgment. *Psychological Review, 96*, 58–83.

Stein, R. T., & Heller, T. (1979). An empirical analysis of the correlations between leadership status and participation rates reported in the literature. *Journal of Personality and Social Psychology, 11*, 1993–2002.

Stogdill, R. M. (1963). *Manual for the Leader Behavior Description Questionnaire—Form XII.* Columbus, OH: Ohio State University, Bureau of Business Research.

Thomas, A. B. (1988). Does leadership make a difference to organizational performance? *Administrative Science Quarterly, 33*, 388–400.

Uleman, J. S., Newman, L. S., & Moskewitz, G. B. (1996). People as flexible interpreters: Evidence and issues from spontaneous trait inference. In M. P. Zanna (Ed.), *Advances in Experimental Social Psychology* (Vol. 28, pp. 211–279). New York: Academic Press.

Weiner, B. (1985). Spontaneous causal thinking. *Psychological Bulletin, 97*, 74–84.

Wittenbrink, B., Judd, C. M., & Park, B. (1997). Evidence for racial prejudice at the implicit level and its relationship with questionnaire measures. *Journal of Personality and Social Psychology, 72*, 262–274.

Wofford, J. C., & Goodwin, V. L. (1994). A cognitive interpretation of transactional and transformational leadership theories. *Leadership Quarterly, 5*, 160–186.

Yammarino, F. J., & Dubinsky, A. J. (1994). Transformational leadership theory: Using levels of analysis to determine boundary conditions. *Personnel Psychology, 47*, 787–811.

Zaccaro, S. J., Foti, R. J., & Kenny, D. A. (1991). Self-monitoring and trait-based variance in leadership: An investigation of leader flexibility across multiple group situations. *Journal of Applied Psychology, 76*, 308–315.

Zaccaro, S. J., Gilbert, J. A., Thor, K. K. & Mumford, M. D. (1991). Leadership and social intelligence: Linking social perspectiveness and behavioral flexibility of leadership effectiveness. *Leadership Quarterly, 2*, 317–342.

9

Training Effectiveness: Assessing Training Needs, Motivation, and Accomplishments

Kurt Kraiger and Herman Aguinis
University of Colorado at Denver

The objective of this chapter is to consider how people evaluate others in organizations and the processes by which these evaluations are used as input into training and development systems within organizations. Specifically, we examine the processes by which supervisors, trainers, and others evaluate employees' learning and developmental needs, make decisions affecting their career motivation or expectations for training, and track their progress through training. Our emphasis is on the effects of interpersonal perception and evaluation processes on employee training and development, particularly in terms of diagnosing training needs, facilitating trainee learning, and measuring training transfer or impact.

Broadly then, this chapter is on the relationship between interpersonal perception and evaluation and training effectiveness. Training effectiveness refers to the individual and organizational factors that influence employee learning, development, and transfer (Tannenbaum, Mathieu, Salas, & Cannon-Bowers, 1991). Unlike classic instructional systems models (e.g., Gagne & Briggs, 1974), training effectiveness models put a premium on social influences as determinants of the extent to which trainees learn and apply training content. Therefore, training effectiveness becomes an ideal framework for understanding the impact of person perception and interpersonal judgment on training-related processes. Robert Benchley once wrote, there are two kinds of people in the world—those who classify the world as two kinds and those who don't. In this chapter, we make one important distinction: There are two broad classes of determinants of training effectiveness: Factors that are related to processes of interpersonal perception and evaluation and factors that are not. Included in the latter category are critical variables, such as organizational support (often financial) for training, the training medium (e.g., instructor-led vs. computer-based), the quality of training design, and the quality of training delivery. As important as these variables appear to be, theory and research on training effectiveness over the past 15 years has highlighted other motivational, perceptual, and attitudinal variables that seemingly play as large a role in determining training success. These are the factors that we highlight in this chapter.

One assumption we make in the chapter is that classroom-style instruction is the predominant form of organizational training.[1] Thus, perceptions of learners by trainers and of trainers by learners are a critical component of the learning environment. A second assumption is that the design, conduct, and evaluation of training and development programs usually relies on various forms of input from organizational members: input on training needs, participation in training (as learner or instructor), evaluation of training impact, and decision making regarding the need for new or more training (Baldwin & Magjuka, 1997). This is not always the case, as training can be done from habit or spring from management decree. At best, though, training is built with social input. Supervisors continuously make assessments regarding subordinates' skills, abilities, learning and development needs, motivation, accomplishments, and so forth. In addition, supervisors observe career progress, provide subordinates with information regarding goal achievement, provide feedback regarding their training and overall performance, and track subordinates' progress over time. These assessments and behaviors occur in the context of a unique supervisor–subordinate dyadic relationship (e.g., Aguinis, Nesler, Quigley, Lee, & Tedeschi, 1996). By understanding the dynamic nature of the interpersonal factors inherent in relationships such as these, one can evaluate better the accuracy and usefulness of human input into training systems.

---

[1] Although alternative forms of training (such as technology-based training) are increasingly popular, a recent survey by the American Society of Training and Development confirms that instructor-led training remains by far the most prevalent form of organizational training (McMurrer, Van Buren, & Woodwell, 2000).

We organize the chapter as follows: discussion of interpersonal perception and evaluation factors affecting training success at three temporal stages (a) pretraining, (b) during training, and (c) post-training. For each stage, we identify and define relevant person perception constructs that would most likely have an impact on individual attitudinal variables that, in turn, are likely to affect employee learning and development.

INTERPERSONAL PERCEPTION AND EVALUATION INFLUENCES ON PRETRAINING PROCESSES

According to common training effectiveness models, there are two sets of pretraining influences on training effectiveness: organizational and individual factors (Noe, 1986; Tannenbaum et al., 1991). Organizational support for training is an example of the former set and individual motivation to learn is an example of the latter. Because needs assessment and (to a lesser extent) training design are formal processes that should examine and account for both sets of variables, it is valuable to consider the effects of interpersonal perception and evaluation on decisions made during these steps. We propose that, in general, interpersonal judgments will affect pretraining variables that in turn affect employee motivation, attitudes, and propensity for learning.

Decisions made during the needs assessment and design steps influence the quality of training. When correctly implemented, a needs assessment determines if there is a performance problem, whether training is the best solution to that problem, who should be trained, and what specific tasks or knowledge, skills, and abilities (KSAs) should be trained. During training design, critical decisions are made regarding how tasks or KSAs should be trained, who should train, and how the learning environment can be optimized. Ideally, these decisions are made by matching available training techniques to training needs, given available instructional resources. Decisions are guided by knowledge of intended outcomes (Kraiger, Ford, & Salas, 1993), learning principles (Ford & Kraiger, 1995), and perceptions of learners' baseline knowledge, abilities, or learning styles (Hayer & Allinson, 1997).

An important, untested assumption of the needs assessment step is that participants (analysts, job experts, supervisors, and incumbents) are accurate and unbiased reporters of job-related phenomena (Ford & Kraiger, 1995). An important assumption of the training design process is that designers hold accurate, unbiased perceptions of learner motivation and capability. To the extent that interpersonal perception and evaluation factors distort either set of judgments, participant decisions about training and training content may result in less than optimal learning and transfer.

Motivational and Attitudinal Variables

Proponents of training effectiveness models advocate that concurrent with the formal training development, there are equally important informal processes by which future trainees interact with their environment and form attitudes and perceptions about training or themselves. These attitudes and perceptions have a direct impact on their receptivity to training and potential for learning. Among the most potent variables are trainee self-efficacy and motivation to learn (Mathieu & Martineau, 1997). Thus, an important pretraining objective should be to conduct assessment and design activities in such a way that these individual attributes are maximized. From the perspective of this chapter, an important consideration is how interpersonal evaluation processes may interact with formal organizational efforts to undermine or enhance pretraining states.

Trainee Self-Efficacy.   Trainee self-efficacy is defined as the belief in one's capacity to organize and execute actions necessary to attain specific types of performance (e.g., succeed in training; Baldwin & Magjuka, 1997). Trainee self-efficacy is related to decisions to enroll in training (Hill, Smith, & Mann, 1987), effort and persistence in training (Quiñones, 1995; Travillian, Baker, & Cannon-Bowers, 1992), performance in training (Gist, Schwoerer, & Rosen, 1989; Gist, Bavetta, & Stevens, 1990; Tannenbaum et al., 1991), and trainee reactions to training (Gist et al., 1989; Tannenbaum et al., 1991). In general, trainee self-efficacy is enhanced through self-determination, goal setting, successful performance, positive feedback, and perceptions of confidence held by others. Trainee self-efficacy is diminished when these conditions are not met (e.g., unsuccessful performance or lack of positive feedback); further, self-efficacy can be diminished through inaccurate, negative feedback from others. The influence of perceptions and feedback by others on trainee self-efficacy suggests that it is useful to consider how consistent errors or biases in the judgments of others may inadvertently affect trainees' perceptions of self-efficacy.

Trainee Motivation to Learn.   Training motivation refers to the direction, effort, intensity, and persistence that trainees apply to learning-oriented activities before, during, and after training (Salas &

Cannon-Bowers, 2000). Motivation to learn and attend training affects learning during training, as well as retention and trainee willingness to apply the newly acquired KSAs back on-the-job (e.g., Quiñones, 1995). Trainee motivation to learn is affected primarily by individual characteristics such as cognitive ability, self-efficacy, anxiety, and conscientiousness but is also influenced by goal setting and self-determination, as well as individual perceptions of situational variables such as feedback from others (Mathieu & Martineau, 1997).

Interpersonal Influences on Trainee Motivation and Attitudes

Perceptual and attitudinal biases related to interpersonal perception and evaluation factors may affect trainee self-efficacy or motivation to learn. For example, both self-efficacy and motivation develops from positive feedback. However, will supervisors offer the same accurate, useful feedback to all of their subordinates?

Research on leader–member exchange theory (LMX) indicates that relationships between a supervisor and his or her subordinates are heterogeneous (Dansereau, Graen, & Haga, 1975). Supervisors develop a relationship with one subordinate and perhaps a different relationship with another one (Farmer & Aguinis, 1999). These relationships develop very early because supervisors quickly categorize subordinates (Liden, Wayne, & Stilwell, 1993). This categorization often leads to labeling a subordinate as a member of the in-group or out-group, with in-group members evaluated more positively than out-group members (Turner, 1985). To the extent that supervisors rely on cognitive heuristics such as categorization to evaluate their subordinates' career progress, they risk making erroneous assessments.

The fundamental attribution error refers to the tendency to believe that subordinates' behaviors are caused by their enduring personal characteristics, dispositions, or attitudes and are not a result of unstable situational factors (Aronson, Wilson, & Akert, 1997; Baron & Byrne, 1997; Fiske & Taylor, 1991). The context in which behaviors and events occur is not as salient to observers as the dynamic behavior of others. Thus, supervisors underestimate the role external circumstances play in subordinates' actions and automatically attribute dynamic behavior to the type of person they are; this leads to the overestimation of dispositional causes (Fiske & Taylor, 1991). A related error, the self-serving bias, refers to individuals' propensity to take credit for success and to deny responsibility for failure (Baron & Byrne, 1997; Fiske & Taylor, 1991). Subordinates and supervisors each attribute their successes to dispositional causes (e.g., ability), but associate failures with external forces (e.g., bad luck). Finally, the false-consensus effect refers to the tendency of supervisors to overestimate the number of subordinates who hold the same beliefs as they do or who see things in the same way (Fiske & Taylor, 1991). Instead of using consensus information (e.g., evaluations and judgments of subordinates) when making judgments, supervisors assume that subordinates would react as they would.

Because training needs assessment is often done as a response to perceived performance problems, the focus of the analysis is to isolate root causes. Unfortunately, the prior discussion suggests that the source most likely to be consulted, the supervisor, may be prone to overevaluate the likelihood that a problem exists, believe that it is attributable to internal (i.e., employee) deficits in skills and abilities, and feel that there is agreement within the work group as to the extent of the problem. Collectively, these attribution errors may cause analysts to overstate the nature of severity or prevalence of the performance deficit.

Not as obvious is the predicted indirect effects of these errors on the motivation and attitudes of future trainees. An employee and supervisor observing the same performance problem are likely to reach different conclusions as to its root cause. By both the fundamental attribution error and the self-serving bias, supervisors are likely to attribute performance problems to skill deficits in subordinates (e.g., "He should be more accurate in his financial forecasts"), whereas employees are more likely to attribute the same problem to situational factors (e.g., "Why can't they buy me a better forecasting program"). If the employee is assigned to training, depending on the interpretation of that decision, there is a risk of needlessly undermining his or her self-efficacy (e.g., "Perhaps I am not as effective as I thought") and/or motivation for training (e.g., "What good will this do me given the real problem;" Quiñones, 1995). Although research results are inconsistent, there is at least some evidence suggesting that the decision to mandate training may have a negative impact on trainee motivation (see Baldwin & Magjuka, 1997). Negative interpretations may be more pronounced for individuals holding a performance orientation (i.e., perceiving training as an opportunity to demonstrate personal capability) compared to those holding a mastery orientation (i.e., perceiving training as an opportunity for learning new skills; Dweck, 1986). Assignment to training for individuals holding a mastery orientation may be interpreted as a lack of confidence in them by management (Farr & Middlebrooks, 1990). Thus, generalizations by supervisors regarding inadequate performance or the need for training in subordinates based on faulty attributions may lower overall trainee motivation.

Failure to account for cognitive heuristics during needs assessment and design phases may result in faulty decisions about the need for training or undermine trainee self-efficacy and motivation to learn. The obvious prescription for avoiding these errors is to collect and reconcile data from multiple sources; however, this is often not realistic given time or budget constraints. Therefore, it is advisable that training analysts and course designers at least be aware of the possible deleterious effects of these attribution errors, challenge statements of causality by supervisors or incumbents (e.g., ask for supporting documentation), or anticipate and correct for the impact of these evaluations on employee attitudes.

INTERPERSONAL PERCEPTION AND EVALUATION INFLUENCES ON TRAINING PROCESSES

From the perspective of training effectiveness models, there are three general sets of factors concurrent with training that influence training success: organizational support for training; the abilities, attitudes, and motivations of participants during training; and the training itself (Tannenbaum et al., 1991). Organizational support includes direct support for participants (e.g., offloading work responsibilities) and policies and practices related to the value placed on training (e.g., linking employee development to manager appraisals). Although interpersonal perception and evaluation processes may affect organizational support, the impact is likely only minimal and indirect. The primary factors related to training participants are ability factors (e.g., general intelligence) and nonability factors, such as trainee motivation, self-efficacy, and expectations for training (Tannenbaum et al., 1991). Because interpersonal perception and evaluation factors affecting employee attitudes and motivation were discussed in the prior section, we limit our discussion here to the impact of interpersonal factors on training processes. Similar to the prior discussion, we propose that, in general, these variables will affect training-related variables that in turn will affect employee motivation, attitudes, and learning.

Research stemming back to the late 1950s has consistently supported the impact of instructor-related variables on trainee learning (Campbell, 1971). Instructors can influence trainee learning primarily through the perceptions of their credibility, similarity and status in the minds of trainees; the quality of their instruction; and the nature of their interactions with the trainees. The impact of interpersonal perception and judgment factors on instructor variables is considered in the following section.

Learner Perceptions of Instructors

In traditional instructor-led settings, trainee motivation to learn and receptivity to training content is a function of identification with and respect for the instructor. For example, behavioral modeling studies indicate that learning is enhanced when the model (demonstrating correct behaviors) is perceived as high status, competent, and demographically similar to the trainees (Decker & Nathan, 1985). Social categorization processes may influence trainee perceptions of the credibility of trainers and the relevance of training materials. For example, Aguinis et al. (1996) found that graduate students who identified with their faculty supervisors were more likely to report that (a) they had a higher quality relationship with their professors, and (b) their professors had higher levels of credibility. Trainees are likely to form immediate impressions of instructors that include an in-group or out-group designation. Because there are likely differences in prior knowledge of content area between the instructor and trainees, many instructors receive immediate out-group designation by trainees. This designation may be further engrained if the instructor differs from most trainees in age, race, or gender, or when the instructor comes from outside the organization or has not held the same job as trainees. Initial perceptions and judgments may need to be overcome for the training to be successful. For example, one of the authors has conducted numerous training sessions for organizations that provide job readiness training to welfare-to-work populations. The training begins with an open-ended discussion of trainees' on-the-job problems and goals for training. Because most trainees were social workers and persons of color, the (implicit) purpose for the discussion was to give the trainees an opportunity to judge whether a white trainer from academia could understand their needs well enough to present useful job-related information.

Interactions Between Instructors and Learners

Ideally, the learning environment is a dynamic one in which instructional style and content vary as a function of interactions between learners and the instructor. For example, if the trainer perceives that material is too difficult, he or she might slow down the rate of presentation, or allow learners additional time to ask questions or practice concepts. In general, the perceptions of learners by instructors serve as primary input into the dynamic relationship of the two. Prior to, or near the beginning of, a training program, the instructor explicitly or implicitly evaluates the readiness and proficiency of either the class as a whole or learners as individuals. As the program unfolds, better instructors monitor learner achievement, seek feedback, and adjust instructional styles accordingly. It is valuable then to consider the impact of interpersonal perception and evaluation processes on instructors' perceptions of learners during training.

Initial Perceptions.   On the basis of either pretraining assessment or personal judgment, an instructor may evaluate trainees on a number of dimensions that in turn, affect what and how material is presented. Key evaluation variables include: general ability levels of trainees, skill deficits (related to training content), and perceptions of learning styles or preferences. Different learning environments (e.g., perceptually oriented vs. behaviorally oriented) may be enacted depending on instructor perceptions of trainees (Kolb & Lewis, 1986). To the extent that this information is collected informally through instructor perceptions, the instructor risks committing judgment errors that may undermine training effectiveness.

As a social process, stereotyping is pervasive enough (see Dovidio & Fiske, this volume), that it is likely instructors may often use stereotypes or general impressions of training groups to guide initial impressions of trainees' aggregate ability or skill levels. This may be particularly true if the trainer is brought in from outside the organization. Given the cognitive demands of starting a training class while getting to know a large number of trainees, instructors may rely on simple social categories or stereotypes to form baseline impressions of trainee attributes (e.g., a graduate instructor may observe that an incoming class reminds her, demographically, of a previous class that was particularly strong academically). Through representativeness bias, instructors may judge how likely it is that a person belongs to a certain group on the basis of whether his or her characteristics are similar to the characteristics associated with the category (Aguinis & Adams, 1998; Fiske & Taylor, 1991). That is, the more an individual resembles the average or typical member of a category, the more likely it is that the instructor will believe that he or she belongs to that category. Thus, a management trainee who dresses too casually for training may remind the instructor of other trainees who have washed out of similar programs. Unfortunately, this heuristic can lead to incorrect assumptions because there are always exceptions to a category; thus this heuristic leads supervisors to overlook relevant information like base rates (Baron & Byrne, 1997). Fortuitously, accurate categorization allows instructors to make good decisions with minimal information about how to introduce material. However, stereotyping may also result in inaccurate or unfair decisions about the group as a whole (see Dovidio & Fiske, this volume).

When trainers have access to formal information about trainees (e.g., data from a needs assessment or pretest), other interpersonal biases or errors may occur. The personal validation phenomenon refers to the tendency to believe that vague descriptions, which could apply to or be true of anyone or any group, are unique to the individual or group to which they are being attributed (Latkin, Littman, Sundberg, & Hagan, 1993). Thus, general statements made within the organization ("Workers today are lazy") may be taken as indicative of a specific training group. Unfortunately, using this heuristic leads to a failure to search for disconfirming evidence and failure to see that the description is generic enough to apply to others than those whom to whom they are attributed.

As instructors form rapid impressions of trainee attributes, committing the fundamental attribution error may lead them to attribute the trainees' presence in training to dispositional (e.g., ability deficits) rather than situational (e.g., escalating job demands) characteristics. To the extent that instructors hold implicit personality theories (Schneider, 1973) about the interrelationship of these traits and other characteristics related to learning styles, the instructors may adopt inappropriate or inefficient instructional tactics. For example, an instructor may believe that workers with difficulties mastering certain basic tasks are also those most likely to benefit from hands-on training.

The consequences of erroneous judgments of trainees' abilities, skills, or learning preferences can be severe. In traditional classroom settings, behavioral confirmation (or "self-fulfilling prophecies") have been well-documented; given incorrect initial impressions of student aptitude by instructors, instructors may act in such a way that they elicit (for better or worse) the characteristics that confirm their preconceived biases (Eden & Ravid, 1982; Rosenthal & Jacobson, 1968).

Thus, we are suggesting that given the cognitive demands of beginning a new training program and incomplete data on trainees, trainers may rely on stereotypes or commit attribution errors or judgment biases that lead them to misperceive learners' capabilities and preferences for learning. As a result, the trainer may either "dumb-down" material, or present information too rapidly or too superficially for trainees in attendance. Not only will these conditions undermine trainee learning but also will affect trainee motivation, which will further hamper in-class learning.

To avoid these consequences, trainers must realize the importance of collecting as much information as objectively as possible. For example, inventories can be administered during pretraining to assess trainee learning styles (e.g., Hayer & Allinson, 1997). As training starts, instructors should be aware of the potential for errors and biases introduced from the use of stereotypes and cognitive heuristics, and they should make the effort to see learners as individuals rather than as a homogeneous group of trainees.

Midtraining Perceptions.　During the course of training, instructors may explicitly or implicitly seek feedback on trainee mastery of the content, or trainees' comfort with the style or rate of training. This may be done formally through quizzes, tests, or training reaction forms, or informally through perceptions of trainee learning or interest. The more the instructor relies on informal data collection, the more likely he or she is to make judgment errors that in turn will affect the quality of training.

At the beginning of a course, there may be several types of errors or biases committed by instructors that result in misperceptions of trainee performance. These largely parallel those probable at the onset of training with two exceptions. First, instructors' judgments of current performance in training may be influenced by judgments or knowledge of past behavior. Thus, to the extent that trainees struggle (or do exceptionally well) at the beginning of training, instructors' evaluations of their performance levels in the middle or at the end of training may be inaccurate. Further, by demonstrating an anchoring and adjustment bias, trainers may start with an initial reference point or anchor for their judgments (based on pre- or initial training states) and adjust their estimate or decision away from the anchor (Aronson et al., 1997). Unfortunately, this judgment is strongly tied to the initial anchor and often it is not adequately adjusted away from this value.

Second, judgments of high or low achievement during training by trainees may hold negative repercussions for both trainees and trainers. Trainers who anticipate giving negative feedback to trainees at the end of training may distort evaluations because of anxiety over anticipated exchanges. Also, trainee evaluations may be consciously or unconsciously affected by a social motive to present a positive image to self or others in the organization. Instructors may be more likely to commit self-serving

biases, in which they take credit for any improvements in trainee performance but blame trainee traits for lack of progress. Because classroom
training is largely a dyadic experience, instructors may also be guilty of
self-centered bias and take more credit for outcomes that were produced in
conjunction with others than they deserve (Fiske & Taylor, 1991). Unlike
the self-serving bias, it does not matter if the outcomes are a success or a
failure. That is, trainers will claim responsibility for joint outcomes regardless of their favorableness. The consequence for learners is that they may
not get proper reinforcement for their own effort and accomplishment.

Again, we suggest that trainers make attribution errors or judgment biases that lead them to misperceive and under-represent learner accomplishment. As a result, the trainer may fail to make midcourse adjustments that
correct for learning deficits and may fail to adequately prepare learners to
transfer newly acquired skills. That is, if the judgment of the instructor
is that learning is slow but is the result of unintelligent or unmotivated
trainees, then he or she would respond differently than if the perception
was that learning was on-track or that lack of learning was attributable to
the difficulty of the material. Similarly, the subliminal message that the
material is simply too hard for trainees may undermine their motivation
to transfer. As in the case of initial training perceptions, the remedy is for
instructors to be as aware as possible of potential biases and to anchor
perceptions on objective data as much as possible.

INTERPERSONAL PERCEPTION
AND EVALUATION INFLUENCES
ON POST-TRAINING PROCESSES

The training effectiveness literature suggests that successful transfer is
primarily a function of three sets of factors: initial learning during training, trainee motivation or readiness to transfer, and direct organizational
or interpersonal support for transfer (Tracey, Tannenbaum, & Kavanagh,
1995). In general, the greater the learning during initial training, the greater
the potential for successful transfer (Noe, 1986). The effects of interpersonal perception and evaluation factors on learning during training were
addressed in the prior section. Consistent with previous sections, we again
propose that, in general, processes of interpersonal perception and judgment may affect post-training support variables that in turn affect employee
motivation to transfer.

Motivation to Transfer

Beyond direct support from managers and peers, training effectiveness models posit that transfer of training is also facilitated by broad organizational support. Organizational support may be conceptualized primarily in terms of organizational transfer climate, defined by Rouillier and Goldstein (1993) as situations or consequences that inhibit or help trainees apply trained skills back on the job. Generally, these include situational cues (prompting application at appropriate times) and linking consequences (including feedback) to performance. Research on transfer climate suggests that climate matters at least in part because of its effects on trainee characteristics: Facilitating climates increase trainee focus, motivation, and intentions to transfer (Tracey et al., 1995; Rouillier & Goldstein, 1993). Thus, it is valuable to understand the influence of interpersonal perception and judgment processes on employee motivation to transfer.

Given some learning during training, trainees' transfer of that learning back to the job is largely a function of two mutually influencing factors: readiness or motivation to transfer (i.e., is there willingness to try to apply what was learned) and organizational and managerial support for transfer (i.e., will efforts to transfer be reinforced or maintained). Trainee readiness to transfer refers to the willingness to try to apply newly learned skills and knowledge to the job; it is based on the value trainees attach to training, their expectancies that transfer will be successful, and their perceptions of the training climate (Noe, 1986).

Perceptions of the value of training and expectancies for success are largely affected by encoding the reactions, perceptions, and evaluations of others. Trainees' perceptions of the perceived importance (to the organization) of training, the quality of the training itself, and the value supervisors or other workers place on training affect motivation to transfer. Van Maanen (1978), among others, noted the tendency of veterans to warn newcomers to, "forget everything they learned in training." Other motivational states or dispositional traits may influence trainee readiness to transfer. Trainees with clear expectancies regarding post-training outcomes may be more likely to apply newly trained skills, as may trainees who have well-defined behavioral goals (often called action plans by trainers). Ford, Quiñones, Sego, and Sorra (1992) found that employees high in self-efficacy were more likely to seek out opportunities to apply newly trained skills. Finally, although the notion is untested, it is likely that trainees holding a mastery orientation would be more willing to try to apply new skills to the job and be more likely to persist in new behaviors should they encounter performance difficulties.

How might interpersonal perception and evaluation factors influence employee readiness to transfer? As with pretraining motivation to learn, errant attributions by supervisors (through the fundamental attribution error) when conveyed to the subordinate may undermine expectancies regarding improvements in post-training error. Specifically, if the initial poor performance is attributed to dispositional causes (e.g., "You're not smart enough") rather than to situational ones (e.g., "You haven't been trained on this new equipment"), then trainees may lack self-efficacy returning to the job environment. Further, self-serving biases may cloud supervisors' judgments regarding the role they played in the initial problem; accordingly, trainees may return to the job anticipating that many of the same pretraining obstacles to performance are still in place (Latham & Crandall, 1991).

Support for Transfer

Other research has shown that supervisory support for trainees before or after training may facilitate motivation to transfer (see Baldwin & Magjuka, 1997). Ford et al. (1992) found that supervisors gave some employees more opportunities to perform newly trained skills than they gave to other employees. Baldwin and Magjuka (1991) reported that trainees entering training expecting some kind of supervisory follow-up displayed stronger intentions to transfer what was learned to the job.

Given the important role of the supervisor in conveying expectations and assigning work, it is valuable to reconsider potential leader–member exchange effects. Recall that LMX theory posits that supervisors will establish unique dyadic relationships with each subordinate, in part, because of social categorization of subordinates as in-group and out-group members. Accordingly, it is reasonable that subordinates returning from training may receive differential support, expectations, or job assignments from the same supervisor. An interesting research question, but perplexing practical problem, is whether in-group or out-group designation moderates transfer of training through effects on employee motivation and perceived support.

There have been some research efforts but few institutionalized attempts to measure trainee perceptions of transfer climate. The preceding discussion would suggest that such efforts might have considerable value in that unanticipated differences in employee readiness to transfer may emerge. That is, organizations may assume that employees differ in their capacity to apply trained skills on-the-job but only in relationship to differences in initial learning. By measuring trainee motivation to transfer and perceptions of perceived organizational and managerial support, organizations may identify other sources of variance in transfer readiness that result from interpersonal evaluation and judgment factors. Supervisors of workers with low readiness can provide additional training or support even if natural interpersonal processes have not "greased the pump" in the past.

SUMMARY

The objective of this chapter was to speculate on how to the consider the effects of interpersonal perception and evaluation processes that may influence judgments made by supervisors, trainers, and others during formal and informal aspects of employee training programs. Our analysis was done from the perspective of training effectiveness models that highlight the impact of social influences on training outcomes. According to these models, training success is affected by both organizational and individual factors before, during, and after training. Employee attitudes and motivation, particularly self-efficacy and motivation, mediate relationships between antecedent factors and employee learning. At each stage of training, supervisors, trainers, and other organizational members may make judgments about trainees' capabilities, accomplishments, and readiness to learn or transfer. These judgments may be affected by numerous attribution errors or biases consistent with those reported in the cognitive heuristics literature. As a result, employee attitudes and motivation may be affected, and employee learning may be minimized. To counteract these effects, organizations are encouraged to rely on multiple sources of information and question the veracity of judgments made about trainees.

ACKNOWLEDGEMENTS

Kurt Kraiger, Department of Psychology, University of Colorado at Denver; Herman Aguinis, Graduate School of Business Administration, University of Colorado at Denver.

Correspondence concerning this chapter may be addressed to Kurt Kraiger, Department of Psychology, University of Colorado at Denver, Campus Box 173, P. O. Box 173364, Denver, Colorado 80217. Electronic mail may be sent to kkraiger@carbon.cudenver.edu.

REFERENCES

Aguinis, H., & Adams, S. K. R. (1998). Social-role versus structural models of gender and influence use in organizations: A strong inference approach. *Group and Organization Management, 23*, 414–446.

Aguinis, H., Nesler, M. S., Quigley, B. M., Lee, S., & Tedeschi, J. T. (1996). Power bases of faculty supervisors and educational outcomes for graduate students. *Journal of Higher Education, 67*, 267–297.

Aronson, E., Wilson, T. D., & Akert, R. M. (1997). *Social psychology* (2nd ed.). Reading, MA: NY: Addison-Wesley.

Baldwin, T. T., & Magjuka, R. J. (1991). Organizational training and signals of importance: Linking pretraining perceptions to intentions to transfer. *Human Resource Development Quarterly, 2*, 25–36

Baldwin, T. T., & Magjuka, R. J. (1997). Training as an organizational episode: Pretraining influences on trainee motivation. In Ford & Associates (Eds.), *Improving training effectiveness in work organizations* (pp. 99–127). Mahwah, NJ: Lawrence Erlbaum Associates.

Baron, R. A., & Byrne, D. (1997). *Social psychology* (8th ed.). Boston: Allyn & Bacon.

Campbell, J. P. (1971). Personal training and development. *Annual Review of Psychology, 22*, 565–602.

Dansereau, F., Graen, G., & Haga, W. J. (1975). A vertical dyad linkage approach to leadership within formal organizations. *Organizational Behavior and Human Performance, 13*, 46–78.

Decker, P., & Nathan, B. (1985). *Behavior modeling training.* New York: Praeger.

Dweck, C. S. (1986). Motivational processes affecting learning. *American Psychologist, 41*, 1040–1048.

Eden, D., & Ravid, G. (1982). Pygmalion vs. self-expectancy on trainee performance. *Organizational Behavior and Human Performance, 30*, 351–364.

Farmer, S., & Aguinis, H. (1999). Antecedents and outcomes of subordinate perceptions of power in supervisor–subordinate relationships: An integrated model. *Academy of Management Best Paper Proceedings, OB*, E1–E6.

Farr, J. L., & Middlebrooks, C. L. (1990). Enhancing motivation to participate in professional development. In S. L. Willis & S. S. Dubin (Eds.), *Training and development in organizations* (pp. 195–213). San Francisco: Jossey-Bass.

Fiske, S. T., & Taylor, S. E. (1991). *Social cognition* (2nd ed.). New York: McGraw-Hill.

Ford, J. K., & Kraiger, K. (1995). The application of cognitive constructs and principles to the instructional systems models of training: Implications for needs assessment, design, and transfer. In I. Robertson & D. Cooper (Eds.), *The International Review of Industrial and Organizational Psychology, 10*, 1–48. New York: Wiley.

Ford, J. K., Quiñones, M. A., Sego, D. J., & Sorra, J. A. (1992). Factors affecting the opportunity to perform trained tasks on the job. *Personnel Psychology, 45*, 511–527.

Gagne, R. M, & Briggs, L. J. (1974). *Principles of instructional design.* New York: Holt, Rinehart & Winston.

Gist, M. E., Schwoerer, C., & Rosen, B. (1989). Effects of alternative training methods on self-efficacy and performance in computer software training. *Journal of Applied Psychology, 74*, 884–891.

Gist, M. E., Bavetta, A. G., & Stevans, C. K. (1990). Transfer training method: Its influence on skill generalization, skill repetition, and performance level. *Personnel Psychology, 43*, 501–523.

Hayer, J., & Allinson, C. W. (1997). Learning styles and training and development in work settings: Lessons from educational research. *Educational Psychology, 17*, 185–193.

Hill, T., Smith, N. D., & Mann, M. F. (1987). Role of efficacy expectations in predicting the decision to use advanced technologies: The case of computers. *Journal of Applied Psychology, 72*, 307–313.

Kolb, D., & Lewis, L. H. (1986). Facilitating experiential learning: Observations and reflections. In L. H. Lewis (Ed.), *Experiential and simulation techniques for teaching adults. New directors for continuing education* (No. 30, pp. 99–107). San Francisco: Jossey-Bass.

Kraiger, K., Ford, J. K., & Salas, E. (1993). Application of cognitive, skill-based, and affective theories of learning outcomes to new methods of training evaluation. *Journal of Applied Psychology, 78,* 311–328.

Latham, G. P., & Crandall, S. (1991). Organizational and social factors. In J. Morrison (Ed.), *Training for performance: Principles of applied human learning* (pp. 259–285). Chichester, England: Wiley.

Latkin, C. A., Littman, R. A., Sundberg, N. D., & Hagan, R. A. (1993). Pitfalls and pratfalls in research on an experimental community: Lessons in integrating theory and practice from the Rajneeshpuram Research Project. *Journal of Community Psychology, 21,* 35–48.

Liden, R. C., Wayne, S. J., & Stilwell, D. (1993). A longitudinal study on the early development of leader–member exchanges. *Journal of Applied Psychology, 78,* 662–674.

Mathieu, J. E., & Martineau, J. W. (1997). Individual and situational influences in training motivation. In J. K. Ford and Associates (Eds.), *Improving training effectiveness in work organizations.* (pp. 193–222). Hillsdale, NJ: Lawrence Erlbaum Associates.

McMurrer, D. P., Van Buren, M. E., & Woodwell, W. H, Jr. (2000). *The ASTD state of the industry report.* Washington, DC: American Society of Training and Development.

Noe, R. A. (1986). Trainee attributes and attitudes: Neglected influences on training effectiveness. *Academy of Management Review, 11,* 736–749.

Quiñones, M. (1995). Pretraining context effects: Training assignment as feedback. *Journal of Applied Psychology, 80,* 226–238.

Rosenthal, R., & Jacobson, L. (1968). *Pygmalion in the classroom.* New York: Holt, Rinehart & Winston.

Rouillier, J. Z., & Goldstein, I. L. (1993). The relationship between organizational transfer climate and positive transfer of training. *Human Resource Development Quarterly, 4,* 377–390.

Salas, E., & Cannon-Bowers, J. B. (2000). The science of training: A decade of progress. *Annual Review of Psychology.*

Schneider, D. J. (1973). Implicit personality theory: A review. *Psychological Bulletin, 79,* 294–309.

Tannenbaum, S. I., Mathieu, J. E., Salas, E., & Cannon-Bowers, J. A. (1991). Meeting trainees' expectations: The influence of training fulfillment on the development of commitment, self-efficacy, and motivation. *Journal of Applied Psychology, 76,* 759–769.

Tracey, J. B, Tannenbaum, S. I., & Kavanagh, M. J. (1995). Applying trained skills on the job: The importance of the work environment. *Journal of Applied Psychology, 80,* 239–252.

Travillian, K., Baker, C. V., & Cannon-Bowers, J. A. (1992, March). *Correlates of self- and collective efficacy with team functioning.* Paper presented at the 38th Annual Meeting of the Southeastern Psychological Association, Knoxville, TN.

Turner, J. C. (1985). Social categorization and the self-concept: A social cognitive theory of group behavior. *Advances in Group Processes, 2,* 77–121.

Van Maanen, J. (1978). People processing: Strategies of organizational socialization. *Organizational Dynamics, 7,* 18–36.

10

Coaching in Organizations

James W. Smither
LaSalle University

Susanne P. Reilly
Right Manus Consultants, Stanford, Connecticut

The prevalence of coaching in organizations has recently seen a renaissance. Part of the interest in coaching stems from the increasing popularity of executive coaching. Graddick and Lane (1998) note that the use of external executive coaches is an increasingly popular trend in corporations. Other evidence concerning the popularity of coaching can be found by perusing any large bookstore's inventory. A recent search at the online bookstore Amazon.com found 16 popular books on the topic of executive coaching (e.g., Hargrove, 1995; O'Neill, 2000), and a search of the online bookstore at the Center for Creative Leadership found 58 publications dealing with coaching.

The renewed interest in coaching is not limited to external executive coaching. The role of internal coaching (managers serving as coaches) has recently been highlighted by Waldroop and Butler (1996). At one large corporation, supervisors are now routinely referred to as coaches (e.g., "I need to talk to my coach" rather than "I need to talk to my supervisor").

The surge in coaching's popularity has been accompanied by a somewhat modest rise in scholarly interest concerning the topic. An October 1999 search of the PsycINFO database found 17 articles in peer-reviewed journals explicitly dealing with executive coaching or coaching skills in general. Of these, 12 articles appeared in a single journal, *Consulting Psychology Journal: Research and Practice*. Many of the articles approach the topic of executive coaching from the perspective of counseling psychology (e.g., multimodal therapy or psychodynamic theory), and rely on case studies as illustrations or sources of evidence (Diedrich, 1996; Goodstone & Diamante, 1998; Kilburg, 1996, 1997; Levinson, 1996; Peterson, 1996; Richard, 1999; Saporito, 1996; Tobias, 1996; Witherspoon & White, 1996).

Kilburg's (1996) study provides a useful review of the coaching literature. His work points out that there is very little empirical, rigorous study of the effects of coaching in business. Kilburg has noted that the application of coaching to the art and practice of management has been growing rapidly although the scientific basis for these applications is limited at this time.

In this chapter, we argue that social psychological theory and research can provide a valuable foundation for research and practice in this area. We first define coaching and then present a five-stage model of coaching. This model incorporates recent theory concerning executive coaching while also reflecting our own experiences as practitioners in this area. We then discuss each stage in succession. For each of the five stages, we describe how social psychological research can help enhance our understanding of critical issues associated with the stage, directions for research, and implications for practitioners.

DEFINING COACHING

Kilburg (1996) defined executive coaching as:

> A helping relationship formed between a client who has managerial authority and responsibility in an organization and a consultant who uses a wide variety of behavioral techniques and methods to help the client achieve a mutually identified set of goals to improve his or her professional performance and personal satisfaction and, consequently, to improve the effectiveness of the client's organization within a formally defined coaching agreement (p. 142).

A less formal definition from Hall, Otazo, and Hollenbeck (1999) states that executive coaching is "a practical, goal-focused form of personal one-to-one learning for busy executives. It may be used to improve performance, to improve or develop executive behaviors, to work through organizational issues, to enhance a career, or to prevent derailment" (p. 40). Harris' (1999) definition says simply that executive coaching is "an on-going, one-on-one learning process enabling people to enhance their job performance" (p. 38).

Referring to managers as coaches (i.e., internal coaches), Kinlaw (1996) defined coaching as "a disciplined conversation, using concrete perfor- mance information, between a leader and an individual or a team that results in the continuous improvement of performance" (p. 21). Waldroop and Butler (1996) described coaching as just plain good management, re- quiring such generic management skills as keen powers of observation, sensible judgment, and an ability to take appropriate action.

STEPS OR STAGES
IN EFFECTIVE COACHING

Table 10.1 presents a summary of the key steps or stages in effective coaching as seen by a variety of authors. There is considerable overlap among the descriptions that these writers offer.

Several common themes emerge from a review of Table 10.1. First is the importance of establishing a relationship between the coach and the person who is being coached. Second, assessment of the person (i.e., strengths, limitations, etc.) and the context in which the person is working is an essential component of effective coaching. Third, effective coaching in- cludes goal setting and developmental planning. Fourth, the centerpiece of coaching involves implementation—the person tries new behaviors (e.g., to address performance problems), meets regularly with the coach, and gradually gains a sense of behavioral mastery or cognitive control over the problems or issues he or she is facing. Fifth, the coach and the person being coached monitor and evaluate the person's progress and the coach- ing relationship. On the basis of these common themes (and our own ap- plied experience in this area), we organize this chapter around a five-stage (or five-step) model of effective coaching: (a) establishing the coaching relationship, (b) assessment, (c) goal setting and development planning, (d) implementation, and (e) evaluating progress and the coaching relation- ship.

Next, we describe how social psychological research can help enhance our understanding of critical issues associated with each of these stages. It is of course beyond the scope of this chapter to describe all of the social psychological phenomena that might be relevant to coaching processes. Instead, we describe the relevance of several phenomena as a way of

TABLE 10.1

Steps or Stages Associated With Effective Coaching

Harris (1999)
1. Assessment (typically using a 360-degree feedback survey or various personality tests)
2. Feedback
3. Planning
4. Implementation
5. Follow-up

Foster and Seeker (1997)
1. Helping to monitor performance
2. Diagnosing performance problems and deficiencies
3. Determining directions for performance improvement
4. Sharing constructive feedback
5. Creating a supportive environment

Kilburg (1996)
1. Developing an intervention agreement (e.g., establishing the goals, time commitment, resource commitment, methods, confidentiality constraints, and in the case of external coaches, payments)
2. Building a coaching relationship
3. Creating and managing expectations of success
4. Providing an experience of behavioral mastery or cognitive control over the problems and issues (i.e., the heart of coaching—addressing performance problems, dealing with emotions, using feedback and disclosure, emphasize what will work most effectively with the best long-term outcomes, confronting acting out and ethical lapses in a tactful way)
5. Evaluating coaching success or failure (e.g., assessing coaching sessions and periodically looking back over what has been accomplished)

Graddick and Lane (1998)
1. Precoaching (i.e., meeting with the executive, his or her supervisor, and the coach to discuss specific issues the coaching should address; calibrating expectations and setting goals)
2. Data gathering (i.e., from the executive as well as others in the organization to diagnose and develop action plans—in-depth background interviews, personality inventories, and 360-degree assessment either by survey or interviews with the executive's peers and direct reports)
3. Coaching (i.e., meeting regularly—often 2 to 4 times a month—for several months to review the data, develop a plan of action, and monitor progress)

Saporito (1996)
1. Setting the foundation (i.e., understanding the context in which the person is working and the behaviors required for success in that context)
2. Assessing the individual
3. Developmental planning
4. Implementation

Peterson (1996)
1. Forging a partnership (i.e., building trust and understanding so people want to work with the person)
2. Inspiring commitment (i.e., helping people focus their energy on goals that matter)
3. Growing skills (i.e., finding the best way for the person to learn)
4. Promoting persistence (e.g., building stamina and discipline to make sure learning lasts on the job)
5. Shaping the environment (e.g., to reward learning and remove barriers)

---

illustrating how social psychology in general can provide important insights for coaching research and practice. Although we draw on research and theory from many areas of social psychology, we especially emphasize literature dealing with person perception and interpersonal judgment. Major themes, applications to coaching, and directions for research are summarized in Table 10.2.

ESTABLISHING THE COACHING RELATIONSHIP

We recently interviewed six executives about their experiences being coached by others. One common theme that emerged in their comments was the critical role of trust. For example, we were repeatedly told that a successful coach "had my welfare in mind" and provided feedback that was "in my best interest." These executives also said that effective coaching was characterized by a sense of reciprocity—there was a two-way relationship. They also described how successful coaches helped build the relationship, for example, by becoming vulnerable in some way (perhaps by discussing feedback they had received about their own limitations or by discussing issues they were facing).

Social psychological research also points to the critical role that relationships play in behavior change. For example, when people try to change themselves, their interpersonal connections play a critical role. Successful change is often instigated by others or by observing someone else change (thereby pointing to the role of reciprocity in successful coaching) and is accompanied by considerable help and support from others.

Unfortunately, establishing a relationship that can provide a strong foundation for subsequent coaching is not necessarily a straightforward matter. For example, Swann (1992) and others have found that people choose, like, and retain partners (in close relationships) who see them in a way that is consistent with their self-views. Indeed, people remain longest and happiest in relationships with partners who share their inflated views of themselves (Baumeister, 1998b, p. 712). This finding can pose a problem for coaches who may often find themselves trying to establish a relationship with an employee who has an unrealistic (inflated) self-evaluation (Baumeister, 1998b, p. 709). Table 10.2 summarizes several issues that are likely to be relevant as a coach seeks to establish a relationship with an employee who will be coached.

TABLE 10.2

Examples of Social Psychological Phenomena Related to Each Stage of the Coaching Process

Social Psychological Phenomena	Description	Examples of Application to Coaching	Research Questions
		1. Establish the Coaching Relationship	
Schemas shape attributions	Person schemas (i.e., certain traits and behaviors go together), role schemas (i.e., how persons in specific roles usually act and what they are like), and event schemas or scripts (i.e., what is supposed to happen in a given setting) may affect attributions.	An employee whose role schema of a manager does not include coaching may react with skepticism to the manager's unexpected efforts to coach the employee. Event schemas or scripts will guide expectations concerning when and how coaching conversations should occur. Employees are likely to be cautious about accepting expectancy—disconfirming behavior. "Why is my manager suddenly trying to coach me, when he or she has never before expressed interest in helping me? Maybe the manager has an ulterior motive."	What are the schemas and scripts that employees and coaches hold about coaching? Do these schemas and scripts create unrealistic expectations or obstacles that limit the coaching relationship?
Motives for self-knowledge	Motives can include a healthy curiosity about the self (appraisal), a wish for favorable information about the self (self-enhancement), and a desire to confirm what we already know about ourselves (self-consistency). Accurate self-appraisal would seem the most useful motivation, but self-enhancement appears to be the strongest motive.	It is important for coaches to understand employees' expectations about the coaching experience. Coaches can help employees become comfortable with the heightened self-awareness that may accompany the coaching process. The coach can help employees keep their illusions small or turn them off when employees have an important decision to make.	How do the employee's motives affect the quality of the coaching relationship and the outcomes of coaching?

| Impression management tactics | Efforts at self-presentation are a trade-off between creating a favorable impression versus plausibility. Ingratiation efforts can be successful in getting others to like one, but they have a much smaller effect on getting others to think one is competent. | What are the tactics used by effective coaches to create a relationship where the employee views the coach as likeable, trustworthy, and competent? |
| The role of liking and reciprocity in compliance and persuasion | Compliance and persuasion are affected by liking, reciprocity, and authority. The reciprocity principle indicates that people like those who like them, cooperate with others who cooperate with them, etc. | The most successful tactic tends to be other-enhancement (i.e., making the other person look good), but some tactics may not be feasible in some coaching circumstances. Transparent ingratiation efforts may boomerang with the target (employee) reacting negatively.

To enhance employee cooperation, the coaching relationship needs to be characterized by reciprocity and liking. Employees are more likely to comply with requests from a coach whom they like and who has previously provided a favor or concession to them. | How do effective coaches create a sense of reciprocity that increases the likelihood of subsequent cooperation by the employee? |

2. Assessment

| The influence of the coach's schemas on the assessment process | Traits and categories become more accessible and thus likely to capture ambiguous behaviors through long-term frequency or recency of use. Those concepts that are applied again and again in the controlled perceiving and judging of self and others eventually become automatized. | Coaches with different educational or work histories (e.g., counseling psychology, OD, I/O psychology, executive development) may attend to different employee behaviors or categorize the same behaviors in very different ways. | How do coaches' work and educational histories affect the way they attend to and categorize employee behaviors? |

(Continued)

TABLE 10.2
(Continued)

Social Psychological Phenomena	Description	Examples of Application to Coaching	Research Questions
Correspondent inference	People routinely underestimate the power of situations and overestimate the power of dispositions in governing behavior. Culture shapes the likelihood of making dispositional versus situational attributions for behavior.	Coaches need to work hard at appreciating the situational constraints that face the person being coached. Internal coaches face the difficult task of seeing themselves as part of the situation that influences the person's performance.	To what extent are coaches' attributions and evaluations influenced by correspondent inferences, self-image bias, and hedonic relevance? Do effective coaches learn about "invisible" (e.g., social norms) situational factors that shape employees' behaviors? Are internal coaches (relative to external coaches) more or less sensitive to external factors that shape employee behavior? Are coaches' attributions shaped by cultural differences?
Self-deception and inflated self-views	People are likely to make internal attributions for their success and external attributions for failure, discover flaws in evidence that depicts them in an unflattering light, minimize the amount of time they spend processing critical feedback, selectively	Once employees have formed an opinion (usually a positive opinion) about themselves it is typically quite resistant to change. Addressing and resolving differences between the employee's self-evaluation and attributions (vs. those made by the coach)	How do effective coaches address and resolve differences between the employee's self-evaluation and attributions versus those made by the coach?

	forget failure feedback while recalling positive information, compare themselves against others that make them look good, sort through memory in a biased way to find evidence that they have desirable traits, think their good traits are unusual while their faults are common, and dismiss criticism as motivated by prejudice.	will play a central role in the success of the coaching relationship.	Does participation in coaching diminish the tendency for employees to sustain inflated self-views?
Receptivity to feedback	Interpersonal circumstances can affect how information about the self is processed even though the implications of the information for the self-concept are identical.	The coach's mere knowledge of the feedback may limit an employee's self-deceptive strategy, yet interpersonal circumstances do not always elicit more accurate and balanced processing of information.	

3. Goal Setting and Developmental Planning

Goal setting theory and control theory	Goal-setting theory directs attention to the importance of goals that are specific and difficult as well as to the critical role that goal acceptance, commitment, and feedback play in behavior change. Control theory shows how self-appraisal relative to a standard and feedback loops are central to self-regulation.	Coaches may focus the employee's attention on attaining success rather than merely avoiding failure. A focus on succeeding tends to increase effort and confidence whereas a focus on failure tends to increase anxiety.	Are effective coaches more likely to frame goals in terms of attaining success rather than avoiding failure?
Implementation intentions	Implementation intentions specify the when, where, and how of responses that can lead to goal attainment. They have the structure, "When situation X arises, I will perform response Z."	Coaches can help ensure that goal setting also includes the formation of implementation intentions. Implementation intentions help people achieve their goals despite tempting distractions, bad habits, and competing goals.	Are successful coaches more likely to ensure that employee goals are accompanied by implementation intentions?

(Continued)

TABLE 10.2
(Continued)

Social Psychological Phenomena	Description	Examples of Application to Coaching	Research Questions
Promotion versus prevention focus in self-regulation	Self-regulatory focus can be viewed as a personality variable (shaped by interactions with one's parents) or a situational variable (depending on how tasks and feedback are framed). A promotion focus orients the person toward maximizing the presence of positive outcomes and addressing nurturance needs. A prevention focus orients the person toward maximizing the absence of negative outcomes and addressing security needs.	When coaches overemphasize attention to negative events, they may enhance an employee's concerns with conformity, tradition, and security. Framing goals and feedback in terms of attaining success may help focus employees on self-direction and stimulation. Coaches may encourage employees to frame goals as learning goals (learning how to perform a task or develop a skill) rather than performance goals (finding out how capable the employee is).	To what extent does the employee's self-regulatory focus (as a personality variable) shape the goals that are set and the subsequent success of coaching? Are effective coaches more likely to shift the employee's self-regulatory focus (as a situational variable) from prevention to promotion (and if so, how do they do this)?

4. Implementation

Social Psychological Phenomena	Description	Examples of Application to Coaching	Research Questions
Self-efficacy	Self-efficacy refers to one's belief in his or her ability to act effectively in a given situation and influences whether one is willing to act and persist in such actions.	Coaches may foster employee self-efficacy by expressing confidence, breaking apart large tasks and assigning one part at a time, celebrating small successes, and providing people with the opportunity to accomplish successively more difficult tasks.	What tactics do effective coaches use to increase employees' self-efficacy?
Self-fulfilling prophecies	Expectancy concerning another may affect one's behavior toward the other which in turn shapes the other's behavior so that the other person ultimately behaves in a way that is consistent with one's expectation.	When coaches believe the employee will be successful and communicate this expectation either directly or indirectly, the probability of employee success will likely increase.	Are effective coaches more likely to communicate positive expectations to employees (thereby triggering self-fulfilling prophecy effects)?

Irrational persistence	Commitment generated by sunk costs (investments of time, energy, care, or other resources) creates counterproductive persistence (e.g., refusal to change wrong opinions or to cancel unsuccessful programs). People appear to think, "We must continue to pursue this alternative (even though it now seems less desirable) because we have already invested X and if we do not continue, we will have wasted our initial investment."	Coaches may reduce irrational persistence by encouraging employees to make careful and accurate calculations about their contingencies, telling them about the dangers of becoming entrapped in a persistence situation, pointing out others who have suffered because of costly persistence, and showing how others may think well of them if they withdraw.	How do effective coaches enhance employees' rational persistence while helping employees to avoid irrational persistence (e.g., because of sunk costs)?
Self-handicapping	In self-handicapping, individuals deliberately create handicaps that will interfere with their performance. Such a handicap (if plausible) reduces the likelihood of success but serves as an excuse that permits the person to attribute failure to a source other than his or her competence (thereby preserving the person's self-esteem).	Coaches can recognize that self-handicapping is most likely to occur when employees have experienced noncontingent success. Coaches can discuss the credibility of such excuses with employees (for example, challenging the attributions that employees make concerning their performance) and detect self-handicapping early in the performance cycle so that obstacles and potential excuses can be removed while working to increase the employee's self-efficacy.	Are effective coaches more alert for self-handicapping? How do effective coaches detect self-handicapping early in the performance cycle so that obstacles and potential excuses can be removed?

(Continued)

231

TABLE 10.2
(Continued)

Social Psychological Phenomena	Description	Examples of Application to Coaching	Research Questions

5. Evaluating Progress and the Coaching Relationship

Social Psychological Phenomena	Description	Examples of Application to Coaching	Research Questions
Schematic versus aschematic	One person may be schematic (e.g., viewing himself or herself as risk-averse vs. risk-oriented) but another person may be aschematic (i.e., lacks any view of himself or herself as one or the other). Schematic people are quicker than others to spot information relevant to the domain (or trait) in others, show greater processing of details, and are better able to integrate it with previously acquired information.	Coaching may affect the employee's self-concept, for example, by making the employee schematic about domains for which he or she was previously aschematic. This, in turn, influences the way the employee attends to and processes information about the self and others.	To what extent does the coaching experience make employees schematic about domains for which they were previously aschematic?
Possible selves	One has multiple concepts of how one might turn out (cognitive representations of the individual's hopes and wishes for the self). Information that one doesn't have the necessary skill to be one of the possible selves is of limited importance when one has many rather than few possible selves.	Effective coaches may ultimately limit the employee's vulnerability to feedback by increasing the number of possible selves that the employee can realistically envision.	Does coaching increase the number of possible selves that employees can realistically envision?

Attributions About the Other Person's Motives

The coach and the employee are likely to make attributions about the other's reasons (goals and motives) for pursuing the coaching relationship (Hilton, 1998). Is the coach interested in the employee's welfare, or does the coach have unstated and perhaps self-serving motives? Does the employee seek coaching as a way to attain some extrinsic reward (or escape an anticipated punishment), or is the employee motivated by more intrinsic goals (e.g., the value of becoming more skillful for its own sake)?

In the case of a manager as coach, the relationship between coach and employee is likely to be reciprocally contingent (Fiske, 1998). That is, the employee depends on the manager for tangible rewards but the manager depends on the employee to accomplish important tasks. In general, the more A's behavior is contingent on B, the greater the need for inferences about B's motives and personality (Fiske, 1998). This suggests that attributions about the motives of the other participant are likely to be especially important when an internal coach and employee begin a coaching process.

As illustrated in Table 10.2, each person's schemas are likely to shape the attributions he or she makes about the other (Baron, Byrne, & Johnson, 1998). Once established, schemas and scripts save one a great deal of mental effort because they tell one what to expect and how others are likely to behave (Baron et al.). They affect attention (what is noticed), encoding (process by which information gets stored in memory), and retrieval (recovering information from memory). Also, when perceivers (e.g., employees) begin to question the interaction goals of a target (e.g., a coach), they are likely to be cautious about accepting expectancy—disconfirming behavior. For example, an employee might think, "Why is my manager suddenly trying to coach me, in view of the fact that he or she has never before expressed interest in helping me develop skills or advance my career? Maybe the manager has an ulterior motive."

Employee's Motives for Participating in the Coaching Process

Another factor likely to affect the success of this stage of the coaching process is the reason why the employee enters into a coaching relationship. Sometimes, employees may be asked to participate as a result of poor or declining performance. In such instances, it may be especially difficult for the coach and employee to establish a trusting relationship because the employee has not asked for and does not welcome the coaching (perhaps feeling coerced into participation). Such a prediction follows from reactance theory (Brehm, 1966). The self resists loss of control; when people feel their freedom is threatened, they may respond by aggressing toward the person who has restricted their freedom or try to reassert what is being taken from them (Baumeister, 1998b, p. 714). In such cases, the likelihood that subsequent stages of coaching will be successful is seriously diminished.

At other times, the employee may welcome the coaching and be eager for feedback and the opportunity to grow skills. In some instances, employees may seek coaching for extrinsic reasons (external rewards or benefits). In other instances, employees may pursue coaching for intrinsic reasons (Deci & Ryan, 1991), such as a need for competence (controlling the environment and seeing oneself as capable and effective), a need for autonomy (experiencing an internal locus of causality for one's actions rather than being controlled or directed by external forces), and a need for relatedness (constructing satisfying relationships with others—knowing and caring for others and believing they care about oneself).

Social psychologists (e.g., Baumeister, 1998b, p. 689) point to three possible motives for self-knowledge (see Table 10.2). Although accurate self-appraisal would seem to be the motive most conducive to a constructive coaching experience, self-enhancement motives may often be stronger. Although self-enhancing beliefs, even if unfounded, may help breed persistence (which may produce genuine success), the benefits of positive illusions such as good adjustment and mental health (Taylor & Brown, 1988) may be outweighed by the dangers of illusions (e.g., overconfidence may breed fruitless persistence or dangerous risk taking). In sum, employees may enter into coaching experiences with the hope of enhancing their self-views, a situation likely to detract from the outcomes of coaching.

Although motives for self-knowledge are often self-enhancing, Swann (1992) coined the term *self-verification* to describe people's quest for feedback that would confirm their view of themselves. People desire stable predictability above all else and changes to one's self-concept are therefore unwelcome—in most cases, the consistency motive overlaps with self-enhancement.

Regardless of the motive for entering into the coaching relationship, the heightened self-awareness that often accompanies coaching (as the employee receives feedback and becomes more preoccupied with assessing his or her behavior and progress) may be uncomfortable. For example, Duval and Wicklund (1972) argued that self-awareness will generally be an aversive state because people will generally fall short of the standards against which they compare themselves (Baumeister, 1998b, p. 685). In sum, an important task at this stage of the coaching process is for coaches to understand and manage employees' expectations about the coaching experience (e.g., helping employees become comfortable with heightened self-awareness and helping them keep their illusions small; Baumeister, 1998b, p. 690).

Impression Management Strategies Used When Establishing the Coaching Relationship

For reasons outlined in this section, coaches need to be seen as likeable, trustworthy, and competent. But how do effective coaches establish trust, liking, and perceptions of competence? We know that efforts at impression formation can exert lasting effects on social thought and social behavior (Baron et al., 1998). Gordon (as cited in Baron et al., 1998) found that the success of different ingratiation tactics across studies varied widely (see Table 10.2). But some tactics (e.g., making the other person look good) may not be feasible, especially for external coaches who initially know little about the person being coached. It is also difficult for a coach to make the employee look good in instances when the need for coaching has been precipitated by the employee's poor performance. Also, although people generally present themselves as favorably as they think they can get away with, internal coaches are constrained to be consistent with what the employee already knows about the coach (Baumeister, 1998b, pp. 705–706). Moreover, ingratiation efforts can be successful in getting others to like one but they have a much smaller effect on getting others to think one is competent (Baron et al., 1998). This is a critical concern for coaches. Ingratiation tactics carry a potential risk for coaches—transparent ingratiation efforts may tend to boomerang with the target (employee) reacting negatively (Baron et al.).

How the Coaching Relationship Affects the Coach's Ability to Influence the Employee at Later Stages of the Coaching Process

Building a productive relationship sets the stage for success in later stages of the coaching process. For example, the relationship established at stage one of the coaching process can affect the likelihood that the employee will be persuaded by or comply with the coach's advice during later stages. Cialdini (as cited in Baron et al., 1998, p. 193) suggests that all forms of compliance rest to some extent on six basic principles. One principle focuses on the role of *friendship or liking*. That is, one is more willing to comply with requests from friends and people whom one likes. The ingratiation tactics discussed above represent one (albeit difficult) avenue for coaches who want employees to like them. A second principle points to the role of *reciprocity* in compliance. Recent evidence also suggests that reciprocity plays a role in persuasion, specifically, one tends to change one's attitude in response to persuasion from others (e.g., a coach) who have previously changed their attitudes in response to one's efforts at persuasion. Thus, one way a coach can help create an effective coaching relationship is by showing early on that he or she is open to being influenced by the person being coached (Baron et al., p. 116). The opportunity for such reciprocity may be more available for internal than for external coaches. Moreover, it would be helpful to better understand the tactics used by effective versus ineffective coaches to create liking and a sense of reciprocity.

ASSESSMENT

This stage of the coaching process generally involves assessment of the employee's strengths and limitations, as well as understanding the context in which the employee operates. Generally, the coach will be assessing aspects of the employee's behavior and performance while also encouraging the employee to engage in ongoing self-evaluation. External executive coaches may gather data by interviewing the employee's coworkers and by using psychological instruments (e.g., personality inventories) that can help profile the employee's dispositions and leadership style. In contrast, internal coaches may use a less formal approach to assessment, often relying on the rich data they collect merely by observing the employee during day-to-day interactions.

In many organizations, the assessment stage begins with a 360-degree feedback process where the manager receives structured feedback from peers, direct reports, and the manager (Graddick & Lane, 1998; Hall et al., 1999; Hollenbeck & McCall, 1999). Such feedback may increase self-awareness (Goodstone & Diamante, 1998; London & Smither, 1995), and because a discrepancy between the person one is and the person one wants to be can be upsetting (Baron et al., 1998, p. 78), it is expected that 360-degree feedback can motivate efforts at behavior change. All of this is consistent with Higgins' (1998) view that self-knowledge is pursued for the sake of adaptive benefits of improving person–environment fit (Baumeister, 1998a). In coaching, knowing the self is a means and not an end in itself.

The assessment stage is also shaped by the purpose of coaching. For example, Graddick and Lane (1998) found two major reasons why executive coaches are hired: First, to help talented executives who are "in trouble" because of behavioral or style deficiencies, and second, to help executives through critical transitions, such as having to lead a major change effort. Internal coaches are also likely to begin the coaching process because the employee is facing a difficult situation.

In such circumstances (when confronted with unexpected, difficult, or unpleasant events), coaches and employees are especially likely to engage in careful attributional analysis. Unfortunately, attributional processes often lead to erroneous inferences and people act in accordance with those inferences (Hilton, 1998). The success of subsequent stages of coaching will depend on the ability of the coach and the employee to accurately diagnose the employee's skills and the situational constraints that are likely to shape the employee's behavior. For the reasons detailed in the next section, such an accurate assessment of the employee and the situation is likely to be a frustrating and difficult endeavor.

The Coach as Assessor

It is likely that coaches with different educational or work histories (e.g., counseling psychology, organization development, industrial and organizational psychology, or executive development) may attend to different employee behaviors or categorize the same behaviors in very different ways. For example, it is likely that a coach who routinely uses the Myers-Briggs Type Indicator (with dimensions of sensing–intuitive, thinking–feeling, perceiving–judging, and extraverted–introverted) might attend to different behaviors than a coach who uses the Fundamental Interpersonal Relations Orientation instrument (with dimensions of need for affection, inclusion, or control), or a coach who uses a personality inventory that focuses on the five-factor model of personality (i.e., emotional stability, agreeableness, extraversion, openness to experience, and conscientiousness). As noted in Table 10.2, this is because traits and categories become more accessible and thus likely to capture ambiguous behaviors through long-term frequency or recency of use. Thus, trait accessibility produces automatic behavior-to-trait encodings just as if the behavior was not ambiguous but instead clearly diagnostic (Wegner & Bargh, 1998). Moreover, when people are asked to evaluate targets about whom information is available on several dimensions, primed dimensions are given more weight in overall evaluations (Wegner & Bargh), again pointing to the influence that the coach's schemas are likely to have in the assessment process.

Self-image bias can also affect the coach's assessments. That is, one tends to judge others according to the traits on which one looks good (Baumeister, 1998b). For example, if a coach has excellent interpersonal skills but weaker decision-making skills, the coach may place more emphasis on interpersonal skills and less emphasis on decision-making skills when judging others. Accessibility is a common factor here—attributes the self emphasizes operate as highly accessible categories for interpreting others' behavior. These effects are much more likely to operate when information about a target person (e.g., employee) is ambiguous (Baumeister, 1998b).

One critical problem that coaches face is suggested by Jones and Nisbett's (1971) well-known notion of correspondent inference, that is, people routinely underestimate the power of situations and overestimate the power of dispositions in governing behavior (see also Heider's notion of behavior engulfing the field; Heider, 1958). Indeed, Gilbert (1998) argued that correspondent inferences appear to be made automatically and considerable effort is usually required to correct them, although others have argued that dispositional inferences are sometimes automatic and sometimes controlled (Kunda, 1998). In this context, Ross (1977) noted that the most important task of lay psychology is distinguishing situational causes from personal ones. Coaches need to work hard at appreciating the situational constraints that face the person being coached. Internal coaches face the difficult task of seeing themselves as part of the situation that influences the employee's performance. Of course, this may be difficult for internal coaches who are likely to make self-serving attributions that deny their potential role in contributing to the employee's poor performance. Internal coaches also need to overcome the influence of hedonic relevance (the other's behavior has implications for the perceiver for good or ill), which may increase the likelihood of attributional distortions (Jones & Davis, 1965). Because the behavior of an employee often has implications for internal coaches (e.g., the employee's manager), internal coaches may be especially likely to make internal attributions for the success of a coworker who is liked while blaming that person's failures on external constraints. That is, like most people, internal coaches may want friends to be given dispositional credit for successes and situational dispensation for failures

(Miller, 1998). In contrast, the internal coach may make internal attributions for the failure of a coworker who is disliked and attribute that person's success to external factors.

Relative to an internal coach, external coaches may be at a disadvantage here because they generally know less about the situation facing the employee. Because the salience of the situation has repeatedly been shown to affect one's willingness to make dispositional inferences (Nisbett, 1998), external coaches need to take special steps, for example, by focusing on "invisible" situational factors such as social norms (Gilbert, 1998) to appreciate the situation as the employee sees it. On the other hand, relative to internal coaches, external coaches are less likely to be juggling multiple organizational issues. Because their attentional capacity is not loaded elsewhere, attributions made by external coaches are more likely to be influenced by clear situational constraints (Wegner & Bargh, 1998).

Both internal and external coaches need to remember that when people choose constraining circumstances, those situations do not mask their dispositions but instead provide evidence of them (Gilbert, 1998). Thus, when a manager chooses repeatedly to work in fast-paced, aggressive business cultures, it makes less sense to argue that the manager's behavior is shaped by the organization rather than by the manager's dispositions.

One important caveat needs to be considered here. There is evidence that culture shapes the likelihood of making dispositional versus situational attributions for behavior. For example, Asians generally live in societies where tradition and role expectations (coupled with the need for group harmony) are greater than is typical for most Americans. Thus, in many Asian cultures there are fewer choices to make and less of a requirement that behaviors be consistent with attitudes. People in Asian cultures may therefore be more inclined to understand their own and others' behavior as being shaped by outside forces rather than being an expression of free will. Asians therefore appear to be less susceptible to correspondence bias. As Nisbett (1998) eloquently stated:

> Societies that preach independence are more industrially-based and provide multitudes of choices and decisions, and draw attention toward the isolated individual, independent of the field and its forces as the causal agent. The processes associated with more agricultural, interdependent, and collectivist societies, on the other hand, integrate the individual in the field of social roles and constraints and, therefore, appropriate causality to forces in that field (p. 193).

The Employee's Self-Evaluation

The employee being coached will, of course, form his or her own assessments and make attributions concerning the causes of his or her behavior. There are good reasons for employees to develop accurate self-assessments. For example, managers who overrate themselves appear to be the least effective (Yammarino & Atwater, 1993) and the most likely to suffer from career derailment (McCall and Lombardo (1983). Yet a host of social psychological phenomena make it difficult for one to arrive at accurate self-knowledge and make accurate self-assessments or attributions. For example, the false consensus effect points to a widespread tendency to assume that others are more like one (and share one's views) than they actually are, whereas the false uniqueness effect points to a tendency to see oneself as more unique than one really is in terms of possessing highly desirable qualities (e.g., being smarter than average; Baron et al., 1998). Self-esteem also affects the attributions one makes about one's behavior. For example, people with high self-esteem show more self-serving bias in their responses to feedback and other events (Baumeister, 1998b).

Self-deception and inflated self-views seem to derive from several processes summarized by Baumeister (1998b, see Table 10.2 for a summary). In sum, employees will tend to seek out evidence that confirms their positive opinions about themselves and will distrust, criticize, or reject contrary evidence. In this context, it is noteworthy that feedback about how others performed shows a clear primacy effect (people make up their minds about others quickly), whereas feedback about the self may show a recency effect (people remain open-minded to upward revision of their self-appraisals). This is consistent with the actor–observer effect by which people more rapidly draw dispositional inferences about others than about themselves (Baumeister, 1998a, 1998b).

The result is that employees are likely to develop and sustain positive self-views, even when coaches see the employee as behaving badly or ineffectively. Overcoming the tendency toward biased self-views is likely to be a major challenge at this step of the coaching relationship. Addressing and resolving differences between the employee's self-evaluation and attributions versus those made by the coach will play a central role in the success of the coaching relationship. There are several ways that coaches may have a positive impact here. First, coaches can help employees attend to unflattering information that might otherwise be ignored. Second, coaches can change the standards against which employees compare themselves (focusing attention on optimal behavior rather than typical or average behavior).

Third, coaches can increase the amount of time that employees spend processing negative feedback. Fourth, coaches can discount implausible attributions (e.g., pointing out that others performed well despite facing the same situational constraints). Fifth, coaches can more precisely define the behaviors or criteria associated with abstract concepts (e.g., "good management"). Sixth, as noted previously, the relationship between the coach and employee (when it is based on liking, reciprocity, etc.) can enhance the coach's ability to persuade the employee to consider and accept other viewpoints and interpretations.

The Employee's Receptivity to Feedback

The coach's mere knowledge of the feedback may limit an employee's self-deceptive strategy. For example, research has found that the time people spent reading either unfavorable or favorable personality feedback depended on whether the feedback was private or known to someone else (an interaction partner). When feedback was private or confidential, people followed the standard self-deceptive strategy of skipping through less favorable information. But when feedback was public, the tendency to ignore unflattering information was eliminated and reversed (Baumeister, 1998b). When others know unfavorable information about one it cannot be ignored because it gains "social reality"; thus, interpersonal circumstances in general, and the coaching relationship in particular, can affect how information about the self is processed even though the implications of the information for the self-concept are identical.

Of course, interpersonal circumstances do not always elicit more accurate and balanced processing of information. For example, people sometimes make more defensive, self-serving attributions for their outcomes when others had monitored the performance than when no one had watched (Baumeister, 1998a). Thus, it would be useful to understand how coaches affect the attributions that employees make and the receptivity of employees to negative feedback.

GOAL SETTING
AND DEVELOPMENTAL PLANNING

Once the coach and employee have assessed the employee's strengths and limitations, along with the situational constraints facing the employee, the next step involves setting goals and formulating developmental plans to guide behavior change. Self-regulation is central to this step in the coaching process. Self-regulation involves controlling thoughts, feelings, impulses, actions, and performances to change the self and make it conform to its own goals (Baumeister, 1998b). Self-regulation acknowledges that rats may simply respond to an experimenter's reward and punishment contingencies but people sometimes set their own contingencies (promising to reward oneself for completing a task). Moreover, self-regulation and self-control (unlike self-esteem) seem to be nearly always good. There seem to be almost no instances where self-control is systematically disadvantageous to the person. Still, people have a limited but renewable capacity to control themselves. Efforts to control multiple things at once may be ill-advised and the imposition of new self-regulatory demands may undermine control in other spheres (Baumeister, 1998b). Thus coaches need to limit the person's attention to one or two goals at a time. Of course, the voluminous research on goal-setting theory (Locke & Latham, 1990) directs our attention to the importance of goals that are specific and difficult, as well as to the critical role that goal acceptance, commitment, and feedback play in behavior change. Here we discuss several streams of social psychological research (summarized in Table 10.2) that are relevant to the goal setting and developmental planning process. These include control theory, implementation intentions, and Higgins' (1998) influential work on the effects of having a promotion versus prevention focus in self-regulation.

Control Theory

Carver and Scheier's (1981, 1982) work on control theory and feedback loops is central to self-regulation. People begin with self-appraisal relative to a standard. If one is short of the standard one operates on the self to change; one then conducts another test to see whether the standard has been reached. If it has not, then one resumes efforts to change; if it has, then the control process ends and one exits the loop (and begins thinking about something else). There is a hierarchy of such feedback loops—higher levels refer to broader units of behavior, whereas lower ones refer to smaller units. Lower levels are often means toward the goals of higher levels. When one is blocked in one's efforts to reach a goal at one level, self-awareness shifts to a lower level in order to find and solve the problem. Because people are always falling short of some of their goals yet not always feeling bad, Carver and Scheier proposed that emotion is generally a response to the first derivative (over time) of one's standing vis-à-vis these goals. That is, one feels good when one is moving toward one's goals, and one feels bad when one is moving away from them or moving toward them too slowly. The feedback loop model illustrates that successful self-regulation requires clear and visible standards, effective monitoring of the self, and some potent means of operating on the self. These concepts can provide an organizing framework for coaching relationships and episodes. Carver and Scheier (like Higgins, 1998, see discussion later in this chapter) point out that sometimes one tries to minimize the distance between the self and some positive standard (moving toward success), but sometimes one tries to maximize the discrepancy between the self and a negative standard (moving away from failure). The same task can be framed either way in terms of succeeding versus failing with very different results. A focus on succeeding tends to increase effort and confidence, whereas a focus on failure tends to increase anxiety. This points to the importance of coaches focusing the employee's attention on attaining success rather than merely avoiding failure.

Implementation Intentions

Gollwitzer's (1999) study has recently drawn attention to the importance of implementation intentions. Implementation intentions are subordinate to goal intentions such as, "I intend to reach x," which are the focus of Ajzen's (1991) theory of planned behavior. Implementation intentions specify the when, where, and how of responses that can lead to goal attainment. By forming implementation intentions, people can switch from conscious and effortful control of their goal-directed behaviors to being automatically controlled by situational cues. Gollwitzer has shown how implementation intentions can allow people to make use of a good opportunity that presents itself only briefly even when they are busy with other things. In this way, implementation intentions help people achieve their goals despite tempting distractions, bad habits, and competing goals. Moreover, implementation intentions appear to create instant habits and their effects have been shown to operate days or weeks after they have been initially formed (Gollwitzer, 1999). In one study, a motivational intervention that focused on increasing self-efficacy to exercise, the perceived severity of and vulnerability to heart disease, and the expectation that exercising will reduce the risk of coronary heart disease raised compliance from 29% to only 39%. When this motivational intervention was coupled with the formation of implementation intentions, compliance increased to 91% (see Gollwitzer for a summary of research). In sum, coaches need to ensure that goal setting also includes the formation of implementation intentions. Doing so could be especially helpful for employees who are otherwise absorbed in an ongoing activity and who would therefore otherwise miss an opportunity to act on their goals.

Promotion vs. Prevention Focus in Self-Regulation

Higgins (1998) has emphasized the role of regulatory focus in cognition and adjustment. Sometimes, *promotion focus* guides self-regulation. At other times, self-regulation is guided by a *prevention focus*. He argues that self-regulatory focus is shaped by caretaker–child (usually parent–child) interactions. Higgins' self-discrepancy theory proposes that a nurturant mode of caretaker–child interaction (where parents hope their child will possess valued attributes and reward a match between their expectations and the child's behavior with positive outcomes such as hugs or kisses) creates a promotion focus and ideal-self guides that orient the person toward maximizing the presence of positive outcomes. In contrast, a security mode of caretaker–child interaction (where parents emphasize the child's duties and obligations and punish a mismatch between their expectations and the child's behavior) creates a prevention focus and ought-self guides that orient the person toward maximizing the absence of negative outcomes. As a personality variable, people can develop general viewpoints about the world where they become strongly nurturance-oriented or security-oriented because of their (parental) socialization during childhood. However, Higgins notes that both systems (promotion/nurturance and prevention/security) are adaptive and thus all people possess both. Still, different (parental) socialization experiences cause one system to predominate in self-regulation. Moreover, personality differences at the general level of regulatory focus appear to influence perception and memory for social events (Higgins, 1998).

Self-regulatory focus can also be viewed as a situational variable, rather than as a personality variable, such that framing a performance task with a promotion focus should produce greater persistence than framing the same task with a prevention focus. For example, in one laboratory study, participants in a positive or promotion focus condition received feedback such as "Right, you got that one," when they solved a problem, or "You didn't get that one right," when they did not solve the problem. Participants in the negative or prevention focus condition received feedback such as "You didn't miss that one," when they solved a problem, or "No, you missed that one," when they did not solve the problem. Students in the promotion focus condition solved more problems and persisted longer in trying to solve unsolvable problems than participants in the prevention focus condition

(Roney, Higgins, & Shah, 1995). This study illustrates that situational manipulations can make one or the other self-regulatory focus more accessible (at least temporarily) and thereby influence the goals that people set, as well as their achievement and persistence. This points to a potentially critical role for coaches. To the extent that coaches can make a promotion focus more accessible (perhaps by the way they frame goals and feedback to move toward success rather than away from failure), they can help shape the behavior of the employees they coach in subtle but powerful ways.

In sum, coaches can play a critical role at the goal-setting and planning step of the coaching process. First, coaches can help ensure that goals are specific, challenging (Locke & Latham, 1990), and proximal rather than distal (Bandura & Schunk, 1981). They can help employees frame goals as learning goals (i.e., learning how to perform a task or develop a skill) rather than performance goals (i.e., finding out how capable the employee is; Dweck, 1996). Coaches can frame goals using a promotion focus (achieving a positive outcome rather than preventing a negative outcome). Also, coaches can help people anticipate obstacles and remove competing temptations (Latham & Frayne, 1989). They can help them cope with conflicting goals, perhaps by identifying ways that they can be reconciled or combined (Cantor & Blanton, 1996). For example, the goal of investing time to learn a new skill and the goal of spending more time with friends or colleagues is reconciled by identifying and collaborating with colleagues who also want to learn the skill. Finally, coaches can ensure that goals are accompanied by implementation intentions.

IMPLEMENTATION

It is beyond the scope of this chapter to discuss all of the social psychological research conceivably relevant to implementing behavior change. Instead, we focus on a few areas that we think are especially interesting for understanding the success of coaching.

Self-Efficacy

Bandura (1977) has argued that a person's beliefs about self-efficacy (one's belief in his or her ability to act effectively in a given situation) are crucial determinants of action. Other things being equal, one's self-efficacy beliefs can determine whether one is willing to act and persist in such actions. Stated simply, when people are confident that they can make a desired response, that is, they have high self-efficacy, they are better able to make that response. When they believe they cannot make the response, this prevents them from acting in a way that can produce the desired outcomes (similar to learned helplessness). This suggests that illusions of control (Langer, 1975) may be helpful because it is better to assume one has control when one objectively does not than to assume one does not have control when one could have had it. Indeed, self-efficacy is by no means fixed and unchanging. For example, positive feedback about skills makes self-efficacy likely to rise (Baron et. al, 1998), and fostering self-efficacy (see Table 10.2 for examples) is seen as a key step in empowering employees (Whetten & Cameron, 1998). In sum, coaches' efforts to increase employees' self-efficacy are likely to play a critical role at this step in the coaching process.

Self-Fulfilling Prophecies

It has long been established that people are influenced by the expectations of others. For example, Rosenthal and Jacobson (1968) showed teachers' initially false expectancies about their students' abilities led to changes in the performance of the students that confirmed those expectancies. The first two of these outcomes appear to be more common than the third. This stream of research points to the critical role that the coach's expectations are likely to play in the employee's implementation of behavior change efforts. It would be helpful to know whether effective coaches deliberately communicate their positive expectancies to employees and avoid directly or indirectly communicating their doubts.

Irrational Persistence

As employees try to implement changes in their behavior and pursue new courses of action, coaches are likely to emphasize the value of persistence. Yet not all persistence is adaptive. For example, persistence is harmful when it creates an obstinate refusal to change wrong opinions, to cancel unsuccessful programs, to stop investing money in unsound enterprises, or to stop treating people in ways that routinely backfire. One factor that contributes to such counterproductive persistence is the feeling of commitment generated by sunk costs (see Table 10.2). People often feel that they will lose all of the investment if they quit now. As a result, they persist far beyond the point where it seems rational to continue (Baumeister, 1998b). Indeed, there are examples of irrational persistence where decision makers have decided to continue a project even though the value of the completed project was less than the amount yet to be spent to complete it (Dawes, 1998). It is also noteworthy that people are more likely to persist in a losing course of action when the initial decision had been their own instead of someone else's, especially if the initial decision had been made in the face of other people's objections. Apparently, we don't want others to say, "I told you so" (Baumeister, 1998b).

Here too, coaches can play a pivotal role (see Table 10.2) by encouraging people to make careful and accurate calculations about their contingencies, pointing to the dangers of becoming entrapped in a persistence situation, and showing them that an audience will think well of them if they withdraw (Baumeister, 1998b). These findings suggest a somewhat counterintuitive role for coaches. On the one hand, coaches want to enhance self-efficacy and rational persistence when the employee confronts challenging, albeit unanticipated, obstacles. At the same time, coaches need to be vigilant of signs that the employee is engaging in irrational persistence perhaps because of perceived sunk costs.

Finally, sunk costs and escalation of commitment have a group-level parallel referred to as collective entrapment—the tendency of groups to cling to unsuccessful decisions or policies even in the face of overwhelming evidence that the decisions are bad ones. Coaches can help limit this tendency through second-chance meetings (where members are asked to express any lingering doubts), skepticism (adopting devil's advocate approaches where each alternative is carefully questioned), and by asking different groups of persons than those who made the initial decision to decide whether to continue with it (Baron et al., 1998).

Self-Handicapping

Another phenomenon that may affect the likelihood of successfully implementing behavior change (and that is grounded in the attributions that actors make concerning their own performance) is self-handicapping. In self-handicapping, individuals deliberately seek out or create handicaps that will interfere with their performance. This approach can serve a short-term interest, namely, preserving the person's self-esteem. But it does so at the expense of the long-term interest of achieving a successful outcome (Arkin & Oleson, 1998). Self-handicapping is most likely to occur when people have experienced noncontingent success. In such a circumstance, the employee may feel like an impostor or pretender and fear that success, because it was attributed to luck, cannot be repeated or sustained.

Self-handicapping makes failure meaningless and forestalls drawing un- flattering attributions about oneself. Self-handicapping is a clever strategy because it protects against failure and enhances success. For example, low effort means failure is not diagnostic of low competence, whereas success would indicate the person is very talented because he or she succeeded despite not trying hard (Baumeister, 1998b).

The self-handicapping phenomenon has implications for coaching. For example, effective coaches may be especially likely to attend carefully to the attributions that employees make in their day-to-day conversations and thereby detect whether employees are creating obstacles or excuses to reduce the risk of failure or enhance the value of success. Effective coaches may also focus the employee's attention on the attributions that he or she makes concerning success or failure, discussing and perhaps challenging the credibility of such excuses with the employee. By doing so, coaches may detect self-handicapping early in the performance cycle so that obstacles and potential excuses can be removed, while at the same time working to increase the employee's self-efficacy.

EVALUATING PROGRESS
AND THE COACHING RELATIONSHIP

Many of the concepts introduced earlier (e.g., the role of attributions in evaluations, control theory, etc.) play a role in the ongoing evaluation of behavior change and the coaching relationship. In this section, we focus on the extent to which the coaching relationship ultimately changes employ- ees' mental frameworks and thereby, in a fundamental way, changes how employees think about themselves and their organizational roles.

One's self-concept can be thought of as a collection of beliefs and feel- ings about oneself (Baron et al., 1998). People have a great deal of infor- mation about the self that is stored in a very loose fashion. In this sense, it is more appropriate to think about an aggregate of self-schemas than about a single conception of the self (Baumeister, 1998a). Markus (1977) introduced the concept of being aschematic (see Table 10.2). We suggest that effective coaching will affect the employee's self-concept, for exam- ple, by making the employee schematic about domains for which he or she was previously aschematic. For example, the coaching process may make managers schematic about important constructs associated with ef- fective leadership. This may occur because traits and categories become more accessible through long-term frequency or recency of use. Thus, those concepts that are applied again and again (e.g., during coaching discussions) in the controlled perceiving and judging of the self and others eventually become automatized. Changing employees' schemas and scripts shape how they expect themselves and others to behave in specific situations (Baron et al., 1998). Moreover, constructs that become chronically accessible ultimately capture and encode behaviors that are ambiguously relevant to the trait and thereby influence one's impression of the target or self on the trait (Wegner & Bargh, 1998).

Another way in which effective coaching can bring about deep change is by affecting what Markus and Nurius (1986) referred to as possible selves (i.e., cognitive representations of the individual's hopes and wishes for the self). Moreover, people who have a very limited number of possible future selves are emotionally vulnerable to relevant feedback (Baron et al., 1998). For example, information that reveals lack of the necessary skill to become one possible self is of limited importance when one has many rather than few possible selves. In this sense, having or imagining more possible selves (i.e., assuming the possible selves are realistically grounded) is more emotionally beneficial than having a very simple view. Thus, effective coaches may ultimately limit the employee's vulnerability to feedback by increasing the number of possible selves that the employee can realistically envision.

CONCLUSION

Our purpose has been to illustrate how social psychological research, especially person perception and interpersonal judgment research, can help enhance understanding and guide research concerning coaching in organizations. At each stage of the coaching process, social psychological research points to critical issues that effective coaches must address. Also, if coaching in organizations is to avoid being characterized as a transient fad, then it must increasingly be grounded in research concerning the psychological processes and mechanisms that distinguish effective from ineffective coaching. We hope that this chapter has served to direct attention to some of these key research issues.

REFERENCES

Ajzen, I. (1991). The theory of planned behavior. *Organizational Behavior and Human Decision Processes, 50*, 179–211.

Arkin, R. M., & Oleson, K. C. (1998). Self-handicapping. In J. M. Darley and J. Cooper (Eds.), *Attribution and social interaction: The legacy of Edward E. Jones* (pp. 313–347). Washington, DC: American Psychological Association.

Bandura, A. (1977). Self-efficacy: Toward a unifying theory of behavior change. *Psychological Review, 84*, 191–215.

Bandura, A., & Schunk, D. H. (1981). Cultivating competence, self-efficacy, and intrinsic interest through proximal self-motivation. *Journal of Personality and Social Psychology, 41*, 586–598.

Baron, R. A., Byrne, D., & Johnson, B. T. (1998). *Exploring social psychology*. Needham Heights, MA: Allyn & Bacon.

Baumeister, R. F. (1998a). The interface between intrapsychic and interpersonal processes: Cognition, emotion, and self as adaptations to other people. In J. M. Darley and J. Cooper (Eds.), *Attribution and social interaction: The legacy of Edward E. Jones* (pp. 201–224). Washington, DC: American Psychological Association.

Baumeister, R. F. (1998b). The self. In Daniel T. Gilbert, S. T. Fiske, and G. Lindzey (Eds.), *Handbook of social psychology* (pp. 680–740). New York: Oxford University Press.

Brehm, J. (1966). *A theory of psychological reactance*. New York: Academic Press.

Cantor, N., & Blanton, H. (1996). Effortful pursuit of personal goals in daily life. In P. M. Gollwitzer & J. A. Bargh (Eds.), *The psychology of action: Linking cognition and motivation to action* (pp. 338–359). New York: Guilford.

Carver, C. S., & Scheier, M. F. (1981). *Attention and self-regulation: A control theory approach to human behavior*. New York: Springer-Verlag.

Carver, C. S., & Scheier, M. F. (1982). Control theory: A useful conceptual framework for personality-social, clinical, and health psychology. *Psychological Bulletin, 92*, 111–135.

Dawes, R. M. (1998). Behavioral decision making and judgment. In Daniel T. Gilbert, S. T. Fiske, and G. Lindzey (Eds.), *Handbook of social psychology* (pp. 497–548). New York: Oxford University Press.

Deci, E. L., & Ryan, R. M. (1991). A motivational approach to self: Integration in personality. In R. Dienstbier (Ed.), *Nebraska symposium on motivation* (Vol. 38, pp. 237–288). Lincoln: University of Nebraska Press.

Diedrich, R. C. (1996). An iterative approach to executive coaching. *Consulting Psychology Journal: Practice & Research, 48*, 61–66.

Duval, S., & Wicklund, R. A. (1972). *A theory of objective self-awareness*. New York: Academic Press.

Dweck, C. S. (1996). Implicit theories as organizers of goals and behavior. In. P. M. Gollwitzer & J. A. Bargh (Eds.), *The psychology of action: Linking cognition and motivation to action* (pp. 69–90). New York: Guilford.

Fiske, S. T. (1998). Goal taxonomies: Then and now. In J. M. Darley and J. Cooper (Eds.), *Attribution and social interaction: The legacy of Edward E. Jones* (pp. 153–161). Washington, DC: American Psychological Association.

Foster, B., & Seeker, K. R. (1997). *Coaching for peak employee performance*. Irvine, CA: Richard Chang Associates, Inc.

Gilbert, D. T. (1998). Speeding with Ned: A personal view of the correspondence bias. In J. M. Darley and J. Cooper (Eds.), *Attribution and social interaction: The legacy of Edward E. Jones* (pp. 5–36). Washington, DC: American Psychological Association.

Gollwitzer, P. M. (1999). Implementation intentions. *American Psychologist, 54*, 493–503.

Goodstone, M. S., & Diamante, T. (1998). Organizational use of therapeutic change: Strengthening multisource feedback systems through interdisciplinary coaching. *Consulting Psychology Journal: Practice & Research, 50*, 152–163.

Graddick, M. M., and Lane, P. (1998). Evaluating executive performance. In J. W. Smither (Ed.), *Performance Appraisal: State-of-the-Art in Practice*. San Francisco: Jossey-Bass.

Hall, D. T., Otazo, K. L., & Hollenbeck, G. P. (1999). Behind closed doors: What really happens in executive coaching. *Organizational Dynamics, 27*, 39–52.

Hargrove, R. (1995). *Masterful coaching: Extraordinary results by impacting people and the way they think and work together*. San Francisco: Pfeiffer & Co.

Harris, M. (1999). Practice network: Look, it's an I-O psychologist . . . No, it's a trainer . . . No, it's an executive coach! *The Industrial-Organizational Psychologist, 36*, 38–42.

Heider, F. (1958). *The psychology of interpersonal relations*. New York: Wiley.

Higgins, E. T. (1998). From expectancies to worldviews: Regulatory focus in socialization and cognition. In J. M. Darley and J. Cooper (Eds.), *Attribution and social interaction: The legacy of Edward E. Jones* (pp. 243–269). Washington, DC: American Psychological Association.

Hilton, J. L. (1998). Interaction goals and person perception. In J. M. Darley and J. Cooper (Eds.), *Attribution and social interaction: The legacy of Edward E. Jones* (pp. 127–152). Washington, DC: American Psychological Association.

Hollenbeck, G. P., & McCall, M. W. (1999). Leadership development: Contemporary practices. In A. I. Kraut and A. K. Korman (Eds.), *Evolving Practices in Human Resource Management* (pp. 172–200). San Francisco: Jossey-Bass.

Jones, E. E., & Davis, K. E. (1965). From acts to dispositions: The attribution process in person perception. In L. Berkowitz (Ed.), *Advances in experimental social psychology* (Vol. 2, pp. 220–266). New York: Academic Press.

Jones, E. E., & Nisbett, R. E. (1971). The actor and the observer: Divergent perceptions of the causes of behavior. In E. E. Jones, D. Kanouse, H. H. Kelley, R. E. Nisbett, S. Valins, & B. Weiner (Eds.), *Attribution: Perceiving the causes of behavior*. Morristown, PA: General Learning Press.

Kilburg, R. R. (1996). Toward a conceptual understanding and definition of executive coaching. *Consulting Psychology Journal: Practice & Research, 48*, 134–144.

Kilburg, R. R. (1997). Coaching and executive character: Core problems and basic approaches. *Consulting Psychology Journal: Practice & Research, 49*, 281–299.

Kinlaw, D. (1996). *Coaching: The ASTD trainer's sourcebook*. New York: McGraw-Hill.

Kunda, Z. (1998). Parallel processing in person perception: Implications for two-stage models of attribution. In J. M. Darley and J. Cooper (Eds.), *Attribution and social interaction: The legacy of Edward E. Jones* (pp. 115–126). Washington, DC: American Psychological Association.

Langer, E. J. (1975). The illusion of control. *Journal of Personality and Social Psychology, 32*, 311–328.

Latham, G. P. & Frayne, C. A. (1989). Self-management training for increasing job attendance: A follow-up and replication. *Journal of Applied Psychology, 72*, 411–416.

Levinson, H. (1996). Executive coaching. *Consulting Psychology Journal: Practice & Research, 48*, 115–123.

Locke, E. A., & Latham, G. P. (1990). *A theory of goal setting and task performance*. Englewood Cliffs, NJ: Prentice-Hall.

London, M., & Smither, J. W. (1995). Can multisource feedback change perceptions of goal accomplishment, self-evaluations, and performance-related outcomes? Theory-based applications and directions for research. *Personnel Psychology, 48*, 803–839.

Markus, H. R. (1977). Self-schemata and processing information about the self. *Journal of Personality and Social Psychology, 35*, 63–78.

Markus, H., & Nurius, P. S. (1986). Possible selves. *American Psychologist, 41*, 954–969.

McCall, M. W., & Lombardo, M. M. (1983). *Off the track: Why and how successful executives get derailed*. (Tech. Rep. No. 21) Greensboro, NC: Center for Creative Leadership.

Miller, A. G. (1998). Some thoughts prompted by "Speeding with Ned." In J. M. Darley and J. Cooper (Eds.), *Attribution and social interaction: The legacy of Edward E. Jones* (pp. 37–52). Washington, DC: American Psychological Association.

Nisbett, R. E. (1998). Essence and accident. In J. M. Darley and J. Cooper (Eds.), *Attribution and social interaction: The legacy of Edward E. Jones* (pp. 171–200). Washington, DC: American Psychological Association.

O'Neill, M. B. (2000). *Executive coaching with backbone and heart : A systems approach to engaging leaders with their challenges*. San Francisco: Jossey-Bass.

Peterson, D. B. (1996). Executive coaching at work: The art of one-on-one change. *Consulting Psychology Journal: Practice and Research, 48*, 78–86.

Richard, J. T. (1999). Multimodal therapy: A useful model for the executive coach. *Consulting Psychology Journal: Practice & Research, 51*, 24–30.

Roney, C. J. R., Higgins, E. T., & Shah, J. (1995). Goals and framing: How outcome focus influences motivation and emotion. *Personality and Social Psychology Bulletin, 21*, 1151–1160.

Rosenthal, R., & Jacobson, L. (1968). *Pygmalion in the classroom.* New York: Holt, Rinehart & Winston.

Ross, L. (1977). The intuitive psychologist and his shortcomings. In L. Berkowitz (Ed.), *Advances in experimental social psychology* (Vol. 10, pp. 173–220). New York: Academic Press.

Saporito, T. J. (1996). Business-linked executive development: Coaching senior executives. *Consulting Psychology Journal: Practice and Research, 48*, 96–103.

Swann, W. B. (1992). Seeking "truth," finding despair: Some unhappy consequences of a negative self-concept. *Current Directions in Psychological Science, 1*, 15–18.

Taylor, S. E., & Brown, J. D. (1988). Illusion and well-being: A social psychological perspective on mental health. *Psychological Bulletin, 103*, 193–210.

Tobias, L. L. (1996). Coaching executives. *Consulting Psychology Journal: Practice & Research, 48*, 87–95.

Tversky, A., & Kahneman, D. (1986). Rational choice and the framing of decisions. *Journal of Business, 59*, S251–S278.

Waldroop, J., & Butler, T. (1996, November–December). The executive as coach. *Harvard Business Review, 74*, pp. 111–117.

Wegner, D. M., & Bargh, J. A. (1998). Control and automaticity in social life. In Daniel T. Gilbert, S. T. Fiske, and G. Lindzey (Eds.), *Handbook of social psychology* (pp. 446–496). New York: Oxford University Press.

Whetten, D. A., & Cameron, K. S. (1998). *Developing management skills.* New York: Addison-Wesley.

Witherspoon, R., & White, R. P. (1996). Executive coaching: A continuum of roles. *Consulting Psychology Journal: Practice & Research, 48*, 124–133.

Yammarino, F. J., & Atwater, L. E. (1993). Understanding self-perception accuracy: Implications for human resource management. *Human Resource Management, 32*, 231–247.

11

Understanding, Assessing, and Intervening with Problem Employees

Zvi Strassberg
State University of New York at Stony Brook

In recent years there has been an increasing appreciation of interpersonal skills as a key determinate of job performance. Strikingly, over half of the approximately 60 billion dollars spent per year on organizational development is devoted to training in interpersonal skills ("Industry Report," 1997). Simultaneously, professionals within organizations as well as management and organizational consultants and researchers have been striving to refine services for preventing and intervening in problems of interpersonal difficulties, including those aimed toward optimizing interpersonal skills (e.g., Gist & Stevens, 1998; Hollenbeck & McCall, 1999).

In order to "put a face" on the issue of interpersonal skills, imagine the following scenarios:

- Roger is a factory line worker who becomes angered quite easily and lashes out at coworkers. He has been shifted among work teams in an ongoing effort to find a group in which he can function cooperatively.
- Meredith is a supervisor who often uses the threat of disciplinary actions including termination as a means for controlling personnel.

253

- Bob is a manager who lashes out at peers (other managers at his organizational level) with verbal "potshots" over disagreements when planning or working on cross-unit projects and also bullies his own supervisors continually.

Roger, Meredith, and Bob differ from each other in the job titles and duties. However, they are similarly identified as "problem employees," that is, their impaired social skills and aggressive behavior are counter-productive to their own and others' job performance; their behavior is therefore detrimental to the well-being of the organization. The bulk of this chapter focuses on aggressive behavior in the workplace, although the principles and practices to be discussed apply to a breadth of interpersonal skill issues (e.g., communication, sexual harassment, and diversity).

Despite the burgeoning interest in interpersonal skills and job performance and an extensive literature on social cognitive bases of social behavior in general (i.e., thought processes about the self and others; cf. Bandura, 1986; Fiske & Taylor, 1991), management scholars have not yet developed a model that emphasizes the role of social cognition in the origins and remediation of interpersonal difficulties. Indeed, a search of the organizational literature on interpersonal skills reveals precious few empirical reports on social cognition, despite the face-valid notion that various aspects of social cognition are applicable to and implicit in various training and coaching activities. For example, in the area of person perception, attributions (Kelly & Michela, 1980; Ross, 1977), self-efficacy (Bandura, 1986), and stereotyping (Judd & Park, 1988; Linville & Jones, 1980) are theoretically central to topics such as conflict and aggression management, assertiveness, and team building. It therefore seems timely to propose a model that provides a comprehensive understanding of social cognitive functioning, describes the cognitive mechanisms of social competence versus interpersonal difficulties (emphasizing aggression), and which can and has been used successfully for facilitating positive behavioral change.

In fact, theory and research from contemporary clinical psychology provides a well-articulated cognitive perspective for understanding, assessing, and intervening in problems of social maladjustment. This perspective has been variously cast as a model of stress inoculation (Meichenbaum, 1985), social skills (McFall, 1982), problem solving (d'Zurilla, 1986), or a social information processing model of social competence (Dodge, 1986; Strassberg & Dodge, 1989). Dodge's social information processing model is perhaps the most well-researched (especially concerning aggressive behavior), encompassing variables from the other related models, and will thus be the focus of this discussion.

Note that Baron and Neuman (1997) recently proposed an integrative model of aggression in the workplace. Whereas their model appears quite useful, the Dodge model is preferred for present purposes because it is meant for application to a broad variety of interpersonal skills, has demonstrated predictive validity in research, and conceptualizes and describes cognitive factors in greater detail than does the Neuman and Baron model.

There are three interrelated goals for the remainder of this chapter: (a) to apply a social information processing model of social functioning toward understanding interpersonal skills and difficulties in the workplace (note that the dearth of empirical literature on social cognition specific to workplace aggression, and even workplace interpersonal skills more generally, requires the use of illustrative findings from samples of aggressive youth and adults outside the work setting); (b) to discuss the model's use in planning and implementing interventions for social maladjustment; and (c) to suggest applications of the model to the demands placed on professionals concerned with education, training, coaching, and counseling within organizations.

SOCIAL COMPETENCE AND PROBLEM BEHAVIOR: A SOCIAL INFORMATION PROCESSING MODEL

Basic Principles

According to Dodge's model (Crick & Dodge, 1994; Dodge, 1986; Strassberg & Dodge, 1989), during interpersonal exchanges an individual receives a set of social cues from another person (or other people), and then engages in cue-relevant cognitive processes that stimulate a behavioral reaction. The behaviors generated by one person then serve as cues for the other person in an ongoing interaction in which the participants are continually processing information and producing behavioral responses until the exchange is terminated. It is hypothesized that behavioral differences between individuals, including differences between those who display aggressive behavior versus those who display nonagressive behavior, can be understood through an analysis of their social cognitive patterns.

An individual comes into interpersonal situations with a cognitive database—or storehouse of knowledge—about oneself, others, and the world that serves as a resource for understanding and acting upon those situations. A person's cognitive database is developed through their own particular experiences with people and events and is organized in the brain as coherent informational units, known as *schema* (cf. Fiske & Taylor, 1991). Examples of schema might include but are not limited to those for the self, others in general, specific individuals, events (e.g., relations between what one does and how others react), and the organizational culture. Differences between people in the contents of various schema in the cognitive database are proposed to lead to differences in behavior, such as differences between individuals who display aggression versus nonagression. For example, in the problem employee scenarios presented earlier in this chapter, Roger's "coworker schema" is likely to include a preponderance of negative assumptions (viz., others are motivated to undermine his work, make him look bad in front of the supervisor, and irritate him).

However, cognitive databases are not simply generalized mind-sets. Rather, in social situations, specific schema are activated and used as guides and resources for the content of cognition in a sequence of information processing steps that are stimulated by social cues and consequate with behavioral reactions, such as aggressive versus cooperative or competently assertive reactions during conflict. The sequence of steps in the model, use of schematic knowledge, and differences between individuals who display aggressive and nonaggressive behavior in the contents of their social information processing are discussed in the next section and depicted in Fig. 11.1.

Please note the use of the term "person who displays aggressive behavior" is meant to denote an individual who engages in higher rates of aggresssion than most other people, not an immutable personality type. Indeed, aggression is often influenced by situational, relationship, and mood factors (as mentioned later), and can be modified through changes in social information processing patterns.

Before moving to the details of the model, please note that information processing may tend to occur as (a) a conscious, controlled activity in situations that are novel or complex; (b) in a rapid and automatic manner largely outside of conscious awareness in situations that are very familiar, such as during repeated discussions of a particular topic, or in ongoing relationships (Schneider & Schiffrin, 1977); or (c) when an individual's social schema are chronically activated in preparation for defense, as is the case with younger people who display aggression (Graham & Hudley,

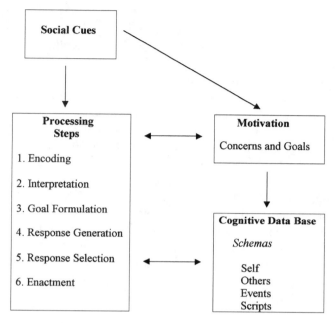

FIG. 11.1. A social information processing model.

1994). However, as described later, a key approach to remediating deviant social information processing patterns is to bring them under conscious control so that they can be monitored and adjusted.

Structure and Dynamics of Processing

As depicted in Fig. 11.1, a person comes to a given situation with a cognitive database of social knowledge, as well as a motivational set (of concerns and goals). Motivational factors may be nonspecific and of general importance, such as avoiding harm, being a helpful person, and being successful in one's job or they may be specific and of immediate importance, such as achieving a particular task or getting a coworker to be more cooperative. In either case, the cognitive processes that occur in a given situation will be influenced by and aimed toward attaining one's motives.

A primary function served by the cognitive database is to guide selective attention to social and other environmental cues that are the most relevant to the individual's motivation at that time. This function is depicted in Fig. 11.1 as the flow of information from environmental input through motivation and the cognitive database to attention and perception of specific cues.

Once cues are perceived, the cognitive database serves as a resource for understanding and acting on those cues.

The first two action steps in the model—cue encoding and interpretation—are "input" cognition; that is, they are oriented toward taking in and making sense of environmental events. During encoding, perceived cues are registered in the brain and stored in short-term memory. Types of cues that might be encoded include but are not limited to a person's physical posture, their vocal tone, and the content of what they say. Individuals with aggressive behavior show deficits in efforts to search for relevant situational cues (Dodge & Newman, 1981), as well as biases in the form of cue distortions, such as encoding of others' neutral facial expressions as those of anger (Dodge, Murphy, & Buchsbaum, 1984).

Encoding deficits and biases are thought to originate with schemas that represent and filter others' behavioral cues in a negative light. Thus, others may be "seen" at a given moment as producing behaviors that they actually haven't generated, such as an angry expression or tone of voice or their words. Because such cues are confirmatory of preexisting schematic notions brought into the interaction, further cue search may be precluded as extraneous.

At the interpretation step, encoded cues are integrated into the cognitive database and assigned personal meaning. One type of well-studied interpretation is that of causal attribution, or the presumed reasons for another person's action (e.g., their intention for criticizing your work, or for not following through with a directive in a timely manner). There is substantial evidence that aggressive individuals are prone to negativistic attributional biases in interpreting the intentions of others, such as attributions of oppositional resistance (Berkowitz, 1989; Strassberg, 1995), blaming (Graham & Hudley, 1994), and hostility (Dodge, 1986; Holtzworth-Munroe & Hutchinson, 1993; Strassberg, 1997), including that which is personalized (Bauer & Twentyman, 1985). Personalized attributions for the intentions and motives presumed to underlie evaluative feedback in the workplace may be especially problematic, as risk factors for revenge (Baron, 1988; Kramer, 1995).

In general, attributional biases are correlated with angry, aggressive overreactions to actual or perceived negative events (Dodge, 1991). Such attribution-driven "reactive aggression" conceptually maps onto Berkowitz' (1989) frustration–aggression model. The patterns of angry aggression described at the beginning of this chapter for Roger the factory worker (lashing out in anger), and for Bob the manager (taking verbal potshots at other managers), provide examples of reactive aggression and of individuals who are likely to suffer from negativistic attributional biases.

The next set of processing steps can be thought of as "output" cognition, as they are oriented toward producing behavioral responses to the interpreted cues. The step following cue interpretation is goal maintenance, revision, or selection. An individual's interpretation of a situation might well be consistent with their goals. This would be the case, for example, if the personnel were compliant with directives issued by Meredith, the supervisor who was mentioned at the beginning of the chapter. However, Meredith might interpret employees' water-cooler chat or nervous laughter in her presence as a lack of respect—each of these activities might lead to expectations of "trouble." If so, Meredith might revise her original goal of simply obtaining workers' compliance to her directives to now include asserting psychological dominance over them, which would be consistent with her pattern of threats. Of course, benign attributions for chat or laughter (e.g., that they build camaraderie or that authority figures make people nervous in general) would presumably not lead to such goal revision. There is no current research base on this processing step, but it is consistent with literature on other aspects of processing to hypothesize that the goal revision and selection tendencies of individuals with patterns of antisocial behavior would include themes of dominance and retaliation.

Having produced a situational interpretation and maintained, revised, or selected a new situational goal, the individual then engages in response generation by accessing the cognitive database for potential goal-relevant behavioral response options. Then, having generated a number of response options, the individual engages in response decision (i.e., selecting the response or responses deemed most likely to help attain the goal). This selection process involves evaluating potential positive and negative consequences of each behavioral option accessed during response generation. The decision process relies on attitudes about the self, such as self-efficacy for the ability to perform a given response, in other words, the belief that one can perform the response with skill (e.g., to explain something in a patient manner; Bandura, 1986) and attitudes about others, such as outcome expectancies for whether a given response will actually produce a desired change in another person's behavior (e.g., whether someone will actually do what is wanted if asked nicely vs. in a demanding manner; Perry, Perry, & Rasmussen, 1986). Put differently, self-efficacy addresses the question, "How well can I perform a given response?" Outcome expectancies address the question, "Will it work the way I want it to if I try it?" Presumably, at least a modicum of positive self-efficacy and outcome expectancy for a given response are necessary to attempting the response, with the probability of engaging in the response increasing along with increases in self-efficacy, outcome expectancy, or both.

Compared to socially competent individuals, individuals with aggressive behavior display deficits in the generation of competent response options such as reasoning and negotiation (Rubin & Krasnor, 1986; Guerra & Slaby, 1989), express low self-efficacy for competently assertive responses and high self-efficacy for aggression (Perry et al., 1986), express positive outcome expectancies for aggression (Perry et al.), and tend to select aggressive responses as the most desirable (Dutton & Browning, 1988). Further, such response generation and decision processes are specifically correlated with proactive, domineering and bullying aggression (Dodge, 1991), and conceptually map onto Bandura's (1986) proposals for the cognitive underpinnings for the social learning of aggression. The patterns of bullying aggression described at the beginning of this chapter for Meredith the supervisor (control through threats) and for Bob the manager (intimidating supervisors), provide examples of proactive aggression and of individuals who are likely to suffer from impaired response generation, evaluation, and selection cognitions.

The final step in the sequence is behavioral enactment or performance of the selected response. Enactment, although clearly a behavioral phenomenon, is also considered a cognitive phenomenon. This is because verbal and motor skills require *action schema* or mental scripts and protocols for their performance (i.e., memory for how to do things like ask for permission or be assertive, which are developed through observation and rehearsal in exchanges with others). Thus, once a response is selected, performance-relevant behavioral scripts are accessed and engaged, leading to the actual production of the behavioral response. Individuals who have aggressive behavior demonstrate difficulty enacting verbally competent responses to conflict, even when specifically directed to do so (Dodge, 1986), indicating deficits in their mental scripts for appropriate response patterns. Fig. 11.2 provides a summary of social information processing deficits and biases displayed among samples of individuals who have aggressive behavior.

Summary

In theory, social cognition "drives" reaction patterns toward others in the course of behavioral exchanges. Indeed, individuals who display aggressive behavior can be differentiated from individuals who display nonaggressive behavior at various steps in the social information processing sequence. Input cognition is related most closely to reactive, angry aggression, and output cognition is related most closely to proactive, bullying aggression.

Encoding
Search deficits;
Negative distortions

Interpretation
Attribute negative
intentions;
Personalize

Goal Formulation
To be investigated

Response Generation
Repertoires deficient
in competent options;
Over-representation
of aggression

Response Selection
Low self-efficacy and
outcome expectancies for
competent behavior,
reverse for aggressive;
Choose aggressive over
competent

Enactment
Deficient in competent
assertion skills

FIG. 11.2.   Summary of processing deficits and biases among aggressive samples.

Understanding of these social information processing and behavioral patterns provides an entrée into promoting positive change among employees who show problematic behavior patterns.

CLINICAL ASSESSMENT
AND INTERVENTION

Assessment and intervention are complementary aspects of a process aimed toward reducing problematic behavior and stimulating positive change in interpersonal skills. Assessment is concerned with identifying points for change, whereas intervention is concerned with effecting the changes themselves. Application of the social information processing model to enhance interpersonal skill is perhaps best explained by illustrating the principles and practices of assessment and intervention within a case study. As with all cognitive-behavioral interventions, the overarching goal in the following case is to assist the client in becoming autonomously well-functioning, that is, to develop the cognitive and behavioral skills for coping effectively with everyday challenges, as well as with those events that are particularly stressful and difficult (cf. Spiegler & Guevremont, 1993). The reader should keep in mind that the following represents a formalized set of procedures typical of clinical practice. In organizational application, it may be that the various assessment and intervention components are addressed in a similarly structured manner or more informally embedded in direct interaction with and observation of relevant parties across time and situations.

Overview

Bob, the manager mentioned previously in this chapter, ascended rapidly through the corporate ranks. His quick mind and advanced technical skills overshadowed his reputation for being irritable and critical of others. However, these antagonistic and aggressive tendencies had become more frequent and severe in recent months. In fact, other managers had complained to the human resources department, and a vice-president had overheard Bob berating a company supervisor in the parking lot. After an initial screening, Bob was referred to a psychologist with the goal of improving his cooperation and leadership skills.

Assessment

Target Behaviors.   The clinician interviewed the human resource professional making the referral of Bob's case and determined that the most problematic behaviors in which Bob engaged were those of verbal aggression. Specifically, he was prone to delivering angry insults to other managers, for example, "You're such an idiot!" and giving directives in a demeaning manner to supervisors, such as, "Is that simple enough for you to do by tomorrow, Einstein?"

Bob felt justified enough in his behavior that he did not initially construe it as aggression and was at first resentful of being held accountable for what he saw as "other people's problems." However, he also recognized that he was essentially being required to change and agreed that there was nothing to be lost on learning how to effectively manage relationships and create a better working environment for himself and others.

Situational–Contextual Approach. Rather than representing a generalized behavior pattern in a classic personality sense, it is known that aggression tends to occur in certain circumstances, such as in response to actual or potential/anticipated provocations (Dodge, McClaskey, & Feldman, 1985; Wright & Mischel, 1987), often within specific relationships (Chase, O'Leary, Treboux, & Strassberg, 1998), and can be stimulated by emotional moods or states such as fear or anger (Parke & Slaby, 1983; Smith & Lazarus, 1990). Correlaries to such behavior patterns are found at the social-cognitive level of analysis, in situation-specificity of social information processing deficits and biases (Dodge, 1986), relationship-specific negativity in attributions (Hymel, 1986; Snarr & Strassberg, 2000), and exacerbation of hostile attributional biases under conditions of threat and anger (Dodge & Somberg, 1987). It is thought that adversarial relationships and threat or anger states guide selective attention toward conflict-relevant cues; increase the likelihood that negavistic schemas for others will act as filters that distort cues (so that the individual might "see" schema-consistent behaviors that have not actually taken place, such as anger expressions); prime defensive and hostile attributions; restrict the accessing of competent responses and increase the accessing and positive evaluation of aggressive responses; and impair behavioral skills for appropriate responding (Dodge & Somberg, 1987; Graham & Hudley, 1994; Strassberg & Dodge, 1989).

In the initial interview with Bob, the clinician was able to identify three systematic contextually relevant patterns. The first was that Bob's angry outbursts tended to occur situationally, in response to disagreements with other managers during collaborative projects (a common event in the company). The second was that his demeaning directives tended to occur within certain relationships in being aimed toward those supervisors whom he perceived as capable enough to present potential threats to take his job. The third was that his insults and demeaning directives became exacerbated under emotional arousal, as both increased in frequency and severity when he was experiencing stress and anxiety because of performance pressure from executives. Consultation with the referring human resource professional confirmed Bob's reports that these were indeed primary problematic stiuations or contexts for him.

Social Information Processing Contributions. Having linked Bob's aggression to specific problematic situations or contexts, the next step was to identify the social information processing patterns that might underlie his behavior in those circumstances. The clinician assigned

Bob to keep a diary of events and cognitions following aggressive reactions in the identified problematic situations and contexts, including questions corresponding to information processing steps: Encoding, "What did he do that made you react negatively?" Interpretation, "Why did the other person(s) act as they did?" Goal formulation, "What did you want to have happen?" Response generation, "What did you think of as things to do?" Finally, response decision and evaluation, "What did you choose to do and why?" The diary also included descriptions of Bob's aggressive behavior and how others reacted to his aggression. Others' reactions were recorded in order to make salient to Bob the self-defeating nature of his own aggression.

On the basis of data from the diary, the clinician determined that Bob's angry insults were most closely linked to input cognition. During relatively low-stress periods, Bob interpreted other managers' opinions and disagreements as representative of total indifference to his performance goals for himself and his unit. During higher stress periods, Bob's more frequent and severe attacks on other managers were associated with more malignant interpretations that other managers not only neglected his best interests but also were deliberately sabotaging his leadership efforts.

Further, Bob's angry attacks were linked with other managers' reactions that escalated from simple disagreement to retaliation with their own anger toward Bob (which Bob actually initially saw as justification and confirmation of his initial negative attributions).

During relatively low-stress periods, Bob's demeaning directives toward specific competent supervisors were most closely associated with the output cognitions of (a) the goal of maintaining his authority, and (b) the selection of psychologically abusive tactics, which he evaluated positively for their potential to both obtain compliance and demoralize his "competition." However, Bob was able to generate and contemplate less cynical response options, which he did occasionally utilize. During higher stress periods, the increase in frequency and severity of Bob's demeaning behavior was associated with the same goal formulation and response selection patterns as during lower stress periods, but the alternative response generation skills that occasionally acted as buffers against his verbal aggression seemed to become impeded.

Further, Bob's demeaning treatment of supervisors appeared to impair their motivation and performance, as evidenced by reductions in their requests for clarification and guidance and a decline to only moderate quality work. However, Bob initially took these signs of motivation and performance as indicators that he had "been right all along about them trying to get my job, because they're not helping as much as they could."

Enactment Skills. The final point for assessment was Bob's behavior enactment skills. The use of a diary is inadequate for such assessment because, even though it is possible to provide general self-reports on behavior patterns such as times when one is not aggressive, individuals are unlikely to be reliable and valid reporters of the nuances in their own behavior skills. The clinician therefore asked Bob to role play a variety of socially appropriate collaborative and leadership strategies (e.g., requests, negotiation, simple directives, and constructive criticism), both in a calm mood and under conditions of emotional arousal (using fear and anger induction techniques such as asking Bob to imagine an upsetting event from his work life before beginning the role play).

In the sequence of role plays, the clinician played the part of another manager or a supervisor (as appropriate) during a series of hypothetical work-related situations, and Bob "played" himself. For each role play, the clinician instructed Bob to enact the variety of socially appropriate strategies expected of him (e.g., negotiation with another manager or directives with a supervisor). Bob proved fairly adept in these skills, indicating that his mental scripts for appropriate behavior were adequately developed.

Formulation. Bob displayed a negativistic attributional bias for other managers' intentions toward him at times when differences of opinion emerged. This bias was exacerbated when under pressure from executives. Bob also displayed self-protective goals and a bias to evaluate and select responses that would achieve such protection through injuring the perceived competition. Although he did evidence competent options in his response repertoire and used them at times, when under stress this ability was not used. Finally, Bob's aggressive behavior was self-defeating; it created an atmosphere in which peers were antagonistic toward him and his supervisors were either unwilling or unable to work as efficiently as needed.

Bob was therefore judged as a candidate for coaching that emphasized the development of social information processing skills in interpreting the intentions of others; formulating goals using response repertoire resources; and evaluating and selecting leadership methods that were appropriately assertive and productive rather than aggressively destructive.

Intervention

Objectives. Change goals must include not only a reduction in target behaviors but also an increase in specific desired behaviors. Bob arrived on two goals in discussion with the clinician. First, to decrease angry re-actions toward other managers to one per week for the first month, then to eliminate them by the end of the second month, and instead to uti-lize positive assertiveness (e.g., reasoning, explanation, and negotiation) as his primary communication method. Second, to reduce his demeaning directives to supervisors in accord with the same schedule, while utilizing appropriately authoritative delegation and leadership (e.g., simple direc-tives, and offers of clarification, encouragement, and praise) as his primary communication method.

Anchored Training.   As might be expected from the foregoing description, the clinician focused on coaching Bob in new social infor-mation processing patterns for (a) coping with disagreement with other managers, and for (b) delegating assignments to especially competent em-ployees. In order to facilitate generalization of new social information pro-cessing patterns to stressful circumstances, coaching was conducted under both emotionally unaroused and aroused conditions. Creating conditions of emotional arousal in therapy utilized the same emotion-induction tech-niques used during the assessment phase, such as having Bob recall and imagine himself in stressful or conflictual work situations that had recently taken place.

Change Strategies.   The clinician used strategies in a sequence of phases aimed toward facilitating Bob's change goals. As an overview (with details to follow), the function of didactic instruction was to provide Bob with a conceptual framework for his participation in the intervention. The function of modeling and imitation during coaching sessions for social in-formation processing was to elaborate upon and restructure the self, other, and event schemas in Bob's cognitive database. The function of rehearsal within and across sessions, and in his daily life, was to improve access to his storehouse of knowledge for use in social information processing, as the frequency and recency with which schema are activated increases their accessibility (Fiske & Taylor, 1991). Clinician feedback toward refinement of Bob's information processing skills addressed both the content of and access to his storehouse of substantive knowledge, through broadening of the cognitive resources in Bob's cognitive database and developing proce-dural strategies for using the knowledge when required. Specific strategies were as follows:

The first phase was didactic instruction, which covered explanation of the social information processing model, the problematic processing patterns in which Bob was engaging, their relation to his behavior (the clinician had touched on these topics only superficially during the assessment phase to avoid inducing a response set during the assessment), and the effect his behavior had on others reacting negatively to him.

The second phase was direct modification of Bob's problematic processing at each of the relevant steps, using modeling-and-imitation, rehearsal, and corrective feedback (including under conditions of emotional arousal). During this phase of training, the clinician role played Bob, while Bob took the role of another manager. The clinician then engaged in talk-aloud attribution processes, in which he modeled alternative thinking. During the first such session, the clinician "brainstormed" a variety of possible interpretations for other managers disagreeing or making conflicting suggestions to Bob's ideas, emphasizing the possibility of relatively benign interpretations, such as "He heard the idea from someone else and thought it might work," "She was trying to help out but didn't know some important details," and "He's new and doesn't really understand what is appropriate here." The clinician then presented Bob with a similar situation, and Bob imitated the clinician's alternative interpretive thought processes.

Bob was initially stuck on a set of fairly pessimistic interpretation options because he was convinced that he was correct. In fact, there may at times be credence to someone's pessimistic attributions—sometimes others do act with malice. However, thinking very broadly about the causes for another's behavior, including taking responsibility for needing to be more flexible and creative in approaching the person (e.g., "I didn't approach this in a way that would please her," or "I needed to appeal to his interests as well") can balance being accurate with being adaptive, that is, moving beyond the other person's hostility toward positive resolution.

In order to get Bob "unstuck," the clinician led him through another modeling-imitation sequence, in which the clinician added a self-correction prompt for Bob to use if he found himself persevering on negativistic interpretations, "Stop and think. Why else would they do that?" Bob was then able to produce a variety of benign and reasonable interpretations for other managers' disagreements with and suggestions for him, including interpretations emphasizing Bob's responsibility for how others react toward him.

Bob and the clinician then used the same type of modeling-imitation exercise for goal formulation, response generation, and response evaluation and selection regarding Bob's treatment of his supervisors. The clinician modeled formulating goals that were oriented toward task completion and engendering positive motivation in supervisors; generating an array of potential responses supportive of these goals (including responses of encouragement, explanation, and performance rewards); evaluations antic-ipating and contrasting supervisors' likely responses to various strategies (e.g., condescension vs. encouragement); and then consciously selecting positive leadership strategies. Next, the clinician presented Bob with similar situations, and Bob imitated the clinician's goal formulation and response cognition processing.

Subsequent coaching sessions took place over a period of 2 months, pro-viding opportunities for Bob to continue rehearsing the new information processing patterns, apply them in his working life, and report back to the clinician for feedback and assistance in dealing with difficult application situations. Within the first 2 weeks, Bob was able to regularly produce adap-tive cognition without modeling from the clinician, although the clinician provided corrective feedback and redirection or prompting techniques when Bob stumbled (e.g., at times positively evaluating dominance-oriented re-sponses). Through repetition and feedback from the clinician, Bob became adept at each of the information processing steps.

Evaluation.   Coaching in social information processing is a means to an end (i.e., improved job performance). Therefore, it is necessary to actually evaluate whether there has been a positive change in behavior. The clinician found agreement between Bob's own reports and those of the human resources referral source who interviewed managers and supervisors at regular intervals during and after the 2-month coaching period. There had been a steady decrease in Bob's aggression and a corresponding increase in his interpersonal skills. Further, he was increasingly valued as a collaborator with other managers, and his unit's productivity increased.

Follow-Up.   There were two instances of Bob "slipping" during his otherwise steady progress. These two instances occurred during partic-ularly stressful periods for the company. The clinician therefore supple-mented Bob's coaching regimen with sessions in stress management, focus-ing on relaxation techniques for coping with the physiological symptoms of anxiety, and using his new social information processing skills.

WORKPLACE APPLICATIONS

The bulk of this chapter has been concerned with cognitive-behavioral and social information processing principles and practices that have tra-ditionally been the domain of psychotherapeutic and psychoeductional interventions. It has thus far been assumed that the reader would intu- itively perceive points of value in this perspective for infusion into their own work. For example, as discussed earlier, research on cognitive pro- cesses in organizations can use the social information processing model to integrate a variety of theoretical perspectives and variables into a unified model.

In addition, however, there are some basic contributions to applied or- ganizational practice that may be worth noting explicitly. Familiarity with cognitive-behavioral principles and practices can orient human resource professionals, managers, executives, and consultants in handling a broad range of critical issues beyond aggression, specifically including but not limited to communication, gender and sexual harassment; culture and di- versity; team functioning; and the relation between family life and work performance. The remainder of this discussion therefore speaks to inter- personal issues and job performance at a general level, and does so with reference to a few examples of professional functions. The reader is invited to think creatively about additional workplace applications.

Intervention Support

Support for referral-based counseling (e.g., Bob's) can be provided with a minimum of extra effort, such as having a human resource professional "on- call" for consultation in dealing with glitches in implementing therapeutic strategies, or providing positive feedback for behavioral change through evaluation questionnaires. Although some training or continuing education may be required to expand human resource capabilities in this area, the potential benefits are evident.

Executive Coaching

In Bob's case, the terms "counseling" and "coaching" were used inter- changeably, as generic terms indicating individualized attention to his problems. Another contemporary use of the term coaching is in refer- ence to consultation with executives. Indeed, the principles and practices detailed earlier can be applied to coaching of job-related interpersonal skills for those in executive positions. On one hand, executives may sim- ply seek to improve their job performance, satisfaction, or both, through enhancing interpersonal competencies. On the other hand, they may be either beginning to experience or have already established a pattern of job- related interpersonal difficulties associated with the unique and intensive demands of the position. In either case, the individualized, ideally short-term and goal-focused nature of executive coaching efforts (Kilburg, 1996) are well-suited to the client-focused, here-and-now, task-oriented nature of cognitive-behavioral therapy (although coaching can be an ongoing process, moving from one goal to the next). Executive coaching can use the social information processing model as a centerpiece of a cognitive-behavioral approach for addressing any interpersonal topic germane to job performance. Alternatively, the model can be used as an ancillary tool to a primarily behavioral approach; for example, helping the individual to recognize that "hot" cognitions, such as hostile attributions, might trigger anger and in turn undermine the appropriate use of assertiveness skills in delegation and negotiation.

Training

Trainers often aggregate materials from a variety of sources, such as training literature and educational courses. Topics are varied, including conflict management, communication skills, decision making, and sexual harassment (to name a few), and trainers often struggle with how to present material in an easily comprehensible and applicable manner. The social information processing model can be used as a tool for organizing instructional materials into a coherent whole for most topics. As an example, diversity training (working with different cultural groups including other organizational cultures) curriculum might include (a) interpretation, that is, the role of stereotypes in counter-productive interpretations, (b) the meaning of behavioral cues across different cultural groups, (c) response processing or what types of "friendly" or "helpful" behaviors would be considered insulting to certain groups, and why, and (d) enactment or culturally sensitive ways of communicating desires and ideas. By using the model, trainers and trainees would be able to work within a perspective that "ties everything together" in an efficiently applicable package.

A final innovative and compelling approach to enhancing organizational functioning through training would be to engage psychologists to train cohorts of supervisors or managers in a cognitive-behavioral and social information processing approach for dealing with employees who are problem performers. Training would focus on improving cognitive and behavioral skills for the variety of organizing and leadership tasks facing supervisors and managers, using the assessment and change strategies outlined here. Going one step further, however, such training need not always be a reaction to impaired supervisory and management skills, but could be applied proactively because of the inherently stressful and challenging nature of supervisory and management jobs. The end result should be an overall increase in the performance of specific individuals and the organization as a whole. For ethical and practical reasons, such training should be construed as a means to supplement supervisor and manager capabilities for performing their existing leadership duties, rather than as training to become on-site counselors or psychotherapists.

CONCLUSION

The perspective presented in this chapter is simultaneously established and speculative. It represents an established base of theory and empiricism from clinical psychology (including influences from social, cognitive, and developmental psychology on the social cognitive mechanisms of behavior). It also speculates that cognitive-behavioral and social information processing theory and methods can be applied to research, programs, policies, and various training and coaching endeavors aimed toward improving how organizations and the individuals within them function. If the literature on cognitive-behavioral and social information processing contributions to human functioning in general are any indication, then such application would prove to be a very productive and worthwhile investment.

REFERENCES

Bandura, A. (1986). *Social foundations of thought and action: A social cognitive theory*. Englewood Cliffs, NJ: Prentice-Hall.

Baron, R. A. (1988). Attributions and organizational conflict: The mediating role of apparent sincerity. *Organizational Behavior and Human Decision Processes, 69*, 272–279.

Baron, R. A., & Neuman, J. H. (1997). Aggression in the workplace. In R. A. Giacalone & J. Greenberg (Eds.), *Antisocial behavior in organizations* (pp. 37–67). Thousand Oaks, CA: Sage.

Bauer, W. D., & Twentyman, C. T. (1985). Abusing, neglectful, and comparison mothers' responses to child-related and non-child related stressors. *Journal of Consulting and Clinical Psychology, 53*, 335–343.

Berkowitz, L. (1989). Frustration-aggression hypothesis: Examination and reformulation. *Psychological Bulletin, 106*, 59–73.

Chase, K., Treboux, D., O'Leary, K. D., & Strassberg, Z. (1998). Specificity of dating aggression and its justification among high-risk adolescents. *Journal of Abnormal Child Psychology, 26*, 467–473.

Crick, N. R., & Dodge, K. A. (1994). A review and reformulation of social information processing mechanisms in children's social adjustment. *Psychological Bulletin, 115*, 74–101.

Dodge, K. A. (1986). A social information processing model of social competence in children. In M. Perlmutter (Ed.), *Minnesota Symposium on Child Psychology* (Vol. 18, pp. 77–125). Hillsdale, NJ: Lawrence Erlbaum Associates.

Dodge, K. A. (1991). The structure and function of reactive and proactive aggression. In D. Pepler & K. Rubin (Eds.), *The development and treatment of childhood aggression*. Hillsdale, NJ: Lawrence Erlbaum Associates.

Dodge, K. A., McClaskey, C. L., & Feldman, E. (1985). Situational approach to the assessment of social competence in children. *Journal of Consulting and Clinical Psychology, 53*, 344–353.

Dodge, K. A., Murphy, R. M., & Buchsbaum, K. (1984). The assessment of intention cue detection skills in children: Implication for developmental psychopathology. *Child Development, 55*, 163–173.

Dodge, K. A., & Newman, J. P. (1981). Biased decision-making processes in aggressive boys. *Journal of Abnormal Psychology, 90*, 375–379.

Dodge, K. A., & Somberg, D. R. (1987). Hostile attributional biases are exacerbated under conditions of threats to the self. *Child development, 58*, 213–224.

Dutton, D. G., & Browning, J. J. (1988). Concern for power, fear of intimacy, and aversive stimuli for wife assault. In G. Hotaling, D. Finkelhor, J. Kirkpatrick, & M. Straus (Eds.), *Family abuse and its consequences: New directions in research* (pp. 163–175). Newbury Park, CA: Sage.

d'Zurilla, T. J. (1986). *Problem-solving therapy: A social competence approach to clinical intervention.* New York: Springer.

Fiske, S. T., & Taylor, S. E. (1991). *Social cognition.* New York: Random House.

Gist, M. E., & Stevens, C. K. (1998). Effects of practice conditions and supplemental training methods on cognitive learning and interpersonal skill generalization. *Organizational Behavior and Human Decision Processes, 75*, 142–169.

Graham, S., & Hudley, C. (1994). Attributions of aggressive and nonaggressive African-American male early adolescents: A study of construct accessibility. *Developmental Psychology, 30*, 365–373.

Guerra, N., & Slaby, R. (1989). Evaluative factors in social problem solving by aggressive boys. *Journal of Abnormal Child Psychology, 17*, 277–289.

Hollenbeck, G. P., & McCall, M. W., Jr. (1999). Leadership development: Contemporary practices. In A. I. Kraut & A. H. Korman (Eds.), *Evolving practices in human resource management* (pp. 172–200). San Francisco: Jossey-Bass.

Holtzworth-Munroe, A., & Hutchinson, G. (1993). Attributing negative intent to wife behavior: The attributions of maritally violent versus nonviolent men. *Journal of Abnormal Psychology, 102*, 206–211.

Hymel, S. (1986). Interpretations of peer behavior: Affective bias in childhood and adolescence. *Child Development, 57*, 431–445.

Industry Report. (1997, March). *Training, 34*, pp. 33–34, 36–37.

Judd, C. M., & Park, B. (1988). Out-group homogeneity: Judgments of variability at the individual and group levels. *Journal of Personality and Social Psychology, 54*, 778–788.

Kelly, H. H., & Michela, J. L. (1980). Attribution theory and research. *Annual Review of Psychology, 31*, 457–501.

Kilburg, R. R. (1996). Toward a conceptual understanding and definition of executive coaching. *Consulting Psychology Journal: Practice and Research, 48*, 134–144.

Kramer, R. M. (1995). The distorted view from the top: Power, paranoia, and distrust in organizations. In R. Bies, R. Lewicki, & B. Sheppard (Eds.), *Research on negotiation in organizations* (Vol. 5, pp. 119–154). Greenwich, CT: JAI.

Linville, P. W., & Jones, E. E. (1980). Polarized appraisals of out-group members. *Journal of Personality and Social Psychology, 38*, 689–703.

McFall, R. M. (1982). A review and reformulation of the concept of social skills. *Behavioral Assessment, 4*, 1–33.

Meichenbaum, D. H. (1985). *Stress inoculation training.* Elmsford, NY: Pergamon.

Parke, R. D., & Slaby, R. G. (1983). The development of aggression. In P. H. Mussen (Ed.), *Handbook of child psychology* (Vol. 4, pp. 547–621). New York: Wiley.

Perry, D. G., Perry, L. L., & Rasmussen, P. (1986). Cognitive social learning mediators of aggression. *Child development, 57*, 700–711.

Ross, L. (1977). The intuitive psychologist and his shortcomings: Distortions in the attribution process. In L. Berkowitz (Ed.), *Advances in experimental social psychology* (Vol. 10, pp. 173–220). New York: Academic Press.

Rubin, K. H., & Krasnor, L. R. (1986). Social cognitive and social behavioral perspectives on problem solving. *Minnesota Symposium on Child Psychology, 18*, 1–68.

Schneider, W., & Schiffrin, R. M. (1977). Controlled and automatic human information processing: 1. Detection, search, and attention. *Psychological Review, 84*, 1–66.

Smith, C. A., & Lazarus, R. S. (1990). Emotion and adaptation. In L. A. Pervin (Ed.), *Handbook of personality: Theory and research* (pp. 609–637). New York: Guilford.

Snarr, J., & Strassberg, Z. (2000, August). *Maternal interpretations of emotion expressions by oppositional preschool boys.* Paper presented at the 109th Annual Conference of the American Psychological Association, Washington, DC.

Spiegler, M. D., & Guevremont, D. C. (1993). *Contemporary behavior therapy* (2nd ed.). Pacific Grove, CA: Brooks/Cole.

Strassberg, Z. (1995). Social information processing in compliance situations by mothers of behavior-problem boys. *Child Development, 66*, 376–389.

Strassberg, Z. (1997). Levels of analysis in cognitive bases of maternal disciplinary dysfunction. *Journal of Abnormal Child Psychology, 25*, 209–215.

Strassberg, Z., & Dodge, K. A. (1989). Identification of discriminative stimuli for aggressive behavior in children. *The Behavior Therapist, 12*, 195–199.

Wright, J. C., & Mischel, W. (1987). A conditional approach to dispositional constructs: The local predictability of social behavior. *Journal of Personality and Social Psychology, 53*, 1159–1177.

V

Interpersonal Interactions

Person perception influences how people interact with each other. This last section of the book examines how person perception influences multicultural relationships, negotiations, and team processes.

In chapter 12, Sumita Raghuram introduces the interface between culture, person perception, and organizational practices. She proposes that the frames people hold of employees' expectations and needs are culturally based. These, in turn, influence how people are likely to react to different human resource practices. She focuses particularly on flexible employment practices such as telework, flexible work schedules, part-time work, temporary work, and overtime. These are likely to have a differential effect on employee productivity depending on how well they fit with cultural values. She reviews four dominant cultural values (uncertainty avoidance, power equalization, masculinity–femininity, and collectivism–independence), and hypothesizes how reactions to flexible employment practices are potentially affected by each value dimension. For instance, in collectivistic cultures in which employees expect their employers to look after their needs, use of temporary or contract work may be viewed negatively. In cultures where interpersonal relationships are more important than task, telework may be seen as severing ties with employers and coworkers.

Jeff Casey's treatment of negotiation processes (chapter 13) introduces a new aspect of person perception: analyzing the economic value (gain or loss) of the parties involved in a negotiation. Negotiators develop their own frames of reference in approaching a negotiation (e.g., the solution or outcome they are prepared to accept and the point above or below which they will interpret the outcome as a gain or loss). They represent their position in a way that will convey their frame of reference, or convey a frame that they believe will be most beneficial to them in the long run. This is called *positional framing*. They also develop frames about the opposing party's frame of reference—a process called *frame attribution*. Casey explains how this operates and proposes what might happen when a party in the negotiation misinterprets the other party's intentions or desires.

Casey notes that people vary in how they view losses. Some people are loss averse, whereas others are risk seeking. People's orientation to loss emerges when outcomes are framed as losses rather than foregone gains. Because losses carry more weight than gains, negotiators who frame their position negatively seem to have more power in avoiding making concessions and in asking for concessions from the opposing party. Negatively framed negotiators maintain their ground longer and put more pressure on the other party to concede, although this increases the likelihood of impasse. A negative bluff may be quite effective for negotiators who understand the other party's loss aversion. The other party might perceive the bluff, or may incorrectly assume that the other party is bluffing, thereby leading the negotiation to impasse. Casey discusses how these dynamics raise questions for research and practice, such as how do negotiators communicate about framing, and how do they try to manipulate each other's framing in relation to their view of the other party's loss aversion or risk seeking?

Teams have become an increasingly important way to get work done in organizations. Such teams include quality circles, self-managing manufacturing teams, and cross-functional project teams. The need for teams stems from an increasing reliance on sophisticated technology for design and manufacturing and on global marketing strategies in changing economies and differing cultures. Chapter 14 examines shared cognition in work teams, in particular, how person perception influences group dynamics. The authors, Stephen Fiore, Eduardo Salas, and Janis Cannon-Bowers, note that shared cognition and person perception are probably the least understood components of teamwork and the most difficult to research. They suggest that person perception affects the degree to which information is shared and the level of coordination achieved in a newly formed team. This determines the development of a shared mental model, which in turn influences team productivity.

Fiore, Salas, and Cannon-Bowers indicate that teams may benefit from process gains—improvements in team performance through shared cognition over and above the simple combination of individual members' skills and knowledge. Team performance is related to the degree that team members possess multiple models of the environment in which they are operating. Identifying the shared mental models of productive groups suggests training methods to enhance team productivity. In newly formed teams, early interaction processes are important to the development of a team's shared mental model. Preprocess coordination focuses on how initial shared expectations are created in anticipation of team interaction. This preplanning is influenced by perceptions based upon experience with teammates, the task, or external sources such as organizational reputations preceding team interaction. Early information sharing contributes to the development of shared mental models. The authors examine how team-specific attitudes, such as the desire to remain in the group (*group cohesion*) and the belief that the group can accomplish its goals (*collective efficacy*), affect process coordination efforts, belief in the importance of the team's work (*collective orientation*), and interpersonal trust. They also discuss the effects of team-specific cognitions, such as comparing members' competencies and members' familiarity with each other. As team research and theory grow to more fully understand the relationships between shared cognition and group dynamics, the more team effectiveness can be enhanced through team member training and group process facilitation.

In chapter 15 on leadership and member interactions in virtual teams, Bruce J. Avolio, Surinder Kahai, Rex Dumdum, and Nagaraj Sivasubramaniam extend ideas from person perception in face-to-face groups to geographically dispersed teams limited to communicating through advanced information technology. In particular, the chapter examines how leadership and collaborative technologies interact to influence trust development and performance in virtual teams. Computing and telecommunications technologies have allowed organizations to establish teams that are not restricted by geography, time, or organizational boundaries. These *virtual teams* work together both synchronously and asynchronously to accomplish their tasks. This raises questions about how interpersonal perceptions form in virtual teams, the implications for trust formation and performance, and how leadership and information technology interact to influence trust formation and performance in virtual teams. The authors present a model linking leadership and technology to the development of trust.

In a virtual team, just as in an in-person team, the members develop a shared mental model about what the team is and what it does. This requires that team members learn about each other's background, intentions, beliefs, aspirations, and goals. Members learn from each other about the challenges faced by the team, the norms for acceptable and unacceptable behavior, what members expect of each other, and how leadership will operate in the cyberspace environment. This provides the cognitive framework for team members to create a joint definition of the social situation. Unlike face-to-face groups, virtual teams are unable to freely exchange information. They may have trouble developing a common image of roles, work requirements, and how they must work together to accomplish the team's goals. The core components of virtual team interaction are leadership, the nature of information exchange among team members, and trust. Leadership affects the conditions for initial trust and interactions that will likely affect the level of trust, interaction, and performance of the team. Virtual teams are dynamic in terms of membership and location, so a key issue is how a geographically dispersed team can achieve sufficient synergy to make the team members work well together and accomplish the team's objective. Leadership and collaboration technology work together to make this happen. Specifically, leadership affects initial perceptions of ability, benevolence, integrity, and the emotions and mood expressed by the group. Collaboration technology affects the formation of conditional trust by influencing the group's perceptions of other members' ability, benevolence, and integrity. The members' interactions through technology shape their experiences with each other, which in turn influences their perceptions of each other.

12

Cultural Frames and Values Affecting Employment Practices

Sumita Raghuram
Fordham University

With increased globalization of business, there is a correspondingly increased need to understand the implications for human resource management. A question worth exploring is, "To what extent does one differentiate in one's approach of the human resource management (HRM) programs among countries?" In this chapter, I first give a broad overview of the perspectives that suggest the importance of making HRM programs culturally relevant. I take up the specific example of flexible employment practices and propose linking these to country culture. I then provide examples of companies who have attempted to synchronize their practices with country culture.

It may be somewhat puzzling to think that certain practices (e.g., merit based pay), found to be effective in motivating employees in one culture may be ineffective in another. This discrepancy may be better understood from a framing perspective. There is a vast literature that describes the influence of frames in fields such as cognition (e.g., Argyris, Putnam, & Smith, 1985), strategic analysis (e.g., Allison, 1971), and the evolution of science and technology (e.g., Kuhn, 1970). Common to all, is the idea that in order to make progress in any situation, one needs to define a focus of

interest (i.e., develop a "frame"). With a frame, as in the case of a picture frame, attention automatically focuses on the content within, tending
to ignore the content outside the frame (Bateson, 1972). As people and
organizations unconsciously rely on particular frames for perceiving and
interpreting the world, they almost guarantee that there will come a time
when they are faced with situations they have not anticipated and fail in
their understanding (Walsh & Ungson, 1991). These events will occur more
frequently because environments are changing and firms are operating in
global arenas that require managers to deal with the challenge of culturally contrasting rather than culturally shared frames (Dunbar, Garud, &
Raghuram, 1996).

Culture is often defined as a shared system of meaning (Shweder &
LeVine, 1984) or mental programming (Hofstede, 1991), thus creating a
cultural frame of reference about people's characteristics and needs and
organization's practices in response to those needs. Those who are outside
of this cultural frame, and furthermore have their own distinctively different
frame, are unlikely to fully comprehend the meaning of these practices.

An example of how cultural frames may alter the meaning of human
resource practices comes from the strategic HRM research. Researchers
attempt to develop linkages between HRM practices and strategic typolo-
gies (e.g., Porter, 1980, or Miles & Snow, 1978), with the understanding
that these practices will evoke behavior consistent with the needs of the typology (e.g., Schuler & Jackson, 1987; Guthrie & Olian, 1991). Developed
from a U.S. frame of reference, the HRM practices may be less relevant in
some other parts of the world (e.g., Russia), where the concept of business
strategy itself may have limited application.

Or consider the example of yet another frame developed in the United
States: individual-job fit. According to this frame, individuals are assessed
for their individual knowledge, skills, and abilities (KSAs) at the time of
selection, and appraisal or training and decisions made on these assessments
are considered fair and appropriate. However, in cultures where teamwork
and collective performance is more important, the applicability of this
model is limited in guiding HRM decisions (Erez & Earley, 1993).

Using the cognitive perspective, Erez and Earley (1993) focused on
the employer–employee relationships. They suggested that adaptation to
changes in a complex environment requires an analysis of cognitive mechanisms of information processing. These mechanisms explain how employees interpret and evaluate a given situation, and how these processes
affect their work motivation and work behavior. Knowledge about one's

cognitive processes is captured by the self that interprets managerial practices and motivational techniques according to accepted cultural values and norms and in fulfillment of self-generated needs. Accordingly, the self processes information, interprets it within a framework of internalized criteria, and activates the response patterns accordingly (Markus & Wurf, 1987). On the basis of their evaluations employees develop intentions and make commitments to their immediate jobs and to the organizational goals.

The intentions and interpretations of an employee may however be inconsistent with employer expectations. Instead of interpreting merit pay as a vehicle for rewarding individuals equitably, as the employer might have intended, individuals from a group-oriented culture might perceive merit pay as a vehicle for creating differences and unfair treatment (Erez & Earley, 1993). Such misunderstandings may in fact turn into a vicious cycle where perception of unfairness can lead to feelings of distrust between employers and employees and so on. Misinterpretations may perhaps never get clarified because of the lack of trust compounded by problems with cross-cultural communication. To the extent that employees have few exit options into other jobs, their feelings of inequity may lead them to either withdraw psychologically from the organization or to withdraw their efforts (Raghuram & Garud, 1996). The interacting dynamics of perceptions of people, organizations, and their interrelationships bring into focus the importance of choosing human resource practices carefully in a cross-cultural setting and not leaving them to a process of trial and error.

HUMAN RESOURCE MANAGEMENT PRACTICES AND COUNTRY CULTURE

Researchers in the past have been cognizant of the need to contextualize human resource practices in order to ensure positive employee outcomes. Some have advanced theoretical arguments for the need to adopt human resource practices appropriate to the cultural context to achieve strategic advantage (Schuler, Dowling, & De Cieri, 1993; Luthans, Marsnik, & Luthans, 1997). Schuler et al. (1993), focused on the unique aspects of multinational firms that have implications for strategic HRM. They focused on four major areas: interunit linkages, internal operations, human resource functions, and human resource policies and practices. They then described the exogenous and endogenous factors that influence the nature of the activities in those four areas. Luthans et al. (1997) postulated a contingency matrix relating country context and the human resource practices of recruitment, selection, training, compensation, labor relations, and job design. Others (e.g., Newman and Nollen, 1996), explored the cultural fit empirically. They found that a firm's financial performance was higher when management practices, such as participation and merit-based pay, were congruent with national culture.

I take up as an example one human resource practice—flexible employment—that is relatively understudied in the international context. Using the cognitive perspective developed by Erez and Earley (1993), I develop propositions suggesting that the impact on employee work behavior (e.g. employee performance) will be positive when flexible employment is consistent with country culture. I use employee performance broadly in developing the propositions here, because different dimensions of employee performance may be more or less salient in a country. High employee performance may therefore be interpreted to mean team orientation, organizational commitment or conformity to organizational and cultural norms, among other possible indicators.

FLEXIBLE EMPLOYMENT PRACTICES AND COUNTRY CULTURE

People are witnessing a tremendous growth in the use of flexible employment practices such as temporary work, part-time work, and telework (e.g., Feldman, Doerpinghaus, & Turnley, 1994; Greengard, 1994). In particular, these practices make it possible for an employer to access the appropriate type and quantity of skills, reduce labor costs, increase employee commitment, and attract a desirable human resources pool (Pfeffer & Baron, 1988). These benefits are particularly appealing in the face of increased competitiveness because they enable an organization to respond rapidly to environmental demands. Although several factors present in a country, such as institutional, economic or political, may prompt an employer to adopt a flexible employment practice, its acceptance and effectiveness is likely to be dependent on congruency with cultural factors.

Flexible employment includes work arrangements other than the standard 8-hour day job for all working days in a year. Some of the arrangements have been in use for several years (e.g., overtime work) and others are fairly recent (e.g., telework). I consider a wide spectrum of flexible practices that include temporary work, part-time work, contract work, and telework. The benefits offered by each flexible employment practice are varied. For instance, individuals who have significant nonwork demands (e.g., family or education) find part-time work useful in meeting work and nonwork requirements (Rodgers, 1993).

Temporary work facilitates the employer in meeting temporary workload demands. The output expected from the employees is well-defined, time bound, and planned. Temporary workers may be channeled through an agency and the individual may face no limits on the length or repetition of employment.

Telework is a relatively new work form that offers freedom of workplace and time to employees. Teleworking is a broad term denoting, "working from a distance." It includes working out of home, out of clients' offices, out of telecenters or any other location (Fritz, Higa, & Narasimhan, 1995). Employing organizations realize benefits in the form of increased client face-time, reduced real estate costs, and stronger attraction for high-skilled workers.

Flexible practices in one way or the other alter the interpretation of the employer–employee relationships and this interpretation is likely to vary from culture to culture. Practices that are inconsistent with the expected norms of employer–employee relationships may be interpreted as a breach of the implicit contract that employees develop with their employers. For instance, in a culture where the employer–employee relationship is paternalisitic, employees expect their employers to look after their needs over their lifetime. Adoption of temporary work or contract work (more so as a substitute for permanent employment) is likely to elicit strong negative reactions among the employees. Temporary work or contract work symbolize the employer as being manipulative rather than as a provider through good and bad times. Employee reactions may include psychological withdrawal from the organization, as well as withdrawal of effort. Similarly, in a culture where interpersonal relationships take precedence over task, introduction of a work form such as telework is likely to be interpreted as severing ties with the employers and coworkers, thus removing the very basis through which work is accomplished.

I apply Hofstede's (1980, 1984, 1991) conceptualization of national cultures to suggest that consistency between cultural values and flexible practices may lead to higher individual performance. Hofstede's study has been shown to have appealing attributes, namely, the size of the sample, the codification of cultural traits along a numerical index, and its emphasis on attitudes in the workplace. This values framework has been widely used both for theory building and research in international HRM (see Luthans, Marsnik, & Luthans, 1997; Newman & Nollen, 1996).

Uncertainty Avoidance

Uncertainty avoidance is defined as the extent to which the members of a culture feel threatened by uncertain or unknown and ambiguous situations. This feeling of threat may be expressed through nervous stress, a need for predictability, and a need for written or unwritten rules. In organizations, uncertainty avoidance is manifest in increased clarity of reporting relationships, procedures, and systems so as to reduce employees' feelings of anxiety associated with unknown situations. Emphasis is placed on punctuality and precision.

In cultures characterized by high uncertainty avoidance, rule bound and structured work is likely to make the employees feel more comfortable and less anxious about their employment relationship. Employees may expect their employers to take on greater control in determining the work arrangement and let rules and procedures govern their work habits. Employers, too, may feel more comfortable with a work arrangement that prevents uncertainties in employees' behavior. Overtime work provides an extension of the traditional employer–employee roles that are prevalent under regular work hours. Hence the rules, procedures, and supervision continue to apply in the same manner. Contract work enables employers to structure the work specifications and monitor the output as per their requirements.

Comparatively, in low uncertainty avoidance cultures where structures and rules are less important in guiding employee behavior, employers may feel less anxious delegating authority and control. Employees, too, expect an employment relationship that provides them freedom and the informality in solving problems and carrying out their work. The employees are more comfortable in experimenting with new methods of organizing their work that can lead to higher productivity.

Work arrangements such as job sharing, flextime, part-time work, and telework create ambiguity and uncertainty in the employer–employee relationship because the employees are working under looser boundaries of time and space. The boundaries of time and space may or may not coincide with those of the supervisor, peers, or both. Monitoring performance of employees who are job-sharing, working part-time, or working at a distance is consequently more difficult. For these employment practices to be effective, formal rules and procedures have to be replaced by a high level of employer–employee trust and delegation of authority. From the employee perspective, in particular, these work arrangements require that they assume the responsibilities of delivering the output with minimal rules guiding their behavior. Consequently, their comfort level is determined to an extent by the value placed on uncertainty avoidance. Cultures that subscribe to low uncertainty avoidance may therefore be more supportive of job-sharing, flextime, part-time work, or telework.

In sum, in high uncertainty avoidance cultures employees may experience greater motivation in performing their jobs when organizations use overtime and contract work. Similarly, in low uncertainty avoidance cultures, individual performance may be high when there is increased use of telework and flexible schedules.

Power Distance

Power distance is the extent to which the less powerful members of institutions (e.g., family, school, and community) and organizations (place of work) expect and accept that power is distributed unequally. In organizations, power distance influences centralization, participation, leadership style, and use of status symbols.

In cultures characterized by high power distance, employees are likely to feel comfortable in work arrangements that maintain organizational hierarchy. Those in senior positions are expected to make decisions and those in the lower rungs of hierarchy are expected to implement these decisions. Overtime work maintains such an authority structure and the hierarchy in an organization. Employees in cultures subscribing to high power distance are likely to view overtime as a directive from the higher ups and a decision outside of their role and therefore interpret it to be consistent with their employment contract. Although not entirely motivating (except for the additional earnings attached to working overtime) employees are likely to accept it and be productive while working overtime. I would therefore expect increased use of overtime to be congruent with attributes of high power distance culture.

In cultures characterized by low power distance superiors, the ideal boss is a resourceful, respected democrat. The employees expect employers to treat them as equals and employers expect employees to demonstrate initiative. Telework, flex-schedules, and contract work dilute the hierarchical structure of an organization by transferring the supervisory role to the employee. Under telework, and to some extent under job-sharing and flex-schedules, individuals have greater autonomy to choose the process, the time, and the place of work. Under contract work, the primary focus is on the independent production of output or project completion rather than development of a long-term superior–subordinate relationship. I would, therefore, expect the attributes of telework, flex-schedules, and contract work to be congruent with low power distance culture. Moreover, as the value system held by the employees and their supervisors is consistent with the increased flexibility that these work modes provide, I would expect employees to experience greater motivation in performing their jobs.

Individualism–Collectivism

Individualism pertains to societies in which the ties between individuals are loose: Everyone is expected to look after himself or herself and his or her immediate family. As its opposite, collectivism pertains to societies in which people from birth onwards are integrated into strong, cohesive in-groups, which continue to protect individuals throughout their lifetime in exchange for unquestioning loyalty.

In cultures characterized by high individualism, the employer–employee relationship is marked by autonomy, individual responsibility for results, contractual relationship with employers and the precedence of task over relationships. Contract work is consistent with the value system of a society that espouses contractual relationships. Contract workers and their employers realize that the employees' links with the organization and their peer group are temporary and therefore both parties focus on the end outcomes of the contract rather than building enduring relationships. This is consistent with the individualistic values of focusing on the task rather than relationship building. Moreover, to the extent that contract work is voluntary, employees are also likely to find contract work motivating. Flex-schedules (including job-sharing) and telework are, in most part, tailored to meet individual needs rather than the needs of a group or an organization as might be expected in a collective society. These needs may include sufficient personal time distinct from work time, and the freedom to choose individual approach toward job accomplishment. When these needs are met with the use of appropriate employment practices, the employees are likely to appreciate the freedom of choice and become committed to performing their best. Another attribute of telework and flex-schedules is that these practices create a temporal and spatial separation between the employees engaged in these work modes and their supervisors and other organizational members. In order to be productive, it is important that the employees feel comfortable working without the presence of other organizational members for at least some of the time during the day. This is most likely to be true under individualistic cultures that espouse autonomy, self-reliance and individual accountability. I would therefore expect individual performance to be determined by congruence between high individualism and increased use of contract work, flex-schedules, and telework.

Collectivism (or low individualism) is manifested in work unit solidarity, group responsibility for results and moralistic or family-like relationships with employers. Employers and employees expect relationships to take precedence over task and to be cemented first. Relationships at work can be strengthened best when employees have the opportunity to interact with each other and share each others' concerns. This is best enabled if they work together in the same physical space and time. When employees work overtime, they not only share the same physical space and time they may even continue working in the same groups as during normal work hours. This work arrangement may strengthen their sense of group cohesion and is therefore consistent with collective values. Further, employees may perceive overtime work as an act of loyalty that helps them fulfill their moral obligations toward their employer. They are therefore more accepting of the notion of overtime work and view it as symbolic of the welfare of the collective.

In sum, in cultures high on individualism, employees are likely to perceive the use of contract work, telework, and flexible schedules to be consistent with their values, and in cultures low on individualism, employees may perceive use of overtime to be consistent with their culture. Consistency in both cases is, therefore, likely to generate higher individual performance.

Masculinity–Femininity

Higher levels of masculinity are associated with greater importance attached to earnings, recognition, advancement, and challenging work. The feminine dimension on the other hand is associated with good relationships with supervisors, cooperation, quality of life, and employment security. Within the masculine cultures, the employer–employee relationship is likely to be built around emphasis on performance, competitiveness, and work itself as compared to nonwork. Hofstede (1991) suggested that the work ethos in masculine societies tends toward "live in order to work." As a consequence, employers may expect work accomplishment and advancement of the business as the most important aspect of life. Employees, too, are likely to feel more comfortable in a work environment that primarily focuses on their achievements at work and less on their personal needs. Contract work and overtime work are both output oriented. In the process, the two flexible practices offer a less expensive and more efficient option to the employer for achieving output compared to other flexible practices. Consequently, use of overtime or contract work may be a better fit for cultures that value masculinity.

A high quality of life is an important goal for employers and employees in cultures subscribing to feminine values. Both flexible scheduling and telework help in creating greater balance between the work and non-work life of employees. An employer's offer of these work arrangements is likely to be perceived by the employee as an act of cooperation, where the employer is helping the employee in meeting personal needs. This also fosters stronger employer–employee relationships. When employers offer flexible scheduling or telework, they shift their focus from a direct concern about business advancement to helping employees manage their personal lives; in the long run (indirectly), this may create employee commitment and provide other organizational benefits.

In sum, individual performance may be high when cultures high on masculinity use contract work and overtime work. Similarly, individual performance may be high when there is increased use of flexible schedules and telework in cultures low on masculinity. This will be a result of the increased motivation to perform when employees perceive consistency between the work arrangements and their values. I propose here that individual performance will be contingent upon congruence between flexible employment practices and Hofstede's (1980, 1984, 1991) four cultural dimensions: uncertainty avoidance, power distance, individualism, and femininity. More precisely, in developing proposed linkages between human resource practices and country culture, a possible refinement is to consider the relative importance of all cultural dimensions for each country simultaneously. What this means is that a combination of cultural dimensions may provide a more accurate representation of congruent practices within a country than when each dimension is considered in isolation. For instance, one may expect that a country high on femininity may tend toward adopting telework because it improves the quality of life of the employees. However, if this country is also high on collectivism (e.g. Chile, South Korea, and Thailand), then the cultural forces are likely to play against adoption of telework. Under these circumstances, one will have to assess the relative force of each cultural dimension as well as other factors such as the economy, unionization, and labor laws to anticipate the consequences of using a flexible practice.

RESEARCH IMPLICATIONS

In this chapter, I use flexible employment practices as an illustrative set of HRM practices that may be made culturally relevant. Many other kinds of contingency models using other HRM practices can be similarly developed taking into consideration the cognitive processes of employees in different cultures. An extension of the propositions suggested in this chapter may be to examine the impact of a fit between culture and HRM practice on organizational performance. The assumption is that the work behavior of employees will be reflected in organizational performance. Moreover, contextually salient indicators of organizational performance may be a relevant benchmark. These benchmarks may range from increase in market share and contribution to shareholder wealth to environmental conservation, employment generation, or perhaps even contribution to the country's political agenda.

Researchers have provided several useful theoretical models of cross-cultural HRM (see Schuler et al., 1993; Sparrow & Hiltrop, 1997; Luthans et al., 1997). However, there is a significant gap between development of these theoretical models and empirical evidence examining HRM practices in different countries. Empirical studies on cross-national practices are indeed an expensive and time-consuming process, which explains the relatively few studies across different countries. This increases the value of whatever limited amount of information is indeed available on global HRM practices. In the quest to conduct empirical studies, one needs to be mindful of the different research paradigms and research methodologies present in different parts of the world. One can indeed draw insights from different techniques to get a more balanced perspective on understanding different issues.

Hofstede's (1980, 1984, 1991) indices have by far been the most frequently used in cross-cultural research. His indices have, however, been criticized for a number of reasons especially regarding the internal validity of the dimensions and method of scale construction. Jaeger (1983, 1986) raised criticisms about the generalizability of Hofstede's findings. Schwartz (1992) noted several limitations of Hofstede's value research. Specifically, the value dimensions are not necessarily exhaustive of all relevant dimensions; there have been substantial historical changes since the 1970s when the original data were collected, cultural-level values are derived from individual-level data, and the meaning of values may not be equivalent across cultures. Nevertheless, Hofstede discovered meaningful national differences that corresponded to other cultural dimensions (Triandis, 1982). Other research on different companies found that multinational firms do not reduce national value differences among employees working in different cultures (Laurent, 1983). In addition, Hofstede's value dimensions correspond to other cultural frameworks (Kluckhohn & Strodtbeck, 1961; Triandis, 1982). However, researchers in this area may wish to utilize cultural dimensions other than Hofstede's (see Schwartz & Bilsky, 1990; Schwartz, 1992) to guide their research.

IMPLICATIONS FOR PRACTICE

This chapter presents arguments for why organizations are likely to find their practices more acceptable and effective if they are aware of the cultural context in which frames and values are being utilized. Although this may sound simple, organizations are reluctant to experiment with this, partly because standardization brings with it the benefits of efficiency (e.g. Bartlett & Ghoshal, 1998). Managers may opt for the easy way out and choose to go with a centralized management model as this approach is relatively more efficient than having to think of ways by which each country's practices and policies should be designed. Consequently, multinationals feel a tension between standardization and the need to adapt to local conditions.

A practical approach to solving the dilemma of centralization versus decentralization is presented by Trompenaars (1994). He suggested that perhaps organizations should focus their attention on what is to be decentralized rather than how much is to be decentralized. Accordingly, he proposes centralization of information to bring about cohesion among the dispersed units, and technical specifications of operations (e.g., rules, standards, etc.) to ensure some operational control, and to leave the decision of product features to individual countries. Because human resource practices, of all other organizational practices, are most sensitive to cultural contexts it becomes important that these be decentralized to the extent possible. In doing so, certain human resource goals (e.g., costs vs. revenue generated per employee) can be centralized and their implementation can be left to the managers in each country. The underlying assumption here is that the local managers will find the most suitable method for achieving the results, and that achieving the results per se is not questionable. After all, organizations in different parts of the world do find ways to be effective and productive.

Certain universal human resource practices, however, may prove to be useful for managers across the globe. These include selection of managers who are flexible and open to change, providing overseas assignments, and cross-cultural training, and diversity management. These practices are aimed at familiarizing the individual with different perceptual frames that will enable their appreciation of differences.

CASE EXAMPLES

Some organizations, however, have been successful in adapting their practices to the local conditions. The two that I discuss here, Verifone and Asea Brown Boveri (ABB), have had experience with working in very diverse sets of cultures across the globe. The reason for describing these two organizations is to illustrate the factors that have enabled them to implement human resource management practices that are localized. In both cases, the organization's structure, leadership, and corporate values have played a major role.

Verifone Corporation is in the business of automation and delivery of secure payment and payment-related transactions. Their product offerings include smart card technology for merchants, Internet payment solutions, and products for the emerging home banking marketplace. In 1997, Verifone employees were working in more than 30 facilities around the world (Verifone Website, 1999). Since 1997, Verifone has been a part of Hewlett Packard (HP), although it continues to operate as an independent, wholly owned organization. Verifone owes its successes to its past leader, Hatim Tyabji, who shaped the organization for 12 years before handing it over to HP.

Verifone structure as described by Tyabji is that of a blueberry pancake where all berries are the same size and all locations are created equal. Human resource management is run decentrally out of multiple locations. In the face of all the decentralization, there are at least two identifying factors that keep the company cohesive. These are its heavy reliance on computer networks for communication and coordination, and its strong corporate value system that has been continuously reinforced by the leader. In fact, employees' reliance on e-mail has been described as a social system that transmits the company values, and not just as an information system transmitting routine information (Taylor & Carroll, 1995). During their recruitment and selection processes, managers are guided by the principles of their corporate culture (e.g., results orientation and accountability) in addition to the local needs. Hence they are able to bring both global uniformity as well as local diversity in their human resource practices.

ABB is a Swiss-Swedish electrical engineering firm operating in 100 countries worldwide. ABB's products range from equipment for electrical power generation and transmission to high-speed trains, environmental control systems, and automation (ABB Website 19). Once again leadership, in this case that of Percy Barnevik was responsible for creating a global culture in the organization. Barnevik championed the concept of multidomesticity—leveraging global economies of scale and yet maintaining local market presence. His objective was to operate like a local employer with deep roots in individual countries. Emphasis is on created common values and creating links between division in different countries. Their slogan is "Think globally, act locally." This approach implies that the operations in each country must adapt the company's global vision to local markets and operation needs. Accordingly, ABB is extensively decentralized, and yet maintains a strong global corporate culture. The goals and values of the company that establish corporate values and culture are communicated through what is known as the "ABB bible."

The contradiction between centralization and decentralization is, to an extent, facilitated through ABB's matrix structure. On one dimension, ABB is a global network where business managers around the world make decisions on product strategy and performance without regard to national boundaries. On the other dimension of the matrix, are a large number of traditionally organized national companies deeply entrenched in their respective home markets. Moreover, Barnevik pushed authority, responsibility, and accountability deep down the organization with no more than five people between the CEO and shop floor (Kets de Vries, 1998). Consequently, heads of individual companies around the world are given maximum freedom, but simultaneously report to management divisions organized by geography and by industry (Barth, 1998). Göran Lindahl, the current leader of the enterprise, has been credited with further consolidating the business and centralizing the information systems, thus having greater control over the widespread network of businesses.

Their human resource practices include employee rotation that facilitates cohesion of employees while disseminating the corporate philosophy of local sensitivity. Another interesting practice is their mentorship program. Talented workers are identified to spread management methods and technology to countries within a region. For instance, Poles may be used as mentors in Russia, Kazakhstan, and Ukraine; Indians may be used to mentor in Southeast Asia (Barth, 1998).

There are several common features between these two companies. Both have adopted a decentralized approach in their management, thus enabling individual country operations to adapt to local conditions. The structure in the case of Verifone is described as a "blueberry pie," whereas in the case of ABB it is matrix—both focus on decentralization and few levels of hierarchy. However, in order to maintain a cohesive global identity, the leaders in both organizations played a major role in instilling a common core of corporate values that cuts across national borders and cultures. Well-developed information systems is another common characteristic of both organizations that has enabled centralization and control. These two examples, hopefully, provide indicators for how organizations can indeed decentralize and adapt to local culture while maintaining their own corporate culture.

REFERENCES

Asea Brown Boveri Website. (1999). Available: *http://www.abb.com/global/abbzh/*

Allison, G. T. (1971). *Essence of decision: Explaining the Cuban missile crisis.* Boston: Little Brown.

Argyris, C., Putnam, R., & Smith, D. M. (1985). *Action science.* San Francisco: Jossey-Bass.

Barth, S. (1998). Word trade's executive of the decade. *World Trade, 11,* 42–45.

Bartlett, C. A., & Ghoshal, S. (1998). *Managing across borders: The transnational solution.* Boston, Ma: Harvard Business School Press.

Bateson, G. (1972). *Steps to an ecology of mind.* San Francisco: Chandler Publishing Co.

Dunbar, R., Garud, R., & Raghuram S. (1996). A frame for deframing in strategic analysis, *Journal of Management Inquiry, 5,* 23–34.

Erez, M., & Earley, P. C. (1993). *Culture, self-identity, and work.* New York: Oxford University Press.

Feldman, D. C., Doerpinghaus, H. I., & Turnley, W. H. (1994). Managing temporary workers: A permanent HRM challenge. *Organizational Dynamics, 23,* 49–63.

Fritz, M. E. W., Higa, K., & Narasimhan, S. (1995). Toward a telework taxonomy and test for suitability: A synthesis of the literature. *Group Decision and Negotiation, 4,* 311–334.

Greengard, S. (1994, September). Making the virtual office a reality. *Personnel Journal, 9,* 66–79.

Guthrie, G. P., & Olian, J. D. (1991). Does context affect staffing decisions? The case of general managers. *Personnel Psychology, 44,* 263–292.

Hofstede, G. (1980). *Culture's consequences: International differences in work related values.* Beverly Hills, CA: Sage.

Hofstede, G. (1984). The cultural relativity of the quality of life concept. *Academy of Management Review, 9,* 389–398.

Hofstede, G. (1991). *Cultures and organizations: Software of the mind.* London: McGraw-Hill. (Reprinted in 1994, London: HarperCollins).

Jaeger, A. M. (1983). The transfer of organizational culture overseas: An approach to control in the multinational corporation. *Journal of International Business Studies, 14,* 91–114.

Jaeger, A. M. (1986). Organization development and national cultures: Where's the fit? *Academy of Management Review, 11,* 178–190.

Kets de Vries, M. F. R. (1998). Charisma in action: The transformational abilities of Virgin's Richard Branson and ABB's Percy Barnevik, *Organizational Dynamics, 26,* 6–21.

Kluckhohn, F. R., & Strodtbeck, C. (1961). *Variations in value orientations.* Westport, CT: Greenwood Press.

Kuhn, T. S. (1970). *The structure of scientific revolutions* (2nd ed.). Chicago: University of Chicago Press.

Laurent, A. (1983). The cultural diversity of western conceptions of management. *International Studies of Management and Organization, 13,* 75–96.

Luthans, F., Marsnik, P. A., & Luthans, K. W. (1997). A contingency matrix approach to IHRM. *Human Resource Management, 36,* 183–199.

Markus, H., & Wurf, E. (1987). The dynamics self-concept: A social psychological perspective. *Annual Review of Psychology, 38,* 299–337.

Miles, R. E., & Snow, C. C. (1978). *Organizational Strategy, Structure and Process.* New York: McGraw Hill.

Newman, K. L., & Nollen, S. D. (1996). Culture and congruence: The fit between management practices and national culture. *Journal of International Business Studies, 27*, 753–779.

Pfeffer, J., & Baron, J. N. (1988). Taking the workers back out: Recent trends in the structuring of employment. *In B. M. Staw and L. L. Cummings (Eds.), Research in Organizational Behavior* (Vol. 10, pp. 257–303). Greenwich, CT: JAI.

Porter, M. E. (1980). *Competitive Strategy*. New York: Free Press.

Raghuram, S., & Garud, R. (1996). The vicious and virtuous facets of workplace diversity. In M. N. Ruderman, M. Hughes-James, & S. E. Jackson (Eds.), *Selected Research on Workteam Diversity*. Washington, DC: American Psychological Association.

Rodgers, C. S. (1993). The flexible workplace: What have we learned? *Human Resource Management, 32*, 183–199.

Rosenzweig, P. M., & Nohria, N. (1994). Influences on human resource management practices in multinational corporations. *Journal of International Business Studies, 25*, 229–251.

Schuler, R. S., Dowling, P. J., & De Cieri, H. (1993). An integrative framework of strategic international human resource management. *Journal of Management, 19*, 419–459.

Schuler, R. S., & Jackson, S. E. (1987). Organizational strategy and organizational level as determinants of human resource management practices. *Human Resource Planning, 10*, 125–141.

Schwartz, S. H. (1992). Universals in the content and structure of values: Theoretical advances and empirical tests in 20 countries. In M. Zanna (Ed.), *Advances in Experimental Social Psychology* (Vol. 25, pp. 1–65). New York: Academic Press.

Schwartz, S. H., & Bilsky, W. (1990). Toward a theory of universal content and structure of values: Extensions and cross-cultural replications. *Journal of Personality and Social Psychology, 58*, 87–891.

Shweder, R. A., & LeVine, R. A. (1984). *Culture theory: Essays on mind, self, and emotion*. New York: Cambridge University Press.

Sparrow, P. R., & Hiltrop, J. (1997). Redefining the field of European human resource management: A battle between national mindsets and forces of business transition? *Human Resource Management, 36*, 201–219.

Taylor, W. C., & Carroll, C. (1995, November). At Verifone it's a dog's life (and they love it!). Fast Company, *http://www.fastcompany.com/online/01/vfone.html.*

Triandis, H. C. (1982). Review of culture's consequences: International differences in work-related values. *Human Organization, 41*, 86–90.

Trompenaars, F. (1994). *Riding the waves of culture: Understanding diversity in global business*. Chicago: Irwin, BurrRidge, IL.

Verifone Website. (1999). Available: *http://www.verifone.com/corporate-info/*

Walsh, J. P., & Ungson, G. R. (1991). Organizational memory. *Academy of Management Review, 16*, 57–91.

13

Frame Attribution and Positional Framing in Negotiation

Jeff T. Casey
State University of New York at Stony Brook

Negotiation has become an increasingly important topic in industrial and organizational psychology and human resource management in recent years because of a variety of shifts in the marketplace, including globalization, corporate restructuring, workforce mobility, and the shift toward a service-sector economy (Neale & Bazerman, 1991). Other factors include increases in self-employed contractors, the diversified nature of the workforce, greater use of cross-functional teams, and renegotiation.

"Negotiation is the process whereby two or more parties decide what each will give and take in a relationship" (Bazerman & Neale, 1992, p. 3). Many daily interactions involve an element of negotiation. Consider some examples of negotiations in modern organizational contexts.

- *Choosing and implementing a strategy for the firm.* All levels of an organization from the boardroom to the shop floor may engage in a give-and-take discussion concerning the firm's future.
- *Working with various stakeholder groups.* A company's leaders may negotiate with an environmental group in an attempt to persuade the

environmentalists that the firm's toxic emissions are, or soon will be, within reasonable limits.

- *Cross-functional teams.* Each member of a cross-functional team has a different perspective because of his or her functional specialty. Negotiation is necessary if the team is to reach a consensus concerning the approach it should employ in carrying out the assigned tasks.
- *Working with international partners to exploit global markets.* Commonalities that are taken for granted when doing business within one's home country are suddenly topics for negotiation when the firm expands into foreign markets. Negotiation helps to determine ways in which the firm's culture needs to adapt in order to be successful in a new country.
- *Managing organizational change.* Management may engage employees in a dialogue about how a set of organizational changes will be implemented. This discussion may take the form of a negotiation concerning the "when" and "how" of the change process.
- *Hiring and assignment of tasks.* Organizations routinely negotiate with individuals to whom they have offered jobs. These negotiations may concern, for example, pay and benefits. At the time of hiring, or at some later date, additional negotiations may take place concerning the content and scope of the individual's job description.
- *Ensuring fair treatment of employees.* Fairness is a slippery concept that takes on different meanings in different organizational situations. Employees at different levels of an organization may negotiate to agree upon certain guidelines for fair and ethical treatment of employees.
- *Appraising job performance.* In many performance feedback systems in use in firms, the superior evaluates the subordinate's performance on various criteria and the subordinate also evaluates his or her own performance on the same criteria. The superior and subordinate then discuss the reasons for the similarities and differences in their evaluations. This discussion may produce a negotiated agreement concerning the subordinate's performance that reflects the perspectives of both parties.
- *Labor contract negotiations.* The debate that surrounds the creation of a new labor contract between a firm's management and its labor union is a formal negotiation that addresses, for example, compensation, benefits, hours of work, and job security.

Two of the key areas of behavioral research that have been applied to negotiation are behavioral decision theory and social cognition. During the

1980s and early 1990s, a great deal of research focused on applying behavioral decision theory concepts to negotiation (e.g., Neale & Bazerman, 1991). More recent studies have begun to apply knowledge from social cognition to negotiation (e.g., Kramer & Messick, 1995).

The present work takes an in-depth look at the concept of framing. This concept has its roots in both behavioral decision theory and social cognition. Previous work on framing in negotiation has considered the effect of framing on one dimension only. This work typically considers the framing of the purchase price in a prospective transaction (e.g., Bazerman, Magliozzi, & Neale, 1985). The present work examines framing in greater depth by recognizing that, even in a simple buyer–seller transaction, there are two dimensions—a good or issue and a purchase price—that may be framed the same or differently. In addition, I explore the possibility of *frame attribution*, a process by which negotiators may attempt to identify each other's frames, and *positional framing*, a process by which negotiators may attempt to manipulate each other's frame attributions.

GAIN/LOSS FRAMING

Individuals tend to evaluate outcomes of decisions or negotiations as gains or losses relative to a neutral reference point (Kahneman & Tversky, 1979; Tversky & Kahneman, 1991, 1992). Outcomes inferior to the reference point may produce negative emotional states such as dissatisfaction, disappointment, or regret, whereas outcomes superior to the reference point may produce positive emotional states such as satisfaction, elation, or joy. An individual's reference point on a particular dimension may be determined by the characteristics of the individual and by situational factors. For example, for most people, not receiving one's next paycheck would be experienced as a loss. Thus, the paycheck is negatively framed: Receiving the check does not evoke elation, but failing to receive it evokes strong dissatisfaction. The absence of the check is framed as a loss equal to the amount of the check. The check is in one's *psychological endowment* even before it is actually received. Thus, if the check is not forthcoming, the individual experiences a loss. In contrast, a one-time, year-end bonus may be framed positively. Because the individual is uncertain about whether he or she will receive a bonus and the amount of the bonus, the bonus does not enter the individual's psychological endowment until it is actually received. Receipt of the bonus evokes strong positive feelings, but failure to receive the bonus may evoke only weak negative feelings, particularly if bonuses are rare. In this case, because the bonus is not in the individual's psychological endowment, the bonus is positively framed.

EFFECTS OF FRAMING
ON RATES OF CONCESSIONS
AND NEGOTIATION OUTCOMES

In the literature, treatments of framing in negotiations usually involve only the monetary dimension (cf. Thompson, 1998). For example, consider a negotiation between a prospective buyer and a prospective seller concerning a used computer. Both parties know that, if purchased new, the computer would cost $1000. Thus, if an agreement is reached, then the purchase price will be somewhere between $0 and $1000. The buyer's and seller's situations are considered in turn.

Suppose the buyer has budgeted only $500 for the purchase of a computer. The seller does not have this information. It is likely that the buyer will set $500 as his or her reference point for evaluating different prices. As a result, the buyer will frame any price above $500 as a loss. If the parties were to transact at a price of $600, then the buyer would suffer a $100 loss. Because of loss aversion, the buyer may strive to avoid this loss by starting the negotiation at a low price and conceding slowly. This behavior by the buyer increases the chances that the negotiation will lead to impasse. Impasse may occur if the seller becomes impatient or believes that the buyer will never make an acceptable offer. Any price below $500 represents a gain to the buyer. If the parties happen to transact at a price of $400, then the buyer experiences a $100 gain. If the parties discuss a price of $400, but eventually settle at $500, then the buyer does not experience a loss, assuming the buyer's reference point has not changed from $500. Instead, the buyer foregoes a $100 gain in this situation in order to make the transaction happen.

Suppose the seller believes that he or she can sell the computer via the Internet for $400. The buyer does not have this information. It is likely that $400 will be the seller's reference point for evaluating different prices. Any price above $400 will be appealing to the seller, because prices above $400 represent gains for him or her. Therefore, the seller is likely to reduce his or her offer price more rapidly than the buyer within the range from $500 to $1000. The buyer, on the other hand, is likely to concede faster than the seller within the $0 to $400 range. The reason is that negotiators are quicker to relinquish gains than to accept losses. Finally, the two parties have a *bargaining zone* ranging from $400 to $500. Any price within this zone represents a gain for both parties.

Across a wide range of decision making situations, individuals tend to code decision outcomes and prospective outcomes as gains or losses relative to a reference point (Tversky & Kahneman, 1992). The location of the reference point has been shown to affect decisions in myriad contexts. Concerning the role of framing in negotiation, Bazerman and Neale (1992, pp. 38–40) found that negotiators, similar to the computer buyer in the example above, who framed their own prospective price concessions as losses, as opposed to foregone gains, were less likely to settle quickly and more likely to follow a risky bargaining strategy that puts pressure on the other side to make concessions and increases the probability of impasse.

Framing outcomes as losses, as opposed to foregone gains, affects behavior because individuals tend to be *risk seeking in the domain of losses* and *loss averse*. Risk seeking in the domain of losses refers to the tendency to prefer a gamble over a sure thing in the domain of losses. Suppose that an individual is in the midst of a difficult negotiation and is contemplating two alternatives. Alternative 1 is to accept the other party's most recent offer. This alternative is a sure thing, but it entails a sure loss of $850 to the individual. Alternative 2 is to hold out for a longer period and hope that the other party will acquiesce. This alternative is a gamble, because the individual is not certain as to how the other party will react if he or she holds out. The individual estimates that, if he or she holds out and the other party acquiesces, nothing ($0) will be lost. However, if the other party does not acquiesce, $1000 will be lost. The individual estimates the probability that the other party will acquiesce to be 15%. Thus, a choice between two alternatives must be made:

Alternative 1

- A sure loss of $850.

Alternative 2

- A 15% chance of losing nothing ($0), and an 85% chance of losing $1000.

The concept of risk seeking for losses predicts that individuals, including those who generally regard themselves as risk averse, will choose alternative 2 (Kahneman & Tversky, 1979).

Loss aversion refers to the tendency of individuals to react more strongly to losses than to equivalent gains. For example, consider the following opportunity:

- A 50% chance to win $200, and a 50% chance to lose $100.

Most individuals decline this bet, although its expected value is a gain of $50. Risk aversion is generally not sufficient to explain this behavior. The rule of thumb here is that "losses loom [much] larger than gains" (Kahneman & Tversky, 1979, p. 274).

Framing may be especially important in claiming resources in distributive negotiations. A distributive negotiation is one in which each party can benefit only at the other's expense. Distributive negotiations are often referred to as "win-lose" or "zero-sum" negotiations. Individuals cannot always control their framing of decision outcomes, and frames may behave in a manner similar to that of reversible figures (Kahneman, 1992). However, negotiators who happen to frame their current situations or prospective concessions negatively seem to have greater power and "moral authority" in avoiding making concessions and in asking for concessions from the other side. For example, in a negotiation experiment, Neale and Bazerman (1991) found that buyers outperformed sellers even though the two sides' objective bargaining power was comparable (Bazerman et al., 1985; Neale, Huber, & Northcraft, 1987). This result can be explained by a tendency on the part of buyers to frame the purchase price negatively (as a loss), whereas sellers frame it positively (as a gain; cf. Casey, 1995). As shown later, this point is subtler than it initially appears. The main point here is that framing the purchase price as a loss apparently gave buyers more bargaining power than sellers who did not frame their situations negatively.

BIDIMENSIONAL FRAMING IN NEGOTIATION

It is important to recognize that even the simplest buyer–seller negotiation involves at least two variables: (a) a good, concession, or issue, and (b) a purchase price. These two variables may be framed the same or differently. Table 13.1 shows how buyers and sellers framed the purchase price and the good or issue at stake in experiments reported by Casey (1995).

TABLE 13.1
Transaction Framing

	Transaction		No Transaction	
	Buyer	*Seller*	*Buyer*	*Seller*
Purchase price	Loss	Gain	No loss	No gain
Good or issue	Gain	No gain	No gain	Gain

The buyer frames the good or issue positively and the purchase price negatively, whereas the seller frames both the purchase price and the good or issue positively. The buyer's framing is denoted as G+ P− because the good (G) is framed positively and the purchase price (P) is framed negatively. Negative framing of the purchase price by buyers means that, if a transaction occurs, the buyer feels a strong sense of loss of the purchase price. The strength of this sense of loss is determined by the buyer's degree of loss aversion. The buyer also feels a sense of gain at the receipt of the good purchased. However, because of loss aversion, the loss of the buying price is magnified. Thus, the purchase price must be small in order for the transaction to have positive overall value for the buyer. For the seller, the reverse is not true. The seller feels no sense of loss at giving up the good if a transaction takes place and no sense of loss at not receiving the purchase price if a transaction does not take place. We label the seller's framing G+ P+, because the good and purchase price are framed positively. The selling price does not have to be especially large to offset the seller's giving up of the good or issue (Casey, 1995). Stated another way, the purchase price is a part of the buyer's psychological status quo, whereas the good or issue is not. In contrast, neither the purchase price or the good is in the seller's psychological status quo. Thus, the buyer's reluctance to give up the purchase price is similar to an *endowment effect* (cf. Thaler, 1985; Thaler & Johnson, 1990). In essence, the seller has a smaller ego involvement in the negotiation than the buyer.

The combination of the prospect theory concepts of loss aversion and risk seeking in the domain of losses increases the likelihood that negatively framed negotiators will stand firm for longer periods, thereby increasing pressure on the other side to concede. However, this increased pressure comes at the expense of an increased probability of impasse.

FRAME ATTRIBUTION
AND POSITIONAL FRAMING

It is advantageous for a negotiator to know how the other party frames the various issues under contention. However, the other negotiator may or may not choose to express his or her actual framing of issues. In addition, negotiators may strategically misrepresent their frames. Hence, a distinction can be drawn between positional frames and actual frames. One does not have direct access to the other party's actual frames, but inferences or assumptions may be made on the basis of the party's positional frames and other information.

Past behavioral research has not addressed the possibility of frame attribution and frame misrepresentation in negotiation. Little is known about (a) how Party X attempts to manipulate Party Y's inferences as to Party X's framing of issues, and (b) how individuals infer the other party's framing given that the other party may be attempting to manipulate this inference process. Positional bargaining (Fisher & Ury, 1981) often involves each negotiator describing possible concessions on his or her part as losses to him or her. Thus, the individual's positional framing of one or more issues is negative, although his or her actual frames may be positive or negative. This behavior is, of course, intended to allow the individual to avoid making concessions while extracting concessions from the other party. The implicit notion is that negative-frame negotiators are more deserving of concessions from the other party than positive-frame negotiators. In addition, negative positional framing can help the negotiator put forth a credible threat that he or she will not back down later in the negotiation.

Positional framing: Techniques for manipulating attributed framing. Party X may attempt to manipulate Party Y's inference as to Party X's framing of an issue by establishing a reference point that frames the issue negatively. For each issue, we assume that Party X has a neutral reference point that divides the outcome space into a gain region and a loss region. There are several generic means that Party X may use for persuading Party Y that Party X's framing of an issue is negative and that Party Y should remove Party X's loss by conceding on this issue. First, and most obvious, Party X may communicate his or her positional frame by stating his or her positional reference point and indicating that outcomes below or above this point are losses to him or her. Second, Party X may explain that, over the course of history, he or she has had outcomes equal to or better than the positional reference point. Third, Party X may explain that others in Party X's circumstance have traditionally received outcomes equal to or better than the positional reference point. Fourth, Party X may argue that outcomes worse than Party X's positional reference point are unfair to Party X for one reason or another. Fifth, Party X may argue that he or she has suffered previous losses and that outcomes worse than the positional reference point are insufficient to offset these losses. Sixth, Party X may argue that he or she can obtain an outcome better than or equal to his or her positional reference point by terminating the negotiation with Party Y and negotiating with another party. Of course, any of these tactics may be contrived for the purpose of bluffing. In addition, similar tactics could be used by one party in an attempt to alter the other party's framing.

Frame Misrepresentation

Frame misrepresentation may be one of the most common bluffing tactics. Presenting one's position as negatively framed helps to justify standing firm. To the extent that individuals have an intuitive sense of the effects of loss aversion on preferences and decisions, their use of negative frame bluffs may be quite effective. Like any bluffing technique, however, a negative frame bluff may increase the likelihood that the other party will break off the negotiations.

Concealing Negative Framing

An opposite frame presentation technique is to conceal negative framing of an issue in order to avoid making the other party aware of the heightened importance of that issue. For example, a seller who frames the purchase price negatively may wish to conceal his or her magnified need for the cash that a transaction would provide.

As long as bargainers focus on stated positions, identifying each other's actual frames may be difficult. Even when a positive bargaining zone exists, if both bargainers bluff by insisting that their frames are negative, then impasse is more likely than when one or both negotiators admit to positive framing. Shifting to a focus on underlying interests (see Fisher & Ury, 1981) may reveal individuals' true frames and increase the likelihood of a settlement that meets both sides' resistance points. A negotiator's resistance point is the settlement (e.g., price) that leaves the negotiator indifferent between settling versus walking away. However, in distributive bargaining, this revelation may not be advantageous if the negotiator's true frame is positive, because the other party may now expect more concessions. Thus, it might be predicted that positive frame negotiators will be more likely to engage in positional bargaining than negative frame negotiators. In essence, negative frame negotiators will be more direct about what they stand to lose.

TABLE 13.2
Predicted Effects of Buyer's Bidimensional Framing on Negotiation

Buyer's Framing	*Negotiations*
G+ P+	Buyer is ambivalent about settling. Buyer makes moderately rapid concessions toward an immediate price.
G+ P−	Buyer is not predisposed to settle because P is framed negatively. Buyer makes low offer and concedes slowly.
G− P+	Buyer is strongly predisposed to settle because G is framed negatively. Buyer makes high offer and concedes rapidly.
G− P−	Buyer is ambivalent about settling. Buyer makes moderately rapid concessions toward an intermediate price.

Note. G = Good or issue; P = purchase price; "+" denotes positive framing; "−" denotes negative framing.

PREDICTED EFFECTS
OF BIDIMENSIONAL FRAMING
ON NEGOTIATION

Table 13.2 shows the predicted effects of the various bidimensional framing combinations on a buyer's willingness to settle, rate of concessions, and willingness to pay. These factors are affected by framing, loss aversion, and risk seeking for losses. The individual concedes more slowly if a transaction would entail a loss and more rapidly if a transaction would avoid a loss. These predictions should be tested in future work.

PREDICTED EFFECTS OF ACTUAL
VERSUS ATTRIBUTED FRAMING
ON NEGOTIATION

For the present, assume that individuals have an intuitive understanding of the concept that a good or issue can be in or not in a negotiator's psychological endowment. Thus, it is assumed that negotiators have at least a rudimentary understanding of some of the consequences of framing. Also, it is assumed that framing is one of the variables that negotiators use in assessing the other party's position. The extent of individuals' intuitive understanding of framing is an important topic for future empirical work.

TABLE 13.3
Buyer's Assumptions as to Seller's Framing

	Transaction		No Transaction	
	Buyer	*Seller*	*Buyer*	*Seller*
Purchase price	Loss	No loss	No loss	Loss
Good or issue	Gain	No gain	No gain	Gain

Some combinations of attributed frames and actual frames can lead to situations that threaten the parties' ability to reach an agreement. Recall that G+ P− was the framing used by buyers in Casey (1995). If the seller attributes a different frame to a buyer whose actual framing is G+ P−, the seller may incorrectly attribute bluffing behavior to the buyer. The seller may decide to counter with the same tactic, thus edging the negotiation toward impasse.

If the other party's framing is not obvious, then individuals may make the somewhat egocentric assumption that the other party's framing is the same as their own. This assumption would be a type of false consensus effect (Ross & Nisbett, 1991). It is also closely related to the fixed pie assumption (Neale & Bazerman, 1991). In a simple purchase situation, the buyer may assume that the seller frames the purchase price negatively and the good or issue positively (i.e., G+ P−), as shown in the Table 13.3.

The buyer assumes that the purchase price is already in the seller's psychological endowment, whereas the good is not. Thus, if a transaction occurs, then the seller is assumed by the buyer to experience no loss (the avoidance of a loss) from receipt of the purchase price and no gain (foregoing of a gain) from giving up the good. If a transaction does not occur, then the seller is assumed by the buyer to experience the loss of the purchase price and the gain of the good. The buyer assumes that the seller will be predisposed to reach an agreement in order to avoid the loss of the purchase price, which is magnified by loss aversion. In addition, the buyer will be predisposed not to transact because of the loss aversion associated with giving up the purchase price. Hence, the buyer may expect a relatively quick settlement in which the seller does most of the conceding. However, the buyer's attributed frames for the seller may be incorrect. If, for example, the seller frames both the purchase price and the good positively (G+ P+,

TABLE 13.4
Seller's Assumptions as to Buyer's Framing

	Transaction		No Transaction	
	Buyer	*Seller*	*Buyer*	*Seller*
Purchase price	No gain	Gain	Gain	No gain
Good or issue	Gain	No gain	No gain	Gain

as in Casey, 1995), then the seller faces no prospect of loss. Therefore, the seller will not react as the buyer predicts; loss aversion will not cause the seller to feel pressure to make an agreement. The parties may not reach an agreement because neither is being driven to concede by the force of loss aversion. If they do transact, the purchase price may be low because of the buyer's loss aversion associated with giving up the purchase price.

The seller also may make an inference concerning the buyer's framing. The seller may assume that the buyer's framing matches his or her own (i.e., both parties use $G+ P+$ framing), as shown in Table 13.4.

In this case, the seller is not driven by loss aversion and the seller assumes the same for the buyer. The seller may expect a relatively easy negotiation with reciprocal concessions. However, if the buyer frames the purchase price negatively ($G+ P-$, see Table 13.2), the seller will be surprised that he or she has to do most of the conceding in order to achieve an agreement. The seller may wrongly interpret the buyer's behavior as bluffing.

CONCLUSION

Framing of decision outcomes is usually treated as a construct that researchers attempt to infer from behavior. This chapter proposes the possibility of frame attribution and positional framing and suggests that individuals may attempt to infer and even manipulate others' framing of issues in negotiation. Furthermore, individuals may engage in positional framing by intentionally misrepresenting their own framing of an issue such that the opposing negotiator draws an erroneous conclusion.

The chapter also raises numerous questions that future work might address through laboratory experiments, surveys, or both, of professional negotiators. Some of these questions are: How do negotiators communicate about framing? How do negotiators attempt to manipulate each other's framing? Are parties aware of the role played by the other party's loss aversion and risk seeking for losses? Do negotiators appreciate the extent to which negative framing inhibits concessions? How is frame attribution similar to or different from other types of attribution?

ACKNOWLEDGEMENTS

Correspondence concerning this chapter should be addressed to Jeff T. Casey, W. Averell Harriman School for Management and Policy, State University of New York at Stony Brook, Stony Brook, New York 11794. Electronic mail may be sent to jeff.casey@sunysb.edu.

REFERENCES

Bazerman, M. H., Magliozzi, T., & Neale, M. A. (1985). The acquisition of an integrative response in a competitive market. *Organizational Behavior and Human Performance, 34,* 294–313.

Bazerman, M. H., & Neale, M. A. (1992). *Negotiating rationally.* New York: The Free Press.

Casey, J. T. (1995). Predicting buyer-seller pricing disparities. *Management Science, 41,* 979–999.

Fisher, R., & Ury, W. (1981). *Getting to yes: Negotiating agreement without giving in.* Boston: Houghton Mifflin.

Kahneman, D. (1992). Reference points, anchors, norms, and mixed feelings. *Organizational Behavior and Human Decision Processes, 51,* 296–312.

Kahneman, D., & Tversky, A. (1979). Prospect theory: An analysis of decision under uncertainty. *Econometrica, 47,* 263–291.

Kramer, R. M., & Messick, D. M. (1995). *Negotiation as a social process.* London: Sage.

Neale, M. A., & Bazerman, M. H. (1991). *Cognition and rationality in negotiation.* New York: The Free Press.

Neale, M. A., Huber, V. L., & Northcraft, G. B. (1987). The framing of negotiations: Context versus task frames. *Organizational Behavior and Human Decision Processes, 39,* 228–241.

Ross, L., & Nisbett, R. (1991). *The person and the situation.* New York: McGraw-Hill.

Thaler, R. H. (1985). Mental accounting and consumer choice. *Marketing Science, 4,* 199–214.

Thaler, R. H., & Johnson, E. J. (1990). Gambling with the house money and trying to break even: The effects of prior outcomes on risky choice. *Management Science, 36,* 643–660.

Thompson, L. (1998). *The mind and heart of the negotiator.* Englewood Cliffs, NJ: Prentice-Hall.

Tversky, D., & Kahneman, A. (1991). Loss aversion in riskless choice: A reference-dependent model. *Quarterly Journal of Economics,* 1039–1061.

Tversky, D., & Kahneman, A. (1992). Advances in prospect theory: Cumulative representation of uncertainty. *Journal of Risk and Uncertainty, 5,* 297–323.

14

Group Dynamics and Shared Mental Model Development

Stephen M. Fiore and Eduardo Salas
University of Central Florida

Janis A. Cannon-Bowers
*Naval Air Warfare Center, Training Systems Division
Orlando, Florida*

Moving toward the 21st century, teams continue to be a dominant presence in industry (Guzzo & Salas, 1995). Created for tasks as varied as designing a product to selecting a new CEO, they have a life expectancy that can range from the length of a given meeting to the duration of a corporation (e.g., Cannon-Bowers, Tannenbaum, Salas, & Volpe, 1995). Clearly, the last decades have seen a tremendous increase in the use of teams. As such, the implementation, use, or both, of teams as a definable organizational unit has substantially increased—beginning with the periodic use of quality circles and project teams and ending with the current popularity of self-managed teams. Surveys of medium to large corporations reveal that the "team presence" in industry has risen from 5% in the early 1980s to over 50% in the mid-1990s (Savoie, 1998). Similar results were found by an American Society for Quality Control (ASQC) Survey (1993) that polled over 1,200 employees, revealing that 80% were involved in one or more teams in their company.

The reasons for the increase range from global competitiveness driving a need for employee involvement (e.g., Savoie, 1998), to increases in task complexity requiring that multiple employees work interdependently (e.g., Salas & Cannon-Bowers, in press). Specifically, as layers of middle management have disappeared in American industry, organizations have focused on the potential of employee involvement; this has resulted in the increase in the number of self-managed teams (e.g., Cohen, Ledford, & Spreitzer, 1996; Dunphy & Bryant, 1996). Additionally, the increasing complexity of many organizational activities demands that a number of employees work interdependently in order for tasks to be accomplished. Similarly, the importance of various decisions associated with organization strategy are better handled by, not only the collective knowledge of a team, but the shared responsibility it engenders (Salas & Cannon-Bowers, in press).

Because of this prevalence of teams in industry today, many are formed without much forethought along with the expectation that only gains in productivity can result from teamwork (Hackman, 1990). Although there are substantial benefits associated with teamwork (e.g., Cannon-Bowers & Salas, 1998), the reality is that there is little guarantee of success, as many teams fail for any number of reasons (e.g., Hackman, 1998). Thus, given this increasing reliance on teams, it is critical that a full understanding of the factors impacting team effectiveness be delineated. In this chapter we first define what we mean by a team. Second, we examine a relatively recent theoretical approach to team training, discussing how shared cognition (e.g., team mental models), is argued to be directly related to team performance (Cannon-Bowers & Salas, 1998). Third, we discuss how factors associated with person perception may influence the development of shared mental models (SMM).

THE UTILITY OF TEAMS

An early characterization of teams states that they are "interdependent collections of individuals who share responsibility for specific outcomes for their organizations" (Sundstrom, de Meuse, & Futrell, 1990, p. 120). A more specific definition states that a team is composed of "two or more individuals who must interact and adapt to achieve specified, shared, and valued objectives" (Salas, Dickinson, Converse, & Tannenbaum, 1992, p. 4). Thus, although numerous definitions have been offered, it is generally accepted that for a team to exist there needs to be a clear level of interdependence coupled with clearly articulated roles and goals (e.g., Swezey & Salas, 1992). In order to be effective, then, team members must not only possess task-relevant knowledge but a shared understanding of each of these factors (Cannon-Bowers, Salas, & Converse, 1993).

An ongoing debate in the literature on team effectiveness is the presence or absence of *process gains*. Process gains are defined as the improvement in team performance over and above the simple combination or summation of individual members' skills and knowledge (Steiner, 1972). A similar idea from the decision-making literature states that, if working in a team is truly facilitative (rather than merely additive), then there should be a bonus associated with group performance—termed *assembly bonus effects* (Collins & Guetzkow, 1964). Indeed, the often cited cliché "two heads are better than one" appears to be reason enough for the proliferation of committees in administrations and organizations. Gains in productivity are postulated to occur for any number of reasons, for example, from a particular composition of the group (e.g., Moreland, Levine, & Wingert, 1996) or from a group interaction effect (e.g., synergy, Hall & Watson, 1970; brainstorming, Osborne, 1957) to increases in motivation (e.g., social facilitation effects, Hendrick, 1987). Essentially, interrelationships within the team are thought to facilitate collective evaluation, idea generation, goal commitment, and so on, such that team performance, effectiveness, or both, increases (Hackman, 1987). In the next section we discuss the theoretical development of the shared mental model construct, which is often used to explain effective team performance (i.e., process gains).

SOCIAL COGNITION

During the past decade, cognitive science has substantially influenced social psychology, creating the social cognition movement (e.g., Levine, Resnick, & Higgins, 1993). Although definitions vary, social cognition is said to involve "those social processes...that relate to the acquisition, storage, transmission, manipulation, and use of information for the purpose of creating a group-level intellective product" (Larson & Christensen, 1993, p. 6). Additionally, this influence of cognition has had a substantial impact on the study of groups. Indeed, as the above definition suggests, groups are sometimes considered to be information processing units (Hinsz, Tindale, & Vollrath, 1997), in a manner analogous to early views of human cognition (e.g., Newell & Simon, 1972). Although the utility of this characterization is debatable, nonetheless, we focus on one area of social cognition and team effectiveness that has repeatedly proven to be theoretically and practically useful: shared mental models.

Shared Mental Models

Theories of shared cognition have been applied to explain successful team performance in a variety of task situations. *Shared cognition* is the term used to describe how processes at the intraindividual level are dependent upon and interact with processes at the interindividual level (e.g., Cannon-Bowers, Salas, & Converse, 1990; Levine et al., 1993). Definitions of mental models vary somewhat, often dependent upon the domain in question. In the cognitive science literature, mental models are organized memory structures involved in the comprehension of a given phenomenon as one integrates knowledge, and they facilitate one's ability to draw inferences (e.g., Johnson-Laird, 1983). Similar notions are proposed by human factors researchers who argue that mental models allow users to generate descriptions of a system and make predictions about future system states (e.g., Rouse, Cannon-Bowers, & Salas, 1992). From the organizational psychology literature, mental models are said to be representations of knowledge elements in an employee's environment along with the elements interrelations (Klimoski & Mohammed, 1994).

Notions of shared knowledge have recently come to the forefront of research on teams because efficient and effective team performance is often shown to be related to the degree that team members possess multiple models associated with the system, environment, or both, in which they are operating (e.g., Cannon-Bowers et al., 1993; Salas, Cannon-Bowers, & Johnston, 1997). The idea of a SMM has existed in one form or another for a number of years. For example, Wegner's (1987) notion of transactive memory (TAM) can be seen as an early illustration of SMM theory. In TAM theory, a dyad (or group) does not store all aspects of declarative knowledge relevant to their relationship, rather they store who is aware of what information. Essentially, TAM theory suggests that team members form expectations about their teammates' capabilities (e.g., Wegner) or task (e.g., Liang, Moreland, & Argote, 1995). These expectations lead them to assess a teammate's likely contribution to the task and is a way in which members gauge team member role responsibilities (cf. Rouse et al., 1992).

Others have noted how shared expectations about team members, task environments, or both, can affect group performance. For example, Gersick (1988) noted that group interaction is affected by the degree to which members hold preconceived expectations about their task and roles. To the degree that these expectations overlap, rapid development of group norms that drive performance can result. Research with negotiation groups found that shared task scripts, that is, preconceived procedures for appropriate team behavior, influenced the development of group norms and subsequent performance (Bettenhausen & Murnighan, 1985). Essentially, these group processes are composed of "pre-interaction hypotheses about other group members, the task, and the work environment that influence coordination intentions" (Wittenbaum, Vaughan, & Stasser, 1998, p. 179). This body of research suggests that anticipated interaction can influence later group process and can be facilitative when there exists a certain amount of accuracy and overlap to these social interaction hypotheses (see also Levine, Bogart, & Zdaniuk, 1996; Zdaniuk & Levine, 1996).

Team training researchers have most clearly articulated theories involving shared cognition in general and definitions of shared mental models in particular. Initial theorizing on training shared mental models suggested that, for teams to coordinate their actions, they must possess commonly held knowledge structures that allow them to predict team behavior based upon shared performance expectations (Cannon-Bowers et al., 1993; Stout, Cannon-Bowers, & Salas, 1996). Specifically, according to shared mental model (SMM) theory, members of effective teams possess a shared set of knowledge that facilitates their interaction. In particular, highly effective teams must hold compatible knowledge structures about a variety of facets of the team task. First, they must have a shared understanding of their teammates' roles, that is, knowledge pertaining to their individual responsibilities and required actions. Second, they must maintain a shared understanding of the team task at a level sufficient to integrate their actions. Last, they must share an understanding of the potential situations they may encounter. The convergence of these interrelated knowledge structures is said to be a SMM for the team task (Cannon-Bowers et al., 1995). In the actual task environment, that is, in the context of dynamic decision making, this SMM allows the team to explicitly or implicitly coordinate their behavior dependent upon situational demands. Specifically, to the degree that the team possesses a SMM, they will be able to generate overlapping expectations as task-related situations unfold. In turn, these expectations are used to generate predictions for appropriate performance behaviors during routine or novel situations (e.g., Cannon-Bowers et al., 1993; Orasanu, 1990). In sum, SMMs consist of interrelated sets of knowledge that teams utilize to quickly adapt their behavior depending upon task demands (Cannon-Bowers et al., 1993; 1995; Orasanu, 1990; Salas & Cannon-Bowers, in press).

By emphasizing SMM theory, researchers have uncovered productive team training programs. For example, high performing teams were found to possess a shared vision in which member attitudes are in agreement as to the goals and direction the team should take (Cannon-Bowers et al., 1995; Niehoff, Enz, & Grover, 1990). From such findings, training programs were developed to ensure the formation of shared knowledge with respect to the task goals and team-task expectations, and often prove to be more effective (e.g., Cannon-Bowers et al., 1995; Fredericksen & White, 1989; Kozlowski & Salas, 1997; Orasanu & Salas, 1993). Such theorizing has produced a number of additional training interventions designed to foster the development of shared knowledge structures. For example, "cross-training" (e.g., Volpe, Cannon-Bowers, Salas, & Spector, 1996), training designed to encourage compatible mental models with respect to team member roles and responsibilities, has recently shown promise in shared mental model development (e.g., Blickensderfer, Cannon-Bowers, & Salas, 1998). Additionally, training programs using SMM theory to emphasize efficient information transfer showed performance improvements in the form of more effective crew coordination (Blickensderfer, Cannon-Bowers, & Salas, 1997; Cannon-Bowers, Salas, Blickensderfer, & Bowers, 1998; Serfaty, Entin, & Johnston, 1998; Volpe et al., 1996).

In sum, the aforementioned research, although demonstrating the utility of SMMs with respect to team performance, has more clearly emphasized the cognition side of the social cognition movement. In the next section of this chapter, we attempt to remedy this by discussing how a number of issues relating to team interaction behaviors and person perception can influence the development and use of SMMs.

SOCIAL COGNITION AND SHARED MENTAL MODEL THEORY

The complexity of the context in which teams operate in organizational environments requires that a rubric be developed with which to understand team performance in a variety of settings. Heretofore, methods such as delineating team competencies under SMM theory have been discussed (e.g., Cannon-Bowers et al., 1995; Salas & Cannon-Bowers, in press). In this section we discuss such issues, but we relate them to person perception. We argue that when cognitions are interdependent (Ickes & Gonzalez, 1994), the importance of issues associated with person perception become particularly acute. Specifically, person perception factors affecting individual cognition (e.g., trust) are amplified when socially shared cognition is mandatory. Essentially, previous work has focused upon the notion that team performance is the result of possessing the appropriate competencies for a given task. Training programs have therefore emphasized the development of such competencies. We suggest that antecedent conditions dependent upon person perception may also be foundational to team training. In particular, what is critical, but often ignored, is how social cognition can impact the development, use, and/or acceptance of these competencies; an issue we begin to address here.

In order to specify the focus of this section, we constrain our discussion to only a portion of the variables associated with SMMs and team effectiveness. First, we focus specifically on developing teams, that is, relatively young teams composed of members who may be unaware of each other's task, team competencies, or both. Such teams are in the initial phases of their evolution and this designation encompasses either teams created for a particular organizational need (e.g., process redesign) or teams formed and in training for critical operational environments (e.g., aircrews). Issues associated with person perception become particularly salient in such teams because the early interaction processes are critical to the development of a team's SMM. Second, we emphasize team coordination efforts and we distinguish between preprocess and in-process coordination behaviors. Third, we discuss information sharing behaviors and how they influence shared mental model development. In our closing section, we illustrate how person-perception constructs affect these team interaction behaviors and SMM development.

Team Coordination

In this section, we describe arguably one of the most critical aspects of team performance behaviors, that is, team coordination. As mentioned, researchers have proposed that effective teams develop a shared understanding or SMM with which they are able to anticipate each other's actions and needs, as well as fluidly adapt to dynamic task demands (Cannon-Bowers et al., 1993). Specifically, what is foundational to SMM theory is the notion that effective teams seamlessly integrate their behavior to facilitate team interaction. In order for such integration to take place, teams must possess shared models of various aspects of their team's responsibilities. It is this aspect of team coordination on which we focus, that is, the ability to coordinate actions with or without explicit communication. We argue that in order to understand the complex manner in which person perception impacts shared mental models, we need to first understand this fundamental aspect of team performance.

Analyses of effective teams continually illustrate that coordinated behaviors on the part of a team lead to successful performance (Kleinman & Serfaty, 1989; Nieva, Fleishman, & Reick, 1978; Orasanu, 1990). Furthermore, such coordination can occur both implicitly and explicitly in dynamic team interaction (e.g., Stout, Cannon-Bowers, Salas, & Milanovich, 1999). Coordination varying in explicitness pertains to the degree to which team members must articulate their behaviors (e.g., plans, routines) or interact in the absence of verbal communication. Specifically, implicit team coordination describes team interaction behavior that is coordinated in the absence of overt communication (cf. Entin & Serfaty, 1999). Conversely, explicit team coordination describes interaction involving overt team communication. For implicit coordination to take place, research suggests that teams must share an understanding of expectations for each member, assessments of task demands, and/or appropriate allocation of resources (e.g., Urban, Weaver, Bowers, & Rhodenizer, 1996; Wittenbaum, Stasser, & Merry, 1996).

The degree to which coordination need be implicit or explicit often depends on either the task, or the context of the task situation. In many situations, explicit coordination can be beneficial to team performance. For example, a number of aviation accidents resulted from inadequate information transfer, a type of failure in crew coordination relating to communication (Foushee, 1982). Furthermore, evidence suggests that more effective cockpit managers increase crew coordination by verbalizing intentions, ensuring that all members share the correct information and could plan actions accordingly (Helmreich, Foushee, Benson, & Russini, 1986). Others have shown that effective aircrew captains articulate plans and strategies, increasing both coordination and the likelihood that a SMM of the task, the situation, or both, develops (Orasanu, 1990).

At the same time, the literature on team coordination suggests that implicit interaction behaviors are just as critical to effective team performance. In particular, implicit coordination is typically relied on most during demanding situations (e.g., high workload) without a corresponding decrease in performance (Cannon-Bowers et al., 1998; Entin & Serfaty, 1999; Kleinman & Serfaty, 1989). Such findings suggest that implicit coordination allows teams to effectively deal with this workload through a decrease in overt communication.

Preprocess and In-process Coordination

Although definitions of coordination in teams vary somewhat, here we emphasize the distinction between coordination occurring prior to, and during, team interaction (Wittenbaum, Vaughan, & Stasser, 1998). Specifically, timing of coordination pertains to the presence of coordination efforts prior to, or during, team interaction (i.e., preprocess or in-process). In-process coordination occurs during interaction and it involves the integration of individual member contributions (and is therefore more akin to that proposed by SMM theory to describe efficient team performance). Critical to person-perception issues, though, is this notion that coordination can occur prior to team interaction (e.g., Gersick, 1988; Wegner, 1987; Wittenbaum et al., 1996). Preprocess coordination describes how initial shared expectations are created in anticipation of team interaction. Thus, although we acknowledge the criticality of in-process coordination to team effectiveness, we equally emphasize the importance of preprocess coordination.

A substantial body of literature suggests that individual team members may engage in some form of preplanning (i.e., preprocess coordination) as they prepare for eventual interaction. Thus, we distinguish between the timing of the coordination in order to illustrate the differing effects person perception can have on the development and utilization of SMMs. In particular, we differentiate these constructs because the actual construction and use of a SMM will vary in these differing contexts and this may depend on associated person-perception issues. We next discuss a portion of the research that investigated the group dynamics associated with coordinated actions.

Anticipatory tacit coordination is the term used to describe preprocess coordination implicitly engaged by team members (Wittenbaum et al., 1996). This involves the covert adaptation of member actions in order to efficiently coordinate team behavior. Initial research on preprocess coordination was done in the area of "routine" behaviors. Group dynamics researchers noted that coordination in teams is often facilitated by the early development and rapid use of task routines—habitual behaviors in which a group engages. Gersick and Hackman (1990) defined a *habitual routine* as occurring "when a group repeatedly exhibits a functionally similar pattern of behavior in a given stimulus situation without explicitly selecting it over alternative ways of behaving" (p. 69). A consistent body of research provides evidence that the spontaneous tendency of a group is to utilize such routines and focus in on a particular shared behavior process. Habitual routines may facilitate team interaction because they represent shared plans which can aid in coordinating the execution of a plan of action.

Though routines are more often considered to occur in established work groups, evidence suggests that they can easily arise in newly formed groups. Evidence for this was originally found by Maier (1963) who showed that groups quickly set themselves into a certain routine of solving a problem. Others later noted that, "groups seemed to settle very early on a particular line of attack, and alternative work procedures were seldom explored in the group discussion" (Campbell, 1968, p. 209). Additionally, research suggests that groups are clearly unwilling to alter a task routine once it has begun (e.g., Hackman & Morris, 1975). As an indication of this unwillingness, researchers have found that newly formed groups consider explicit coordination activities to be a low priority and typically make task performance the main prerogative (Shure, Rogers, Larsen, & Tassone, 1962). More recent research suggests that such routines can be either rapidly acquired norms for behavior or norms developed from anticipated interaction and perceptions of the team and task (Gersick, 1988; Gersick & Hackman, 1990). Thus, preprocess coordination can be directly affected by person-perception issues associated with team members' knowledge of their teammates, the task, or both.

A related body of research, focusing more on explicit coordination efforts, demonstrates that members of a team will infer the abilities of a team member and, in anticipation of interaction during task performance, modify the manner in which they prepare. Knowledgeable team members, on the basis of "other members' past behavior, expertise and interest . . . can adjust their own behavior to facilitate the group's task completion" (Wittenbaum et al., 1996, p. 130). Thus, to the degree this perception is accurate, team task performance may be facilitated. For example, when expecting a decision-making task requiring unanimity, group members engaged in more information processing. This increased information processing led to a better understanding of each member's expertise, and, presumably, their contribution to the discussion. Research investigating minority and majority influence and anticipatory interaction has found analogous results. For example, participants preparing for a group discussion vary their prepatory behavior dependent upon their perception of group faction size (e.g., Levine et al., 1996). When told that they would be in the minority position, participants spent more time studying material relevant to their own position and this effort increased when the participants perceived the opposing faction size to increase (Levine & Russo, 1995). In studies where participants are asked to articulate their thoughts prior to group discussion, they are more likely to list thoughts indicative of less bias when they perceive their group to be in opposition to their own views (Zdaniuk & Levine, 1996).

Additional evidence that preprocess coordination takes place can also be found in the literature on TAM systems (Wegner, 1987; Wittenbaum et al., 1996). This body of research finds that prepatory behavior on the part of team members will later influence performance. For example, how one perceives their teammate's expertise can influence the level of effort put forth in preparation for a team task. Participants who believed their teammate was less expert in a given area, spent significantly more time studying that topic area in preparation for the group task (Wegner). Analogous results are found in the applied literature. In an investigation of air-traffic control teams, Smith-Jentsch, Kraiger, Cannon-Bowers, and Salas (2000) noted that initial assessments of teammate specific knowledge (that is, perception of a teammate's level of expertise) can be influenced by worker reputations.

Interestingly, research additionally suggests that preprocess coordination will differ depending upon perceptions of not only the team but also the task. On the one hand, if the perception is that the task calls for unique input, then team members will focus on what they believe to be their idiosyncratic contribution. On the other hand, if the task is thought to require collective action, then team members may focus their input on what they believe to be shared abilities. Thus, initial perceptions about group members may drive individual preparation and this may interact with task perceptions.

In sum, preprocess coordination, whether implicit (e.g., Wittenbaum et al., 1996) or explicit (e.g., Levine et al., 1996), is influenced by perceptions based upon experience with teammates, the task, or external sources such as organizational reputations preceding team interaction. Essentially, these initial perceptions result in a "profile" of the target person(s) that will influence preprocess and, subsequently, in-process coordination. This body of research has a number of implications for the development and utilization of a SMM. For example, such perception issues will impact SMM development in that, a priori, members begin to devise a shared understanding of the team and the task. To the degree that their perceptions are accurate, team members' shared understanding will be facilitative. Conversely, if their perceptions are inaccurate, then there are two possible consequences: (a) the team may use initial meeting time in an attempt to construct an accurate shared understanding of their task and abilities, or (b) the team may forge ahead unaware that their perceptions are inaccurate. Obviously this latter case is much more detrimental to team performance and research suggests that this is often the case in team problem-solving. For example, Fiore, Ferketish, Schooler, and McConnell (1998) noted that problem-solving teams often enter their first meeting erroneously believing that they possess a shared understanding of the team task. Only through facilitated interaction, where perceptions of the team and the task are explicitly articulated, do team members realize that their initial perceptions may be inaccurate.

With respect to the utilization of a SMM, such perceptions may negatively affect team coordination. To the degree that a team member's perception of a teammate's roles, skills, or both, are inaccurate, the team member will be less likely to engage in behavior that would facilitate team performance. For example, research on dynamic team interaction finds that effective teams freely engage in task sharing. Specifically, when one team member is under a heavy workload, they may pass certain responsibilities to a teammate they believe can manage them (e.g., Cannon-Bowers & Salas, 1998). Thus, if a team member has an inaccurate perception that his or her teammate is knowledgeable in a particular task, this "hand-off" could negatively impact performance. Similarly, if a team member has an inaccurate perception that his or her teammate is not knowledgeable, they may not engage in a coordinated hand-off and their own performance may suffer. Note, therefore, that the valence associated with this inaccuracy is independent of the outcome. Specifically, if one's perception of their teammate is inaccurate, either positive (i.e., unduly favorable) or negative (i.e., unduly harsh), the hand-off will have negative consequences.

Information Sharing

In this section, we discuss how information sharing behaviors among team members influence the development of a SMM. Thus far we have implicitly suggested that the act of sharing information among team members is a critical component of effective teamwork. Here we argue that the information sharing process is foundational to the development of a SMM and we explicitly discuss the research that has investigated this process within interacting groups. Because we now discuss behaviors associated with actual interaction, we focus on what would be characterized as in-process coordination efforts.

Assembled teams are often composed of members varying in a number of ways (e.g., responsibility level or roles). Thus, even though they may share a common product or service, during the course of their workday each member is exposed to differing forms of knowledge related to that product or service (Wittenbaum & Stasser, 1996). As such, team members bring with them a variety of knowledge, which theoretically is at the disposal of the entire team. Empirical studies suggest otherwise and over the last decade a substantial body of research has documented this inability of groups to share information in a variety of task situations (e.g., Hollingshead, 1996; Stasser, Stewart, & Wittenbaum, 1995; Straus, 1996). These studies typically involve manipulating the amount of information provided to individuals within a group, such that idiosyncratic information is distributed across members. Results from studies such as these find that asymmetric distribution of task data leads to information sharing of only the overlapping material. Specifically, group members are more likely to discuss the information they hold in common (i.e., transfer similar data), and not the information they hold that is unique.

Others suggest that, in newly forming groups, communication is facilitated by the development of common ground or "a common language for describing tasks" (Liang et al., 1995, p. 386). Analogous to sharing similar information, this process is considered to be a modification of one's "vocabulary schemas" as referential communication is developed (e.g., Fussell & Krauss, 1989). These changes gauge the degree to which collaborators modify their language in order to produce overlap in terminology. Such modifications have been found in linguistic investigations of the development of common ground (e.g., Clark & Wilkes-Gibbs, 1986) and in situations such as collaborative design (Harvey & Koubek, 1998).

We suggest that these findings are in stark contrast to the expected results of group interaction; that is, a collection of individuals each contributing unique input, thus increasing the amount of knowledge the group as a whole possesses. If group members are unable or unwilling to share this information, then clearly there is little benefit of their meeting. Furthermore, evidence suggests that the bias toward discussing only shared information is particularly acute in newly formed teams. In such teams, conformity pressures are often high and the team will therefore emphasize similarities in an attempt to increase cohesion (Worchel, Coutant-Sassic, & Grossman, 1991).

Thus, with respect to information transfer in newly formed teams, there appears to be a confluence of factors mitigating the potential benefits of team interaction. First, teams in their early stages of development may experience self-generated pressures to conform resulting in a desire to seek common ground. Although this may facilitate cohesion within the group (e.g., Worchel et al., 1991), the process forces a decrease in information sharing, that is, it pressures the group to discuss only their similarities. But for a team to be most effective, they must pool their resources (i.e., contribute their idiosyncratic knowledge and be intimately aware of each other's resources). When information sharing fails, the likelihood of such a synergistic effect decreases.

In sum, information sharing is critical to the development of a SMM because in order for team members to be explicitly aware of each other's roles in the team task environment, they must engage in it freely. Furthermore, without an understanding of the responsibilities of each team member, effective coordination cannot take place. Essentially, the resulting team interaction process would be one bereft of utility in that the developed mental model would consist of only shared elements (i.e., it is likely to be incomplete).

TEAMWORK BEHAVIORS
AND PERSON-PERCEPTION PROCESSES

In the context of SMMs the previous sections describe two somewhat correlated constructs associated with team-specific behaviors: team member coordination efforts and information sharing. In this final section, we discuss these behaviorally based constructs but relate them to group dynamics resulting from person perception, and we describe them in the context of the attitudes and cognitions (e.g., Cannon-Bowers et al., 1995; Salas & Cannon-Bowers, in press) associated with team interaction (see Fig. 14.1). In particular, we suggest that person perception will directly impact the

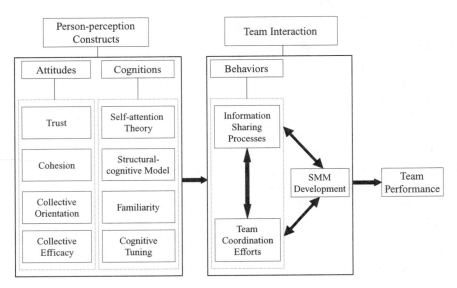

FIG. 14.1. Descriptive relation of person-perception constructs to team interaction behaviors and shared mental model of development.

degree to which information is shared and the level of coordination achieved by the team. This, in turn, may affect the development of a SMM in newly formed teams. We suggest that initial perceptions formed prior to actual teamwork produce anticipatory processing of teammates and this subsequently affects the nature of their interaction. Similarly, perceptions formed during interaction also affect this interaction as team members revise these perceptions and attempt to reach a common ground (i.e., develop a SMM of their team and the task).

Team-Specific Attitudes

Group Cohesion and Person Perception. We present a rather straight-forward conceptualization of *group cohesion*, defined here simply as the willingness to remain in the group (e.g., Mullen & Copper, 1994). Although contradictory evidence exists, the majority of studies suggest that group cohesion can positively impact team effectiveness (see Evans & Dion, 1991). As for the mechanism(s) or factors that lead to cohesion, some have suggested that cohesion depends upon the degree to which group members believe they match a perceived prototype of the typical group member (Hogg, 1987). Thus, cohesion increases as a function of the perceived similarity among group members. Essentially, a form of self-categorization process proceeds whereby member cohesion is dependent upon the degree of category congruency between one's self-concept and their perception of their group (Hogg, 1993; Levine & Moreland, 1990).

Prior to interacting with the team, one would expect that initial perceptions based upon any number of factors (e.g., reputations, rumors, or speculation), may produce preprocess coordination efforts. These efforts, in turn, may lead to the development of a membership category for the team with which one is to work. Thus, the degree of one's accuracy in their perception of the group prototype and self-concept, and one's belief that they match that prototype, may increase the level of cohesion. Note, though, that the accuracy of this perception would be checked by processes occurring during in-process interaction. For example, upon initially meeting with the team, early interactions are crucial in that they may either support or refute one's perceptions of the group prototype. Refutation of the group prototype may decrease cohesion only to the degree that one feels this new prototype is inconsistent with one's own self-concept.

As evidence that in-process coordination efforts may serve to modify one's perception of the group, consider recent efforts to train SMMs. Research in team training found that teams trained in self-correction as a means to improve team performance not only developed better shared expectations but also exhibited greater team cohesion (Blickensderfer et al., 1997). Thus, because of the self-correction training, these teams were better able to coordinate their in-process efforts by forming shared expectations concerning teammate and task performance.

Collective Efficacy and Person Perception.

Collective efficacy is a team's shared belief in their competence to perform a task (Whitney, 1994; see also Bandura, 1986; Guzzo, Yost, Campbell, & Shea, 1994). Others state that collective efficacy is made up of shared beliefs in the team's abilities to communicate and perceive competence for coordinated group activities (Zaccaro, Blair, Peterson, & Zazanis, 1995; see also Paskevich, Brawley, Dorsch, & Widmeyer, 1999). Collective efficacy as a construct will impact mostly in-process coordination efforts. For example, recent research suggests that the degree to which team members attempt to compensate for each other's behavior in dynamic task situations is dependent upon collective efficacy (Smith-Jentsch et al., 2000). These studies found that when teams experience an influx of new member(s), and thus experience a decrease in the level of familiarity (i.e., team-specific competencies), coordination efforts are affected. When team members possess sufficient collective efficacy, though, they compensate for this by more closely monitoring the actions of the new member or by working harder. But such compensation is dependent upon a sufficient shared understanding of their teammate's responsibilities. Without such SMMs one's understanding of their teammate's role will be insufficient to allow them to recognize when increased effort is required.

Collective efficacy is also strongly related to group cohesion and SMMs of one's team and task (Smith-Jentsch et al., 2000). Specifically, teams composed of members high in teammate-specific knowledge showed a greater desire to stay with that team and also a greater belief that the team could persevere in adversity. But Smith-Jentsch et al. found that a team's use of behaviors that were indicative of a SMM was related more to cohesion than to collective efficacy. They argued that in order for a team member to feel self-assured enough to seek assistance, admit error, or both, they must not only believe in the team's ability to provide assistance but also show a high degree of cohesiveness with that team. This finding is analogous to Jones and George's (1998) speculations that "conditional trust" may place constraints on a team member's desire to seek help.

Collective Orientation and Person Perception.

Before group cohesion, collective efficacy, or both, can develop, some researchers suggest that team members must possess a collective orientation (Driskell & Salas, 1992; Salas & Cannon-Bowers, in press), that is, a belief in the importance of teamwork (e.g., Gregorich, Helmreich, & Wilhelm, 1990). Essentially, collective orientation describes the degree to which one values teamwork and is willing to engage in teamwork behaviors (e.g., give and take input). A consistent body of research suggests that, on interdependent tasks, a high degree of collective orientation results in improved performance. For example, early research into negotiation effectiveness found that when negotiators were both cooperatively oriented as opposed to self-centered, overall outcomes improved (Kimmel, 1980). Similarly, collectively oriented team members performed better on a judgment task than did egocentric team members (Driskell & Salas, 1992).

Collective orientation, then, may impact both preprocess and in-process coordination efforts. On the one hand, prior to initial contact, those low in collective orientation may engage in little prepatory behaviors as their interest in team interaction will be low. In-process coordination efforts will be similarly lacking and may actually be inhibitory if one perceives their team in a negative light or the organizational environment is somewhat hostile. For example, research suggests that help-seeking behavior is impacted by the degree of collective orientation in the organization's culture (Lee, 1997). These studies find that, when organizational norms are perceived to favor collective efforts, participants are more likely to seek assistance and thus improve overall performance. On the other hand, those high in collective orientation are likely to spend a considerable amount of time engaging in preprocess coordination efforts. These efforts may include attempts to prepare for the task or attempts to familiarize oneself with the team and may result in facilitated in-process coordination.

Trust and Person Perception.   Trust is an integral part of teamwork specifically because team tasks require a high level of interdependence. This mutual dependency leads to shared respect for team members strengths and fosters open lines of communication (De Vries, 1999). The development of a shared understanding of the team, the task, or both, is analogous to group socialization processes associated with acculturation. The process of acculturation occurs when a new group member learns the set of shared thoughts, values (e.g., trust), and customs for the group (Levine & Moreland, 1990). Others have noted how shared values and beliefs significantly impact effective teamwork by increasing the trust within the team (De Vries), the creation of a common bond, or both—a process suggested to foster the developmental process as "groups" evolve into "teams"

(Jones & George, 1998). These factors lead to an increasing likelihood that supporting behaviors critical to effective teamwork will be implemented. Specifically, interpersonal trust is thought to mediate cooperation and teamwork by increasing confidence in others, as well as increasing help-seeking behaviors and the free exchange of information (Jones & George).

Trust may dually impact preprocess and in-process coordination depending upon whether initial trust is high or low. For example, recent studies illustrate how initial perceptions can mediate the degree to which information among teammates is shared. As mentioned, information sharing is critical to the development of SMM specifically because of its necessity in developing teammate- and task-specific knowledge (e.g., Smith-Jentsch et al., 2000). When trust expectations were manipulated in experimental settings such that initial perception of team members was positive or negative, it significantly influenced performance (Butler, 1999). Furthermore, this impact was greater than a later measure of "climate" of trust. Thus, initial perceptions of trust may mediate and play a greater role in information sharing than overall team climate.

As further evidence that trust will impact coordination efforts, consider findings from research into the utility of TAM systems. Research suggests that a shared understanding of who knows what is important specifically because team members can trust their teammates to provide accurate information on a topic with which they are unfamiliar (Liang et al., 1995). Furthermore, it allows them to coordinate their behavior more effectively because of the increased likelihood that they will anticipate each other's needs. Additionally, studies suggest that antecedent effects such as team trust, can mediate team performance by impacting the level of dissatisfaction in the group. For example, in an investigation of over 350 product innovation teams, Nerkar, McGrath, and MacMillan (1996) found that social dissatisfaction affected what they termed to be *team deftness*, that is, the ability of the team to share information and trust one another enough to fluently execute their task.

Recently, trust was found to play a mediating role in what could be considered in-process coordination efforts directly relevant to the development of a SMM. Trust was argued to mediate two facets of cooperation within the team: coordination and helping (Dirks, 1999). In particular, it was suggested that a team's ability to "harmoniously combine actions (i.e., be coordinated) is likely to be contingent on the extent to which individuals can depend on their partners and can predict their partners' behaviors" (p. 447). Results from this study found that trust mediated the degree to which a team would share and commit to ideas in a decision-making task and impacted the degree to which teams cooperated (i.e., coordinated actions and helped each other). Essentially, the low trust group worked more as individuals and directed their efforts toward individual goals, whereas high trust groups exhibited behaviors more consistent with collective effort.

The level of trust perceived among team members, thus, is essential for the effective utilization of a SMM. Specifically, because there is often a critical need for dynamic reallocation of efforts in team coordination (i.e., handing-off of task responsibilities); this will manifest itself only to the degree that there is a shared level of trust within the group. For example, teams in highly dynamic environments, such as cockpit crews, often times must interact implicitly in order to seamlessly integrate their actions. If the team does not hold the same level of trust for one another, then one teammate may be less inclined to pass on a task when their workload has exceeded a safe level. Note, that this assumes a level of shared understanding of each other's roles in that task reallocation is only possible when each team member possesses an appropriate level of knowledge associated with their teammate's task.

Team-Specific Cognitions

Self-Attention Theory and Person Perception. Group membership may lead to intragroup comparisons that directly or indirectly influence performance. According to Mullen's (1987) *self-attention theory*, across a wide variety of social situations the phenomenon of self-attention leads people to match or evaluate themselves in comparison to other group members. The larger the difference in the *other-total ratio*, the more matching or self-evaluation takes place.

Self-attention theory has been applied to in-process coordination efforts (e.g., social facilitation effects). Specifically, as the other-total ratio increases, that is, as the "performer" becomes proportionately more rare, they are increasingly self-attentive; thus, their performance effort increases. Similarly, the model has been applied to social loafing. This would occur when the other-total ratio decreases such that as the performers become proportionately less rare they become less self-attentive.

Structural-Cognitive Model and Person Perception. According to the *structural-cognitive model* (Humphrey, 1985), members of large groups (e.g., organizations) have difficulty adequately perceiving each others' talents and abilities. Thus, when placed in a team situation one's attempts at preprocess coordination will be stymied. In particular, structural factors associated with an organization may modify the information one has about potential teammates. Additionally, because of information processing limitations, one cannot adequately correct for any potentially biased sources of information. Thus, according to the structural-cognitive model of human behavior, intragroup impressions are heavily influenced by often inaccurate factors (e.g., perceived roles), and not entirely on abilities and dispositions. As such, this model explains how organizational factors can influence person perception and affect preprocess coordination efforts.

Familiarity and Person Perception.   Recently, a number of studies have begun to systematically address the degree to which ad hoc groups may differ from actual groups, particularly as they relate to familiarity between members. For example, recent studies have illustrated the effectiveness that can take place when groups are composed of members who are more than just acquaintances (Jehn & Shah, 1997). Specifically, the degree of familiarity was manipulated such that comparisons were made between groups composed of friends versus groups composed of acquaintances. On both decision making and motor tasks, Jehn and Shah found that friendship groups outperformed acquaintance groups—an effect attributed to increases in both commitment and cooperation. Furthermore, friendship groups were more likely to monitor their task performance, thus increasing the likelihood that they would engage in a group-level self-evaluation process.

Others have shown that friends preconceived expectations about a group task (i.e., whether negotiation or problem solving) can be affected by a form of collective orientation (Thompson & DeHarpport, 1998). In particular, friends high in "communal orientation" were more likely to focus on joint interests and equally allocate their resources. More recently, Smith-Jentsch et al. (2000) noted that familiarity breeds teamwork "by increasing teammates' willingness to ask for and accept assistance and performance feedback" (p. 39).

In the context of the present discussion, in-process coordination efforts are substantially improved when members are friends. Specifically, we emphasize these studies because they illustrate the degree to which both coordination (in the form of cooperation) and group-level awareness (in the form of critical evaluations) can facilitate performance when members are more than just acquaintances. Thus, familiarity appears to be a necessary but not sufficient precondition for SMM development.

Cognitive Tuning and Person Perception.   Transmission of information among team members is critical to team performance (e.g., Stout et al., 1999). In addition to difficulties associated with the content of the information transmitted or shared (i.e., whether unique or similar), also affected by person perception is the process by which that information is transmitted. Specifically, social psychologists have distinguished between a number of differing transmission processes. For example, Zajonc (1960) described cognitive tuning processes whereby a sender attempts to take into account the receiver's perspective and modify the message to maximize comprehension. This concept of cognitive tuning is particularly salient with respect to SMM development and person perception when considering Hardin and Higgins (1996) expansion of the Zajonc definition. In particular, they described three types of tuning, each dependent upon characteristics associated with the sender–receiver relationship (e.g., agreeableness, animosity, or indifference). Here, we discuss these factors as they relate to team coordination efforts.

Supertuning is the process whereby the sender is highly motivated to tailor the message for the receiver. In such situations, the sender's perception of the target's level of knowledge will be first and foremost in influencing the manner in which the message is constructed and conveyed. Effective team interaction, whereby team members communicate on a level appropriate to each other's understanding, is only possible to the degree that the team members are aware of each other's level of knowledge. Thus, team process interventions (e.g., cross-training) may have an impact in that a shared understanding of a teammate's task will affect the manner in which the message is conveyed. Additionally, when the level of trust, cohesion, or collective orientation is high within the team, more effort may be put forth in order to maximize the likelihood that information is properly transmitted. These factors will simultaneously affect the development of a SMM and the level of coordination achieved. Specifically, the development of an accurate SMM is only possible to the degree that information transmission is as accurate as possible. Similarly, if information is incorrectly transmitted, coordination efforts will be stymied; a situation we discuss next.

Antituning is the process whereby the sender deliberately fails to tune the message because a level of animosity exists among the team members. For example, if there is a low level of trust within the team or the team has low cohesion, this will affect the degree to which team members are motivated to achieve effective levels of performance. Similarly, if a given team member is apathetic toward meeting team goals, (e.g., has low collective orientation) he or she may not communicate a message appropriate for their team (e.g., leave out critical information). As with supertuning, any of these factors will simultaneously affect the development of a SMM and the level of coordination achieved. In this case, the development of an accurate SMM is hindered because of purposeful inaccuracies in the data transmission; team members will thus build inaccurate mental models of the team, the task, or both, which in turn hinders coordination.

Last is *nontuning,* the process whereby the sender constructs a message based upon prior beliefs. In such situations, a message may be faulty not because of distrust but rather because of inaccurate mental models. For example, if previous experience with a team has led to misperceptions about a given teammate, then communication methods may be altered in a manner the sender believes is appropriate. Alternatively, this misperception may be because of inaccuracies associated with the task. In either case, inappropriate information may be transmitted and both the development of a SMM and coordination efforts of the team will suffer. Note, though, that nontuning may be directly related to the team evolution process. With increasing interaction experience, the team becomes more aware of each other's roles and tasks (i.e., they develop an accurate SMM), and they are better able to integrate their actions. Thus, as a team matures, communication may be more appropriately tailored and coordination efforts become more integrated.

CONCLUSION

Teams have become a way of life in most organizations. Therefore, as their importance grows, it becomes imperative that one understands how to design, manage, and compose effective teams. More specifically, there is a need to continue to determine which factors contribute to effective team functioning and teamwork and better specify how and why they contribute. As we have discussed, much of the literature suggests that teamwork is comprised of related knowledge (i.e., cognition), behaviors (i.e., skills), and attitudes. In this chapter, we focused on shared cognition and person perception specifically because it is probably the least understood component of teamwork and the most difficult to research. Nonetheless, the implications of knowing how team members "think" in a group situation (e.g., perceive others), are far-reaching.

The more researchers understand for example, implicit coordination and the mechanisms that allow team members to function effectively without overt strategizing, the better able they will be to offer human resources practitioners interventions, tools, and guidelines for managing and training teams. Similarly, increased understanding of collective orientation may, in due time, increase the ability to design, develop, and test highly specific selection protocols. For example, to the degree that organizations desire team-based management, assessment methods that are able to select employees who would be better "team players" could be implemented.

In sum, the deeper the thinking, and the better specified the research, the more likely it is that researchers can develop and offer accurate principles and guidelines as well as effective tools and interventions that facilitate organizational functions. We hope this chapter takes us closer, and motivates others, to continue to investigate the complex relationship between shared cognition and group dynamics.

ACKNOWLEDGEMENTS

Stephen M. Fiore and Eduardo Salas, Department of Psychology, University of Central Florida; Jannis A. Cannon-Bowers, Naval Air Warfare Center, Training Systems Division.

Correspondence concerning this chapter should be addressed to Eduardo Salas, Department of Psychology, University of Central Florida, P. O. Box 161390, Orlando, Florida 32816. Electronic mail may be sent to esalas@pegasus.cc.ucf.edu.

REFERENCES

American Society for Quality Control. (1993). Teaming Up for Quality. Gallup Survey. Milwaukee, WI: ASQC.

Bandura, A. (1986). The explanatory and predictive scope of self-efficacy theory. *Journal of Social & Clinical Psychology, 4*, 359–373.

Bettenhausen, K., & Murnighan, J. K. (1985). The emergence of norms in competitive decision-making groups. *Administrative Science Quarterly, 30*, 350–372.

Blickensderfer, E., Cannon-Bowers, J. A., & Salas, E. (1997). Fostering shared mental models through team self-correction: Theoretical bases and propositions. In M. Beyerlein, D. Johnson, & S. Beyerlein (Eds.), *Advances in interdisciplinary studies in work teams* (Vol. 4, pp. 249–279). Greenwich, CT: JAI.

Blickensderfer, E., Cannon-Bowers, J. A., & Salas, E. (1998). Cross-training and team performance. In J. A. Cannon-Bowers & E. Salas (Eds.), *Making decisions under stress: Implications for individual and team training* (pp. 299–311). Washington, DC: American Psychological Association.

Butler, J. K. (1999). Trust expectations, information sharing, climate of trust, and negotiation effectiveness and efficacy. *Group & Organization Management, 24*, 217–238.

Campbell, J. P. (1968). Individual versus group problem-solving in an industrial sample. *Journal of Applied Psychology, 52*, 205–210.

Cannon-Bowers, J. A., & Salas, E. (1998). Individual and team training under stress: Theoretical underpinnings. In J. A. Cannon-Bowers & E. Salas (Eds.), *Making decisions under stress: Implications for individual and team training* (pp. 17–38). Washington, DC: American Psychological Association.

Cannon-Bowers, J. A., Salas, E., Blickensderfer, E. L., & Bowers, C. A. (1998). The impact of cross-training and workload on team functioning: A replication and extension of initial findings. *Human Factors, 40*, 92–101.

Cannon-Bowers, J. A., Salas, E., & Converse, S. A. (1990). Cognitive psychology and team training: Shared mental models in complex systems. *Human Factors Bulletin, 33*, 1–4.

Cannon-Bowers, J. A., Salas, E., & Converse, S. A. (1993). Shared mental models in expert team decision making. In N. J. Castellan, Jr. (Ed.), *Current issues in individual and group decision making* (pp. 221–246). Hillsdale, NJ: Lawrence Erlbaum Associates.

Cannon-Bowers, J. A., Tannenbaum, S. I., Salas, E., & Volpe, C. E. (1995). Defining competencies and establishing team training requirements. In R. A. Guzzo & E. Salas (Eds.), *Team effectiveness and decision making in organizations* (pp. 333–380). San Francisco: Jossey-Bass.

Clark, H. H., & Wilkes-Gibbs, D. (1986). Referring as a collaborative process. *Cognition, 22*, 1–39.

Cohen, S. G., Ledford, G. E., & Spreitzer, G. M. (1996). A predictive model of self-managing work team effectiveness. *Human Relations, 49*, 643–676.

Collins, E. G., & Guetzkow, H. (1964). *A social psychology of group processes for decision-making.* New York: Wiley.

De Vries, M. F. R. (1999). High-performance teams: Lessons from the pygmies. *Organizational Dynamics, 27*, 66–77.

Dirks, K. T. (1999). The effects of interpersonal trust on work group performance. *Journal of Applied Psychology, 84*, 445–455.

Driskell, J. E., & Salas, E. (1992). Collective behavior and team performance. *Human Factors, 34*, 277–288.

Dunphy, D., & Bryant, B. (1996). Teams: Panaceas or prescriptions for improved performance? *Human Relations, 49*, 677–699.

Entin, E. E., & Serfaty, D. (1999). Adaptive team coordination. *Human Factors, 41*, 312–325.

Evans, C., & Dion, K. (1991). Group cohesion and performance: A meta-analysis. *Small Group Research, 22*, 175–186.

Fiore, S. M., Ferketish, B. J., Schooler, J. W., & McConnell, K. (1998, August). *Why process mapping works: A cognitive componential analysis of the systems approach to problem identification in teams.* Paper presented at the 24th International Congress of Applied Psychology, San Francisco, CA.

Foushee, H. C. (1982). The role of communications, sociopsychological, and personality factors in the maintenance of crew coordination. *Aviation, Space, & Environmental Medicine, 53*, 1062–1066.

Fredericksen, J., & White, B. (1989). An approach to training based upon principled task decomposition. *Acta Psychologica, 71*, 89–146.

Fussell, S., & Krauss, R. (1989). The effects of intended audience on message production and comprehension: Reference in a common ground framework. *Journal of Experimental Social Psychology, 25*, 203–219.

Gersick, C. (1988). Time and transition in work teams: Toward a new model of group development. *Academy of Management Journal, 31*, 9–41.

Gersick, C., & Hackman, J. R. (1990). Habitual routines in task-performing groups. *Organizational Behavior & Human Decision Processes, 47*, 65–97.

Gregorich, S. E., Helmreich, R. L., & Wilhelm, J. A. (1990). The structure of cockpit management attitudes. *Journal of Applied Psychology, 75*, 682–690.

Guzzo, R. A., & Salas, E. (1995). *Team effectiveness and decision making in organizations*. San Francisco, CA: Jossey-Bass.

Guzzo, R. A., Yost, P. R., Campbell, R. J., & Shea, J. P. (1994). Potency in groups: Articulating the construct. *British Journal of Social Psychology, 32*, 87–106.

Hackman, J. R. (1987). The design of work teams. In J. W. Lorsch (Ed.), *Handbook of organizational behavior* (pp. 315–342). Englewood Cliffs, NJ: Prentice-Hall.

Hackman, J. R. (1990). *Groups that work (and those that don't): Creating conditions for effective teamwork*. San Francisco, CA: Jossey-Bass.

Hackman, J. R. (1998). Why teams don't work. In R. S. Tindale (Ed.), *Theory and research on small groups: Social psychological applications to social issues* (Vol. 4, pp. 245–267). New York: Plenum Press.

Hackman, J. R., & Morris, C. G. (1975). Group tasks, group interaction process, and group performance effectiveness: A review and proposed integration. *Advances in Experimental Social Psychology* 45–99.

Hall, J., & Watson, W. H. (1970). The effects of a normative intervention on group decision-making performance. *Human Relations, 23*, 299–317.

Hardin, C. D., & Higgins, E. T. (1996). Shared reality: How social verification makes the subjective objective. In R. M. Sorrentino & E. T. Higgins (Eds.), *Handbook of motivation and cognition, Vol. 3: The interpersonal context* (pp. 28–84). New York: Guilford.

Harvey, C. M., & Koubek, R. J. (1998). Toward a model of distributed engineering collaboration. Paper presented at the 23rd International Conference on Computers & Industrial Engineering, Chicago, March 29-April 1.

Helmreich, R. L., Foushee, H. C., Benson, R., & Russini, W. (1986). Cockpit resource management: Exploring the attitude-performance linkage. *Aviation, Space, & Environmental Medicine, 57*, 1198–1200.

Hendrick, C. (1987). *Review of personality and social psychology*. Newbury Park, CA: Sage.

Hinsz, V. B., Tindale, R. S., & Vollrath, D. A. (1997). The emerging conceptualization of groups as information processors. *Psychological Bulletin, 121*, 43–64.

Hogg, M. A. (1987). Social identity theory and group cohesiveness. In J. Turner (Ed.), *Rediscovering the social group: A self-categorization theory* (pp. 89–116). Oxford, England: Basil Blackwell.

Hogg, M. A. (1993). Group cohesiveness: A critical review and some new directions. In W. Stroebe & M. Hewstone (Eds.), *European review of social psychology* (Vol. 4, pp. 85–111). London: Wiley.

Hollingshead, A. B. (1996). The rank-order effect in group decision making. *Organizational Behavior & Human Decision Processes, 68*, 181–193.

Humphrey, R. (1985). How work roles influence perception: Structural-cognitive processes and organizational behavior. *American Sociological Review, 50*, 242–252.

Ickes, W., & Gonzalez, R. (1994). "Social" cognition and social cognition: From the subjective to the intersubjective. *Small Group Research, 25*, 294–315.

Jehn, K. A., & Shah, P. P. (1997). Interpersonal relationships and task performance: An examination of mediation processes in friendship and acquaintance groups. *Journal of Personality and Social Psychology, 72*, 775–790.

Johnson-Laird, P. N. (1983). *Mental models: Toward a cognitive science of language, inference, and consciousness*. Cambridge, MA: Harvard University Press.

Jones, G. R., & George, J. M. (1998). The experience and evolution of trust: Implications for cooperation and teamwork. *Academy of Management Review, 23*, 531–546.

Kimmel, M. J. (1980). Effects of trust, aspiration, and gender on negotiation tactics. *Journal of Personality and Social Psychology, 38*, 9–22.

Kleinman, D. L., & Serfaty, D. (1989). Team performance assessment in distributed decision-making. In R. Gibson, J. P. Kincaid, & B. Goldiez (Eds.), *Proceedings of the Interactive Networked Simulation for Training Conference* (pp. 22–27). Orlando, FL: Naval Training System Center.

Klimoski, R., & Mohammed, S. (1994). Team mental model: Construct or metaphor? *Journal of Management, 20*, 403–437.

Kozlowski, S. W. J., & Salas, E. (1997). A multilevel organizational systems approach for the implementation and transfer of training. In J. K. Ford, S. W. J. Kozlowski, K. Kraiger, E. Salas, & M. S. Teachout (Eds.), *Improving training effectiveness in work organizations* (pp. 247–290). Hillsdale, NJ: Lawrence Erlbaum Associates.

Larson, J. R., & Christensen, C. (1993). Groups as problem-solving units: Toward a new meaning of social cognition. *British Journal of Social Psychology, 32*, 5–30.

Lee, F. (1997). When the going gets tough, do the tough ask for help? Help seeking and power motivation in organizations. *Organizational Behavior & Human Decision Processes, 72*, 336–363.

Levine, J. M., Bogart, L. M., & Zdaniuk, B. (1996). Impact of anticipated group membership on cognition. In R. M. Sorrentino & E. T. Higgins (Eds.), *Handbook of motivation and cognition: The interpersonal context* (Vol. 3, pp. 531–569). New York: Guilford.

Levine, J. M., & Moreland, R. L. (1990). Progress in small group research. *Annual Review of Psychology, 41*, 585–634.

Levine, J. L., Resnick, L. B., & Higgins, E. T. (1993). Social foundations of cognition. *Annual Review of Psychology, 44*, 585–612.

Levine, J. M., & Russo, E. (1995). Impact of anticipated interaction on information acquisition. *Social Cognition, 13*, 293–317.

Liang, D., Moreland, R., & Argote, L. (1995). Group versus individual training and group performance: The mediating factor of transactive memory. *Personality & Social Psychology Bulletin, 21*, 384–393.

Maier, N. R. F. (1963). *Problem solving discussions and conferences: Leadership methods and skills.* New York: McGraw-Hill.

Moreland, R. L., Levine, J. M., & Wingert, M. L. (1996). Creating the ideal group: Composition effects at work. In E. H. Witte & J. H. Davis (Eds.), *Understanding group behavior: Small group processes and interpersonal relations* (Vol. 2, pp. 11–35). Mahwah, NJ: Lawrence Erlbaum Associates.

Mullen, B. (1987). Self-attention theory: The effects of group composition on the individual. In B. Mullen & R. Goethals (Eds.), *Theories of group behavior* (pp. 125–146). New York: Springer-Verlag.

Mullen, B., & Copper, C. (1994). The relation between group cohesiveness and performance: An integration. *Psychological Bulletin, 115*, 210–227.

Nerkar, A. A., McGrath, R. G., & MacMillan, I. C. (1996). Three facets of satisfaction and their influence on the performance of innovation teams. *Journal of Business Venturing, 11*, 167–188.

Newell, A., & Simon, H. A. (1972). *Human problem solving.* New Jersey: Prentice-Hall.

Niehoff, B. P., Enz, C. A., & Grover, R. A. (1990). The impact of top management actions on employee attitudes and perceptions. *Group and Organization Studies, 15*, 337–352.

Nieva, V. F., Fleishman, E. A., & Reick, A. (1978). *Team dimensions: Their identity, their measurement, and their relationships* (Tech. Rep. No. DAH19-78-C-0001). Washington, DC: Advanced Research Resources Organizations.

Orasanu, J. (1990). *Shared mental models and crew performance.* Cognitive Science Laboratory Report #46. Princeton, NJ: Princeton University.

Orasanu, J., & Salas, E. (1993). Team decision making in complex environments. In G. Klein, J. Orasanu, R. Calderwood, & C. E. Zsambok (Eds.), *Decision making in action: Models and methods* (pp. 327–345). Norwood, NJ: Ablex.

Osborne, A. F. (1957). *Applied imagination.* New York: Scribner's.

Paskevich, D. M., Brawley, L. R., Dorsch, K. D., & Widmeyer, W. N. (1999). Relationship between collective efficacy and team cohesion: Conceptual and measurement issues. *Group Dynamics, 3*, 210–222.

Rouse, W. B., Cannon-Bowers, J. A., & Salas, E. (1992). The role of mental models in team performance in complex systems. *IEEE Transactions on Systems, Man, and Cybernetics, 22*, 1296–1308.

Salas, E., & Cannon-Bowers, J. A. (2000). The anatomy of team training. In S. Tobias & J. D. Fletcher (Eds.), Training and Retraining: A handbook for business, industry, government, and the military (pp. 312–335). New York: Macmillan Reference.

Salas, E., Cannon-Bowers, J. A., & Johnston, J. H. (1997). How can you turn a team of experts into an expert team?: Emerging training strategies. In C. Zsambok & G. Klein (Eds.), Naturalistic decision making (pp. 359–370). Hillsdale, NJ: Lawrence Erlbaum Associates.

Salas, E., Dickinson, T. L., Converse, S. A., & Tannenbaum, S. I. (1992). Toward an understanding of team performance and training. In R. W. Swezey & E. Salas (Eds.), Teams: Their training and performance (pp. 3–29). Norwood, NJ: Ablex.

Savoie, E. J. (1998). Tapping the power of teams. In R. S. Tindale (Ed.), Theory and research on small groups (pp. 229–244). New York: Plenum.

Serfaty, D., Entin, E., & Johnston, J. H. (1998). Team adaptation and coordination training. In J. A. Cannon-Bowers & E. Salas (Eds.), Making decisions under stress: Implications for individual and team training (pp. 221–245). Washington, DC: American Psychological Association.

Shure, G. H., Rogers, M. S., Larsen, I. M., & Tassone, J. (1962). Group planning and task effectiveness. Sociometry, 25, 263–282.

Smith-Jentsch, Kraiger, K., Cannon-Bowers, J. A., & Salas, E. (2000). Familiarity breeds teamwork: A case for training teammate-specific competencies. Unpublished manuscript.

Stasser, G., Stewart, D. D., & Wittenbaum, G. M. (1995). Expert roles and information exchange during discussion: The importance of knowing who knows what. Journal of Experimental Social Psychology, 31, 244–265.

Steiner, I. D. (1972). Group processes and productivity. New York: Academic Press.

Stout, R. J., Cannon-Bowers, J. A., & Salas, E. (1996). The role of shared mental models in developing team situational awareness: Implications for training. Training Research Journal, 2, 85–116.

Stout, R. J., Cannon-Bowers, J. A., Salas, E., & Milanovich, D. M. (1999). Planning, shared mental models, and coordinated performance: An empirical link is established. Human Factors, 41, 61–71.

Sundstrom, E., de Meuse, K. P., & Futrell, D. (1990). Work teams: Applications and effectiveness. American Psychologist, 45, 120–133.

Swezey, R. W., & Salas, E. (Eds.). (1992). Teams: Their training and performance. Norwood, NJ: Ablex.

Thompson, L., & DeHarpport, T. (1998). Relationships, goal incompatibility, and communal orientation in negotiations. Basic & Applied Social Psychology, 20, 33–44.

Urban, J. M., Weaver, J. L., Bowers, C. A., & Rhodenizer, L. (1996). Effects of workload and structure on team processes and performance: Implications for complex team decision making. Human Factors, 38, 300–310.

Volpe, C. E., Cannon-Bowers, J. A., Salas, E., & Spector, P. (1996). The impact of cross-training on team functioning. Human Factors, 38, 87–100.

Wegner, D. (1987). Transactive memory: A contempory analysis of the group mind. In B. Mullen & G. R. Goethals (Eds.), Theories of group behavior (pp. 185–208). New York: Springer-Verlag.

Whitney, K. (1994). Improving group task performance: The role of group goals and group efficacy. Human Performance, 7, 55–78.

Wittenbaum, G. M., & Stasser, G. (1996). Management of information in small groups. In J. L. Nye & A. M. Brower (Eds.), What's social about social cognition? Research on socially shared cognition in small groups (pp. 3–28). Thousand Oaks, CA: Sage Publications.

Wittenbaum, G. M., Stasser, G., & Merry, C. (1996). Tacit coordination in anticipation of small group task completion. Journal of Experimental Social Psychology, 32, 129–152.

Wittenbaum, G. M., Vaughan, S. I., & Stasser, G. (1998). Coordination in task-performing groups. In R. S. Tindale & L. Heath (Eds.), Theory and research on small groups: Social psychological applications to social issues (Vol. 4, pp. 177–204). New York: Plenum.

Worchel, S., Coutant-Sassic, D., & Grossman, M. (1991). A developmental approach to group dynamics: A model and illustrative research. In. S. Worchel and W. Wood (Eds.), Group process and productivity (pp. 181–202). Newbury Park, CA: Sage.

Zaccaro, S., Blair, V., Peterson, C., & Zazanis, M. (1995). Collective efficacy. In J. E. Maddux (Ed.), *Self-efficacy, adaptation, and adjustment: Theory, research, and application* (pp. 305–328). New York: Plenum.

Zajonc, R. B. (1960). The process of cognitive tuning in communication. *Journal of Abnormal & Social Psychology, 61*, 159–167.

Zdaniuk, B., & Levine, J. M. (1996). Anticipated interaction and thought generation: The role of faction size. *British Journal of Social Psychology, 35*, 201–218.

15

Virtual Teams: Implications for E-Leadership and Team Development

Bruce J. Avolio, Surinder Kahai,
Rex Dumdum, and
Nagaraj Sivasubramaniam
Binghamton University

There is an ongoing transformation in organizations toward developing comprehensive team-based systems (Townsend, DeMarie, & Hendrickson, 1996; Ulrich, 1998). Indeed, for many organizations today, teams have become the primary unit of performance (Katzenbach & Smith, 1993; Mohrman, Cohen, & Mohrman, 1995). Some of the dramatic and ongoing transformations in organizational design and structure have been made possible through the availability of collaborative information technologies. These technologies have enabled organizations to rapidly form teams that are not restricted by geography, time, or organizational boundaries. Advances in computing and telecommunications technologies have allowed many organizations to deploy teams consisting of members at distant locations and, in some instances, other organizations to work together both synchronously and asynchronously to accomplish their tasks. These new teams have been called *virtual teams* (Lipnack & Stamps, 1997; Townsend et al., 1996; Townsend, DeMarie, & Hendrickson, 1998).

Ironically, while many organizations are still struggling with the best ways to configure work done in face-to-face teams, they must now address a new level of complexity in the form of virtual teams and organizations comprised of members from different cultures, time zones, and in some instances organizations. Going virtual is likely to be a key challenge for organizations in the near future. Trends toward going virtual are likely to accelerate over the next 5 to 10 years as new information technology and global expansion rapidly transform the way organizations do business (Boudreau, Loch, Robey, & Straud, 1998).

The interest in virtual teams has grown exponentially over the last several years attributable in part to the rapid globalization of world markets, the emergence of e-commerce, and the growth in mergers and acquisitions (Boudreau et al., 1998; Hughes, Ginnett, & Curphy, 1999; Lipnack & Stamps, 1997). The interest in virtual teams has also been fueled by a general belief that this type of organizational architecture may have greater productive potential than using more conventional team structures (Townsend et al., 1998).

The shift toward using virtual teams in organizations raises several fundamental questions: How do interpersonal perceptions form in virtual teams? What are their implications for trust formation and performance? How do leadership and information technology interact to influence trust formation and performance in virtual teams? How will early impressions of leadership at a distance affect each team member's efficacy to perform? Does the emergence of leadership in this context parallel what has been observed in teams working face-to-face? How does the leadership in a virtual team learn to understand and develop its members' needs, show consideration, inspire, create innovative thinking, and set an example for members to follow? What type of virtual or "e-leadership" will have the most positive impact early on in a team's formation of trust versus later in the team's development cycle? Do such teams need to meet face-to-face for leadership to develop at all, or can leadership evolve at a distance solely through the use of advanced information technology?

The formation of virtual teams provides an interesting platform for examining social cognitive processing in organizations. For example, the creation of virtual teams will not necessarily eliminate the impact that stereotypes have on how members in a team perceive and treat one another. Because many virtual teams are comprised of members from different cultures, one needs to understand how differences across cultures in how team members perceive one another can affect how team members build trust, efficacy, and ultimately the team's performance.

Addressing all of the questions presented is important to harnessing and integrating the collective intelligence, creativity, and know-how of human resources working in virtual teams (Hughes et al., 1999; Tapscott, 1996). Many of the answers to these questions may parallel what has already been learned about human perception and interactions in face-to-face teams. However, these questions have gained new relevance because they have never been examined with a focus on the type of human interactions in organizations that now occur on a daily basis in virtual teams. Hence, in addition to a new set of questions on how to best use this new technology to enhance human interactions, many traditional questions concerning human perception and social cognition need to be revisited and reexamined in this new context.

We begin by defining what constitutes a virtual team and how such teams differ from and are similar to face-to-face teams. This discussion is followed by an examination of how trust contributes to the development of virtual teams and their performance. Following this, a model linking leadership and technology to the development of trust is presented. This model describes the core component processes that are expected to affect the development of virtual teams along with several key propositions to help guide future research projects on this topic.

VIRTUAL TEAMS

Currently, there is no common "working definition" of what constitutes a virtual team. Thus, we begin with what constitutes a team using Katzenbach and Smith's (1989) operational definition. We then extend their definition of a team by embedding the team in a virtual context. According to Katzenbach and Smith (1993), a team is a small number of people with complementary skills who are committed to a common purpose, performance goals, and approach for which they hold themselves mutually accountable. Embedding teams in a virtual context typically results in some members being situated in dispersed locations. These dispersed locations can be in the same building, in different buildings, in different cities, and in many cases located in different organizations and countries.

Interactions that occur among virtual team members primarily take place electronically. These electronic communication processes increasingly rely on multiple communication channels that involve text, graphic, audio, and video communication. For example, one can now conduct a team meeting from different locations and see and hear each member's input, work jointly on an electronic white board to develop some model, and send text notes to each other via e-mail.

Virtual team members typically interact with each other both synchronously and asynchronously. Synchronous interaction occurs when team members communicate at the same time, as in chat sessions or desktop video conferencing. Asynchronous interaction occurs when team members communicate at different times, as in e-mail or bulletin boards.

Virtual teams are frequently quite fluid in terms of their membership with individuals joining and leaving teams very rapidly. Also, in many organizations, employees can belong to several virtual teams simultaneously. Finally, the standard process for working together has usually been based on a collaborative form of leadership (Jarvenpaa & Leidner, 1998; Kimball & Eunice, 1999).

There are numerous examples of virtual teams that have emerged in the last several years. Many of the software teams used by companies like Microsoft work 24 hours-a-day. How is this possible? It is possible when team members are geographically located in the United States, United Kingdom, India, and the Pacific Rim. These virtual teams pass software around the globe, building on each other's products 24 hours-a-day. Such geographically dispersed teams rely almost exclusively on technology to support their interactions (Kimball & Eunice, 1999).

Another example of a virtual team is a Computer Emergency Response Team (CERT), which first began as a concept, nearly a decade ago at Carnegie Mellon University. The primary goal of a CERT is to prevent or address attacks on the Internet. The main product of a CERT is to inform Internet users of an impending attack, or what to do if an attack has already occurred on the Internet. The composition of such teams is typically based on the particular challenges being confronted by the team. Members can be pooled from different locations and organizations around the globe.

A third and increasingly more common example is the virtual manufacturing team. Such teams are often comprised of some combination of members from design, development, production, marketing, suppliers, and customers. The team generally has a specific project to work on, with a time schedule and project deliverables. Many of these teams are comprised of members from multiple organizations who work in a strategic partnership to design and develop new products.

In sum, virtual teamwork is goal-oriented, knowledge intensive work, oftentimes undertaken by individuals separated by geography, organizational affiliation, and culture (Kimball & Eunice, 1999). If we consider teams along a continuum, at one end of that continuum are teams that come from the same organization, same location and interact face-to-face on a regular basis. At the other extreme end, are teams of people who come from different organizations, geographical regions, cultures, and time zones, and are interacting via computer-mediated technology.

A virtual team has many of the same challenges as a face-to-face team. Virtual teams have the challenge of building norms of conduct, a common mission, cohesion, alignment, appreciating each member's ideas and talents, developing trust in team members, and developing each other's capacity to take on additional challenges and opportunities. However, because virtual teams typically have much less opportunity to interact with each other face-to-face, the challenge of developing a high-performing team may be much more difficult in the virtual team context. For example, whether any team is virtual, without a common belief in what's important to work on, it will have difficulty developing the synergy required to be successful.

Virtual teams, like face-to-face teams, must develop a common sense or shared model of how to work together effectively, how to optimally exchange information, how to evaluate the team's results, and how to continue to advance the development of its members. Such shared mental models once established, can provide a virtual team with a sense of coherence concerning its collective expectations, intentions, and beliefs. The shared mental model can provide a basis for understanding how to work with each other effectively and ultimately impact the development of trust that team members have in each other.

The development of a shared mental model about what the team is and what it does requires that team members learn about each other's background, intentions, beliefs, aspirations, and goals. The type of learning that takes place involves the following: how members of the team perceive the challenges confronting the team; what norms are acceptable and unacceptable behavior in the team; what members expect of each other in terms of each other's contribution to the team's work; what members perceive as being their responsibilities for developing each other; how the leadership of the team is supposed to guide its interactions together, and so forth.

Given the absence of face-to-face interactions, a fundamental question is how does a virtual team develop a "shared" mental model that provides the framework for optimizing its interpersonal interactions? Without a shared mental model of expectations, it will be difficult if not impossible for virtual teams to build sufficient trust among its members to exchange the necessary information that is required to address the team's important challenges and objectives (Coutu, 1998; Lipnack & Stamps, 1997).

The development of a shared mental model also provides the cognitive framework for team members to create a joint definition of the social situation in which they are embedded. The challenge to developing a common mental model is true of all teams, however in the global virtual team context, the platform for interactions offers some new and interesting challenges for developing a shared mental model of what constitutes one's team that needs to be explored in future research.

INTERPERSONAL REQUIREMENTS
OF VIRTUAL TEAMS

Virtual teams must create the "gel" or sense of belonging that provides the basis for synergy and optimum exchange of information among diverse members (Handy, 1995; Melymuka, 1997). This is also true of teams that work face-to-face but perhaps is more critical with virtual teams because members are situated in multiple locations and therefore lack social and nonverbal cues; this can slow down the formation of deeper interpersonal relations among team members (Weisband & Atwater, 1999). Some evidence already indicates that teams that interact virtually report their members have less attraction to each other, or less of a gel that holds them together (Kimball & Eunice, 1999). Kimball and Eunice note that a common problem with virtual teams is that their conversations deal less with relationship building and more with logistics and task requirements. Over time, a lack of attention to building the interpersonal processes associated with effective team development may lead to less effective interactions and exchanges of information (Warkentin, Sayeed, & Hightower, 1997). As noted above, without an adequate exchange of information a virtual team has little chance of building trust and being successful with either its most basic or more challenging tasks (Townsend et al., 1996).

Where team members are unable to freely exchange information, they will have difficulty developing a common image in their mind of what is required, what their roles are, and how they must work together to fulfill their task and mission requirements (Cannon-Bowers, Salas, & Converse, 1993). Developing a shared mental model of the task and what constitutes effective teamwork is important for achieving coordination and synergy among team members. Where virtual teams are able to develop a shared mental model concerning mission, requirements, and responsibilities, we expect they would be more capable of exchanging information, learning from each other, and executing tasks.

If team members are unable to freely exchange information in a virtual team context, then they will be less capable of developing interpersonal perceptions that provide the basis for trust formation. Thus, how information about the team, its membership's capabilities, and the work is exchanged can affect the conditions for trust formation, which, in turn, can affect subsequent interactions and ultimately team performance.

Here is where leadership can have a significant impact on virtual team development. The leadership in a virtual team can help facilitate the establishment of norms and expectations to guide initial and subsequent interactions. For instance, transactional leadership can help to clarify what is acceptable and unacceptable behavior in the team, as well as what the goals are to be achieved (Avolio, 1999). Transactional leadership of the team can support progress toward goals by providing reinforcement and encouragement to team members.

Through the use of transactional leadership, virtual teams can build a history of interactions, which develops knowledge about each other and a base for members to build initial levels of trust. McKnight, Cummings, and Chervany (1998) refer to this form of trust building as being knowledge-based, which then becomes an integral part of the team's shared mental model of expectations of one another. As such, the leadership of the team creates a set of expectations for interaction that produce a historical repository of data on the team that can be incorporated into each team member's image of the team and the trust they are willing to assign to each other.

We define trust here as, "the willingness of a team member to be vulnerable to the actions of other team members based on expectations that the others will perform a particular action important to the trustor, irrespective of the ability to monitor or control other team members" (Mayer, Davis, & Schoorman, 1995, p. 712). Trust forms the glue that holds relationships together over time, distance, and diverse cultures. Without a sufficient level of trust, team members will expend time and energy protecting, checking and inspecting each other as opposed to collaborating to provide value-added ideas (Cooper & Sawaf, 1996).

Building trust in virtual teams may be even more critical to the team's development versus face-to-face teams, because direct supervision and monitoring is much more difficult in the virtual team context. Yet, given the importance of trust to the development of teams in general, there has been only a handful of studies that have directly examined how trust forms in virtual teams (e.g., Jarvenpaa, Knoll, & Leidner, 1998).

In Fig. 15.1, a conceptual model of virtual team development is presented as a framework for the remainder of our discussion in this chapter. This model is offered to help focus future research on several core components that comprise the development of virtual teams. These core components include leadership, the nature of information exchange among team members, and trust. We take the position here that leadership can influence the

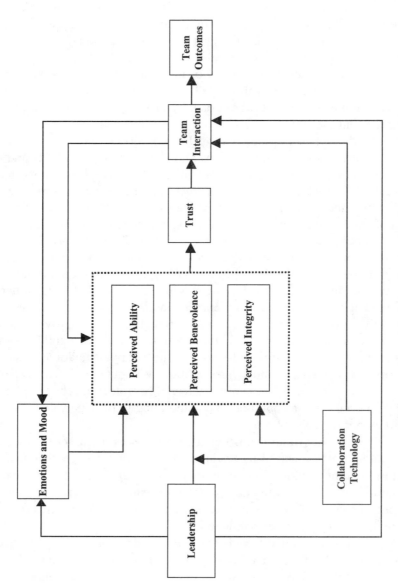

FIG. 15.1. A model of virtual team development.

conditions for initial trust and interactions that will likely affect the level of trust, interaction, and performance of the team.

Because virtual teams are connected via information technology, another issue to be addressed and presented in the model is how technology can affect the type of interactions virtual teams have and their impact on the development of trust. Because of space limitations, we focus our discussion on the effects of richness of information technology on trust, interaction, and team performance. We begin our discussion by operationally defining the construct of trust in virtual teams, followed by an examination of how leadership and technology affect trust formation, interaction, and performance in virtual teams.

THE EVOLUTION OF TRUST IN VIRTUAL TEAMS

Because virtual teams are very dynamic entities in terms of membership and location, more traditional conceptions of trust need to be expanded to understand how such teams form and function in organizations. Our discussion of trust in virtual teams builds on the work of Jones and George (1998), Mayer et al. (1995), Meyerson, Weick, and Kramer (1996), and Lewicki and Bunker (1996). We add to these discussions, how leadership and collaborative information technologies affect trust formation in virtual teams.

Meyerson et al. (1996) examined the formation of trust in teams that had limited interaction history. According to Meyerson et al., trust in temporary systems is not simply conventional trust scaled down to brief encounters among group members. Although it may represent that form of trust in part, they argued that trust in temporary teams is a "unique form of collective perception" that is based on broad expectations imported from other settings. These expectations then form the basis for broad categorizations that help identify group membership. For example, as a member of a virtual team, one can learn the experience and skill sets that other members bring to the team. Electrical engineers have certain skill sets that members assume are present at the outset. Added to these skills, the engineers on one's team may have extensive experience building the type of equipment that the team is working on together. Their educational background and experience may provide sufficient information to categorize them as "experts one can rely on" to build the team's product.

Alternatively, in a culturally diverse team some of the same electrical engineers described above may come from a third-world culture. For members coming from a more advanced culture, the engineers who are from the third world may be stereotyped as not having "state-of-the-art" knowledge. Such categorizations can lead to lowering expectations for their contribution to performance and trust in their abilities.

The knowledge of team members' education or experience can provide a basis for a more "depersonalized" form of trust building that has been called *conditional trust* (Jones & George, 1998). Conditional trust is based on a contractual or transactional model whereby trust in others is contingent upon certain conditions being satisfied. For example, all other things being equal, if members of a newly formed virtual team have the skills required to do their tasks, then the conditions for trust among members may be present to meet its goals.

Building on our example, conditional trust can be assigned to members of the team because of their expertise, credentials, and roles that they've imported into the team. Conditional trust requires that there are clear expectations of what is required of team members. Then, the expectation of who is qualified to be a team member provides the categorical boundaries in which trust can be assigned to new team members. Hence, credentials and expertise imported into the team can form the basis upon which one member knowing little else about another can conditionally trust the person to "get the task done."

Meyerson et al. (1996) argued that virtual teams during formation operate under an assumption that the selection of its members was based on a prespecified set of qualifications. Knowing the set of a priori qualifications provides a basis for trust formation as members "belong to a group" that presumably has the core competencies to work together. In this way, the prior history of members can be incorporated into the team's early development, helping to build conditional trust in other team members. With such a prespecified set of qualifications, the stereotype of third-world team members may be overridden with the idea that they were picked to work on the team because of their knowledge and expertise regardless of where they came from in terms of geographical location.

Social identity theory provides another basis for explaining the formation of conditional trust (Jarvenpaa & Leidner, 1998). In a virtual team context, initial impressions may be formed on criteria that are different than in the more typical face-to-face interactions. For example, if interactions among team members are initially founded on text based e-mail messages, then one's physical appearance, age, gender, and race are of little consequence to the initial impressions formed by team members. Thus knowing a member's educational or experiential background may provide the basis for categorizing team members as "acceptable" or "unacceptable." Building on the example mentioned above, if all team members are electrical engineers, then they can more quickly categorize each other's characteristics if they perceive members as being similar to themselves. These similarities initially determine the boundaries of people who can and cannot be trusted (Brewer, 1981). In other words, the members are part of a group that each member can relate to or perhaps have had some history of interactions.

In contrast, where members come from very different disciplines or cultures, it becomes more difficult to identify with each other and to classify each other's behavior. In this situation, the identity of group members may be formed on the basis of the leadership of the team highlighting the team's common purpose or mission. Specifically, although they all stem from diverse and perhaps unique backgrounds, the leader can emphasize that the team exists to accomplish a particular mission. The mission may provide an initial basis for identification, which team members can then build on as they get to know each other's unique strengths and capabilities.

Once initial similarities are identified, the other attributes associated with group membership may be invoked affecting how members ultimately perceive each other. To the extent that membership is positively valued in the group that is being used for categorization, a positive impact on trust formation is likely to be seen.

Depending on the nature and quality of repeated interactions within the team, conditional trust evolves into unconditional or developmental trust (Jones & George, 1998; Lewicki & Bunker, 1996). As intentions and capabilities are uncovered through repeated interactions, and those intentions and capabilities are viewed as positive, unconditional trust is formed among team members. Unconditional trust once formed is commonly referred to as "trusting someone or a group of individuals without question." Shamir, House, and Arthur (1993) suggest that at the core of deeper levels of trust associated with unconditional trust, is a higher level of identification among team members. Specifically, members of a team come to identify with each other's purpose, mission, and goals resulting in a deeper level of trust, which indicates they are "all together on the inside" in working towards a common mission or vision (Avolio, 1999). Unconditional trust is formed in a work context that (a) promotes positive attitudes and positive moods and emotions, and (b) encourages the exploration of shared values (Jones & George, 1998).

How trust develops in teams is critical to understanding how to make virtual teams successful. Unfortunately, at present, there has been very little research examining how trust forms in virtual teams. Jarvenpaa and colleagues (1998) examined the development of trust in global virtual teams. The teams in their study were student teams working on class projects. One of their goals was to determine how trust was developed in virtual teams with members located in different geographical regions and cultures. They examined how perception of team members' benevolence, integrity, and ability affected the level of trust in 75 temporary, global teams that interacted over a 2-month period.

Jarvenpaa and her colleagues found that contrary to their initial expectations, trust developed rather quickly in global virtual teams without any face-to-face interactions. However, the trust that was formed was not very deep, or as described previously—unconditional—and had to be continually reinforced with task-related communications that maintained a clear sense of what the team's purpose, responsibility, and tasks were with regard to their projects.

Maznevski and Chudoba (2000) also investigated the development of trust in global virtual teams. Their data were collected over nearly 2 years and were based on extensive observations of global virtual teams interacting around work projects. Maznevski and Chudoba reported that teams with stronger and more consistent shared expectations needed less interaction and information to make decisions over time. The results regarding shared expectations point to the importance that leadership can play in developing virtual teams. Specifically, leadership in teams is seen as a core process that builds shared expectations upon which team members can then build trust in each other (Avolio, 1999; Bass, 1998; Sivasubramaniam, Murry, Avolio, & Jung, in press).

For example, Sivasubramaniam et al. (in press) demonstrated that undergraduate teams that exhibited more collective transformational leadership within the first 3 to 4 weeks of their formation exhibited higher levels of group potency a month later, as well as higher performance 3 months after the team's formation. The more transformational led teams spent time clarifying their mission, setting expectations and norms, understanding each other's needs, questioning each other's ideas to be more creative and reinforcing each other's efforts. Moreover, the type of collective leadership that formed in these student teams within the first 3 weeks was highly predictive of the leadership observed 3 months later. Teams that were transformational early on in their development evaluated themselves as transformational 3 months later. Whereas, teams that initially were more passive or corrective in leadership orientation, evaluated themselves as passive 3 months later. These latter teams also had the lowest levels of performance on student projects.

In the following section, we examine more deeply how leadership style can contribute to the development of trust in virtual teams, the type of interactions observed, and ultimately the team's performance.

EFFECT OF LEADERSHIP STYLE ON TRUST DEVELOPMENT IN VIRTUAL TEAMS

One of the core issues underlying our discussion of trust is how a geographically dispersed team can achieve the synergy that makes the team greater than the sum of its parts (Melymuka, 1997). Specifically, our challenge is to understand how virtual team members can "work out task interdependencies, resolve issues involving tradeoffs among various perspectives, and develop solutions and approaches that build upon the diversity of expertise" to accomplish its collective goals (Mohrman et al., 1995, p. 64). What little we do know about virtual teams indicates that an important component of building synergy and trust involves leadership and the use of collaborative information technologies with virtual teams (Jarvenpaa et al., 1998; Lipnack & Stamps, 1997; Townsend et al., 1998).

Systematic research examining the interaction effects of leadership and collaborative information technologies on the formation of trust in virtual teams is almost nonexistent. Figure 15.1 summarizes the effects of leadership and collaborative technology on the development of trust in virtual teams. The model extends the work of Mayer et al. (1995), as well as Jones and George (1998) on the evolution of trust in teams by adding leadership and collaboration technology as important determinants of trust formation, interactions among team members, and the outcomes produced by virtual teams.

According to the *interactionist model* proposed by Jones and George (1998), trust is a dynamic experience in which values, attitudes, moods, and emotions interact to produce an overall state of trust or distrust. Specific attitudes involved in the formation of trust are perceptions of other members' ability, benevolence, and integrity (Mayer et al., 1995). Ability refers to the group of skills that enable an individual being trusted (i.e., a trustee) to be competent in a certain domain. Benevolence represents a positive orientation of a trustee towards the trustor, whereby the trustee wants to do good to the trustor by showing interpersonal care and concern. Integrity refers to a trustee's adherence to a set of principles that the trustor finds acceptable. Emotions and mood refer to feelings of individuals as they go about their daily activities. Emotions are intense feelings that interrupt on-going cognitive processes and behaviors, which are tied to particular events or circumstances. Moods are less intense but pervasive feelings that are not linked to any particular events or circumstances (Jones & George, 1998).

Leadership contributes to the formation of trust by influencing initial perceptions of ability, benevolence, and integrity as well as the emotions and mood expressed by the group. Collaboration technology may also influence the formation of conditional trust by influencing the group's perceptions of other members' ability, benevolence, and integrity. As individuals interact via technology, their experiences with each other are expected to shape their moods and emotions as well as their perceptions about or attitudes toward each other. Over time, the nature of interactions can be instrumental to the development of unconditional trust or distrust in others. Leadership style and collaboration technology are both expected to influence the nature of interaction that evolves and subsequent levels of trust that will be achieved in virtual teams. We will limit our focus here on leadership to the effects of transformational and transactional leadership on virtual team development (see Bass, 1998 and Avolio, 1999 for a more detailed discussion of these styles).

Effects of Transformational and Transactional Leadership on Trust and Team Interactions

In the model presented in Fig. 15.1, we expect both transactional and trans-formational leadership to affect perceptions of other team members' ability, benevolence, and integrity both directly as well as indirectly through influ-ence on the team's pattern of exchanges, interactions, or both, over time. Transactional leaders use goal setting and contingent rewards to motivate followers to achieve agreed upon levels of performance. Their exchanges of information revolve around the clarification of task objectives, such as who is responsible for a task, who is accountable and who determines the goals that are desired. Transactional leaders link the goals once achieved by group members to appropriate levels of recognition and rewards. Such leaders are expected to contribute to the early formation of trust by demon-strating that members are fair with each other and consistent in working toward stated objectives and goals. As such, transactional leadership can contribute to initial perceptions of member integrity and the formation of conditional trust.

Compared to transactional leadership, transformational leadership is likely to be associated with perceptions of higher ability and benevolence among members in a virtual team and, therefore, a higher level of trust among members that was labeled unconditional trust in the preceding section. Transformational leaders augment transactional leader behaviors by instilling confidence among team members about their collective ability to accomplish the team's challenges and goals (Bass & Avolio, 1994; Sosik, Avolio, & Kahai, 1997). By encouraging team members to work as a team and by helping team members see the importance of transcending their own self-interest for the sake of achieving the team's objectives, a transformational leader is likely to instill greater confidence among team members about other members' benevolence.

Transformational leaders use individualized consideration when encouraging team members to consider the input provided by every member of the team and its relevance to the task at hand. They promote comments that encourage an understanding and deeper appreciation of input provided by each team member. They encourage interactions that indicate peer support, and hence perceptions of benevolence, while also emphasizing the collective action that is needed to achieve exemplary performance (Kramer, Brewer, & Hanna, 1996). By promoting intellectual stimulation, which encourages a questioning of assumptions and a reframing of traditional thinking, a transformational leader can increase the level of information exchange among team members. Increases in information exchange among members can reveal information about other members' ability, benevolence, and integrity (Jarvenpaa et al., 1998), forming unconditional trust and ultimately higher levels of collective performance.

A transformational leader is also likely to influence perceptions of team members' ability, benevolence, and integrity through his or her influence on team members' emotions and mood. The use of individualized consideration is likely to promote positive emotions and moods among team members in that the leader is showing concern for each member's needs and aspirations. Positive emotions and moods can also result through inspirationally motivating messages, which provide meaning and challenge to team members' work together.

By framing the importance of the team's task or mission, a transformational leader can help build member identification that the challenges confronting the team can be successfully addressed. Such leaders enhance the significance of the work in the eyes of team members. They demonstrate how each member has the requisite ability to make a difference in achieving the team's goals, enhancing the individual and collective efficacy of the team. By setting a positive role model and establishing high expectations, the transformational leader of a virtual team can enhance each team member's sense of collective identity and in turn the quality of member interactions. According to Jones and George (1998), by creating positive emotions and moods within the team, members will more readily develop positive perceptions about each other's ability, benevolence, and integrity, ultimately resulting in greater trust among team members.

We expect that transformational leadership in virtual teams will help the team identify a common sense of purpose as it creates a shared mental model of the challenges and opportunities that the team is working on. Transformational leaders create an exciting vision and articulate it to team members to develop a shared set of expectations, which provides a broad framework for interpersonal interactions. Members are reinforced for sharing their expertise and knowledge and for supporting each other to achieve the mission and vision. By providing a clear line of sight to the ultimate goals for the team, and supporting interactions that help the team to identify its strengths and weaknesses, the transformational leader is able to build a more highly developed and high performing team.

In sum, a virtual team working at a distance from each other with a transformational leader is likely to exhibit a greater number of team member comments that indicate individualized consideration, intellectual stimulation, and inspirational motivation. Transformational leadership is expected to create perceptions of higher team member ability, benevolence, and integrity both directly as well as indirectly through positive emotions and moods. Perceptions of higher ability, benevolence, and integrity promoted by a transformational leader will contribute to the formation of unconditional trust among members of a virtual team.

Effect of Collaboration Technology on Trust Formation and Team Interactions

Another factor affecting the development of trust in virtual teams is the level of media richness associated with the collaboration technology used to connect virtual team members. Media richness refers to a collaboration technology's capacity for immediate feedback, the number of cues and channels used for information, level of personalization, and language variety (Daft & Lengel, 1986).

Media richness is expected to influence trust formation by influencing the perception of ability, benevolence, and integrity. To the extent media richness is low, establishing perceptions of team member ability, benevolence, and integrity will be inhibited (Ridgeway, 1987) and, hence, formation of trust will be hindered. Furthermore, to the extent media richness is low, more in-depth interactions among team members will be inhibited (Kahai & Cooper, 1999). These less effective interactions can reduce the information about team members' ability, benevolence, and integrity, thereby hindering the formation of conditional trust.

In contrast with the views expressed above, the use of lean media for initial interactions among virtual team members may also help members categorize each other more quickly into task relevant groups. Specifically, if members are not able to identify member attributes that are irrelevant to their task (e.g., gender or race), then conditional trust may form because of the ability of team members to forgo stereotypes and classify attributes of team members that are relevant to team performance. Focusing a virtual team during its formation on member attributes essential to the team's work may be one way of mitigating stereotypes that can potentially slow down a virtual team's development and also lower its performance.

Being unaware of the typical individual cues that are present in face-to-face interactions, virtual team members using information technology low in media richness may be able to establish an initial group identity more quickly that builds conditional trust. For example, with a software design group, one can conclude that members are all engineers with a certain degree of expertise, and it is this expertise that is evident and forms the basis for conditional trust.

Finally, the absence of socio-emotional cues for teams interacting through leaner information technology media, can also enhance the salience of the team when inspirationally motivating comments by a transformational leader emphasize the team as a whole (e.g., we can create synergy by working together as a team; Lea & Spears, 1991). Making the team's collective mission more salient to its members is likely to help create a shared identity that can facilitate the formation of unconditional trust among team members (Kramer et al., 1996).

Social categories are fundamental tools for how people perceive and classify each other. Categories such as race or gender are used to quickly classify people and to assign meaning to the individual based on category membership (Operario & Fiske, this volume). By using categorization processes, people are more efficient in classifying others and in assimilating new information. However, although categorizing people into groups is a more efficient form of information processing that may create a greater sense of group identify in the initial formation of a virtual team, it may be ineffective to the degree that it minimizes important objective differences among members.

One advantage of using lean media with initial virtual team interactions is that it reduces the amount of information that needs to be processed by team members. Indeed, such media can be used to focus on the type of task relevant information that may facilitate the development of conditional trust among team members. It may also explain why global teams examined by Jarvenpaa and her colleagues that had formed trust swiftly had communications that were more relevant to the task.

Currently, the available research linking media richness to the formation of trust in virtual teams does not provide a clear basis for drawing any firm conclusions. However, there are several alternative possibilities that need to be explored in future research on this topic. First, we expect that collaborative technology that is characterized by higher media richness will be associated with the formation of conditional trust among members of a virtual team who are more homogenous in terms of member attributes. Specifically, providing team members with additional information that reinforces their similarities will serve to build higher social identification within a team and trust among its members. Alternatively, collaborative technology that is characterized by lower media richness is expected to be associated with the formation of conditional trust among members of a virtual team who are more diverse in terms of member attributes. In this context, the sharing of task-relevant knowledge can form the basis for categorization as opposed to member characteristics, which may focus members on "how different they are" versus the team's common purpose or mission. In this situation, the transactional leader can help members see what task expectations they have, their responsibilities, and their goals based on the content of the leader's communication with the team.

Transactional leaders formulate agreements and specify requirements linking each member to his or her specific responsibility. Transformational leadership builds on transaction by creating an image in team member's minds of how they can work together, what they have in common, how they can leverage their differences, and ultimately why their work is important to the organization.

In sum, at present there is no available research linking the type of media used to connect virtual team interactions and its impact on how members of the team view one another. Nor is there any available research examining how the interaction of leadership, media richness, and team composition effects the development of virtual teams. This area represents a huge opportunity for future work on virtual team development.

Effect of Team Interaction on Team Outcomes

For the purpose of illustration, this chapter defines team effectiveness and team potency as representing team outcomes in our model. Potency is defined as a group's collective belief that it can be effective (Guzzo, Yost, Campbell, & Shea, 1993). Guzzo, et al. argue that transformational leadership directly influences group potency by boosting the confidence of team members and developing in them the belief they will succeed. Several other authors have argued for a similar relationship between team leadership and potency (cf. Shamir et al., 1993), however, only one study examines the effect that collective leadership behavior of teams has on the formation of group potency and performance (Sivasubramaniam et al., in press). Sivasubramaniam et al. reported that collective transformational leadership exhibited by teams directly influenced group potency and indirectly influenced group effectiveness through group potency. Specifically, each team member rated how their team's leadership as a whole influenced team interactions. Team members rated each other using the team as the unit of analysis. For example, team members rated how often members questioned each other's assumptions on the best ways to proceed with work. They defined leadership "by" the team or collective as opposed to "of " the team by an individual.

Sivasubramaniam et al. (in press) speculated that the transformational leadership formed within the first several weeks of team interaction became the basis for subsequent team interactions over the next 3 months. Teams that rated themselves as more transformational demonstrated that they had a clearer sense of purpose and higher potency within the first 3 weeks. By showing a greater concern for each other's needs, a willingness to challenge each other's ideas, and a more positive attitude toward each other, the leadership in these teams appeared to enhance perceptions of team member ability, motivation, and ultimately competency to perform.

SOME EXTENSIONS OF THE MODEL OF VIRTUAL TEAM DEVELOPMENT

The model in Fig. 15.1 provides a top-down view of how leadership and collaborative information technology can interact to create conditional and unconditional trust in virtual teams. Leadership style can interact with collaborative technology affecting perceptions of team member ability, benevolence, and integrity. Also modeled in Fig. 15.1, is how emotion and mood affects team member perceptions of ability, benevolence, and integrity.

We now propose several possible extensions of the model presented in Fig. 15.1 that we were unable to discuss in detail in this chapter. Extensions to the model include constructs such as each team member's disposition to trust, the complexity of the task or project being undertaken, situational stability or normality, the culture of the organization, and national culture. For example, if some members of a virtual team come from cultures that are low versus high in uncertainty avoidance, then we might expect that the formation of conditional trust would be more difficult to achieve (Hofstede, 1980).

The cultural component in the model can also reflect the culture of the organization. For example, in an organization where fear pervades and people point fingers at each other for making mistakes, the formation of conditional trust will also be more difficult to establish. Both examples regarding culture highlight the importance of considering the context in which virtual teams are embedded in order to determine how trust is developed. As noted above, this embedded context also includes the level of change or situational normality confronting a team's work together. Because many virtual teams, by definition, span different work contexts and cultures, and oftentimes work on projects in rapidly changing global markets, researchers must integrate the "embedded context" into their models when attempting to explain how both transactional and transformational leadership affects the formation of trust in virtual teams.

SOME PRACTICAL IMPLICATIONS AND CONCLUSIONS

The increasing globalization of world markets will no doubt increase the prevalence of virtual teams in organizations. This trend combined with the increasing reliance on collaborative information technologies to connect team members across time and distances will fuel the growth of virtual teams as a central structure in organizations. We have attempted here to clarify what constitutes a virtual team and to present a model to explain how leadership and collaborative technology affect the formation of trust in such teams, and their subsequent impact on interaction and performance. We have also argued here that going to virtual teams takes the concept of team to a higher level of complexity.

The necessity for forming virtual teams is being dictated by the practical challenges confronting organizations today that are working in multiple locations across different cultures to achieve the synergies required to compete in a global marketplace. Researchers are at the beginning of studying a whole new phenomenon of groups in organizations that requires a rethinking of teams, team leadership, the formation of trust, and the team's development. This new virtual context for interaction at work provides the opportunity to import earlier models of human perception and behavior into this new context to help explain how virtual teams form, interact, and perform. Identification of the boundaries of those earlier models in terms of explaining virtual team development provides the next platform for creating new models and methods to explain human interactions in virtual team contexts.

REFERENCES

Avolio, B. J. (1999). *Full leadership development: Building the vital forces in organizations.* Thousand Oaks, CA: Sage.

Bass, B. M. (1998). *Transformational leadership: Industrial, military and educational impact.* NJ: Lawrence Erlbaum Associates.

Bass, B. M., & Avolio, B. J. (1994). *Improving organizational effectiveness through transformational leadership.* Thousand Oaks, CA: Sage.

Brewer, M. B. (1981). Ethnocentrism and its role in interpersonal trust. In M. B. Brewer & B. E. Collins (Eds.), *Scientific inquiry and the social sciences.* San Francisco: Jossey-Bass.

Boudreau, M., Loch, K. D., Robey, D., & Straud, D. (1998). Going global: Using information technology to advance the competitiveness of the virtual transnational organization. *Academy of Management Executive, 12,* 120–129.

Cannon-Bowers, J. A., Salas, E., & Converse, S. (1993). Shared mental models in expert team decision making. In N. J. Castellan (Ed.), *Individual and group decision making: Current issues.* Hillsdale, NJ: Lawrence Erlbaum Associates.

Cooper, R., & Sawaf, A. (1996). *Executive EQ: Emotional intelligence in leadership and organizations.* New York: Grosset/Putnam.

Coutu, D. (1998). Trust in virtual teams. *Harvard Business Review, 76,* 20–21.

Daft, R., & Lengel, R. (1986). Organizational information requirements, media richness, and structural design. *Management Science, 32,* 554–572.

Guzzo, R., Yost, P., Campbell, R., & Shea, G. (1993). Potency in groups: Articulating a construct. *British Journal of Social Psychology, 32,* 87–106.

Handy, C. (1995). Trust and the virtual Organization. *Harvard Business Review, 73,* 40–49.

Hofstede, G. (1980). *Culture's consequences.* Beverly Hills, CA: Sage.

Hughs, R. L., Ginnett, R. C., & Curphy, G. J. (1999). *Leadership: Enhancing the lessons of experience.* Boston: Irwin McGraw-Hill.

Jarvenpaa, S., Knoll, K., & Leidner, D. (1998). Is anybody out there? Antecedents of trust in global virtual teams. *Journal of Management Information Systems, 14,* 29–64.

Jarvenpaa, S., & Leidner, D. (1998). Communication and trust in global virtual teams. *Journal of Computer Mediated Communication 3.*

Jones, G., & George, J. (1998). The experience and evolution of trust: Implications for cooperation and teamwork. *Academy of Management Review, 23,* 531–546.

Kahai, S., & Cooper, R. A. (1999). The effect of computer-mediated communication on agreement and acceptance. *Journal of Management Information Systems, 16,* 165–188.

Katzenbach, J., & Smith, D. (1993). *The wisdom of teams: Creating the high-performance organization.* Boston: Harvard Business School Press.

Kimball, L., & Eunice, A. (1999). The virtual team: Strategies to optimize performance. *Health Forum Journal, 42(3),* 58–62.

Kramer, R. M., Brewer, M. B., & Hanna, B. A. (1996). Collective trust and collective action: The decision to trust as a social decision. In R. M. Kramer & T. R. Tyler (Eds.), *Trust in organizations: Frontiers of theory and research* (pp. 357–389). Thousand Oaks, CA: Sage.

Lea, M., & Spears, R. (1991). Computer-mediated communication, De-individuation and group decision-making. *International Journal of Man-Machine Studies, 34,* 283– 301.

Lewicki, R., & Bunker, B. B. (1996). Developing and maintaining trust in work relationships. In R. M. Kramer & T. R. Tyler (Eds.), *Trust in organizations: Frontiers of theory and research,* Thousand Oaks: Sage.

Lipnack, J., & Stamps, J. (1997). *Virtual teams: Reaching across space, time, and organizations with technology.* New York: Wiley.

Mayer, R., Davis, J., & Schoorman, F. (1995). An integrative model of organizational trust. *Academy of Management Review, 20,* 709–734.

Maznevski, M., & Chudoba, K. (2000). Bridging space over time: Global virtual team dynamics and effectiveness. *Organization Science,* 11, 473–492.

McKnight, D. H., Cummings, L. L., & Chervany, N. L. (1998). Initial trust formation in new organizational relationships. *Academy of Management Review, 23,* 473–490.

Melymuka, K. (1997, April 28). Virtual realities. *Computerworld, 31(17),* 70–72.

Meyerson, D., Weick, K. E., & Kramer, R. (1996). Swift trust and temporary groups. In R. M. Kramer & T. R. Tyler (Eds.), *Trust in organizations: Frontiers of theory and research,* Thousand Oaks: Sage.

Mohrman, S., Cohen, S., & Mohrman, A. (1995). *Designing team-based organizations: New forms for knowledge work.* San Francisco: Jossey-Bass.

Ridgeway, C. L. (1987). Nonverbal behavior, dominance, and the basis of status in task groups. *American Sociological Review, 52,* 683–94.

Shamir, B., House, R. J., & Arthur, M. B. (1993). The motivational effects of charismatic leadership: A self-concept based theory. *Organization Science, 4,* 577–594.

Sivasubramaniam, N., Murry, W. D., Avolio, B. J., & Jung, D. I. (in press). A longitudinal model of the effects of team leadership and group potency on group performance. *Group and Organization Management.*

Sosik, J., Avolio, B., & Kahai, S. (1997). Effects of leadership style and anonymity on group potency and effectiveness in a GDSS environment. *The Journal of Applied Psychology, 82,* 89–103.

Tapscott, D. (1996). *The digital economy: Promise and peril in the age of networked intelligence.* New York: McGraw-Hill.

Townsend, A., DeMarie, S., & Hendrickson, A. (1996, September). Are you ready for virtual teams? *HRMagazine, 41(9),* 122–126.

Townsend, A., DeMarie, S., & Hendrickson, A. (1998). Virtual teams: Technology and the workplace of the future. *Academy of Management Executive, 12,* 17–29.

Ulrich, D. (1998). A new mandate for human resources. *Harvard Business Review, 76(1),* 124–134.

Warkentin, M. E., Sayeed, L., & Hightower, R. (1997). Virtual teams versus face-to-face teams: An exploratory study of a web-based conference system. *Decision Sciences, 28,* 975–996.

Weisband, S., & Atwater, L. (1999). Evaluating self and others in electronic and face-to-face groups. *Journal of Applied Psychology, 84,* 632–639

16

Conclusion

Toward a Comprehensive Understanding of Person Perception in Organizations

Manuel London
State University of New York at Stony Brook

How people perceive and make decisions about each other underlies many of the processes in industrial and organizational psychology and human resource management. Subjective judgment of others enters into selection, performance appraisal, development, and interpersonal processes in organizations. Despite many standard applications with standard measures and procedures that have been tested for reliability and validity, many of the processes actually used in organizations are not problem free. They are subject to a host of biases and distortions stemming from individual cognitions, motivations, and feelings as well as from situational conditions, such as norms and task demands. Also, they entail complex interpersonal interactions that involve the behaviors, motivations, and perceptions of decision makers and the people about whom personnel decisions are made. The purpose of this book was to understand person perception in hopes of improving these key organizational processes. This chapter highlights the major contributions of each chapter in the book.

BASIC THEORY AND RESEARCH

The introductory section reviewed basic theory and research on person perception from social psychology. Klimoski and Donahue's foundation chapter categorized the elements of person perception into an input-processes-output causal model. However, they noted that this is simply a convenient way to organize the components of social cognition. In reality, the components are subject to reciprocal causation and the effects of social and normative forces, such as accountability mechanisms and feelings. They concluded with a dynamic, embedded systems approach that recognizes (a) the arbitrary distinction between cause and effect and (b) the elusive nature of judgment accuracy because of the contingent and volatile nature of perceptions. Instead of worrying so much about accuracy, they recommended that the focus should be on the usefulness of inferences in relation to the demands and clarity of the task and the ego involvement and skill of the perceiver.

Continuing the introduction of basic social psychological phenomena, chapter 2 by Operario and Fiske considered the role of stereotypes in social cognition. Stereotypes have a kernel of truth and may be functional in that they reduce the need for thought and make judgment easier. However, as fixed, static generalizations about groups, stereotypes lead to self-perpetuating biases and inequality. Stereotypes can be controlled by interventions (e.g., training) that take into account their subtlety and pervasiveness.

A theme from these two introductory chapters that is evident in the rest of the book is that subjectivity in judgment is not necessarily bad. Person-perception processes offer functional heuristics that make judgment easier. This is dangerous if key information is ignored, consciously or unconsciously. Fortunately, person-perception processes and the variables affecting them can be recognized, understood, and controlled. Decision makers can be taught to perceive their own cognitive deficiencies. Also, organizations can be guided to structure decisions to limit biased decision processes and to identify and overcome unfair or discriminatory actions and decisions.

EMPLOYEE SELECTION

The shortcomings of person perception are perhaps most evident in employee selection decisions. The employment interview is ubiquitous yet notoriously invalid. In chapter 3 on person perception in the interview,

Parsons, Liden, and Bauer considered the perspectives of both the interviewer and applicant. The interviewer's goal is to make the selection decision, whereas the applicant's goal is to decide whether to join the organization. The interview is a reciprocal exchange of information that is biased by preconceptions, the influence of nonjob-related factors, and cognitive distortions and limitations in information processing. Structuring the questions and standardizing the process are ways of controlling or avoiding the influence of irrelevant information, reducing the effects of erroneous evaluations (for instance, first impressions based on physical appearance), and enhancing the applicant's sense of fairness.

Executive selection is especially ripe territory for person-perception biases. Unlike selecting employees for standardized positions, each executive vacancy is unique, and organizations vary in how they recruit and evaluate external and internal candidates. Selection committees may be used. Recruitment firms may be hired to do the initial identification and screening. Psychologists may be hired to conduct individual assessments of candidates. In global corporations, cultural factors affect decision makers' perspectives, candidate characteristics, and position requirements.

In chapter 4, Sessa summarized her study of numerous executive selection decisions. She found that decision makers are prone to use salient but irrelevant information to categorize candidates, rely on nonpredictive descriptions of past performance, and formulate unrealistic or inaccurate expectations of future performance. Decision makers are subject to common rater biases, such as leniency, halo, and restriction of range. Also, decision makers tend to be highly confident in their judgments. She focused especially on the differences between selecting internal and external candidates. External candidates are perceived more favorably during the selection process, perhaps because there is less information about them than about internal candidates or perhaps because decision makers hope that external candidates will provide a fresh perspective. However, once on the job, external candidates are more likely to fail than internal executives, perhaps because of unrealistically high expectations, or possibly because external executives are more likely to be chosen for especially tough assignments. Sessa concluded her chapter by offering ways to overcome biases in executive selection, such as using selection committees composed of members who have different backgrounds and points of view and are affected by the decision in different ways. The goal is to broaden the pool of candidates who are considered and ensure that a wide array of information is taken into account.

Another method for making selection and job assignment decisions is the assessment center. This is a costly technique that is often used in hiring people for valued entry-level positions (for instance, fast-track management development programs) and collecting data about development needs for current valued employees. The assessment center tries to avoid biases in person perception by observing candidates' performance on standardized exercises that simulate actual job conditions. Multiple trained observers evaluate the candidates on performance dimensions that are important to the organization. In chapter 5, Sackett and Tuzinski reviewed the methods used to collect assessor judgments. They argued that raters do not differentiate performance dimensions within exercises, but rather seem to form overall conclusions about a candidate's performance on an exercise. So the method should recognize that different exercises measure different elements of effectiveness. In the case of an assessment center aimed at measuring managerial performance, for instance, particular exercises may capture different elements of the managerial role. One exercise may focus on negotiation skills, another on organizing or delegation skills, and another on fact-finding skills. Assessors should try to reach consensus on their evaluations for each exercise and dimensions should be exercise specific (that is, the same dimensions should not necessarily be evaluated in different exercises). This builds on assessors' abilities to evaluate effectiveness on specific roles rather than make finely tuned performance evaluations across roles.

PERFORMANCE APPRAISAL

The third section of the book turned to performance appraisal. This is another common function that is likely to be plagued by person-perception errors. Considerable effort is often placed on designing performance rating forms in hopes of standardizing information collection and judgment processes. However, unlike selection processes, which may rely on trained interviewers or assessors, people in all types of jobs appraise others' performance. Typically, supervisors evaluate subordinates at least annually as part of an organization's performance management and compensation system. Increasingly, organizations collect performance judgments from subordinates, peers, and customers (e.g., multisource and 360-degree ratings). The results are fed back to target employees to help guide their development. In addition, the results may be used to make decisions about target employees' pay or future job assignments.

In chapter 6, Janet Barnes-Farrell offered insights and challenges in understanding the role of person perception in performance appraisal. She noted the constraints of memory demands in information gathering, storage, and retrieval as raters sort out and integrate pieces of information. Person-perception processes pose cognitive challenges because of selective attention, schemas, and attribution processes. Raters' goals and ratees' performance history can influence what information is noticed and remembered. For instance, raters are likely to look for negative information about employees with a history of problem performance, whereas raters are likely to look for positive behavior about employees with a history of "star" performance (and look for environmental causes of failure if the stars slip up). Regarding special features of the performance measurement process, Barnes-Farrell emphasized that choosing to spend time on performance appraisal comes at a cost, and that organizations should develop cultures and reward systems that encourage appraisers to reallocate their time and mental energies to facilitate accurate performance measurement. Also, raters should be taught cognitive simplification strategies that might be quite functional. The chapter covered problems of rating multiple targets, having insufficient information (which might be especially likely in rating geographically dispersed employees), information overload, and the challenge of identifying behavior patterns over time, avoiding the tendency to jump to immediate conclusions based on limited information. Another rating challenge is meeting multiple goals, such as rank ordering employees for administrative purposes while also identifying employees' strengths and weaknesses for development purposes. One issue for the future is the increased diversity of the workplace, such that raters have to evaluate people from different backgrounds. Another is rating employees on their contribution to a team outcome and keeping track of the performance of larger numbers of employees given flatter organization structures.

Mount and Scullen (chapter 7) turned to multisource ratings. Employees come to the rating process with schemas of what they expect from the people they rate. These schemas are based on their conceptualization of the ratees' roles (e.g., peers, supervisors, or suppliers) and their relationship to the ratees. Raters' schemas also are based on their implicit conceptualization of personalities and stereotypes. Mount and Scullen outlined components of a rating, such as the rater's general view of the ratee's performance, the rater's view of the ratee's performance on specific dimensions, idiosyncratic effects of the rater influenced by the rater's information processing and rating patterns, the effects of the rater's specific viewpoint or perspective in relation to the ratee, and random error. Idiosyncratic rater effects may be systematic errors (such as a leniency bias) or may reflect valid aspects of the rater's perspective that could be very useful feedback to the ratee. Differences in viewpoint and rating style explain why raters may not agree, even raters who have the same role in relation to the ratee (e.g., part of the same subordinate group). Averaging ratings within groups of raters cuts across rater errors but may reduce the value of the information. Feedback reports therefore may provide average ratings by rater group and also the range of the ratings (lowest and highest) for each dimension for each rater group so that the ratee can think through why raters may disagree.

DEVELOPMENT

The fourth section of the book covered developmental processes—in particular, how person perception influences the way roles, such as "leader," are conceptualized, communicated, and serve as a basis for development. Brown and Lord in chapter 8 considered how the dimensions of leadership stem as much from observers' (e.g., subordinates') conceptualizations and expectations for the role of leader (i.e., the dimensions that comprise leadership and how the dimensions are interrelated) as much, or more than, from actual leader behaviors and the effects of these behaviors on the subordinates. How subordinates process information and their expectations and stereotypes of leadership affect how they react to the leader.

Just as the cognitions of observers are important to conceptualizing leadership, Brown and Lord suggested that the cognitions of the leaders themselves are important to understanding leadership. These cognitions encompass the leaders' schemas of leadership, how people react to them, and how they change their behavior to suit the situation. Leaders monitor their behavior and apply social intelligence to determine the requirements of the situation and the need to vary their behavior to meet changing conditions. These cognitions may be more important to understanding leadership than objective categorizations of leadership traits and behaviors.

In chapter 9 on training and employee development, Kraiger and Aguinis considered how interpersonal relationships and judgments influence directions for training. Supervisors judge their subordinates' capabilities and needs for development. Trainers take this information and form their own judgments about trainees' skill needs and learning capabilities as the educational process begins. These judgments may be biased by various attribution errors and person-perception biases, such as erroneous first impressions and false attributions of the effects of situational conditions, and these errors may build on each other as training and development progresses in courses and on the job. The authors recommend that such errors in judgment, and their consequent effects on poor training design and misdirected career guidance, can be avoided by educating supervisors and trainers about the errors, encouraging them to check evaluations from others, and periodically evaluating learning and correcting for inaccurate conclusions by changing learning methods.

Smither and Reilly, in chapter 10, applied conceptualizations of leadership and feedback to coaching processes. Organizations hire external coaches to work with executives. Also, organizations expect executives and managers to be coaches and developers of their people. That is, an important part of the managerial role is to be a coach and developer. Coaches help managers collect and understand feedback, sometimes by starting with the results of a multisource feedback survey. Coaching is a growing field in human resources and industrial and organizational psychology, yet it doesn't have a strong basis of theory and research. Smither and Reilly's chapter is a seminal piece in applying person perception to the way coaches and those they coach establish a constructive relationship, assess needs, formulate and implement goals and plans, and track progress. A role of the coach is to help the coachee understand how person-perception processes operate, affect their relationship, and influence how information enhances self-knowledge and establishes directions for development. Smither and Reilly applied social psychological theories of person perception (such as goal and control theories, orientation toward maximizing outcomes, self-fulfilling prophecies, and self-handicapping) to how people in the coaching relationship (the coach, coachee, and the people with whom the coachee works) form their expectations, evaluate others, and interact with each other.

In chapter 11, Strassberg examined how supervisors manage problem performers. This is a type of coaching, and it entails understanding the situation, the characteristics of the employee, and how the employee processes information about the situation. The goal is to help the problem performer recognize the need to change, want to change, and establish a direction for change. Strassberg focused on individuals who display aggressive behavior in the workplace. Helping these individuals requires a comprehensive understanding of social cognitive functioning. He outlined a social information processing model that starts with social cues, self-schemas, and information processing mechanisms for encoding and interpreting information, forming goals, and responding. Individuals with aggressive behavior have deficits and biases in their information processing that make them miss or distort cues to how others react to them, possibly misreading others' intentions, personalizing feedback, and deriving satisfaction from their own aggressive behavior. Interventions may include coaching and training to help problem performers recognize and care about their effects on others and how their behavior influences how others view them.

INTERPERSONAL RELATIONSHIPS

The final section of the book covered how people perceive each other in interpersonal situations. Sumita Raghuram's chapter 12 explored how cultural differences affect the impact of flexible employment practices on employee performance. She argued that multinational organizations need to be cognizant of local cultural values in establishing human resource practices, such as various forms of flexible employment. As such, she considered the intersection between organizational practices and individual's expectations and needs manifest in cultural values. The chapter whets the researcher's appetite for understanding how national culture, and cultural characteristics more broadly (e.g., differences between various cultural classifications within countries and companies) affect employees' person perception and interpersonal judgments. Also, the chapter suggests the need for understanding how cultural values influence the human resource practices that are adopted and how these relationships are mediated by stereotypes or prototypes of what people are like and what they expect and need.

In chapter 13, Jeff Casey examined the cognitive underpinnings of negotiations by focusing on the opposing party's frames of economic value for alternative possible outcomes. This introduces a different form of person perception—one that focuses on economic gains and losses. The psychological dynamics are that people vary in their tolerance of risk (they may be risk seeking, risk averse, or risk neutral). They form frames of their own and the opposing party's reference points for gain or loss. Also, they make attributions about the other's accuracy in representing their viewpoint. Because behavioral decision research tells us that "losses loom larger than gains," parties who represent their positions more negatively are likely to stand firm for a longer time and ask for concessions from the opposing party, even though this risks the possibility of impasse. This chapter provided a clear explanation of behavior decision theory applied to buyer–seller negotiation situations. Casey noted at the outset of the chapter that the concepts can be applied to different types of negotiations, including personnel selection and performance appraisal discussions. At the conclusion of the chapter, he left us with key questions for future research, such as, "How do people form their frames and become aware of the other party's loss aversion or risk seeking tendency?" These concepts can be integrated with aspects of person perception (e.g., schemas, stereotypes, and behavioral attributions) involved in evaluating others' personal characteristics and interpreting the reasons for their behavior.

The next two chapters focused on person perception in groups. Chapter 14, by Fiore, Salas, and Cannon-Bowers, considered how shared cognitions evolve as the team members come to the group with initial expectations of their respective roles, the other members' characteristics, and how the group should operate. As the group initiates discussion, the members provide information about each other. In the process, the group forms a shared mental model which affects its productivity. Important variables that develop over time are the members' attitudes about their desire to be a part of the group, their beliefs that the group can succeed, and their feelings that the members can be trusted. Member training and group facilitation can help the team develop a shared mental model that promotes group effectiveness.

Chapter 15 by Avolio, Kahai, Dumdum, and Sivasubramaniam, explored teams whose members are geographically dispersed and interact via computing and telecomunications technologies. This is person perception without face-to-face interaction. In particular, Avolio et al. considered how different forms of leadership (transactional and transformational) interact with the modes of collaboration technology to affect group process. Transactional leaders set goals, establish rules for communication, and track accomplishments for the group. Transformational leaders request ideas and facilitate on-line discussions of group members' feelings about the team. Transformational leaders use the technology to increase the frequency of interaction, encourage joint problem solving, and promote sharing of ideas.

CHALLENGES FOR RESEARCH AND PRACTICE

This book identified ways to improve evaluation methods, overcome person-perception errors, adapt to new person-perception situations, and use technology to enhance person perception. The concepts discussed throughout the book suggested challenges, areas for exploration, and possible solutions as organizations and technology change and as demands for evaluating others increase. In particular:

1. The chapter authors suggested how commonly used evaluation methods, such as the interview, assessment center, performance appraisal, and multisource feedback survey, can be improved to overcome the frailties of social cognition and take advantage of human information processing capabilities. For instance, employment interviews can be structured to have common questions for all applicants and to ask about job-relevant behaviors and experiences. Executive selection processes can be designed to expand the number and types of candidates considered. Assessment centers can measure performance in particular situations. Multisource feedback can highlight performance in specific roles. Continued work is needed to fine tune these techniques.

2. Interventions can be designed and tested to enhance person perception and decision making in organizations. These include training decision makers about information processing errors and encouraging (or requiring) slower, more deliberate information processing. For example, structured group discussions can help to ensure that all information is covered and all viewpoints are expressed and reviewed. Information on cognitions, motivation, and feelings can be collected and fed back to decision makers. Multiple modes of information collection and processing can be used to promote a comprehensive approach to information processing.

3. Person perception needs to be examined in a host of interpersonal situations, especially those that are highly unstructured and complex, including negotiation and conflict resolution, global interactions, and team work. In addition, the interface between these interpersonal situations and personnel decisions can be studied (for instance, negotiation or conflict in a selection committee composed of people from different cultures, or a manager receiving multisource feedback from a geographically dispersed work group representing different countries).

4. Advances in technology communications offer new modes for the study and improvement of social cognition and interpersonal judgment. Recent creative applications of new technology are the use of CD ROMs to present information about job candidates and the use of video, audio, and text as research and training devices (see Sessa's discussion of executive selection; chapter 4). Another new application is the use of the Internet and e-mail to conduct customized multisource surveys when managers feel they need feedback (see Mount and Scullen's review of multisource feedback; chapter 7).

Author Index

Subject Index